THE PUZZLE OF THE WESTERN ZODIAC: ITS WISDOM AND EVOLUTIONARY LEAPS

A PAINFUL ASCENT TO THE TRUTH

ALEX A. GURSHTEIN

authorHOUSE®

AuthorHouse™
1663 Liberty Drive
Bloomington, IN 47403
www.authorhouse.com
Phone: 1 (800) 839-8640

Published by AuthorHouse 12/22/2017

ISBN: 978-1-5462-1901-9 (sc)
ISBN: 978-1-5462-1899-9 (hc)
ISBN: 978-1-5462-1900-2 (e)

Library of Congress Control Number: 2017918152

CONTENTS

PRELUDE

This book is the output of a life-long struggle for insight into the conception and advance of the Western Zodiac. The author's rationale is to reveal that the Western Zodiac is a multipart and challenging piece of the human cultural beat. We shall re-enact its implementation, but in coping with such a challenge we need to involve up-to-date scientific techniques from various academic areas.

As a result, the story you are about to partake in is a synthesis of numerous assorted ingredients. It is an interdisciplinary blend that is equally relevant to both astronomy and ancient history. There are those who christen it a headlong flight of fantasy, others – an intrepid theoretical endeavor.

In our age of narrow disciplinary subdivisions, the study of astronomical practices in the archaic world is the worry of a tiny group of scholars often self-identified as archaeoastronomers. Their backgrounds, by and large, are in astronomy. The general development of humankind through various cultural stages is, on the other hand, fleshed out by much more wide-ranging parties within the Liberal Arts: historians and prehistorians, archaeologists, anthropologists, linguists, ethnologists, students of mythology, historians of religion, etc. Sad though it may be, at times, archaeoastronomers and scholars of the humanities are stuck in opposite corners of the proverbial ring and relate to each other about as well as two boxers.

The lack of mutual understanding impairs the goal to recreate humankind's cultural and intellectual stride as an integrated process. But, if successful, the interdisciplinary approach would create a win-win situation for all of modern science. The successful actualization of this approach with regards to the Zodiac is the ultimate ambition of the current research project.

To combine different modes of understanding the ancient world in a single reconstruction will be no easy task. Despite one's best efforts, it is hardly possible for a single scholar to provide equally exhaustive analyses of data from far-flung fields. No one person can be an impeccable authority in multiple and vastly different areas. I am certainly no Renaissance man. Nevertheless, in an interdisciplinary inquiry, there is no other way but to intertwine together results gathered by completely different methods into one unified mosaic. Such a medley – even if it is not entirely precise at first - is valuable as a work in progress and a pathway to future discussion and development.

Thus, the present book cannot and does not portend to have exhaustive answers to all the problems it raises. It is a mental adventure, which more than anything tries to lay out an entirely new view to how we understand the evolution of the Western Zodiac, which this author considers to be one of the brilliant accomplishments in the ancient history of Western Civilization.

The author would like to believe this book will be of significance for, and enjoyed by, everybody who is interested in a lofty outlook on the progress of human culture. Reading it requires no advanced astronomical, mathematical, or historical background. To achieve this outcome, the author takes the responsibility of introducing, identifying, and explicating every general article that would be of use in his forthcoming arguments. All technicalities involved in this research are explained with the necessary ins and outs and put in plain words.

AN AUTHOR'S NOTE ON HUMANKIND'S CULTURAL HISTORY

Everything new has its roots in the abysmal mists of time.
The past is a prologue.
The past coexists with our present
regardless of whether we are aware of it or not.
It affects psyche and consciousness, man's worldview,
and human behavior.
Entire nations are never at liberty to opt for a future
free of their preexisting complexes;
their cultural development is to some extent
determined even by the most remote past.
This fundamental fact applies as much to historic processes
as it does to individuals and nations.
When applied to astronomy, this principle is at the heart
of the given study.
This book is meant to be
a provocative polemic of pushes
that resulted in the inception of the Zodiac and its evolution
in the Western Tradition.

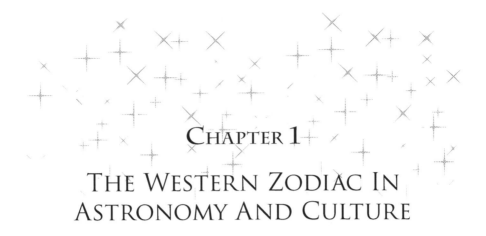

CHAPTER 1

THE WESTERN ZODIAC IN ASTRONOMY AND CULTURE

The term, the *Zodiac*, is striking in multiple languages and has the same Greek primary source as the English *zoo*; the Zodiac means a *circle of animals*. An insight into this term is even more evident in some tongues that have created special words for the Zodiac. In Czech, for example, it is *Zverokruh,* which is plainly and literally a "circle of animals." The same takes place in German (Zodiac = *Tierkreis*).

In contemporary practice, with the trademark Zodiac we address several different entities. Since antiquity, this brand served to denote the belt of 12 constellations that line the annual circular passage of the Sun on its starry background. As it is detectable from the Earth, like a watchful guardian, the Sun throughout the year consistently visits all its celestial subordinates. Today, the starry necklace of the Sun would be more correctly referred to as the ordinary Western Zodiac, and it is the focal point of our interest.

Much later, at the time of cultural mixing, another meaning of the Zodiac took root. The name was extended to label the antique 12-year Chinese calendric cycle. This cycle is employed by many nations of the Asia-Pacific area. The menagerie of the 12-year Chinese cycle serves as curious monikers to distinguish one year from another. Referring to this cycle, it is appropriate to call it the Chinese, or Eastern, Zodiac.

The institution of the Chinese Zodiac is traditionally ascribed to the Yellow Emperor. Some Chinese writers suggest that their nation actually begins with the Yellow Emperor because he is credited with the integration of the country. While the majority of Western historians dismiss the historicity of the Yellow Emperor, most Chinese historians regard him as a real person. Soon after him, the 12 beasts of the Eastern Zodiac surfaced in historic writings (Wu, 1982; Hucker, 1975). Depending on the interpretation of data, the count of the Chinese cycles starts in 2637 or 2697 BCE. Of course, both dates are questionable.

The Chinese Zodiac has nothing in common with the starry sky or any constellations. It is a string of tags applied to successive years, arising out of the particular mythology of the ancient Chinese world. The only commonality between the Western and Eastern Zodiacs is the use of sets comprised of 12 units (a 12-strong set). Otherwise, their respective long histories do not intersect.

The term Zodiac is also often used in referring to the star groupings that were arranged along the track of the Sun by indigenous Mesoamerican cultures (Aveni in Walker, 1996, pp.269-303). However, those cultures were separated from the so-called Old World by the long-impassable Atlantic Ocean and had no influence on Western civilization. Knowledge of extinct Zodiacs of Mesoamerica is not widespread among the modern public, and, more to the point, has no connection with the contents of this book.

The accomplishment that is the conventional Western Zodiac is unique among the highlights of human intellect. In this book, we narrate only the birth of this pattern - the Zodiac in its Western form.

Zodiacs: Solar and Lunar

The Zodiac has many faces, and here is an additional facet. On the high seas of scientific publications, one can be confronted by a baseless assertion that our subject – the Western Zodiac – was preceded in time by a system of *Lunar Lodges*. Some scholars designate the regular 12-strong Western Zodiac as the Solar Zodiac in contrast to Lunar Lodges that compile the Lunar Zodiac. The latter contains 28 (or sometimes 27) starry groups, which in their totality denote the path of the Moon among stars in such a manner that it covers each "Lunar Lodge" in one day. In the sky, the observable path of the Moon is pretty close to the path of the Sun, but the Moon is moving among stars much faster than the Sun, performing one full revolution in about 29.5 days. This means that "Lunar Lodges" have to be about two and a half times smaller than one constellation of the Solar Zodiac.

The Lunar Zodiac has nothing to do with the genuine article, and the idea that it is more ancient is misguided. Moreover, while observations of the waning and waxing of the Moon are easy to conduct, the movement of the Moon among stars is so tangled that each "Lunar Lodge" cannot be determined from simple observations. The new Moon is born each time amongst different starry groups and moves sometimes above, sometimes below the path of the Sun. Finding the regularities of the Moon's motion is a daunting task even for modern astronomers. For the ancients it was nigh impossible. Under these circumstances, the Lunar Zodiac can be considered only as a later upgrade of the genuine Zodiac specifically for lunar observation.

There exist at least two substantial pieces of evidence why the Lunar Zodiac is significantly younger than the genuine Solar Zodiac. Using an analysis of the Chinese sky, this has been convincingly shown by Sun Xiaochun and Jacob Kistemaker (1997).

The second major proof was granted in 2000 by the American astronomer Bradley Schaefer, who published a paper with an evaluation of the date of origin of the "Lunar Lodge" systems on astronomical grounds. He concluded (p. 283) that

> "the best estimate for the date of formation of Chinese lodge system is 3300 BC with a one-sigma [i.e., one standard deviation - A.G.] statistical uncertainty of 480 years. Similarly, the dates for the formation of the Hindu and Arab system are 1750 ± 640 BC and 200 ± 600 BC respectively."

Further in this volume, I shall demonstrate that the offspring of the genuine Zodiacal system is several thousand years older than that. The trace and influence of the Lunar Zodiac in world culture is considerably less meaningful in comparison with the Solar Zodiac, so I shall not touch on the Lunar Zodiac in this book.

Alex A. Gurshtein

The Western Zodiac as an Astronomical Gadget

The Western Zodiac stems entirely from observations of astronomical phenomena. Relative to each other, the stars are practically stationary, while the Sun, the Moon, and the planets wander among them. The Zodiac was designed to denote these movements. Moreover, each zodiacal constellation corresponds to a calendric month, and, through this, the Western Zodiac is clearly related to another astronomical undertaking – the solar calendar.

Having survived in various times and lands, today the Zodiacal dial is a symbolic incarnation of the solar year with its regular rotation of the 12 months. And, though the Zodiac belongs to the science of astronomy, it would be incorrect to consider it as purely a scientific tool. The Zodiac was incorporated into the greater fabric of Western mythology and symbolism, so that in discussing it one must treat it as much more than a mere astronomical utility. In this book, I will be forced to consider the Zodiac in a much broader cultural context.

The Western Zodiac as a Symbolic Contrivance

The Western Zodiac has long ago taken its place among the world's cultural gems. First and foremost, it is a great and complicated symbolical unity. It had to be somehow developed from a simpler assemblage to a more elaborate one. But, so far, such statements are not more than guesses. In current scientific literature, there is not even a hint concerning the original symbolic meanings of the zodiacal constituents.

It is the metaphorical aspect of the Zodiac that requires a multidisciplinary approach that can go far beyond the scope of astronomical phenomena alone.

Prominent experts in symbolism, such as Joseph Campbell (1904-1987), Mircea Eliade (1907-1986), and Marija Gimbutas (1921-1994), have repeatedly demonstrated symbols' tendency to morph and cross the narrow boundaries. For example, a specific agricultural symbol like an ear of corn can gain a wider significance and become a spiritual/religious symbol. This, in turn, enters both the visual culture and the language, spawning other offshoots and contingent symbols. In the end, this symbol is almost omnipresent in a culture even though its origins

4

may well be forgotten. The same is entirely true for the Zodiac. Only an interdisciplinary approach to the understanding of the Western Zodiac can allow scholars to move from the current standstill and achieve new results.

Sometimes, ancient symbolic iconography is easily decoded. It is known to many, for instance, that the Greek sun god, Apollo, drives a *quadriga* chariot. The term of classical times, quadriga, means a chariot drawn by four horses. In Apollo's case, the four horses symbolize the four seasons of the solar year. The symbolic relationship of the sun god Apollo and his four horses is indisputable, but it is unfortunately infrequent that a symbol is so transparent.

The German writer and polymath, Johann Wolfgang von Goethe (1749-1832), gave an instructive definition of symbolism:

> "Authentic symbolism is present when something specific represents something more universal, not as a dream or a shadow, but as a living momentary revelation of what is inscrutable."

In the forthcoming research, the decoding of the zodiacal symbolism will be crucial.

Images of the Zodiac as a latent Clue to its Deciphering

How did a bull, a water-bearer, or a ram first make their way up into the sky as constituents of the Western Zodiac? What is the veiled meaning of the 12 mystic zodiacal icons? To speak metaphorically, when and wherefore did Pisces swim up into the stream of zodiacal emblems? The heavenly fishes are as silent as the earthly ones. Why, for Heaven's sake, have these mutes floated into the waters of the Zodiac?

The more down-to-earth inquiry is why and when were pagan labels projected onto the sky of the Northern hemisphere of the Earth? Are the constellations merely a form of ancient funny comics? Did ancient peoples pin up these images in the sky merely for some form of spiritual satisfaction? Or did the constellations carry out a more terrestrial function for the early sky-gazers, as well?

It is possible that once upon a time somewhere on Earth there was an aged savant cognizant of the clue to those questions. Maybe a hint was buried among the innumerable papyri of the Alexandrine Library, which are now long gone. Today, it is unlikely that we can apprehend that clue from among a few ancient scrolls, palimpsests, or cuneiform tablets that have survived in the museum showcases. If such a finding were possible, any curious digger of archaic writings would have long since recognized it and paid attention to such a sensational artifact.

How, then, can the history of the Zodiac still be supplemented, given that the amount of applicable ancient sources is rather scant and that numerous accomplished scholars have tried to unveil the secrets of the Zodiac with limited success?

In the eyes of this author, there exists a resource that has been underused: the images of constellations themselves, along with their celestial locations, sizes, names and their symbolic filling. *A key to the history of the starry map could be hidden in the starry map itself.* For the Zodiac's decoding, it is imperative to peruse the constituents of the Zodiac itself.

Images of the Sun, the Moon, and stars adorn many Paleolithic caves, though no depictions of constellation maps have yet been found. This, however, does not mean that pre-literate cave dwellers did not connect stars into patterns in the sky. In various museums, among ancient rarities, there are all kinds of mysterious objects claimed to be of astronomical significance. The absence of clear-cut evidence might discourage some from pursuing the subject of pre-written astronomy altogether, but this author believes it is a healthy exercise to stretch our scientific imagination, to use reason and archaeological findings to come up with a plausible working hypothesis on the roots of the 12 pagan images of the Western Zodiac.

Let me allude to the French astronomer and great popularizer of science, Camille Flammarion (1842-1925), who began one of his portrayals of the sky with a very thorough analogy of the constellation nomenclature to the names of streets and squares of an expanding city. Citing Paris, he followed the evolution of the type of its street names from epoch to epoch.

At the dawn of the city's existence, its narrow and curved lanes were designated in keeping with local sights: the Street of Martyrs, the Street of Pits, the Street of Troughs, Oven Street, Bread Street, Fish Street, and so on. During Medieval times and through the 17th century, the streets became longer, broader, and straighter. These were mostly named after saints, as a weapon in the Catholic ideological struggle against the rise of Protestantism. In the 18th century, and the advent of the Enlightenment, came the turn of statesmen, seafarers, and savants.

Regular alterations can be traced in the development of the Parisian map. Like tidal waves came periods of philosophers and military leaders; then distinguished officials and city representatives.

One can readily gather that the social and political concerns of Parisians at any given time were reflected in the names they gave to their physical surroundings. The same is true of celestial names. As Flammarion concludes,

> "Issues that the thoughts and feelings of the people were focused on in various periods of their lives, were mirrored in the names and titles recorded in the Sky as well as on the Earth."

Is Camille Flammarion's judgment adequate? An answer to such a question is not straightforward. An assiduous critic of investigations in this field, Edward C. Krupp, the Director of Griffith Observatory in Los Angeles, noted that over the last century and a half inquiries into the origin of constellations have followed two strategies. In one case, literally following written sources and iconography, researchers reached as far back as Mesopotamia of the 3rd millennium BCE. The other strategy, according to Krupp,

> "involves juggling the properties of constellations as a set, in the belief that the distribution across the sky constrains their origin" (2000, p.46).

This is Flammarion's strategy. It is shaky but exciting because it requires a more generalized abstract view. One has to look at the big picture rather than focus on any individual element. By no means do I want to suggest that the comparison Flammarion draws to the Paris map can alone serve as proof of the possibility of decoding the meanings of the most ancient of constellations. By itself, it is nothing more than an analogy, but Flammarion's parallel concerning constellation nomenclature hits the nail right on the head.

Both the map of Paris and the map of the sky present themselves as patchwork quilts, and they were sewn together and patched up in various times. To me, similarities in these two cases are eye-catching. Flammarion's thought is echoed by a contemporary scholar, Keizo Hashimoto, of Kansai University, Osaka, Japan, who condenses it into two phrases:

> "Constellations are the invention of human imagination. With constellations the sky is a unique document of ancient astronomy and ancient society" (*See* Hashimoto's Preface to Xiaochun and Kistemaker, 1997).

My primary focus in this book is that this paperless but priceless source, the chart of the sky, could be self-sufficient for the investigation of its own genesis. Being the unique product of ancient astronomy and ancient society, the sky map itself might be a clue to its own life story even without recorded data. After all, ancient peoples were not adherents of the scientific method in white lab coats, but weavers of myth and allegory, of tales and poetry.

Transfer of Knowledge and Traditions

To give a green light to our further investigation we need to get down to brass tacks, i.e. to define clearly our basic stance on the transfer of knowledge and cultural traditions. Even when someone looks back into the depths of history, what he will see there is largely predetermined by social and cultural context of one's own time. That is why, over the course of various historic epochs, views regarding the genesis of the Zodiac have fluctuated wildly. For instance, the ancient Greek thinkers, to the best of our knowledge through written sources, paid no attention to the origin of the Zodiac whatsoever. They accepted the existence of the Zodiac for granted regardless of its origin.

Curiously enough, this lack of interest and view of the Zodiac can serve as certain proof of the constellations' great age in and of itself: since the Greeks neither claimed to be the originators of the Zodiac nor doubted its validity and importance, one might easily conclude that its roots went much deeper and by the classical period had made it a permanent fixture in both the astronomical and symbolic vocabularies.

The pivotal point for serious interest in the pre-Christian past was the Renaissance. Literally, the term means *re-birth*, referring to a new rise of interest in Greek antiquity and a desire to return to what were believed to be the cultural values of Greece. It was during the Renaissance that the now-common belief that the Greeks had laid the foundations for every important aspect of Western Civilization - art, philosophy, and science – solidified and took shape. The Greeks were considered to be the godfathers of Western civilization, and the adoration of the miraculous Hellas was spectacular.

More relevantly to this study, the same ideas that pertained to art and culture were also held in regards to astronomy. The starry sky began to be seen as a tapestry of constellations embroidered by the Greeks - a part of their brilliant legacy.

It took centuries to discover the very existence and heritage of the great Mesopotamian cultures and to decode the plethora of cuneiform texts. The development of archaeology and the reading of cuneiform tablets convincingly showed that the Greeks were often nothing more than talented students of the inhabitants from the Valley between Tigris and Euphrates. The Greeks borrowed heavily the skills, knowledge, and cultural traditions of their eastern predecessors. By the early 20th century, the European sky had turned out to be a Mesopotamian bequest, gifted to Europe via Greece. A new trend, called *Panbabylonism* (everything from Babylon), seeped into historic thought at that point.

The detection of the Mesopotamian precursor of Greek astronomy raised the questions of continuity of scientific knowledge and the implementation of older practices into newer ones. As more research shows, many cultures that were previously considered to be pioneering turned out to be successors of one or more predecessors.

As it turned out, transfer of traditions oftentimes did not admit territorial or cultural borders. Suddenly, it became apparent that the model of progress we know to have been true since the Renaissance was equally valid millennia ago: the newcomers dropped their own data onto the piles of information inherited from earlier times, and their vision grew more sophisticated. In astronomy, it may mean no archaic knowledge concerning the sky and luminaries disappeared for good, but passed from age to age and from land to land.

The inheritance and transfer of cultural traditions is a complicated and non-linear process. Sometimes traditions are inherited in their entirety, sometimes they are adjusted partly, or they can be discarded. I want to remind you of just one astronomical example. English, French, and some other modern languages have kept the connection in the names of the days with celestial objects or deities they personified (Sunday – the day of the Sun; Monday – the day of the Moon; etc.). Contrary to this, in most of the Slavic languages, such a connection has been totally lost. Does this mean that the Slavs did not inherit the cultural traditions of Romans? Of course, not. This inheritance, though, did not come directly from Rome but through the later Byzantium, which had already rejected some peculiarities of the Roman culture.

In general, we can state that the paths of cultural continuity are most often unpredictable and arbitrary: one segment of ancient cultural inheritance may be preserved in Culture **A** while another dies in Culture **A** but finds a refuge in Culture **B**. It is impossible to predict which traditions "soak in" from one epoch to another and which ones disappear without a trace.

Under these conditions, it is essential to note that the presence of traditions in at least one succeeding culture obliges us to think that this tradition could have been born in a preceding era. The lack of the same traditions in other parallel cultures does not by itself constitute a reason to deny their presence in a preceding one. We shall examine cultural traditions keeping in mind that they can be obscured. Even one positive case can serve as a jumping-off point for investigation into its roots.

The Process of Cognition: In Search of Universal Integrity Instead of Local Diversities

The proper way to understanding the early history of the sky is not focusing on local diversities but seeking the universal integrity of astronomical knowledge. This is known to be the general way of any science for revealing the laws of logical thinking, or the laws of Nature, as well as the laws of human societal progress. Unfortunately, such a basic methodological principle has never before been applied to the history of ancient astronomy.

It took me decades to grasp clearly that the sky was a unique starry vault, which spread alike over each and every land and various archaic cultures. Proceeding in their steady, continuous, and never-ending development, different people came to comprehend the heavens and the movements of the bright celestial luminaries. During numerous millennia, they accumulated knowledge and transferred it orally from generation to generation, and from one land to another. In this development, local disparities were sure to appear. Nevertheless, the appearance of the sky and the celestial events observed were common among cultures. So, many of their conclusions and concepts should also have been common.

Once a well thought-out novelty had been established, succeeding generations inherited it directly, sometimes adding corrections but rarely introducing radical alterations.

Some remarks that are supportive to my central methodological idea can be found in volumes such as *Astronomy Across Cultures*, edited by Helaine Selin (2000). In particular, Subhash Kak, of Louisiana State University, a computer scientist who was attested as "one of the leading intellectual luminaries of the Hindu-nationalist diaspora" and the author of *Birth and Development of Indian Astronomy*, figures it out:

> "The most important conclusion of the new findings is that there existed a much greater traffic of ideas in all directions in the ancient world than has hitherto been supposed" (p.338).

The continuity of cognition and comprehension was not passive, and older knowledge was creatively altered into new receptacles.

> "[I]n thinking about the "cultural debt" of one group to another, it is imperative not to fall into the trap of seeing one group as the passive recipient of ideas or skills or traditions transmitted by a superior group. What one group takes over from another is always adapted and reinterpreted according to the system of values of the group doing the receiving. Everything they receive from others they transform so as to give the innovations functions and meanings suited to

11

their own purposes and cultural traditions... This is how cultural identity is forged, not by mindless imitation or passive reception," –

these words belong to Prof. Thomas R.Martin (1996) in respect to the development of ancient Greece, but they remain valid and accurate in respect to each and every historic-cultural process.

The various aspects of the concept of universal integrity in human history were successfully advanced in the research accomplished by the social anthropologist, Bronislaw Kasper Malinowski (1884-1942), and by the archaeologist, Vere Gordon Childe (1892-1957). In working out a reliable explanation of the astronomical past, I utilized the results of their breakthroughs, as well as the long collective efforts of many other scholars (Harris, 1968).

Seeking the integrity of astronomical knowledge will be among my leading methodological principles, though I understand that any principle is nothing more than a pushing stimulus. Thus, the reader cannot expect me to present exact evidence of its correctness in advance. A principle can prove its efficiency only in action.

An Evolutionary Scenario Versus an Instantaneous Creationist Origin

Keeping in mind the possible conservation of more ancient traditions within younger ones, we return to the main problem of this book: are the mainstream archaeoastronomers of today right in their willingness to give up on finding the solution to the origin of the Zodiac? Are they satisfied in the knowledge that some zodiacal constellations are listed in the most ancient Mesopotamian texts and that more ancient written references cannot exist due to the nonliteracy of the earlier cultures? These scholars refuse to step on the thin ice of prewritten history, and it does not bother them that such a refusal leaves many aspects of the Zodiac unexplored and unexplained.

Is it possible that the 12 zodiacal constellations represent nothing more than a hodge-podge of accidental entities – people, animals, and things? I will state right now that such a position seems to me absolutely unacceptable and unsound.

Since the time of the first written references to the zodiacal constellations in Mesopotamia through today, the Western Zodiac has existed in the sky for about two and a half millennia. Could it have happened that the cultural memory of many generations of ancient people, people renowned for their symbolic and mythological mentality, preserved a row of meaningless accidents? This author is certain of such a scenario's utter impossibility. The pagan zodiacal system could only be passed from generation to generation if it reflected a specific and significant worldview.

There is yet another important concern in the history of the Zodiac. Is it possible that the complex system of 12 elements could emerge all at once without at least some evolutionary stages? Relying on my methodological understanding of the nature of historical processes, I feel I must answer the question negatively. Among basic principles for this research we need to involve the idea to seek the evolutionary scenario of zodiacal development. This means the suggestion that all 12 zodiacal labels were instituted in a single drive is not self-evident. A symbolic congregation as numerous as 12 elements, seems to me, was gathered in several iterations.

One cannot overstress the fact that in order to crack the puzzles of the Western Zodiac, one will have to face the problem of interpreting ancient symbolism. It is imperative because the Mesopotamian cuneiform tablets do not contain any keys to the understanding of the innermost meaning of the Zodiac and the impeti behind its inception. Granted, we have unimpeachable evidence of the existence of a number of zodiacal constellations in ancient Mesopotamia, but we do not have any reason to rule out the possibility that the birth of the Zodiac predates the period of its first written mentions. In stating this opinion, however, we step on the very thin ice of prehistory that the mainstream archaeoastronomers want to avoid at all costs.

Involving Pre-Written History

In modern scientific vocabulary, the history of humankind means the branch of knowledge that deals with the past as it is documented, though not exclusively, by any kind of recorded source (cuneiform tablets, hieroglyphs, scrolls, etc.). Considering the problem this way, *history* is the privilege of literate societies, but not of earlier cultures. Such a viewpoint justifies the sound title of the famous scientific bestseller, *History begins at Sumer* (Kramer, 1981).

Unlike history, the span of human existence before the advent of written records is called *prehistory* (Stearns, 2001). It is a study of pre-literate societies based on various archaeological findings, tools, skeletal remains, and other material artifacts, including rock paintings found in the 20th century. Prehistoric objects are not always of great antiquity; in some regions of Australia and the Pacific Islands, for example, textual records appeared with the arrival of Europeans only in the 18th century. So, for various regions the borderline between history and prehistory is very uncertain in the absolute time scale.

In this author's opinion, the terminological discrepancy between history and prehistory is misleading. Recorded history and non-literate prehistory are, in reality, equally important segments of a single developmental continuum. Thus, I shall endeavor to avoid the term of prehistory, replacing it with the more tolerant and inclusive term of pre-written history. On the pages of this book, I shall attempt to demonstrate that astronomical heritage may be the most important body of knowledge that we have for bridging the pre-written and recorded history of humankind. This heritage can help us to comprehend our far-gone cultural roots.

Investigations in the area of humanity's pre-written history are particularly difficult because the deeper one digs, the fewer reliable facts are at hand. Nevertheless, we ought not forget that a large number of accomplished researchers participate in these explorations and their results deserve respect and acknowledgment. And the first thing one can do in order to acknowledge their toil is to reject as outdated the opinion that only written sources can be reliable while resources dating to preliterate times are inherently untrustworthy.

Certainly, as far as the early steps of the cultural development of mankind go, so far we have only a few shards of a grand mosaic at our disposal. The interpretation of these pieces is sometimes quite uncertain and controversial. That is why our undertaking will be a laborious and risky business. Among the reasons is that, so far, there exists no conventionally accepted history of archaic astronomy. Also, to this day, there has been no single vision of the history of the cultural development of humankind.

Is it legitimate to recreate archaic astronomy without written sources? For this author, the reconstruction of at least some its aspects seem possible. After all, sooner or later a broken amphora may be glued back together by an archaeologist.

Corroborative Arguments for the Author's Cause

The reader may be wondering on what the author bases his certainty that the celestial map does carry a coded meaning and can be used for its own decoding. I see at least three arguments in favor of this view.

My first argument concerns the practical importance of astronomical observations. Even in the most ancient of times, man had to position himself in relation to the surrounding space (the purpose of navigation) and in relation to time (the purpose of the calendar), the latter problem being especially challenging.

We know that the movements of celestial luminaries across the sky provided a calendar by which ancient gatherers, hunters, herders, and farmers could foresee the change of the seasons. Their survival hung on the thread of knowing when the herds would migrate, when to plant, and when to harvest. The ability to recognize star patterns would have provided some simple mnemonics for seasonal change. Thus, we might expect that stories incorporating mythology, symbolism, and even numerology could hold some insights. Calendars were the mirrors of their corresponding cultural epochs.

Even in historically recent times, the problem of establishing an accurate calendar took up the minds of eminent leaders. It is not by chance that the grand Roman ruler, Gaius Julius Caesar (c.101-44 BCE), the Pontiff Gregory XIII (1502-1585), and the Indian Prime Minister, Jawaharlal Nehru (1889-1964), all of them mighty heads of multiethnic societies, took great pains to resolve calendar problems.

Having a personal commitment to the values of the Egyptian calendar, Julius Caesar took it as a paragon in reshaping the awkward Roman calendar. His reform was purposefully completed by Octavianus Augustus (63 BCE-14 CE).

In 1545 during the Protestant Reformation, the catholic Council of Trent authorized the Pope Paul III to refine the Julian calendar. The final proposition was over by the pontificate of Gregory XIII, and a Papal Bull sanctioned the Gregorian calendar (the New Style) in 1582.

In the 20th century, the first Prime Minister of sovereign India, Nehru, strongly pressed the newly created body of the UN to modernize the Gregorian calendar for international use. He insisted on administrating a new universal calendar. The calendar was a substantial issue that drew attention even during the greatest social upheavals, such as the French Revolution of 1789.

I give examples from various epochs that clearly indicate that the calendar has never been a purely technical time-reckoning device. In all epochs it carried an ideological, social, religious, and political burden. A historian of culture from then Leningrad, E.G.Rabinovich (1978), made an interesting point that the type of calendar forms an important and stable characteristic of culture.

The social ingredient of the calendar was even more important in the archaic world when the calendrial functions were a matter of sacred rites. Being the foundation and the primary driving force of archaic astronomy, the calendar was certain to occupy a central position in the astronomical practice of ancients. The Zodiac being the yearly corridor of the Sun among stars is the quintessence of calendrical issues.

My second argument concerns the nature of language, which has always been an evolving system rather than an ossified one: language has constantly enriched itself with new ideas. During all stages of linguistic development, newly introduced words, terms, and names have always been the products of their time, reflecting the concerns that preoccupied the culture at the moment. Like all new symbols, they were constructed according to the context of their epoch, and this principle should have been fully reflected in the names that were projected into the sky. They were brainchildren of their times.

Finally, was it necessary for ancients to gaze at the sky and study the Universe? The profound French mathematician and thinker, Henri Poincaré (1854-1912), gave a response to this query when he wrote,

> "Governments and parliaments must find that astronomy is one of the sciences which cost most dear: the least instrument costs hundreds of thousands of dollars, the least observatory

costs millions; each eclipse carries with it supplementary appropriations. And all that for stars which are so far away, which are complete strangers to our electoral contests" (English edition of 1982, p.289).

After this disparaging opening, Poincaré declares,

> "Astronomy is useful because it … shows us how small is man's body, how great his mind, since his intelligence can embrace the whole of this dazzling immensity, where his body is only an obscure point, and enjoy its silent harmony. Thus we attain the consciousness of our power, and this is something which can not cost too dear, since this consciousness makes us mightier."

This role must be attributed to the heavens from the very nativity of mankind, of which the Zodiac was an essential part.

The Chart of the Sky Could Get No Interpretation Centuries Ago

Many astronomers of the past occupied themselves with thinking about the history of the sky. An example of vivid interest in this history is a book by Noël Antoine Pluche (1688-1761), a professor in the French town of Rheims. It was published in 1739-41 and has been translated into English as *The History of Heavens considered according to the notions of the poets and philosophers, compared with the doctrines of Moses* (1740). Many other examples can be cited, but, to be honest, because of the absence of clear perceptions of the peculiarities of ancient civilizations, the history of the sky could not be compiled either at that time or centuries later. The history of the sky remained an encrypted page in the tome of ancient history.

A proper basis for investigating the sky has only recently emerged. It happened only after the modern studies of human pre-written history had become a solid area of social sciences. With the design of structural anthropology, Claude Lévi-Strauss (1908-2009) was in the vanguard of achievers in this field.

To sum up the remarks of this Chapter, I have worked on the troublesome problem of understanding the entire historical process: the book in your hands is devoted to ancient astronomy and its interconnection with world history, the main emphasis stressing universal integrity instead of well-known local diversities.

I do not foster an illusion that my importunate and, at times, overzealous claim to attach supplemental millennia to the conscious history of the human race is exhaustively backed by airtight arguments in all of its aspects. Unfortunately, we are really short of facts at hand, and evidence in favor of my concept is scarce and circumstantial. Nevertheless, under fire from skeptics and ill-wishers, I turn to the comfort expressed in a piece of common wisdom: ***absence of evidence is not at all the same as evidence of absence.***

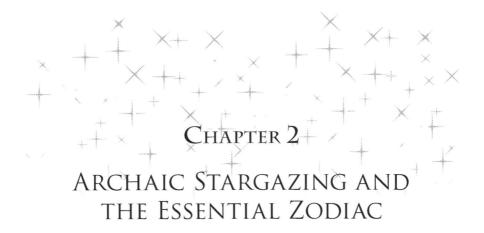

CHAPTER 2

ARCHAIC STARGAZING AND THE ESSENTIAL ZODIAC

Among the nine Greek Muses, the mythological daughters of Mnemosyne and Zeus, only one of them – Urania - was the patron of science. And that science was, of course, astronomy. It is trivial to say that astronomy is the oldest bough on the tree of exact sciences. It is not so trivial to claim that archaic astronomical activity was a launching pad for the making of humankind.

In this Chapter we shall summarize the basic facts of archaic astronomy in such a manner as to clarify it for non-astronomers.

Ancient Humans: Mobility and Time-keeping

At the turn of the 21st century (November-December 1999, pp.542-553), *American Scientist* published a list of 100 of the most influential books that molded the 20th century. Among those was Pierre Teilhard de Chardin's (1881-1955) *The Phenomenon of Man* (1959). This worldview-shaping scholar – a French Jesuit, philosopher, and accomplished researcher – put emphasis on what he considered to be one of Early Man's most amazing features – his restless mobility.

The key argument in favor of mobility: it would seem that as soon as the earliest primitive stone tools come onto the historical scene, they are found not in a few localized spots, but are spread across practically ever major landmass on Earth. It is almost impossible to imagine that such developments could have taken place simultaneously in distant corners of the globe independently of each other. Rather, the evidence would testify that humans set off on a long journey as soon as they got out of the proverbial cradle.

One can argue long and hard as to what exactly pushed early humans in their migratory pursuits, but it seems indisputable that only the "guiding" stars could have directed them to find their whereabouts.

Before preliterate man could start on the path of a settled lifestyle with domesticated animals and crops, he had to familiarize himself with his environment: the mountains, hills, valleys, forests, and water bodies that surrounded him. When he roamed over vast areas in search of food and favorable living, the nomad needed to have some means of orienting himself in space.

> "One measure of the success of different species of animals is the range of environments in which they are able to flourish. In this respect human beings are supreme. In the course of prehistory they occupied or at least became aware of every environmental niche on earth" (Clark, 1992, p.14).

As seasons regularly spun, preliterate man would have inevitably had to navigate himself in time, as well. Time reckoning was a tricky and challenging venture for mankind in its infancy.

Terrestrial markers are not sufficient for orientation in space and time. Only celestial signposts are idoneous for orientation and navigation. In order to locate himself in both space and time, the nomad had to rely on the sky and its features. Thus the making of humankind, i.e., «domestication» of the immediate living space, went hand in hand with the «domestication» of the sky. Astronomical activity escalated at the very dawn of human prehistory simultaneously with human restless mobility.

The sky offered two kinds of occurrences to archaic man. The first were the rare and irregular happenings that instilled fear: horrible solar and lunar eclipses, the appearance of hairy comets, flashes of supernovae, etc. To the list of such irregular and portentous events were added meteorological phenomena such as thunder and lightning, shooting stars and meteor showers, rainbows, halos around the Sun or Moon, St. Elmo's fires. In millennia to come, such celestial happenings, which continued to be considered remarkable well into written history, became omens for divination, a means for communicating with supernatural forces and fortune telling.

The second kind of occurrences were the regular ones, perceptible in their stability, which allowed for the understanding and development of certain governing rules. Among these occurrences were the cyclical changes in the Moon's appearance (lunations), the daily rotation of the entire celestial dome, the movement of the Sun relative to the horizon, the regular changes in the brightness of variable stars. The movement of the planets among the stars is also cyclical, but the changes typically take place for over a year and, in order to be assimilated, require more thorough and systematic observation.

Certainly for their immediate practical purposes, the preliterate nomads chose the simplest of the regular celestial occurrences: the changing phases of the Moon and the movement of the Sun relative to the horizon. Awaking science was engendered not so much by experiences on the turbulent Earth as by the harvesting of knowledge from the sky. As historian of science Alexander Koyré (1892-1964) wittily remarked, science stepped down onto Earth from the heavens (Koyré, 1985).

Lunar Month: The Firstborn of Paleolithic Astronomy

Mother Nature gave living creatures two natural cycles that govern their lives: the day and the solar year. The use by ancient man of the lunar month can be considered a "historical mishap." It was developed and used solely on the basis of simplicity and practical convenience. The Moon in its periodic phases (lunations) hangs as a giant clock face in the sky, visible to anyone in clear weather.

On the vault of heaven, the spectacle of the constantly changing lunar orb is unmatched. From times immemorial, it has been part and parcel of ancient thoughts, mythologies, religions, and traditions. Even in a much later period about which we have a lot of written and archaeological evidence, the Greek Antiquity, the Moon remained a mysterious and special heavenly body. In Aristotle's philosophy, for example, the "sphere" of the Moon served as a meaningful borderline between a mortal and a corruptible Earth (sublunary world) and an immortal, incorruptible, and eternal world of the ideal heavenly bodies beyond the Moon.

Poor material evidence relating to the Moon reached museums from the deepest strata of prewritten history. Nevertheless, it is strongly conclusive, as Daniel M. McDonald (1905-1991) has mentioned in his *The Origins of Metrology* (1992), that not solar years with their uncertain starts and ends, but the rigid, defined lunar phases were utilized to establish the first well-known calendar system: the lunar month with its one-fourth portion, a seven-day subset now known as a week.

Nobody knows precisely when time reckoning with the lunar phases originated. In any case, in the initial lines of the Old Testament we read about the seven-day week. According to the *Holy Scripture*, God created the firmament and the earth, vegetation bearing seed of its kind, two great lights in the sky to shine upon the Earth and to dominate by day and by night, countless living creatures, and man in his own image in six days:

> "And God proceeded to bless the seventh day and made it sacred, because on it he has been resting from all his work that God has created for the purpose of making" (Genesis 2: 3).

Texts of the Old Testament extend over a period from the twelfth to the second century BCE (Roberts, 2004). For their narrators, the seven-day week was as archaic and obvious as the separation of light from darkness, of waters from dry land, and indeed as the creation of all earthly matter. Today, no specialist in the field would challenge the fact that the seven-day period originates from the lunar month, the week being the natural one-quarter subdivision of the total lunar phase cycle.

To every English speaker, it is obvious that "moon" is akin to "month." The same is correct in German, *Mond* and *Monat* are clearly relatives. These two examples are not incidental. Traces of the inseparable connection between the Moon and calendar time units are apparent in most Indo-European languages.

Linguists confirm a more distant affinity. Lithuanian *ménuo* 'moon; month', Old Church Slavonic *měsęcǐ* 'moon; month' and Sanskrit *mās-* 'moon, month' are all derived from the root word *meh$_1$-* 'to measure' (Gurshtein, 2005).

We can say with a high certainty that in archaic everyday life the appearance of the Moon was used as a unit for time keeping. But linguistic evidence is only a few thousand years old. The most ancient substantial proofs are acquired from petroglyphs and bone markings.

It was Alexander Marshack in the USA in 1972 and, in parallel, Boris A. Frolov in the former USSR in 1974, who claimed that a lunar month and a seven-day week date back to the Upper Paleolithic age and are at least 15-20 thousand years old.

Examining many artifacts under the microscope, Marshack found the markings on any piece were not carved in a single session, as one might expect if they were made for ornamentation, but on the contrary had been cut at intervals. This is obvious evidence that the Upper Paleolithic cave dwellers were taking notice of alterations in the sky.

Both Marshack and Frolov agree that ancient game hunters used a kind of a "prearithmetical system" and probably conducted regular observations of the Sun and the Moon. Protracted migrations of the Upper Paleolithic tribesmen necessitated their ability to orient themselves in time and space. This need stimulated astronomical observations, which have been recorded in pictographs on cave and grotto walls. These images include drawings of phases of the Moon and rows of 28-29 incisions. Archaeologists believe that these marks correspond to the days of the lunar month.

What conclusions are self-evident among everything examined here? The first one is that the Moon surely played an essential role in the spiritual life of our archaic predecessors, in the formation of their archaic worldview. As Eliade (1959) noticed, in the mind of archaic man the Moon was a permanent catalyst of the concept of non-linear time, the idea of Eternal Return. The periodic phases of the Moon – appearance, growth, wane, disappearance, followed by reappearance after a few nights of invisibility – served as the archetype for a nascent conceptualization of other great natural cycles of death and rebirth.

The second deduction is that the Moon provided a purely utilitarian solution for reckoning a-few-days-long increments of time. Through celestial observations, archaic man retrieved an eternal clock hanging in front of his eyes: the periodic phases of the Moon. Recent publications date the earliest uses of the Moon as a time-measuring device back to 28,000-30,000 years ago (Macey, 1994, p.75).

The Movement of the Sun Relative to the Horizon

Aside from the lunar month implementation, another fundamental novelty of archaic astronomy was the recognition of the characteristic travel of the Sun relative to the horizon. This formative success was achieved due to the earliest scientific instrument in the history of humanity – a rod inserted vertically into the ground (or a standing stone, or an obelisk).

There existed two similarly easy and efficient solutions to determine the movement of the Sun relative to the horizon. A watcher could either mark the length of the shadow in the course of the day and compare the length of the midday shadow from day to day, or he could mark from day to day the points on the horizon at which the sun rose or set. These methods work in the temperate latitudes of the Northern hemisphere, but that is only an argument in favor of their use since the great cultures with the best known early grasp of astronomy – Mesopotamia, Egypt, China, India – all flourished in these latitudes.

So, every day the Sun rises somewhere in the Eastern section of the horizon, reaches its highest point above the horizon exactly in the South, and sets somewhere in the West. In the midday the Sun passes the local celestial meridian, and this is an exceptional point of its track in the sky. It is no accident that we use the familiar terms A.M. and P.M.: *ante meridiem* (before the passage of the meridian) and *post meridiem* (after the passage of the meridian). In the course of any given day, the shortest shadow is cast by the Sun at exactly midday, when the Sun is at its southernmost point.

If one compares the lengths of the Sun's midday shadows over the course of a year, he can easily spot four special days, which today we call the solstices and the equinoxes. While actual weather conditions in any given place can cause uncertainty as to what season it is, the coming of the solstices and equinoxes can be used as an absolute and impeccable indicator of the change of the time of year.

The second method I mentioned above is just as simple. All one needs to do is note from the same point every day the direction in which the Sun either rises or sets. The place where the Sun rises will swing over the course of the year to the right and left of exact East, and the most extreme points of deviation will mark the longest and shortest days of the year, the two solstices. The middle point between the two extremes would then denote the exact geographic East and would be the location of the Sun's rise two times during the year: these are two equinoxes.

The fact that early astronomical observations of the Sun's position on the horizon were indeed performed has been confirmed numerous times by modern archaeoastronomy (Aveni's *Archaeoastronomy* in Macey, 1994; or Walker, 1996).

The use of either method described above would inevitably lead to two discoveries. The first would be the existence of four cardinal points on the horizon: South, West, North, and East. This discovery would account for the universal belief in the four corners (or four «pillars») of the world. In terms of its age, one can only guess that it dates to the same time as the introduction of the lunar month. The positioning of the bodies of the ancient dead in accordance with the cardinal points of the horizon is unimpeachable proof that they were widely known (for more details, see the article by Lawrence H. Robbins, *Astronomy and Prehistory*, in Selin, 2000).

The second discovery would be the knowledge of the four special days of the year that mark four seasons. Since both discoveries are connected to the same set of observations and have a bearing on each other, we have to acknowledge that the discovery of «openers» for spring, summer, autumn, and winter may be as ancient as the discovery of the four corners of the world. Today, we call the starting points of the seasons equinoxes and solstices. They are corresponded by certain positions of the Sun among the stars. As to the dating of their first use, the *Encyclopedia of Time* (Macey, 1994) notes:

> "a bone plaque dating from about 9000 B.C. is believed to show lunations extending to three and a half years, engraved in a format that may be interpreted as indicating the equinoxes and solstices" (p.75).

The date given here, 9000 BCE, is much younger than the known datings of the earliest lunar calendars, but even so, it is much, much older than any existing written sources. There can be absolutely no doubt that astronomical observations were performed long before the existence of written memory.

Constellating the Stars

Having started to domesticate the sky, ancient man found it necessary to learn how to mark the areas of the sky where certain events took place. Let us remember that during Earth's daily rotation, the stars move around like silver nails impaled to the dome of the sky: their positions relative to each other remain almost entirely constant. Ancient man could use stars and only stars as mnemonic devices in an effort to remember the locales of celestial events. Naturally, at first, individual bright stars would do, but their number in the sky is extremely limited and, therefore, insufficient for regular practical use.

The more logical manner was obvious: to unite dimmer stars into groups, which today we know as the constellations. Using modern terminology, we might say that the ancients projected onto the sky a rudimentary reference system. They may not have thought of it in those terms, but the results, nevertheless, served such a purpose.

The new astronomical practice, to which I refer earlier as constellating, stimulated the introduction of starry groups to be remembered for simpler orientation in the sky. As an aside, one can also conjecture that the same starry groups enabled migratory peoples to navigate in an open topographic landscape and carry the knowledge of certain constellations long distances. The grouping of the stars into constellations with meaningful names marked the second mindstep of celestial "domestication": the conceptualization of the sky.

Discord on the Time of Constellation-forming

Many authors have attempted to date constellation forming and, for the most part, have not made much headway. In the last half of the 19th century, Camille Flammarion in his *History of the Sky* (1872), despite an absence of significant proofs, summarized the investigations of his French colleagues by proposing that the basis for the contemporary nomenclature of the constellations of the Northern hemisphere appeared 60 centuries ago (about 4,000 BCE) somewhere in a place close to 38° Northern latitude and 68° Eastern longitude. This area, according to Flammarion, was populated by a nation that had reached a high level of civilization. Today, it lies in the heart of Asia near the borders of modern-day Afghanistan.

It was Edward Walter Maunder (1851-1928), an Englishman, at the beginning of the 20th century, who proposed the idea that the constellation-makers had lived around 2,700 BCE in the Northern hemisphere of the Earth at a latitude between 36 and 40° (1908, 1913).

Soon after, in 1923, similar conclusions were reached by Andrew Claude De la Cherois Crommelin (1865-1939), another astronomer of Greenwich Observatory. His authoritative survey began with a very precise notice:

> "Astronomy is truly called the oldest of the sciences, for the motions of the Sun and Moon affect the course of human life in so many ways (and did so still more in the simpler conditions of primitive life) that the importance of finding out the periods and laws of their revolutions must have been recognized very early; this would involve the mapping out of the principal star groups, since these would be required as points of reference. Probably the same facts were in many cases learnt independently in different countries" (p.640).

Crommelin was very scrupulous in his conclusions, pointing out that all of them must remain provisional. Meanwhile, he considers that, in the case of ancient Egypt, we have (p. 641)

> "good reasons for believing that the stars had already been mapped out to some extent in 4000 B.C., and that the character both of their daily and annual motions was understood".

His overall determination is that the Chinese had mapped out the constellations at least as far back as 2,500 BCE, and at approximately the same time, an independent system of constellations was devised apparently in or near Mesopotamia:

> "... I also think that Mr. Maunder's deduced latitude of the observers who designed the constellations (36° to 40°) is rather too high... It is fairly evident that the constellations were not wholly, perhaps not even mainly, designed from

fancied resemblances between them and the objects whose names they bear; there is such resemblance in a few cases (for example, the Great Bear and Orion), but in others the figure was chosen as part of a symbolical scheme" (p.645-646).

One can hold his breath in front of monumental serial publications under the general title, *Sternkunde und Sterndienst in Babel* (1907-35), by Franz Xaver Kugler (1862-1929), who was a giant in systematical readings of the ancient cuneiform astronomical tablets. He brought into historical-astronomical studies an incredible wealth of factual material.

After World War II, there appeared an important paper on the origin of the Zodiac (1953) by Bertil L.van der Waerden (1903-1996).

More recently, Michael William Ovenden (1966) sought to demonstrate that the constellations were designated by the Minoans about 2,800 ± 300 years BCE, with the geographical latitude of the constellation-makers being 36° ± 1.5° North and the longitude 26.5° East. As for the Zodiacal constellations, Ovenden dated their origin as 2,600 ± 800 years BCE. At the same time as Ovenden's presentation, Rupert Seeley Gleadow (1909-1974) published a very serviceable book, *The Origin of the Zodiac* (1968).

Archie E.Roy, continuing Ovenden's work in analyzing the list of the constellations in Aratus' poem, *The Phaenomena*, suggested that they had come from Crete in the early Minoan period, being derived from the Sumero-Akkadian astronomer-priests' observations (1984).

Now, most researchers recognize that the Babylonian tradition of the constellations' formulation and naming really came from Sumer and Akkad. According to Willy Hartner (1905-1981), it is actually more ancient and

"had its origin about or even some time before 4,000 B.C. with the prehistoric settlers of Persia, Elam, and Mesopotamia, and it was taken over by the Sumerians and Akkadians, from where it eventually passed over to the Greeks" (1965).

The Case of the Great She-Bear

Today we can make a rough guess that the process of putting stars together into the first constellations started several millennia earlier than was suggested by the aforementioned authors.

For a long time many historians of astronomy thought Ursa Major to be among the most archaic constellations of the world. It is possible to point out the reasons:

1) the same name circulated in many different corners of the Earth among many different cultures;
2) the main part of this constellation has a very characteristic outline with seven bright, sharp structured stars;
3) in the moderate latitudes of the Earth's Northern hemisphere this circumpolar constellation can be observed on every serene night, without any exceptions, in all seasons.

To the best of my knowledge, Owen Gingerich, of Harvard University, was the first to introduce the correct approach for estimating the age of the Great She-Bear on the absolute time scale and date it as far back as the Ice Age (1984; 1992). He drew attention to the fact that - as well as in many other regions of the Earth - this name exists among some native people of Siberia as well as among the native people of Alaska. Gingerich proposed that

> "a celestial bear crossed the Bering Straits with ancient migrants; especially... the same identification is found across Siberia, as has been pointed out to me by Alexander Marshack. Such an early tradition could well have diffused throughout the world from the ancient cave dwellers of Europe... In the widespread mythological connection of the dipper stars with a Great Bear (Ursa Major) we have a hint that a few of the constellations may date back as far as the Ice Ages" (1984).

Consider the geological situation in this part of the Earth at the end of the last Ice Age, known as the Wurm Glaciation. Siberia and

Alaska were covered with a common glacial shield; in the scientific literature this geological formation is named either Beringia or Arctida. It seemed to be a cold, dry climate then, with a serene sky very suitable for astronomical observations. Upon the ice shield there was a thin layer of soil with good grass in summer. There were many different herbivores, which were not afraid of cruel frosts - herds of mammoths, fleecy rhinoceroses, bison, bears - that Paleolithic hunters went after for food and clothing. The Bering Strait was absent, and tribes of Paleolithic hunters were migrating from Siberia to Alaska and vice versa without hindrance. Thus, common linguistic sources appeared.

The situation was radically changed due to global warming; tundra with permafrost appeared in the place of Arctida, the fleecy herbivores died out, the sky became covered with low clouds, and the seas were united by the newborn Bering Strait.

It is obvious that the common linguistic offspring could have been born only before, not after, the Bering Strait appeared and this last date is known well enough geologically; the opening of the Bering Strait occurred 15 thousand years ago (Svitich, Taldenkova, 1993). Consequently, the Great She-Bear is no younger than this figure.

It is inconceivable that once the ancients began to combine stars into groups they would limit themselves to the Great She-Bear. Of course, there had to be several groups with bright distinguishable stars in their midst. Among the more obvious candidates to be the earliest are Orion, Canis Major, Taurus. Due to their startling uniqueness in the sky, the Seven Sisters – the Pleiades – must have been among the most ancient asterisms. It is important to emphasize yet again the fact that in investigating the origins of the constellations, as well as the question of the lunar month, we encounter datings that precede the birth of literacy and the very possibility of these events being mentioned in writing by several millennia.

The Celestial Equator and the Path of the Sun

Having united the stars into groups, ancient sages could not fail to notice that some of the newly created groups were located close to the immobile point around which the entire celestial sphere revolves. These groups never in the course of the year dip below the horizon (non-setting circumpolar constellations). All other stars are only visible in the sky during a certain season (seasonal constellations). Any practitioner of astronomy will tell you that once they put the stars into constellations, the ancient observers would grasp the idea of the celestial pole and a celestial equator, which circumscribes the entire sky. The next mental leap, though not necessarily an easy or fast one, would be to understand that all the wandering celestial luminaries – the Sun, the Moon, and the planets – always roam within a certain span of the sky, which is not along the celestial equator but is tilted relative to it.

Modern man knows that the planet Earth regularly orbits the Sun, the centerpiece of our Solar system, within a period of a solar year. It appears to a terrestrial observer that the Earth is stationary, but in the course of a year the Sun circumnavigates on the background of stars, which are effectively fixed in the sky in relation to each other.

The visible path of the Sun among the stars is called the *ecliptic*. This term for the track of the Sun among "fixed" stars is derived from the same Greek root as the English word *eclipse*, because solar and lunar eclipses can take place only when the Moon passes the ecliptic.

Another fact of importance is that the Moon and planets also move close to the Sun's path, sometimes dipping below it, sometimes floating above it (they move within a narrow belt about ± 9°, including the ecliptic as its central line of symmetry). We can say that the Moon and the planets move through an ecliptic belt, whereas the Sun itself moves strictly along the ecliptic across the same background of stars, never deviating below or above it. Only the path of the Sun among the stars is strictly fixed and easily predictable. The Romans called this path the *Via Solis*.

From Four "Seasonal" Days to Four "Seasonal" Labels in the Sky

Without exception all experts in the field concur that in prehistoric times stargazers had amassed expertise in accurately determining the four «seasonal» days corresponding to two solstices and two equinoxes. The next mental step was easy, obvious, and begged to be taken. It was merely necessary to notice that, during each of the four "seasonal" days, the Sun was surrounded by the same stars, i.e., appears in the same points of the firmament.

This conclusion is so trivial that, strictly speaking, it did not even require a familiarity with the path of the Sun in the sky from month to month. The conclusion could have been made in a purely empirical way, and could have served to ease somewhat the determination of the "seasonal" days of the year. The need for systematic observations of sunrises or sets disappeared, since the entrance of the Sun into a particular group of stars directly indicated the beginning of the corresponding "seasonal" day.

Thus, there existed an unequivocal correlation between "seasonal" days of the year and "seasonal" groups of stars (constellations), which in this case took on the role of celestial labels. In the minds of the ancients, they served probably not as labels but as incarnations of godly providence. The correlation of "seasonal" days to particular constellations remains true for hundreds of generations of stargazers.

Does the above suggest that the method of observing the Sun's rises on the horizon had been exhausted and was completely replaced by observations of the Sun's position? I am not saying this is true. Observations of the Sun among the stars were somewhat simpler, but at the same time less accurate. It is possible that all the methods of observation coexisted and continued to be used simultaneously.

Are there examples of celestial observations helping predict events on Earth? There are many. The simplest: the waxing and waning of the tides. Their moments can be measured empirically as a result of regular preceding observations, but can be determined instantly based on the Moon's position in the sky. The second approach is no less effective than the first.

In light of everything discussed, we arrive at the following concrete conclusion. By the time of the Neolithic revolution, agriculturists realized the critical practical need for reliably determining the changing of the annual seasons independantly of localized and often significant fluctuations in the weather. The simple and convenient solution of this problem was the use of four constellations that served as celestial markers of the "seasonal" days.

For complete clarity, let us reiterate the points. On the eternal dome of the sky, the *celestial sphere*, the relative positions of stars remain practically unchanged for many centuries, and that is why they are indispensable as registration markers to fix the movements of the roving bodies – the Sun, the Moon, and the planets. All of these roving bodies march along the ecliptic within the belt of the Zodiac. And the Zodiac was very evidently furnished for this very purpose: to register the movements of these bodies. Meanwhile, the planets were not the first concern in this respect. Primarily, the Zodiac appeared to mark the path of either the Moon or the Sun. For our cause, it is extremely important to know which was in reality the primary purpose of the Zodiac: the path of the Sun or the path of the Moon?

Certain cuneiform tablets tell us about the constellations along the Moon's path, but these particular texts, of the so-called ^{mul}APIN series, were written relatively late. Besides, the same phase of the Moon can be found at random among different starry backgrounds, making it extremely difficult to correlate lunar phases with the "Lunar Lodges." On the other hand, archaic solar-position observations from Stonehenge and many other ancient European and Middle Eastern locations played a key role in early cultures. Let us, therefore, accept that the ecliptic constellations primarily marked the *Via Solis*.

Let me once more stress two extremely important conjectures. First, we assume that, together with the observation of the phases of the Moon and the Sun's movement in respect to the horizon, the Sun's position on the ecliptic against the starry background had also been adopted at the earliest stages of astronomical observations. Secondly, we assume that the astronomical observation of the Sun's movement along the ecliptic led in time to the identification of the four special points of the ecliptic (or four special configurations of stars).

The same thought can be expressed in reverse order. The calendar was essential for archaic people because of the existence of four different seasons of the solar year. To distinguish seasons, the movement of the Sun along the ecliptic played a central role. Along the ecliptic, four special "seasonal" points determined the location of the Sun, and, therefore, the features of the solar calendar.

A Dozen Zodiacal Constellations

During the Middle Ages and in some fields even today, for example in medical science, Latin served as the international *lingua franca* of religion and science. The International Astronomical Union (IAU) officially approved the names of constellations as they are in Latin, as well. Thus, in this book I shall use those Latin designations, often if necessary with the English translations and explanatory notes in parentheses as needed.

The official names of the Zodiacal constellations in Latin are: Aries (ram), Taurus (bull), Gemini (twins), Cancer (crab), Leo (lion), Virgo (virgin), Libra (scales), Scorpio (scorpion), Sagittarius (archer), Capricorn (sea-goat), Aquarius (water bearer), and Pisces (pair of fish). As a side note, there is a thirteenth constellation along the ecliptic, Ophiuchus (serpent-bearer), but it was never included into the sequence of the Zodiac.

There is a funny rhyme to remember the zodiacal names in proper order (Gleadow, 1968, p.15):

> *The Ram, the Bull, the Heavenly Twins,*
> *And next the Crab the Lion shines,*
> *The Virgin and the Scales,*
> *The Scorpion, Archer, and Sea-Goat,*
> *The Man that bears the Watering-Pot,*
> *The Fish with glittering tails.*

The modern names of the Zodiacal constellations came to us via ancient Greece, but nowadays there are practically no doubts that the Greeks themselves basically lifted the designations straight from older Babylonian sources. We do not know for sure if the Babylonians invented these names or borrowed them from other people.

Fig. 1. An artistic view of the Western Zodiac (drawing by A.Kharitonova).

Zodiacal Signs versus Zodiacal Constellations

As the reader has probably recognized, there is an important difference between the concept of a constellation in ancient times and today. An ancient constellation was a picture in the sky comprised of several noticeable stars and very often there were vacant gaps between constellations. A modern constellation is a certain celestial area. No vacant gaps exist among modern constellations. They share borders exactly the same way as various countries on a geographic map.

As with all other constellations, the configurations of the zodiacal constellations are irregular, exhibiting varying allotments of space along the ecliptic. For practical convenience, the ecliptic of 360° was divided into 12 geometrically equal portions, consisting of 30° celestial longitude each. Contrary to the zodiacal constellations, equal portions of the ecliptic became known as the *signs of the Zodiac.*

The history of the 12 astrologer's signs is deeply entangled with the 12 original zodiacal constellations, which antedate the astrologer's craft. The oldest available cuneiform texts from Mesopotamia with 12 equal Zodiacal signs date to the 5th century BCE (Van der Waerden, 1974); the earliest surviving horoscope with the 12-sign Zodiacal system was calculated for April 29, 410 BCE (Lankford, 1997, in entry on Astrology by Whyte, p. 44).

Earlier records, however, reveal the constellations in the ecliptic were not always evenly spaced. According to B.L. van der Waerden (1974), the oldest historical records on the whole set of 12 zodiacal constellations likely point to approximately the 8th century BCE, but in no way can we rule out the possibility that the zodiacal constellations, or at least some of them, are much older than that. The discrepancy among irregular ecliptic constellations is a clue that these constellations may not have been originally conceived as a complete 12-strong system. Indeed, some of the 12 Zodiacal constellations we know of today were absent in Babylonian times (Gleadow, 1968).

The Phenomenon of Precession

While spinning a top on a table, very soon you notice that its axis of rotation is slowly moving in such a way as to form the shape of a cone. This effect is common for rotating bodies and is called *precession*. The same effect takes place with the daily rotation of the Earth. The conical motion of the Earth's axis of rotation is not noticeable during short intervals of time because its period is about 26,000 years.

In the long run, precession of the Earth's axis changes how the stars appear in the sky. Because it specifically affects the positions of equinoxes, astronomers usually call this phenomenon the *precession of the equinoxes*.

The spatial motion of the Earth's rotational axis describes a cone about the axis of the ecliptic, causing the positions of the four distinct ecliptic points (spring, summer, autumn, winter) to move along the circle of the ecliptic as a rigid system with a period of about 26,000 years. Meanwhile, the plane of the ecliptic, as if glued to the stars, remains practically unchanged in the sky.

Concerning the Zodiac, the main consequence of precession is that the positions of the equinoxes and solstices move along the ecliptic: the four seasonal points shift westward (counterclockwise in the Northern hemisphere) along the zodiacal insignia. On average, each of these four points passes through a Zodiacal constellation about every 26,000/12 = 2,140 years. As a first approximation, I shall consider it a sufficiently accurate value for each of the distinct points to remain within one zodiacal constellation for about 2 thousand years.

Even in very archaic times as, for example, during the Neolithic revolution, for a practitioner in stargazing it was not difficult to determine four special days a year that marked the four seasons: vernal equinox, summer solstice, autumnal equinox, and winter solstice. Consequently, it was not hard for him to identify the four constellations on the track of the Sun where the above-mentioned "seasonal" points were located. Therefore, he made up a certain set of four specific constellations that served just like labels or icons on a modern computer screen.

Due to precession of the equinoxes, two millennia later another practitioner was forced to make up another set of peculiar "icons" for equinoxes and solstices. Affected by precession, renewed sets of four constellations will emerge about every two thousand years.

It does not matter whether ancient practitioners knew about precession of the equinoxes or not. In all probability, we guess they did not. Regardless of this, every two millennia of human history, they made use of a new set of four constellations for equinoxes and solstices. The described situation with celestial "labels" is not theoretical but a practical outcome of direct stargazing.

Springtime and the Head of the Zodiacal Carousel

From a purely geometric point of view, the Zodiac is a belt, which has neither a beginning nor an end. But ancient man, naturally, would have understood the correlations between zodiacal constellations and the months of the solar year, and for him, not all of the constellations had equal significance.

Ancient man's comprehension of the sky differed from modern man's. In days of old – in the absence of city lights – man groveled before the might of the starry sky and worshipped it. With the flourishing of urban civilizations, the city dwellers, not the rural folk, determined the peculiarities of a culture.

Ancient man felt the rhythms of Nature in full force. The calendar was for him not just a piece of paper, but a living testament to his unbreakable bond with Nature. So when did the New Year begin for ancient man: winter, spring, summer, or autumn? As it was once decided in the Roman Senate, for Westerners the New Year begins in the peak of the winter season, on January 1. In China this day jumps around within the confines of a month. For Muslims and Jews, the beginning of the New Year constantly moves around, falling in different seasons of the solar year. Many other variants exist.

Step back for a moment from the calendar peculiarities of modern peoples and try to give a clear and unbiased answer to the question above: when does the New Year begin according to common sense? Let us first agree that the «year» is a real solar period determined by the Sun's movement in the sky, i.e., the changing of the seasons. In this case, the most logical beginning of each natural cycle is the spring. Spring is the rebirth of Nature after the death of winter. It's a time when new energy flows into all things living, a warm morning after the cold darkness of night. It is the obvious starting point for a new yearly cycle.

The importance of spring's symbolism is indisputable, and the positioning of the point of the vernal equinox among the stars could reflect that importance. In the first century CE, this fact was repeatedly emphasized in the writings of the Roman astrologer Marcus Manilius (1977). By his time, the point of vernal equinox was located in Aries, and he wrote repeatedly, "Resplendent in his golden fleece the Ram leads the way..." (1, 263); "The Ram who leads the signs..." (2, 34); "The Ram as chieftain of them all..." (2, 457); "The Ram's distinguished sign, which leads the rest..." (3, 278).

Spring was the start of the new calendric year in republican Rome and, as far as we can tell by the available data, this was the belief for most archaic tribes and nations. From this, it is fair to say that the origin of the zodiacal circle was also the beginning of springtime. This belief is confirmed in all the sources available to us today.

If you agree that the solar year begins in the spring, then surely you will not object that the naming of a lengthy period of time – the world-age – is also given by the Sun's position among the stars during the vernal equinox. Of course, what matters is not the point itself, but rather the constellation that symbolizes the coming of the spring.

Time Odometer: Celestial Imprints of Historic Epochs

As the song from the 1960's musical *Hair* goes, "This is the dawning of the Age of Aquarius"! Go to any Internet search engine, and you will find tens of thousands of references to this momentous event. Both astrologers and astronomers inform us of the coming of the *world-age of Aquarius*. According to astrological calculations, it will begin in several decades, some time between 2060 and 2100.

If one considers the actual location of the vernal equinox on the ecliptic, the world-age of Aquarius will start in several centuries. But the exact beginning is not all that important. What is important is that these dispatches are not some antiscientific mystical rubbish. To switch to the prosaic language of dry facts, some time soon, as a consequence of the phenomenon of precession, the vernal equinox will leave the bounds of Pisces, where it has been located since the time of Jesus Christ, and enter the territory of Aquarius. The Piscean Age will give place to the world-age of Aquarius.

The names of the lengthy periods of time – Geminean, Taurean, Arian, Piscean, Aquarean world-ages – were invented not by us and not today. Astrologers knew them at least at the dawn of our calendar era because of the enormous role spring played and the corresponding symbolism of the vernal equinox.

In an amazing fashion, the echoes of the ancient's sacred attitude towards spring were utilized in Christianity. The ancient celebration of the coming of the spring became the Christian Easter. According to the official decree of the First Ecumenical Council, summoned by Constantine the Great in Nicaea in 325 CE, the celebration of Easter is directly connected to the vernal equinox.

The Council of Nicaea decided that the Christian *pascha* be celebrated on the Sunday immediately following the full Moon that fell on or after the vernal equinox (Ferguson, 1990). This decision is valid to this day, and in the 16th century it was even the cause behind the reform of the Julian calendar so as to determine the vernal equinox more precisely.

What is essential for our cause? Precession influences the position of the vernal equinox regardless of whether the phenomenon itself is understood by the observers or not. During different epochs, the coming of spring occurred in different constellations not as a result of human understanding, but as a consequence of the empirical observations of the location of the vernal equinox.

Each World-age Displays Four Seasonal Symbols

A year is divided into four distinct seasons with varying climactic conditions. The division of the year into four seasons is justified, of course, only for the moderate latitudes, but today, it is commonly accepted that all of the known ancient civilizations developed just there – in the moderate latitudes of the Northern hemisphere.

The importance of the division of the year into four parts is underscored even in the first lines of Genesis:

> "And God went on to say: 'Let luminaries come to be in the expanse of the heavens to make a division between the day and the night; and they must serve as signs and for *SEASONS* [emphasis added] and for days and years...' (Genesis, 1, 14).

Thus, we have every reason to characterize each world-age not by one, but four celestial symbols, which corresponded to spring, summer, autumn, and winter. This thought is also underscored by Manilius. He speaks of the astrological signs of the four seasons:

> "These four signs have great power in the art of which I tell, for as they mark the changing seasons, so do they alter this issue of affairs or that, suffering naught to persist in its initial state" (3, 666-668).

So, each world-age is characterized by four seasonal symbols and, as it turns out, Claudius Ptolemy, working almost two thousand years ago, already showed interest in these symbols. By measuring the Zodiac from the solstices and equinoxes, in the 2nd century CE, Ptolemy derived a system of three "qualities." In his astrological treatise *Tetrabiblos (Quadripartitum)*, he considered that there are three very important quartets (*tetragons*) of the Zodiac: *Cardinal* signs; *Fixed*, or *Solid*, signs; and *Mutable*, or *Common*, signs. Claudius Ptolemy's astrological classification will be practical and priceless in our forthcoming considerations.

Let us summarize. The world-age of Aries is characterized by four distinct points on the ecliptic, which are in Aries, Cancer, Libra, and Capricorn. In Ptolemy's classification, they are *Cardinal* (or, for his time, *Solstitial/Equinoctial) Signs*.

The world-age of Taurus is characterized by four distinct points of the ecliptic, which are Taurus, Leo, Scorpio, and Aquarius. In Ptolemy's classification, they are *Fixed (or Solid) Signs*.

The world-age of Gemini is characterized by four distinct points of the ecliptic, which are Gemini, Virgo, Sagittarius, and Pisces. In Ptolemy's classification, they are *Mutable (or Bicorporeal) Signs*.

The Greatest Intellectual Undertaking

In hindsight, a few ancient accomplishments of humankind even today continue to manifest themselves in our quotidian lives and to serve people. Among them are advanced speech and writing, reckoning of the days due to the phases of the Moon (genuine calendric months), the invention of the wheel, several domesticated animals and grains, the art of pottery and tool making. We can continue the list, but even so, it will not be a protracted one. Would it not be a right idea to include in this esteemed list the enigmatic Western Zodiac?

For many thinkers, the Zodiac deserves to be elevated among the paramount intellectual accomplishments of the ancient world. The anonymous compilers of the Seven Wonders of the World took into account the Egyptian Pyramids, but never considered it worthy to include in this register the Zodiac band in the middle of the sky dome - a memento, which was not a hand-made item per se, but was more archaic and likely much more notable for the history of human culture than any Greek edifice. Considering the Zodiac the eighth wonder of world, what after all do we know about its descriptions and images?

Because of persisting astrological ballyhoo, it is hard to find a Westerner who, during his or her entire life, has not heard about the Zodiac. These monikers are enveloped in a dense smoke screen of mysteriousness and mysticism. Everyone probably knows that there are 12 of them, the same number as the quantity of months, and those 12 celestial insignia have been stamped on thousands of cultural tokens and objets d'art stretching for millennia up to our days.

Multiple references to the Zodiac can be found in contemporary art, and Dante Alighieri included it in his cantos five centuries ago. One can find it on the stained glass windows of Notre Dame de Paris and among decorations of numerous old tower clocks. It has been presented in medieval chronicles, on the walls of Roman structures, on the ceilings of Egyptian cenotaphs and temples, and in the lines of the Revelations and the Rig Veda. It is mentioned in ancient Greek didactic poetry and has been discovered on the Babylonian boundary stones. It appears on the mosaic floors of synagogues in the Byzantine Empire, on Jewish prayer books, on ritual objects, amulets, jewels, even medical instruments.

The descriptions and images of the Zodiac were particularly widespread in ancient Greece and, later, all around the Near East and Europe. And yet, despite such an abundance of written descriptions and images of the Zodiac for almost two and a half millennia, the genesis of the zodiacal constellations and their background have been buried in the depths of time.

Oddities in the Zodiac

As was mentioned, the circle of the ecliptic passes not through 12 but 13 modern constellations. Only 12 of them are known as the zodiacal constellations. For two weeks in winter, from November 30 to December 16, the Sun passes through *Ophiuchus'* torso (Ophiuchus in English means the serpent-bearer). Why does *Ophiuchus,* frozen almost in the pose of the legendary Laöcoon, reside on the ecliptic with his snakes? It is the thirteenth constellation on the ecliptic, but our astronomical ancestors did not traditionally count it among the zodiacal labels. The giant Ophiuchus is the ecliptic outcast. For what reason?

So far, there is only one explanation for this unusual situation. Constellations appeared in the sky long before people marked out the Zodiac along the Sun's path. Due to the conservatism of human thinking and the preservation of traditions, once something made it up onto the sky, it was almost impossible to change. Later in the book, we shall explain this in more detail, but for now, we will limit ourselves to the facts: not being a zodiacal constellation, Ophiuchus holds his snakes on the ecliptic as a forgotten relic of a pre-zodiacal epoch.

The zodiacal strip is full of oddities. Apart from the presence of Ophiuchus, there is the case of *Libra.* The story of the celestial Libra (the Balance*)* is a rarity in that it is more or less explainable.

Many authors, such as the Frenchman Laplace, for instance, told us the story that the ecliptic position of Libra was not accidental. One cannot find Libra in literature before the 1st century BCE (Commentary to Manilius *Astronomica*, 1977, p. xxv). Originally it was named *Chelae –* the claws of the huge constellation of Scorpio. Claudius Ptolemy in the 2nd century CE sometimes continues to name this part of the sky as Chelae, using interchangeably the names Libra and Claws of Scorpio (Toomer, 1984). Incidentally, the same exchange takes place in some Mesopotamian cuneiform texts (Emelianov, 1999).

We do not know who renamed Claws into Libra, but the renaming was purely symbolical. Libra was the symbol of equilibrium: when the Sun reaches this area of the sky, the light/dark duration of the day and night is equal. The Claws were cut off of Scorpio and renamed as a new constellation specifically to mark the autumnal equinox.

Supposedly, Libra jumped into the heavens much later than all the others did (well into times of literacy). By this moment, all of the ecliptic would have long been subdivided into constellations. The creators of Libra had no free space, but saw the symbolic necessity of locating in that spot an independent, meaningful constellation. The most obvious solution was found in amputating Scorpio's claws. This is an insightful example of an adjustment of existing constellations to newly emerging purposes.

In our days, the real movement of the Sun among the zodiacal constellations does not correspond to the astrologers' representation of it since they continue to use ancient and antiquated calculations. The discrepancies between the real Sun and the "astrological" one are significant. In the following chart, we indicate the time of the Sun's location on the ecliptic as it happens today and that time as it is used in astrological predictions.

MODERN LOCATIONS OF THE SUN WITHIN ZODIACAL CONSTELLATIONS AND IN ASTROLOGY

	Real	*Astrological*
Pisces	Mar, 12– Apr, 18	Feb, 18 – Mar, 20
Aries	Apr, 19 – May, 13	Mar, 21 – Apr, 20
Taurus	May, 14 – Jun, 20	Apr, 21 – May, 21
Gemini	Jun, 21 – Jul, 20	May, 22 – Jun, 21
Cancer	Jul, 21 – Aug, 10	Jun, 22 – Jul, 22
Leo	Aug, 11 – Sep, 16	Jul, 23 – Aug, 22
Virgo	Sep, 17 – Oct, 30	Aug, 23 – Sep, 22
Libra	Oct, 31 – Nov, 22	Sep, 23 – Oct, 23
Scorpio	Nov, 23 – Nov, 29	Oct, 24 – Nov, 22
Sagittarius	Dec, 17 – Jan, 19	Nov, 23 – Dec, 21
Capricorn	Jan, 20 – Feb, 15	Dec, 22 – Jan, 20
Aquarius	Feb, 16 – Mar, 11	Jan, 21 – Feb, 17

Reconditioning of the Zodiac that Failed

Indeed, many attempts have been made to rename radically the pagan zodiacal constellations. For example, Christian authors at various times have sought to alter the names of celestial figures to ones drawn from sacred history and its interpretation. In England, the Venerable Bede, in the 7th century CE, substituted the eleven apostles for eleven of the early zodiacal constellations, as the *Corona seu Circulus sanctorum Apostolorum* (Allen, 1963).

It was Gregory of Tours who applied Biblical names in France (McCluskey, 1990). On Julius Schiller's map entitled *Coeli stellati Christiani haemisphaerium posterius* (see, *Atlas Coelestis seu Harmonica Macrocosmica* by Andreas Cellarius, Amsterdam, 1661), the Zodiacal names had been replaced as follows: S.Petrus, S.Andreas, S.Iacobus major, S.Ioannes, S.Thomas, S.Iacobus minor, Philippus, S.Bartholomae, S.Matthaes, S.Simon, S.Iudas Thaddacus, and S.Matthias.

In certain other astronomical publications, in place of the pagan names one finds names from the Testaments (Flammarion, 1872). Sir William Drummond, in the 17th century, turned his constellations into a dozen Biblical patriarchs (Allen, 1963). Around the same time, a professor from Jena University in Germany, E. Weigelius, sought to introduce a *Coelum heraldicum*, in which the ancient zodiacal signs were substituted with the coats-of-arms or insignia of European dynasties and by symbols of commerce (*Encyclopedia Britannica*, the *Constellation*). All the endeavors described suffered failures.

The information we possess on the Zodiac embraces almost two and a half millennia, including the final stage of the Mesopotamian culture, the Antiquity period, the epoch of Hellenism, the birth of Christianity, the rise of Islam, the Middle Ages, the Renaissance, and modern times. The original reasons for adopting the symbols of the Zodiac were completely forgotten at least as far back as Antiquity; nevertheless, the appearance and names of these ancient pagan constellations, despite all the changes of the socio-cultural context, have remained practically inviolable up to now.

In this Chapter, I have collected and clarified some essential astronomical facts about archaic stargazing and the Western Zodiac. These facts will serve as the astronomical context for the working hypothesis that I will soon propose for the reader's judgment.

CHAPTER 3

NAMING THE SKY: FINDINGS FROM WRITTEN SOURCES

The ultimate goal of our study is to rethink the lost pedigree of the Western Zodiac. This goal necessitates an inquiry into ages past and, specifically, an analysis of constellation names that have reached us from ancient days. Archaic sources, however, contain scant information. While the earliest mentions of the zodiacal constellations appear in fragments of Mesopotamian cuneiform tablets (Waerden, 1966), they are segmented, occasional, and, by themselves, utterly inadequate for a reconstruction of the earliest history of the Zodiac.

In order to compensate somehow for the tremendous gaps within existing sources, in this Chapter we shall detour from the avenue of our investigation and consider the history of constellations during the two-plus millennia when it was documented with written sources.

The story of constellation naming documented in writing is just a later stage in an entire odyssey of celestial domestication that cropped up in the preliterate past. The question is for what purpose should we expend efforts to understand events of not so long ago that are registered in writing? The answer: appealing to written records will be instrumental to have a sort of model for extrapolation to reconstruct some universal features of the undocumented part of the story.

An analysis of the peculiarities of the naming of the sky in documented times will yield the key to understanding the regularities of this process in general. These regularities can serve to extend our insight to earlier, undocumented periods, even preliterate time.

Of course, we shall not have any opportunity to prove that, in the preliterate period, the naming of the sky was conducted according to the same rules and along the same regularities we have uncovered for subsequent historical epochs. Nevertheless, it is known that human psychology does not and did not suffer abrupt mutations; thus, there is no reason why, while naming celestial subjects, preliterate folks should have behaved any differently than after the creation of writing. In any case, an extrapolation from uncovered regularities is better than nothing. The method of extrapolation is known to science the world over and has long served as an important tool of scientific research.

The Oldest Documented Account of Constellations

The preserver of the ancients' priceless astronomical heritage - the Greek, *Aratus* - had nothing to do with science but was a didactic versifier. The desire to combine scientific text with poetry led to the Greek, and later on, the Roman so-called *didactic poetry*, Aratus being among the brightest promoters of the genre.

A complete biography of Aratus was published in Russian by G.Dashevsky (1988). The poet was born about 315 BCE in the provincial Greek city of Soli in Cilicia, the small territory on the southern coast of Asia Minor (modern Turkey). He spent his youth in Athens enjoying personal contact with thinkers of various schools. Supposedly young Aratus was even acquainted with the great philosopher, Zeno of Citium (c.334-262 BCE), a disciple of Plato and the founder and prime mover of Stoicism – the influential Stoic philosophical school (Honderich, 1995). While in Athens, Aratus contacted a certain nobleman, Antigonus, the future warlike monarch of Macedonia crowned under the name Antigonus II Gonatus (Lévêque, 1969).

Eager to maintain Macedonian hegemony in Greece as Alexander the Great had done decades earlier, after claiming the Macedonian kingship in 276 BCE, Antigonus contracted his Athenian teacher, Zeno of Citium, to the court in Pella - his capital. Contrary to Aristotle, who had taught Alexander the Great in Pella, Zeno didn't show up. In the very same period, the Macedonian king appointed his other Athenian mate, Aratus, as one of the court literati.

There are a few versions of why and how Antigonus II Gonatus engaged his appointee to compose the didactic poem *Phaenomena (The Appearances)*. According to one of them, Antigonus did appoint two poetic courtiers: Aratus of Soli, interested in medicine, and Nicander of Colophon, basically dealing with astronomy. Being a prankster, the king ordered Nicander to write a didactic poem on medicine while Aratus was instructed to write a didactic poem on astronomy. Whatever happened in reality, the result known under Aratus' name was outstanding. His poem is the oldest in the world surviving account of the complete set of constellations of the time (Evans, 1998). Written about 275 BCE, Aratus' account is full and quite detailed.

The *Phaenomena* is the only complete extant work by Aratus to be consecrated by time. It is written in hexameters and contains 1154 verse lines fractured by publishers into three sections. It opens with a brief vocative hymn to Zeus (lines 1-18). Lines 19-757 put to verse an older astronomical treatise by Eudoxus of Cnidus (c. 390-340 BCE) while lines 758-1154 deal with weather. The style of the poem resembles the old-fashioned hexameters of Homer and Hesiod. Its background is obviously due to Zeno's Stoicism. As for astronomy, one or both of Eudoxus' astronomical books – the *Phaenomena* and the *Mirror* – served as inspiration for Aratus' poetic reproduction.

Aratus' Astronomical Pretext

To place Aratus' work into historical perspective, it is of value to recall the role of astronomy in ancient Greek cultural and intellectual life. Astronomical notes were so widespread as to even appear in great epics. The following hexameters of *The Iliad*'s Book XVIII (*The Immortal Shield*) are rendered into English prose by S.Butler. Hephaistos, the god of fire and smithies, decorates the shield for Achilles:

> "He wrought the earth, the heavens, and the sea; the moon
> also at her full and the untiring sun, with all the signs that
> glorify the face of the heaven – the Pleiads, the Hyads, huge
> Orion, and the Bear, which men also call the Wain and
> which turns round ever in one place, facing Orion, and alone
> never dips into the stream of Oceanus" (Homer, 1952, p.135).

Homer also pointed out the Dog Star, or Orion's Hound (*Ibid.*, p.155). A short list of the constellations is addressed in *The Odyssey*, too (*Ibid.*, The Odyssey, Book V, p.210). The majestic sailor

> "guided the raft skillfully by means of the rudder. He never closed his eyes, but kept them fixed on the Pleiads, on late-setting Bootes, and on the Bear – which men also call the wain, and which turns round and round where it is, facing Orion, and alone never dipping into the stream of Oceanus."

What is the dating of Homer's poems? It is believed that the blind rhapsode described the Trojan War that took place at least 200 years before his birth (9th century BCE). For a certain time onward, Homer's hexameters were distributed by word of mouth, and were probably not put down earlier than the middle of the 7th century BCE (Martin, 1996).

All constellations and asterisms mentioned by Homer survive to this day. But there is a tough question: did Homer exhaust the repertoire? Or did he address only some examples of constellations that specifically "glorify the face of the heaven"? Taking into consideration that Homer varies the constellation and star names in different passages, he could have known more of them. (At this very time a larger group of constellations and star names was known in Mesopotamia, as is evident from cuneiform tablets, but, again, we lack a complete set of them).

Some lines with the celestial names are also present in two other extant didactic spectaculars of ancient Greek literature, *Works and Days* and *Theogony* by Hesiod (c. 8th century BCE). Those two epics are believed to have been created a generation or two after Homer's time. Being concerned with farm life and its calendar, as well as with deities and mythology, Hesiod, like Homer, addresses the Pleiades, Hyades, Orion, the star of Arcturus, the star of Sirius (for more details see, for example, J.Evans, 1998, pp.3-5).

The Heroic Age of Homer and Hesiod preceded the so-called Archaic Age of Greek history (about 750 to 500 BCE). During this epoch Greek people successfully developed a new form of their social-political structure known as the network of city-states.

From the Archaic Age we have more written sources and more thinkers focused solely or partially on astronomy. The oldest dated Greek astronomical observation that has come down to us is that of the summer solstice of 432 BCE performed by Meton and Euctemon at Athens. Meton is also known for his calendric cycle, and Euctemon for his *parapegma* - an ancient Greek star calendar.

We can easily number the larger group of prominent Greek scholars such as Thales of Miletus (c.625-545 BCE), Anaximander of Miletus (ca.610-540 BCE), Pythagoras (c.580-500 BCE), and a plenitude of others. Those scholars didn't deal only with astronomy, and the majority of their writings came down to us either in fragments or in quotations by later authors. Meanwhile, all of them were among the godfathers of ancient Greek astronomy.

At the beginning of the 5th century BCE the Greek-Persian Wars broke out and stimulated the growth of Greek national self-esteem: the dominance of Athens was firmly established, and the Golden Age of Pericles (c.495-429 BCE) started. Athens' supremacy abruptly ended with the Peloponnesian War (431-404 BCE), during which his own compatriots sentenced Socrates to death.

Socrates' cause was upheld by his immediate disciple, Plato (428-348/347 BCE), who founded *The Academy*, the first known organized scientific school of such a sort in mankind's history. Plato kept a plethora of disciples, the most brilliant among them undoubtedly being the universal mind of Aristotle (384-322 BCE), the future tutor of Alexander the Great of Macedonia.

In 323 BCE with Alexander's death, the Hellenistic Age debuted on the world stage (Lévêque, 1969). The term - *Hellenistic Age* – was an invention of the 19th century to designate the period from Alexander's conquests to the death of Cleopatra VII, of Egypt, in 30 BCE; she was the last Macedonian ruler of Egypt, which was oppressed by advancing Romans.

At the dawn of Hellenism, not only Aristotle was among Plato's eminent pupils. One has to keep in mind, for instance, Zeno of Citium, the Stoic, and, of course, Eudoxus of Cnidus. Both are mentioned above, the latter being among the greatest Greek astronomers.

Theory and Practice of Ancient Greek Astronomy

Eudoxus, a son of Aeschines - the originator of Greek scientific astronomy - was born c. 400 BCE in Cnidus, the ancient Greek settlement on the Carian Chersonese, on the southwest coast of Asia Minor (now in Turkey). For a while, he studied at Plato's Academy (inaugurated in 387 BCE) and also spent a 16-month *internship* in the city of Heliopolis in Egypt. There Eudoxus penetrated the priestly wisdom and wrote his first major treatise, *Oktaëteris,* concerning a calendar of a sort based on an eight-year cycle. Nothing certain is known about this book. Moreover, practically none of Eudoxus' works has survived, but they are recognized through ample Greek sources and some comments by Byzantine scholars.

In mathematics, Eudoxus worked out some fundamental ideas in geometry and number theory. It is generally agreed that he was the direct predecessor of the great Greek geometrician, and the greatest geometrician of all times, Euclid (4th-3rd century BCE).

In astronomy, with an advanced geometrical approach, Eudoxus represented the apparent motions of planets and stars. His model served as an important attempt to "save the phenomena" - the regular Greek articulation for scientific modeling. Among his astronomical results is a systematic description of the sky partitioned into a web of constellations. This is precisely the description that Aratus had secured for us.

Was Eudoxus' description a product of his Egyptian internship? As a matter of fact, there is no indication it was Eudoxus who created the new nomenclature of celestial names himself. On the contrary, according to conventional wisdom there are grounds to suppose that Eudoxus used the older system that was in existence, for example, in Mesopotamia for a long time before him. None of the later authors ever claimed that Eudoxus was the genuine author of the celestial pattern.

Anyway, it was Eudoxus of Cnidus who became a forerunner of Greek scientific astronomy. Thus, it should come as no surprise that Antigonus II Gonatus followed the precedents of many mighty and successful monarchs and involved his courtier, the literate Aratus, in popular versification of Eudoxus' scientific prose.

Aratus was not the first to paraphrase Eudoxus in verse. There were several precedents by various authors. Being unanimously praised by all commentators, Aratus unquestionably surpassed the competitors, and it was his opus that achieved the firm features of a canonic tract. In later times, Aratus' poem would be translated into Latin and modern living languages many times.

A detailed comparison of Eudoxus' and Aratus' writings was exposed due to Hipparchus' notes with quotations from both authors. Hipparchus (2nd century BCE) discredited some misconceptions in both books because the real sky didn't match its poetic description. He didn't blame Aratus but only Eudoxus who, contrary to Aratus, was responsible for misconceptions as a professional scholar.

Aratus' Set of Constellations

As for us now, we care nothing for the *Phaenomena*'s literary advantages, its philosophical background, or misconceptions. Our interest is focused on the oldest complete set of constellation names. And, in this connection, it will be necessary to clarify some special features of Aratus star group inventory.

First of all, not all of Aratus' *catasterisms* – the repertoire of names - became modern constellations. As early as even Ptolemy's time, the Bow was incorporated into the figure of Sagittarius, while the Pleiades were appended to Taurus. In current terminology, those are *asterisms*. (The Hyades were deemed an asterism even during Aratus' time).

There is no agreement among classical textualists on the interpretation of some of Aratus' groupings. Aratus pointed out a Beast, or a Wild Animal, which is absent on a modern celestial map. He wrote of it, "another creature very firmly clutched" and "the Wild-beast which the Centaur's right hand holds" as an offering to the gods upon the Altar. It is possible that Aratus' animal is a part of the Centaur (Allen, 1899). Meanwhile, some writers claim that Aratus' Beast is Lupus (the Wolf), so this latter has to be included in Aratus' inventory.

Nowhere does Aratus directly mention Corona Australis (the Southern Crown). But in the broad context he appealed not just to one, but to two Crowns, so the Southern one was likely in his mind. Finally, Aratus used the term Water. However, experts are inclined to consider it as part of Aquarius – Water that is leaking from Aquarius' vessels.

No exact contemporary sketch of Aratus' sky exists, only a verbal account. So uncertainties in Aratus' verbal description are to be resolved by each author in his own way. My vision of Aratus' inventory is summarized and displayed in the following table.

ARATUS' STAR GROUPINGS, OR *CATASTERISMS*

No.	Name	Translation, or Commentary
1	Andromeda	The mythological princess of Ethiopia
2	Aquarius	*The Water-pourer*, or *the Waterman*
3	Aquila	*The Eagle*
4	Ara	*The Altar*
5	Argo (Navis)	*The Ship of Argo*; La Caille split it into three constellations.
6	Aries	*The Ram*
7	Auriga	*The Charioteer*
8	Bootes	*The Shepherd*; otherwise known as Arctophylax *(The Bear-Watcher)*, while its brightest star is known as Arcturus
9	Bow	Now an asterism within Sagittarius
10	Cancer	*The Crab*
11	Canis Major	*The Greater Dog*; for Aratus *the Dog of Orion* or *Orion's Hound*
12	Canis Minor	*The Lesser Dog*; sometimes the constellation of Procyon (the name of the principal star)
13	Capricornus	*The Sea Goat*
14	Cassiopeia	The mythological queen of Ethiopia
15	Centaurus	*The Centaur*
16	Cepheus	The mythological king of Ethiopia
17	Cetus	*The Whale*; for Aratus, *the Sea Monster*
18	Corona Australis	*The Southern Crown*
19	Corona Borealis	*The Northern Crown*
20	Corvus	*The Raven*
21	Crater	*The Cup*

22	Cygnus	*The Swan*; for Aratus, simply *a Bird*
23	Delphinus	*The Dolphin*
24	Draco	*The Dragon*
25	Eridanus	*The river Eridanus*; for Aratus, *a River*
26	Gemini	*The Twins*
27	Hercules	For Aratus, *the Kneeling One*
28	Hydra	*The Water-snake*
29	Leo	*The Lion*
30	Lepus	*The Hare*
31	Libra	*The Balance*, or *the Scales*
32	Lupus	*The Wolf*; for Aratus - *a Wild Animal*, and that is why some authors don't count Lupus as Aratus' constellation
33	Lyra	*The Harp*
34	Ophiuchus	*The Serpent-holder*
35	Orion	Sometimes *the Giant, the Hunter*, or *the Warrior*
36	Pegasus	For Aratus, it is simply *a Horse*
37	Perseus	The Greek mythological hero
38	Pisces	*The Fishes*
39	Piscis Austrinus	*The Southern Fish*
40	Pleiades	Didn't survive as a constellation; now an asterism within Taurus
41	Sagitta	*The Arrow*
42	Saggitarius	*The Archer*, or *the Bow-stretcher*
43	Scorpius	*The Scorpion*
44	Serpens	*The Snake*, or *the Serpent*
45	Taurus	*The Bull*
46	Triangulum	*The Triangle*
47	Ursa Major	*The Greater She-Bear*
48	Ursa Minor	*The Lesser She-Bear*
49	Virgo	*The Virgin*

Of course, it is disappointing that Aratus detailed the constellation pattern without indications as to their locations in the sky. According to ancient writers, Aratus' poem was accompanied by a celestial globe as well as Eudoxus' books. Unfortunately, all those globes are long gone.

In the meantime, we have very solid evidence that Eudoxan/Aratean groupings remained very stable. From post-Aratus time, we have the possibility of checking several important lists of constellations. The first of them, for example, was attributed to Eratosthenes, but experts prefer to name its author as Pseudo-Eratosthenes. His *Catasterisms* were written in the 3rd century BCE, not earlier than 247 BCE (Evans, 1998).

Another valuable message came down from Hipparchus (c.160-120 BCE). We don't possess Hipparchus' star catalogue, but the text of his *Commentary on Eudoxus and Aratus* is priceless in its own right. The next source is a Roman writer, Higinus, who flourished at the beginning of the Common (Christian) Era. Marcus Manilius seconded this latter author in the 1st century CE. All authors mentioned were using practically the same constellations while differing in small details only.

A great piece of evidence was unearthed in the form of a statue of Atlas with a celestial globe on his shoulders. The globe is decorated with constellation figures. This statue was recovered in the 16th century and today is in the *Museo Archeologico Nazionale* in Naples. The statue is a Roman copy of an older Greek masterpiece, which appears to be dated from the 1st century BCE. Once again, all constellations on the globe of this so named Farnese Atlas are of the Eudoxan/Aratean inventory. Such a celestial globe seems to be a direct descendant of the original Eudoxan globe.

Ptolemy's Star Catalogue

The final word of this early story was written about 150 CE, when Ptolemy of Alexandria released a catalogue of star positions for almost the same set of constellations as Aratus presented. Ptolemy omitted two of Aratus' constellations (the Bow and Pleiades), while adding *the Horse Bust* and *Antinous*. The Horse Bust became IAU's Equuleus (the Lesser Horse), but Antinous disappeared for good. The number of Ptolemy's constellations surviving today is 48.

Ptolemy's catalogue was compiled roughly four centuries later than Aratus' poem. Both Aratus and Ptolemy have really the same contents, and all details in Aratus' description of the sky match Ptolemy's catalogue perfectly. This strongly suggests that during these centuries the Eudoxan/Aratean inventory remained stable. As a result of Aratus' and Ptolemy's stellar rosters, the combination of their databases creates a complete body of information including names, images, configurations, and locations for our next drive forward.

Dating of Aratus' Original Rootstock

Since Hipparchus, it has been noted that Aratus' description of the sky doesn't fit the real celestial picture of his lifetime. So the problem appeared to date Aratus' representation properly.

There have been two very sufficient and provocative studies in this field from Great Britain; those of Michael W. Ovenden (1966) and Archie E. Roy (1984). Using a planetarium simulation, Roy followed Ovenden in scrutinizing the constellation list from Aratus' didactic poem. He demonstrated that the poem's observational background, according to astronomical conditions described in it, dated from about 2,000 BCE with an uncertainty of ± 200 years. He concluded that it is

> "conceivably possible that the constellations described by Aratus were part of the legacy left to us by the Minoans who themselves borrowed the system from the constellation-makers, the Sumero-Akkadians" (1984, p.194).

Roy's research was revisited by Russia's Sergei V. Zhitomirsky, who confirmed his predecessor's conclusions (1999, p.499):

> "Accepting the ancient dating of the source used by Eudoxus obliged us to recognize the existence of an unbroken tradition linking the culture of the creators of the description of the starry sky with the founders of originating antique science."

In my mind it is a matter of fact that the Aratus constellation inventory is the crucial source for disclosing archaic astronomical notions. Of course, in scientific literature we have a lot of important investigations of the more ancient cuneiform astronomical tablets but, unhappily, in spite of gigantic efforts and some brilliant results in the field we have no complete and accurate map of the Babylonian sky. We have no complete archaic maps from Egypt nor from China. Some name decodings are conflicting, figures and locales of constellations are yet uncertain, some texts are defective, and in many cases it is impossible to share constellations, asterisms and single stars, etc.

In contrast to cuneiform texts and other obscure sources, Aratus' poem, jointly with Ptolemy's star catalogue, is very noteworthy; not fragmentary but an entire, homogeneous corpus of constellation data with exact names, proper images and precise locations, which may really reflect the archaic roots of a constellation-making process.

Maintaining Traditions

A large body of information regarding constellations has reached us through the works of Arab scholars working at the height of their culture's bloom. If today the constellation names we use are primarily Greek, then the star names are, by and large, of Arabic origin. The latter, however, were not original and tended to follow in detail the Greek traditions. The names of the stars, more often than not, reflect their positions within the Greek constellations. A typical example is the star Betelgeuse, located in Orion, which literally means «the giant's armpit» (the most prolific author in this field is Paul Kunitzsch).

Having established that several distinctly different cultures followed one another in maintaining traditions of star naming, we now touch on the extremely important problem of preserving traditions. The opposition of two trends constantly molds the lifestyle of any given society: the knack for innovation versus conservatism. By conservatism I do not mean ignorant phobia against any innovations. Not at all. Conservatism in the cultural context is a force of habit, or the natural instinct of every man to preserve the best of his ancestors' traditions: for example, the habit of men to dress almost exclusively in pants and women to dress almost exclusively in skirts, to protect the beliefs of predecessors, their symbolic rites, and so on. Tradition provides people with the comfort of predictability and security.

It is tricky to address the question as to which of the stated trends – the tendency to innovate or the dedication to traditions – weighs more on the scales of history. It depends. There have been peoples and times in history particularly sensitive to innovations. There have been exactly opposite situations. History has observed both. In a nutshell, I would like to point out here just one fact: healthy traditionalism in the life of society is as important as the love of innovations.

Without conservative traditionalism, any society will become a horse without a bridle, carrying its rider in an unknown direction. Untested innovations could lead to a dead end, and sometimes could even turn out to be harmful and dangerous, while following set traditions always seems to be more cautious and safe.

The process of counteraction between conservatism and new ideas is well known in science. Science is completely aimed at novelties; even so, it is marked by incredible conservatism intended to keep the boat from being rocked. Conservatism, or, to state it differently, dedication to traditions, has always played a major role in the lives of different peoples, particularly in ancient societies. This premise forms the basis for the science of ethnography.

Formed in the 19th century as a scientific discipline, ethnography is based on the outstanding steadiness both officially adopted and informal traditional rituals and creeds. In its application to archaic man, this is the point as a scientist sees it:

> "The extreme slowness of change, as is borne out by the archaeological record, shows how closely early men clung to tradition in all fields. This was possibly because they felt implicitly the unity of all their culture and the danger of straying from tradition in any part of it. How could they know that any failure to carry out the customary rituals and to say the magic words would not result in the sudden overturning of the whole order of Nature: that it would not cut off the sources of food or bring decease? It was safer not to vary anything unless circumstances made it absolutely impossible to maintain the old tradition" (John Bernal, 1965, Vol. I, p.81).

In this regard, the general tendency of cultural transmission to retain names through the generations is valuable. This seems to be true of the constellations also, which have held their names with a tenacity comparable to that of place-names on the Earth (such as landmarks and bodies of water). In chapter 2, we have already demonstrated that the names and images of the 12 zodiacal constellations are convincing evidence of the stability of cultural traditions.

The *astronyms* (the names of the celestial objects) are characterized by a high degree of stability equal to that of toponyms and hydronyms. Just two modern examples of such a stability. In the modern United States it proved impossible to change Cape Canaveral to Cape Kennedy. In Russia, Leningrad has reverted to its old name of St. Petersburg, as did all the other cities renamed after the 1917 Bolshevik revolution. For more comments of value on this issue, see (Karpenko, 1981, p.44 and *ff*).

In fact, the solid evidence that the constancy of constellation names is meaningful can be used in the analysis of the most ancient epochs because the most ancient civilizations were oriented primarily not towards innovation, but assimilation and transmission of the features that preserved social structure. The Russian historian, I.P.Weinberg (1986, p.50), notes in this connection:

> "The orientation on traditions dominated ancient Oriental society and the culture of the ancient Near East. It was conditioned by the specificity of many of... the premises of cultural development but, most of all, by the essence of mythological mentality, in accordance with which the traditions of the Past and the experience of ancestors were evaluated as the absolute truth and as the model for the following generation... The domination of absolute truth... is connected with... the adherence to the standards that express and reflect this truth, to stable stereotypes of behavior, idioms of speech and formulae, motives and forms of imitative arts. A man possessing a mythological mentality felt himself calm and assured in his familiar environment and usual conditions. That is why his house and utensils, dress and meal barely changed for thousands of years; and that is why the literature and art genres are so stable, each of them having permanent plots, formulae, methods; and this is the reason why new temples were not only constructed in the places of former ones, but also imitated their exterior;

> hence, the general canonicity and the aspiration to repeat the
> experience of predecessors..."

If pre-written societies have survived into historically recorded or modern times due to the conservatism of cultural traditions and their likely similarity on equal stages of progress, ethnographically collected data could be used as the model for the reconstruction of human history before literacy emerged. In Central America, for example, the aboriginal written records were analyzed in conjunction with early European records, archaeological information, and oral traditions. The comparison allowed for recognizing and recreating certain features of prehistoric life in both areas.

Based on unquestionable facts, the assumption of the constancy of traditional astronyms is one of the primary load-bearing pillars in the system of premises to support our forthcoming proposed archaeoastronomical reconstruction, the case of the Chinese sky being a unique exception.

Discovery of the Southern Sky

The Greek and later Arab skies had a gaping hole. Conducting observations on the territories of Mesopotamia, Greece, Egypt, and various parts of the Arab caliphate, one could not see stars that surround the Southern celestial pole. Due to this obvious impediment, the lists of Aratus and Ptolemy encompass only the Northern and equatorial portions of the sky without the Southern circumpolar zone.

The constellations around the Southern pole started to appear much later, and the campaigns for grouping the stars into newer constellations were marked by their own specific flavors. The Dutch provided the first example when several of them pioneered the en masse formation of new constellations in the Southern, then devoid of starry groupings, circumpolar sky at the threshold of the 17th century.

The period of Dutch maritime glory came a century after the first voyage of Columbus (1451-1506). It was by chance that the year of Columbus' arrival in the New World, 1492, coincided with the year that Martin Behaim (1436-1507), a German who served the Portuguese court, a navigator and instrument-maker, completed a terrestrial globe for his native city of Nuremberg, the oldest terrestrial globe extant. At about the same time another German, a majestic painter and engraver, Albrecht Dürer (1471-1528), created an artistic Ptolemaic celestial map that was to become an excellent archetype for all future celestial map-drawers. Neither Behaim nor Dürer could have foreseen that both geography and cartography stood on the threshold of new possibilities.

The European oversea adventurers of the time were mostly Italian, Portuguese, and British sea-traders. They were the first to admire the Southern sky that was invisible from the Mediterranean latitudes. The Florentine Amerigo Vespucci (1454-1512) composed a new star catalogue (Warner, 1979). The first pathfinders, however, did not feel the necessity to introduce any constellations for the sake of navigation.

The Heyday of Celestial Cartography

Celestial cartography advanced with geographic mapping, the best masters being mostly Italians from seaports and natives of the Iberian Peninsula with their famous sea charts, or *portolans*. There were experienced cartographers in Germany, Britain, France, and Switzerland, as well.

It was the German map-maker Martin Waldseemüller (c.1470 – c.1521) who in 1507 issued the American continent its "birth certificate." He updated cartographic knowledge after the expeditions of the late 1400's and early 1500's. One of his sources was Amerigo Vespucci, who trekked to the New World a decade after Columbus. On his globe and a map of 12 separate sheets covering 36 square feet, Waldseemüller was the harbinger in inaccurately labeling the new continent in honor of Amerigo Vespucci. One thousand woodcuts of the map were manufactured and sold, but only one has survived to the present day. It was discovered in 1901 in a southern German castle. Half a millennium after its composition, in 2001 this continental "birth certificate" was obtained by the Library of Congress for $ 10,000,000.

The Dutch took up their ocean-going trade as late as the very end of the 16th century, when the territories across the Atlantic Ocean were divided between Catholic Spain and Catholic Portugal by a papal bull issued by Alexander VI (Borgia) on May 4, 1493 (Stearns, 2001). (The line of demarcation was soon corrected in the Treaty of Tordesillas on June 7, 1494). At this time, the Dutch managed to reach the East Indies (the modern Indonesian archipelago) rather than Columbus' West Indies (Caribbean). It was, therefore, not an accident that in this very period of time, the finest map-making production shifted from warm Southern Europe to the chilly shores of the North Sea.

Senior among map-makers in those lands was Gemma Frisius (1508-1555) of Louvain. His student, Gerhard Kremer, a Belgian, was to become the world leader in the field under the name of Gerardus Mercator (1512-1594). The hallmark of Mercator was the Greek titan Atlas with a globe on his shoulders, the reason why to this day we use the term *atlas* for a collection of terrestrial or celestial maps.

But Gemma Frisius and Mercator were not alone. There existed a large number of gifted individuals that included Abraham Ortelius (1527-1598) of Antwerp, the designer of the first great terrestrial atlas (1570); Willem Janszoon of Alkmaar, who in 1595-96 studied under Tycho Brahe in his Astronomical Observatory and later emerged as a prominent cartographic producer and merchant under the name of Blaeu (1571-1638); van Langren the Son (1600-1675), a Royal Cartographer in Brussels and a pioneer in the charting of the Moon (1645); and some others. This group of outstanding map-makers from the Low Countries had as its member Petrus Plancius (1552-1622), the first cartographer for the newborn Dutch East India company. Plancius was an Amsterdam minister who devoted his attention entirely to adopting astronomical knowledge to the needs of navigation at sea out of sight of land.

All accomplishments in cartography and geodesy of that time were enormous; needless to add, the competition among the professionals in the field was extremely tough, economic significance being the driving force behind the flourishing map-making business.

It came as no surprise that it was the Dutch and not their predecessors in the business of oversea travel who provided the first point-by-point descriptions of the Southern skies. The intensive Dutch cartographic activity served both as the background and as the context for the installation of new constellations in the Southern circumpolar zone. In turn, new celestial names in the sky caught the attention of the educated public and created a proper pretext for the great astronomical boom that occurred soon in connection with the astonishing astronomical discoveries of Galileo.

Constellating the Southern Sky

Let us return, however, to the basic facts. The initial move of the Dutch conquest of the East Indies (Java, Sumatra, etc.) was the so-called "Eerste Schipvaart" (the *First Voyage*) started on April 2, 1595. Apart from commerce, two scientific assignments were imposed upon the expedition: to measure the magnetic deviation of the compass needle and to chart the stars around the Southern celestial pole.

These assignments were set by the aforementioned Petrus Plancius, the cartographer and theologian. He personally instructed a few crewmembers on how to perform astronomical observations and equipped the expedition with the astronomical instruments. It was established beforehand that all scientific accomplishments of the expedition would be exclusive possessions of Petrus Plancius himself. The Amsterdam merchants had ensured the latter right through the States General prior to the departure of the expedition.

The documents preserved to this day show that during the *First Voyage* the experienced navigator, Pieter Dircksz Keyser, executed the majority of the astronomical recordings. There are, however, strong reasons to believe that three other Dutch "lovers of astronomy" also practiced next to Keyser, namely Vechter Willemsz, Frederick de Houtman, and Pieter Stockmans (Dekker, 1987).

Fate willed it so that the leading skywatcher, Keyser, never returned home. The conditions of the Dutch undertaking were rough and when the sailors arrived back home on August 6, 1597, of the 249 initial crewmembers only about 90 had survived. In those long gone times, such occurrences were hardly unusual. Humanity has often had to pay a high price even for the tiniest grains of knowledge.

When the Dutch vessels of the *First Voyage* returned at last, Petrus Plancius secured the astronomical records and promptly proceeded with their primary analysis. Soon afterward, he dispatched his results to Jodocus Hondius, the engraver and producer, who, in turn, rushed to depict on his celestial globe of 1598 the newly recorded southern stars, nicely grouped together into twelve new constellations around the South pole.

Surely, Plancius was the mastermind behind the project, proudly dedicating the globe to the supreme ruling board of the country, the

States General. For this project, Plancius utilized his prior experience in globe making that went back to his cooperation with Jacob Floris van Langren the Father, with respect to the celestial globe of 1589.

Indeed, from 1598 onwards, all of Hondius' celestial globes included twelve new Southern constellations. Obviously, the new constellations were highly valued brainchildren of the motivated and experienced cartographer, Petrus Plancius.

Among the twelve new names of constellations installed under the aegis of Petrus Plancius, not more than three fit even a little into the ancient tradition of celestial nomenclature brought forth by Aratus and Ptolemy. Those three new names were the Phoenix, the Southern Triangle, and Hydrus. As for the other new names, they were called up by the images of the New World obtained through numerous voyages of discovery. These were mainly exotic beasts, some of them mythical and others native to the newly explored Southern countries.

The starry fields next to the South pole, as well as the newly formed constellations, were immediately incorporated into the excellent star atlas *Uranometria* presented by Johannes Bayer of Augsburg (Germany) in 1603. This atlas was well-made and much more popular throughout Europe than the Dutch globes. It is due to this classical product of Bayer's that the new crop of constellation names was brought to the attention of the general public of the time.

Following in Bayer's footsteps, other authors got hastily involved in the formation of the new Southern constellations. To make a long story short, we can definitely conclude that a century after Columbus' first voyage, there were spontaneous common efforts of several celestial cartographers. As a result, in just a few years at the turn of the 17th century, the map of the Southern sky was supplemented by a number of new constellations, fifteen of which have survived to this day. It was a grandiose precedent, a tremendous psychological breakthrough. It became apparent and publicly approved that ancient astronomers could be corrected and supplemented. A door was opened for those who desired to fill the eternal skies with their dreams, fantasies, and even memorabilia of their powerful patrons.

New names were overall very different from the old ones. Follow Flammarion's thoughts on this subject, for they reflected the renewed historical situation born of the stormy epoch of great geographical discoveries. The following is a roster of those fifteen Southern constellation names from the very beginning of the 17th century:

- Apus (the bird of paradise);
- Camelopardalis (the giraffe);
- Chamaeleon (the chameleon);
- Columba (the dove);
- Dorado (the goldfish);
- Grus (the crane);
- Hydrus (the little water-snake);
- Indus (the Indian);
- Monoceros (the unicorn);
- Musca (the fly);
- Pavo (the peacock);
- Phoenix (the Phoenix);
- Triangulum Australe (the southern triangle);
- Tucana (the toucan);
- Volans (the flying fish).

These fifteen names are taken from the *World Map* (1592), by Plancius, the *Celestial Globe* (1597/98), by Plancius with Hondius, and the *Celestial Globe* (1612), designed by Plancius with van den Keere.

New names by Johannes Hevelius of Poland

The Dutch/German example was contagious for their successors. In 1687, a number of new celestial groupings were installed in the Northern sky due to Johannes Hevelius (1611-1687) in his star map (1684) and star atlas, *Firmamentum Sobiescianum* (1690). Of the eleven figures invented by him, these seven have survived up to now:

- Canes Venatici (the hunting dogs);
- Lacerta (the lizard);
- Leo Minor (the little lion);
- Lynx (the lynx);
- Scutum (the shield);
- Sextans (the sextant);
- Vulpecula (the fox).

New names by Nicolas Louis de La Caille of France

Completely different images stood behind the mind of the French astronomer, Abbé Nicolas Louis de La Caille (1713-1762), in the mapping of the Southern skies a century after Hevelius, following his expedition to South Africa in 1751-52. The novelties emerged in his map (1754/55) and the Catalogue (1756) followed by Didier Robert de Vaugondy's map. It was La Caille who dismantled Argo Navis (the ship of the Argonauts) into Carina (the keel of the ship), Puppus (the stern of the ship), and Vela (the sails of the ship). One more ship constellation resides above due to him: Circinus, which is the compass of the ship. This astronomer preferred labels from science and art:

- Antlia Pneumatica (the air pump);
- Apparatus Sculptoris (the sculptor's workshop);
- Caelum Scalptorium (the sculptor's chisel);
- Circinus (the pair of compasses);
- Equuleus Pictoris (the painter's easel);
- Fornax (the chemist's furnace)
- Horologium (the pendulum clock);
- Microscopium (the microscope);
- Mons Mensae (the table mountain, his study place);
- Norma et Regula (the builder's level);
- Octans (the octant invented by Hadley in 1731);
- Pyxis (the mariner's compass);
- Reticulum (the reticule in the eyepiece of a telescope);
- Telescopium (the telescope).

Ear to the Ground

Does it not seem self-evident that the realities and feelings of the epoch were reflected in the constellation names proposed by the Hungarian astronomer Maximillian Hell (1720-1792), Joseph-Jerome de La Lande (1732-1807) of France, and the German astronomer Johann Elert Bode (1747-1826)? For example, they were:

- Globus Aerostatica (the balloon);
- Lochium Funis (the nautical log and line);
- Machina Electra (the electrical machine);
- Officina Typographica (the printing shop);
- Tubus Herschelii Major (greater Herschel's telescope);
- Tubus Herschelii Minor (lesser Herschel's telescope).

Being insufficient in their areas, those last-mentioned failed to stay in the sky in the 20th century after the reform by the IAU.

The process of spontaneous formation of new constellations came to an end in the beginning of the 20th century after the International Astronomical Union (IAU) was created. The Union became the dominating international force in the field of astronomy, an authority subject to no doubts. Cleaning up and cosmetically restructuring the celestial map were on the Union's agenda as top priorities from the get-go.

Right away, at the first General Assembly of the IAU in Rome in 1922, an official roster of 88 constellations was adopted, and it remains unchanged to this day. The task of fixing the boundaries of the constellations was assigned to the astronomer Eugène Joseph Delporte (1882-1955) from the Royal Astronomical Observatory at Uccle (Belgium). His report, *Délimitation scientifique des constellations: (tables et cartes),* was published in 1930. The boundaries between constellations were established along arcs of coordinate circles (right ascension and declination). Because of the slow changes in these circles in respect to the stars, it was specified that boundaries of the constellations were drawn for the epoch 1875, January 1.

The Unique Reshuffling of the Chinese Sky

In all of documented history of constellation naming, there is one solitary precedent when the entire nomenclature of constellations was completely rearranged. This happened in China. An analysis of the given problem is presented in the book *The Chinese Sky During the Han: Constellating Stars and Society* by Sun Xiaochun and Jacob Kistemaker (1997).

The case of the Chinese sky appeared to be entirely different from the case of the sky in the Mediterranean region. In the centuries before the Common Era, the "Empire beneath the Heavens" reached well-being with a rise in national self-consciousness and the making of its own worldview, a perfect example of which is the unique Chinese religion without priesthood (Wu, 1982). Chinese rulers believed that they had gotten a mandate from Heaven to rule over the Earth.

The ideology of imperial China served as the prime mover for a cataclysmic reform of the celestial "megalopolis." Instead of the earlier episodic constellations, Chinese court astrologers of the Han Dynasty (after 200 BCE) thoughtfully peppered the sky with 283 petty asterisms, often comprised of only one or two hard-to-distinguish stars. The network of these newfangled asterisms was molded into the likeness of the Chinese imperial court: the Emperor, Celestial Officials, the Emperor's Facilities, etc. This celestial pileup was propagated by all Chinese royal astronomical institutions of later times. The previous star repertoire was abandoned.

A full reformation of the Chinese sky could only have happened as a consequence of three circumstances of utmost importance:

1) the beliefs of Chinese rulers on receiving a mandate for power from the skies;
2) significant isolation of China from the rest of the civilized world of the epoch; and
3) the presence on a large territory of a mighty central power interested in the radical reform of the sky according to its own social, cultural, and ideological reasons while at the same time possessing the resources to bring such a reform to life with an iron fist.

Nothing of the sort had ever before taken place in earlier Middle Eastern and Mediterranean cultures: they had not been so strongly oriented towards a dependence on the sky, they had not been so strongly isolated from each other, and, finally, they had not controlled significantly large territories to possess the economic might required for performing such a drastic reform. In all likelihood, they never presented themselves with the ideological goal of reflecting their own glory in the sky by instituting their own system of constellations.

For present-day historians of archaic astronomy, the reshaping of the Chinese sky was a stroke of bad luck. The misfortune happened because of the zealousness of Chinese court reformers, who eradicated the legacy of ancient epochs in the sky. Nothing like this took place in what we have dubbed the European tradition. The Mesopotamians followed in the footsteps of their predecessors. Greeks and Romans took the same path.

Were There Revisions in the Sky?

In respect to historic times, denying radical reforms of the starry sky in the Near East and Mediterranean regions, we must immediately make the claim that we by no means rule out partial revisions and adjustments to the celestial map with regard to the necessities of the time. We know of a number of such obvious alterations.

In the previous Chapter we had mentioned that the small constellation of Libra was formed from the claws of Scorpio as a label for the position of the autumnal equinox. There was, most likely, a second goal: to bring the total number of zodiacal constellations to 12; in this case, the number of zodiacal constellations would be equal to the number of calendric months in a year.

Several discrepancies in celestial nomenclature appear between ancient Greek sources and cuneiform texts. For instance, researchers have no doubts that the constellation of Aries did not exist in Mesopotamia. Its place was taken by *hunga* the Hireling (*agru*), an outdoor agricultural worker (see, for example, Gleadow, 1968, pp.172-173). No one has yet managed to determine the time when the Hireling gave way to the Ram.

Leaning on the work of Bobrova and Militarev (1993), A.Yu.Militarev (1995) vehemently argued that in Sumerian texts Sagittarius the Archer was represented as the Old Man or, at least, an Elder Kinsman, while in Virgo's place the texts spoke of the ear of grain (or, less likely, a furrow). It seems that Militarev's examples sooner prove than negate our suppositions. Yes, in ancient times mutations of names took place, but they, as a rule, did not stray far from the original symbolic meaning. Both the Archer and the Elder Kinsman were respected patrilineal members. Both the ear of grain (or furrow) and the Virgin are symbolic embodiments of fertility.

Many more discrepancies exist between the Greek and Egyptian skies. In May 25, 1799, Napoleon's officers in Egypt were amazed when they reached a temple in Dendera. On its ceiling there was a bas-relief with the signs of the Zodiac (Gingerich, 1992, pp.1-6). These signs were easily recognized, and within that band the five naked-eye planets are depicted as gods holding staffs. Meanwhile, among the depictions of the starry sky from Dendera as well as a number of other Egyptian sites, several figures were found that do not appear on the Greek sky, such as a crocodile and a hippopotamus, which had never even been seen in Greece.

The sky has always been a "handwritten manuscript" that could be corrected when necessary. Local diversity, of course, has always existed. However, as far as we can judge from surviving reliable sources, stargazers in general strove to maintain the cultural traditions of their ancestors.

An interesting historical analogy presents itself in the evolution of the symbolism of woman and her birth-giving body (Baring and Cashford, 1991). In the Paleolithic, a birth-giving woman gave a stimulus to the idea of the Mother Goddess. In the Neolithic, the same role was transformed into the Great Goddess of Sky, Earth, and Waters. Later, the equivalent to this role became the Goddess of Life, Death, and Regeneration. In Mesopotamia, this goddess turned into the Great Above and the Great Below. With emerging monotheistic views, the former goddess became Eve, the Mother of all Living. Finally, during the Christian era, the woman symbolism was sublimated within the image of the Virgin Mary.

This story is very enlightening. In various epochs, the same symbolic image appeared under various veils. Something like this took place concerning the constellations. In the sky, there were revisions but no radical reforms.

How Were the Newer Constellations Formed?

So far in this Chapter, we have gathered facts about the process of constellation-making over the course of the last two millennia, starting with the time of Aratus. The time has come to generalize the facts and draw certain conclusions, the first of which is obvious: prior to the birth of the International Astronomic Union, the process of forming new constellations had a spontaneous and unruly nature.

Before, there existed no rules or procedures for the institution and naming of new constellations. Industrious individuals showed initiative. If their results were found to be meaningful and appealed to the other interested persons who started to replicate said results, then they entered into wider usage and grew, with time, into a hallowed tradition. If, however, the new constellation was not popular, the other interested persons simply did not lend it their support. The result did not pass the test of time and disappeared from astronomical practice.

Only the international community, in the guise of the International Astronomical Union, was able to codify the appropriate procedure. Needless to say, no such organization existed prior to the 20th century and could not even be imagined in the time of Aratus or Claudius Ptolemy. Consequently, we reach the general conclusion that not only after Ptolemy, but long before him, as well, which is to say from the very beginning, the process of forming new constellations was unpremeditated and ungoverned.

Conclusion number two relates to the conservatism of astronomical traditions discussed earlier in this Chapter. Despite the addition of a few new constellations over the course of the last two thousand years, especially in the "empty" area around the Southern pole of the sky, the larger part of the sky's constellational repertoire has not even undergone minor changes, the Chinese sky being an exception. This is a serious consideration to take into account, one that must have deep socio-cultural roots in human consciousness.

The Names are Brainchildren of their Epochs

The third important conclusion has to do with the names of the constellations. An analysis of the names introduced into the sky after Claudius Ptolemy clearly shows that they reflected the knowledge and interests of contemporary peoples. They were the brainchildren of their corresponding epochs. Could *Indus, Tucana, Antila Pneumatica, Octans, Microscopium, Telescopium, Reticulum, Machina Electra, Officina Typographica,* etc. appear in the sky before or after the time they actually assumed their positions? Clearly not. Prior to the epoch when these names were used in the sky, their subjects simply did not exist; a few centuries later, these subjects ceased to be fascinating novelties. It is hard to imagine anyone today standing in awe of an air pump or a printing press. In the contemporary world, we see spaceships, computers, and the DNA double helix as the significant symbols of our progress.

Summing up, is it fair to say that the 88 constellations codified by the International Astronomical Union at the beginning of the 20th century could be grouped chronologically using only the peculiarities of their names? Many authors have appealed to such a possibility. Unfortunately, however, neither Flammarion, the author of the important analogy with the Paris city map, nor the other historians of astronomy have tried such an undertaking. None of them pursued this excellent idea in respect to ancient constellations formed before Claudius Ptolemy.

Lacking predecessors in this endeavor, I would now like to broaden and strengthen Flammarion's proposition. Not only specific terms such as toponyms and hydronyms, but language itself in general – a substantial carrier of human culture – is a priceless historical testimony. Living languages never become fossilized. As they live, they grow. Their vocabulary is constantly enriched (though Orwell's Newspeak from the famous novel *1984* may serve as the unique exception). Thus, an analysis of the older astronyms can become a valuable tool in our search for the origins of the zodiacal constellations.

Are we, indeed, capable of extracting anything instructive just from a series of terms and names? Let us turn to another astronomical example that will clarify what I am talking about. I want to discuss the names in the Roman calendar.

As we have mentioned earlier, a radical reform of the tangled, aged Roman calendar was conducted by Julius Caesar and Octavianus Augustus. As the legacy of their innovations, the world has received the current order of names for the 12 months of the year: January, February, March, April, May, June, July, August, September, October, November, and December. What can we deduce from those names even if we know nothing of the reform itself?

First of all, it is evident that the names of September, October, November, and December are the ordinal Latin numbers (*septem*, *octo*, *novem* and *decem*) for the Seventh, Eighth, Ninth, and Tenth. Meanwhile, those months in the current calendar are correspondingly ninth, tenth, eleventh, and twelfth. The conclusion is that these names are relics of the aged calendar, and its old beginning was located at different place.

Several other names of months are relics from ancient Roman gods, but it is not tricky to notice that the seventh month, July, is named in honor of Julius Caesar, while the eighth one is named after the emperor Augustus. Some other vainglorious emperors failed to wedge their names into the calendar, which means that in broad public opinion, only Caesar and Augustus deserved this honor because of their extraordinary achievements in the calendric field. So far, there is enough evidence that may help us even to date the reform in question.

Moreover, there is an antiquated term, *bissextile*, literally in Latin *twice sixth*. It reminds us of an intercalated day in the new Julian calendar, the sixth day before the calends of March being recounted twice every fourth year. Thus, just the linguistic consideration allows to penetrate into the details of calendars before and after Julius Caesar.

The example of the calendric names is certainly not the only case when the names themselves reveal a timeframe for their creation. We can cite another sound example of this sort, the names of the days of the week. In the times of Julius Caesar, the Romans maintained those names as they were derived from the seven planetary gods in the following order:

Sol (the Sun),
Luna (the Moon),
Mars,
Mercury,
Jupiter,
Venus,
Saturn.

Interestingly, the Welsh language protected all those names in accordance with their pronunciation in Latin and without any changes:

Dydd-sul,
Dydd-llun,
Dydd-mawrth,
Dydd-mercher,

Dydd-jou,

Dydd-gwener,

Dydd-sadwrn.

The Gaelic language, a close relative of Welsh, protected the majority of those names but not the day of the Sun, which, in accordance with the Christian influence became the day of the Lord: Di-domhnaich. The same alteration took place for many European languages where Sunday is the day of the Lord: Dimanche – in French, Domenica – in Italian, Domingo – in Spanish and Portuguese.

In Portuguese and the Slavic languages, other days of the week are basically their ordinal numbers. But Northern Europeans adopted the planetary week names, converting them in accordance with the names of native deities. In such a form, we find the names of the week in current English. Wednesday is named after Woden, or Odin (the Norse equivalent of Mercury). Thursday is named after Thunor, or Thor (the Norse equivalent of Jupiter), and Friday is named after the goddess Frigg (the Norse equivalent of Venus). The Norse god who was equivalent to the Roman Mars – Tyr, or Tiw - presented his proper name for Tuesday. We have no specific explanation for why the name of Saturn was not converted but, instead, preserved with its Roman spelling.

Together with F.H.Colson (1926) we can determine:

> "The conclusion seems inevitable that the week was carried into the lands beyond the Rhine and Danube from the still unchristianized Empire, that is to say, not much later and probably earlier than the fourth century. It is quite possible that the remarkably strong Mithraistic zeal which, as inscriptions show, prevailed in the Roman army may have had something to do with this" (p.112).

Because of the conversion of gods' and goddesses' names onto native soils, it is possible to conclude that the week was originally a kind of religious institution. But that is not my main point. Using the cited examples, I want to stress what a rich layer of information can be found in a simple list of names. In both the given examples, the lists of names – for months and days of the week – seem at first glance to be completely homogeneous, but can in fact be easily "layered" into several various historic strata. This is possible because names really do reflect the epochs of their birth, allowing the people who give them to make the world their own. This conclusion will serve us in the later analysis of zodiacal names. We hope to convince the reader just how much can be extracted from the zodiacal images and names in the forthcoming chapters.

Statistics: the Size/Age Correlation

The last, the fourth, derivation from the written history of the newer constellations is of the statistical nature. As noted earlier, the 88 constellations approved by the International Astronomical Union at the beginning of 20th century may be chronologically grouped exactly enough only on the basis of peculiarities of their names. But this characteristic is not measurable. Is there something definite about the peculiarities of those campaigns of constellation naming that can be determined and measured as is customary in the exact sciences?

Constellations do have some measurable parameters. First, there are two celestial coordinates of their dispositions on the celestial sphere. Depending on their dispositions on a given geographical latitude, a constellation may be visible or invisible, either circumpolar, or rising and setting. In accordance with their dispositions, one can sort out the constellations, which are polar, equatorial, zodiacal, Northern, Southern, etc. We have used these parameters many times, but they have little to do with our main problem. There is no real sense in using them for my cause.

One more measurable parameter is the size of a constellation. With regard to our problem, the sizes of the constellations are the only feature that can be exploited by a statistical approach. Does it really make any sense? At a glance, it is absolutely absurd, but let me investigate the problem in more details using the 88 constellations that survived IAU reform at the beginning of the 20th century.

For simplification, we shall use the modern constellations' areas, which are tabulated in modern handbooks. They range from about 1,300 square degrees (Hydra, Virgo, Ursa Major) to some 70-80 square degrees (Crux, Equuleus, Sagitta). Can we rely on using current areas instead of older ones? Yes, because in creating the modern sky map, IAU appointees followed older constellation configurations as closely as possible. Of course, archaic constellations had no strict borders at all. The constellations were a kind of foggy spot, and there are vacant spaces between them. IAU did its best to protect the old constellation configurations, and I can do nothing better. Meanwhile, IAU replaced curved boundaries with celestial meridians and parallels; this action alone had to change the areas of the constellations.

We can estimate the probable difference between average areas of old constellations and their modern representations. Let me suppose that the boundary of any constellation changes by 5° (a highly improbable occurrence). The area of the constellation in this case will then increase or decrease by about 100-150 square degrees. Averaged for the whole sky, it will influence the deviation of the average area by some 25-35 square degrees, which is still insignificant. Even if we admit that some boundaries shift casually within the limits of 10°, we see that the averaged areas of constellations will change by amounts too small compared with the discrepancies between the constellation mean areas.

As a result of this consideration, we can have confidence that the results of the analyzed data do not depend on the fact that the boundaries of the constellations may have had considerable changes in the past. Errors in the areas are not absolute, but relative, and don't exceed 10% of the square. To be applied to the group of constellations, these errors are random but not of systematic character. This means that averaging decreases the final error.

Let us investigate the complete roster of 88 modern constellations in respect to their average area in accordance with the time of their installation. To do so, let me prepare a table of corresponding data.

CONSTELLATIONS BY AREAS

1-3	*	Argo	1,667	46	*	Lupus	334
4	*	Hydra	1,303	47		Sextans	314
5	*	Virgo	1,294	48		Tucana	295
6	*	Ursa Major	1,280	49		Indus	294
7	*	Cetus	1,231	50		Octans	291
8	*	Hercules	1,225	51	*	Lepus	290

9	*	Eridanus	1,138
10	*	Pegasus	1,121
11	*	Draco	1,083
12	*	Centaurus	1,060
13	*	Aquarius	980
14	*	Ophiuchus	948
15	*	Leo	947
16	*	Bootes	907
17	*	Pisces	889
18	*	Sagittarius	867
19	*	Cygnus	804
20	*	Taurus	797
21		Camelopardalis	757
22	*	Andromeda	722
23	*	Auriga	657
24	*	Aquila	652
25	*	Serpens	637
26	*	Perseus	615
27	*	Cassiopeia	598
28	*	Orion	594
29	*	Cepheus	588
30		Lynx	545
31	*	Libra	538
32	*	Gemini	514
33	*	Cancer	506
34	*	Scorpius	497
35		Monoceros	482
36		Sculptor	475
37		Phoenix	469

52	*	Lyra	286
53	*	Crater	282
54		Columba	270
55		Velpecula	268
56	*	Ursa Minor	256
57		Telescopium	252
58		Horologium	249
59		Pictor	247
60	*	Pisces Austrinus	245
61		Hydrus	243
62		Antlia	239
63	*	Ara	237
64		Leo Minor	232
65		Pyxus	221
66		Microscopium	210
67		Apus	206
68		Lacerta	201
69	*	Delphinus	189
70	*	Corvus	184
71	*	Canis Minor	183
72		Dorado	179
73	*	Corona Borealis	179
74		Norma	165
75		Mensa	153
76		Volans	141
77		Musca	138
78	*	Triangulum	132
79		Chamaeleon	132
80	*	Corona Australis	128

38		Canes Venetici	465	81	Caelum	125
39	*	Aries	441	82	Reticulum	114
40	*	Capricornus	414	83	Triangulum Australe	110
41		Fornax	398	84	Scutum	109
42		Coma Berenices	386	85	Circinus	93
43	*	Canis Major	380	86 *	Sagitta	80
44		Pavo	378	87	Equuleus	72
45		Grus	366	88	Crux	68

This is a list of modern constellations as it was approved by IAU (Delporte, 1930) with only one exception; of course, we need to consider Aratus' genuine form of Argo Navis rather than the three small constellations it was dismembered into by La Caille. For convenience, the presence of constellations in Aratus' inventory is marked by an asterisk (the second column). The constellations are placed in order of their areas from the largest to the smallest.

Now let us calculate the averaged areas of constellations during different campaigns of their forming. The collected data are in the next table. Because we have no information on the constellations in pre-Aratus time, we average all Aratean constellations together. There is a nuance because Aratus had mentioned two articles that are not constellations now: Bow and Pleiades. For simplification, I consider the areas of these asterisms to be equal to zero, and therefore I *decrease* the averaged areas. Just in case, I calculate the averaged areas without those two small asterisms (the result is inside the parenthesis).

DISCLOSURE OF AVERAGE AREAS OF MODERN CONSTELLATIONS IN DIFFERENT HISTORICAL WAVES OF THEIR INSTALLATIONS

Informant, or author	Time	*Quantity*	*Average area (sq. degrees)*	*Hemi-sphere*
Aratus of Soli	~275 BCE	49 (47)	631 (657)	Both
Johann Bayer	1603	15	297	South
Johannes Hevelius	1687	7	305	North
Abbé La Caille	1751-52	14	231	South

Very noteworthy and meaningful statistical figures come into view in the last table: the more recent a campaign to form constellations, the smaller in average area (in a statistical sense) those constellations were. Does it make sense? For sure, and this result could even be easily predicted *a priori* on purely theoretical grounds.

Let us imagine that once upon a time the celestial sphere was devoid of constellations. To assemble a constellation, some bright and very noticeable stars were to be bunched together within a certain large region. Fortunately, no restrictions on the size of a constellation existed in those early times. The appropriate tips on constellations installed were carried out by word of mouth from generation to generation. Due to well-known ethnological peculiarities, those firstborn stellar formations remained very stable, essentially forever.

The process under consideration continued developing and less vacant space remained in the sky. Eventually, it became technically impossible to impose new constellations equal in their dimensions to older ones. Two options existed to continue the process: either to introduce smaller constellations, or to partition some older ones. In both cases, the newly formed constellations became smaller than previous ones. This very scenario is pictured in the last table.

There is no reason for trying to deduce an exact mathematical expression for such a process, because laws of mathematics did not regulate it. For our cause it would be satisfactory to limit it with qualitative evaluation. Being statistical in nature, the result of analysis in constellation making is "larger implies older." In the following text, this statistical rule of thumb will be defined as the *size criterion*.

Appealing Analogs for Size/Age Correlation

Is it possible that sometimes a historical process predetermines conditions such that the constituents of the process become smaller as the process develops in time? Yes, such correlations exist, and anyone can find his own examples without hesitation.

Let us consider possible examples. The land fiefs that three to four centuries ago were given to the vassals of the Russian tsars and tsarinas were boundlessly vast. From then onwards, the allotments of private lands in pre-revolutionary Russia grew much smaller, still numbering, however, in hundreds and tens of hectares. The lands given to people in the USSR before the Second World War for *dachas* reached up to one hectare in size, while the garden lots of Khrushchev's era didn't exceed a tiny six hundred square meters.

The dimensions of Russian private lands went down with time. I am sure, in a statistical sense, the same is typical for many countries. As time passes, population grows, and the price of land goes up, while land possessions are fragmented and the average lot of private land decreases.

Startling correlations materialize around us now and then, and we can find an even better example. As the cartographic surveys from space flourished, astronomers received images of Mars, Venus, Mercury, etc. The International Astronomical Union appointed special standing committees that would concern themselves with topographical features of the Solar system bodies. The first objects to be named were the largest ones. As the process went forward, smaller objects were taken into account. As time passed the objects to be named grew smaller and smaller still (see, for instance, Cocks & Cocks, 1995).

This last analogy is especially important because it is absolutely the same process that supposedly took place with the forming of constellations. The earliest constellations, elaborated on the *tabula rasa* of the celestial sphere, on average were greater than those placed later on, possibly on a sphere that had been already filled with many previous constellations. If this assertion is correct, the correlation between the sizes of the constellations and the time of their establishment on the celestial sphere should be a real fact.

Within the earliest constellations, bright and noticeable stars are grouped from vast celestial domains. Due to the authority of ancestral tradition, these early constellations grew more and more rigid as time passed. They came to be known in different corners of the world. Ages rolled by, and new constellations were added that were statistically smaller and smaller. This rule might be incorrect if applied to an individual star group, but, in general, the statistical rule "larger implies older" will supply us with a very efficient clue to the archaic sky.

As an output of the analysis of the written-documented process of formation of the newer constellations in the last two-plus millennia, we have reached four general conclusions.

1. The process of constellation-forming was spontaneous and unpremeditated.
2. Conservative traditionalism prevailed in respect to the names, configurations, and positions of the constellations placed into pre-existing systems; as a rule, constellations did not change their names, configurations, or location in the sky.
3. The names of constellations were imbued with their intellectual context; they were brainchildren of the epochs of their origination and symbolically reflected those epochs.
4. Not more than statistical by its nature, there is a rule of thumb that a larger constellation implies an older one.

Let us stress one more time that at this point, we have no way to prove the validity of these conclusions in the earlier undocumented epochs. It is, however, common scientific practice to extrapolate, and we feel justified in using these conclusions while configuring the working hypothesis on the genesis and evolution of the 12-strong zodiacal entity.

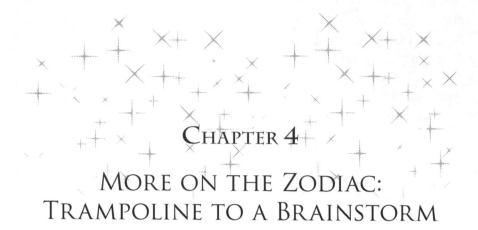

CHAPTER 4

MORE ON THE ZODIAC: TRAMPOLINE TO A BRAINSTORM

The science of astronomy puts at our disposal a description of the Zodiac, exhibits its location in the sky, demonstrates its links to the four seasons, and explains the changes it undergoes due to precession. All of this knowledge was collected in Chapter 2.

However, this is not enough for our forthcoming investigation. As an analogy, it is often not enough to typify an individual with only his physical parameters, height and weight; for a more complete picture one has to consider his profession and emotional qualities. So with the Zodiac, to understand it fully, one has to acknowledge and appreciate the layers of cultural meaning associated with it.

One cannot forget that the Zodiac is a part of the larger picture of the sky, which, besides serving its astronomical function, for the ancients was imbued with special symbolic and spiritual content.

What were Constellation Names?

In the previous Chapter, we reached the conclusion that the names of constellations were their epochs' brainchildren. Now, this is the moment to take the next step and to widen the conclusion, stating that the names of constellations, taken in the context of their time, were not simply abstractions created in a given time, but symbols of vital issues deeply related to that time.

There exists a problem connected with the semantic decoding of the ancient names of constellations. Modern understanding has usually stressed the standard Greek interpretation of the problem, according to which the sky is embroidered with pattern-pictures. In other words, the names of constellations reflect mainly the outward appearance of starry groups. However, there exists a different approach.

Once upon a time, an Englishman of Trinity College, Cambridge, asserted that starry names were created "*for instruction's sake... things cannot be taught without names*" (Allen, 1963, p. v).

The best example of a symbolic name among the zodiacal constellations is that of Libra, which was put in the place of Scorpio's claws to mark the *equilibrium* of the autumnal equinox.

The key aspect of the problem in consideration is: whether the names of ancient constellations were given in accordance with their outward appearance or whether they were memory markers associated with the symbols of certain natural phenomena?

The thesis of the symbolic approach towards the naming of stars and constellations is supported by the folklore of the Australian aborigines, provided over a hundred years ago by E.B.Tylor (1832-1917), an outstanding researcher of primitive culture:

> "The savage names and stories of stars and constellations may seem at first but childish and purposeless fancies; but it always happens in the study of the... races, that the more means we have of understanding their thoughts, the more sense and reason do we find in them. The aborigines of Australia say that... Marpean-Kurrk and Neilloan (Arcturus and Lyra) were the discoverers of the ant-pupas and the eggs of the loan-bird, and taught the aborigines to find them for food. Translated into the language of fact, this simple myth records the summer place of the stars in question, and the seasons of ant-pupas and loan-eggs, which seasons are marked by the stars who are called their discoverers" (1903, Vol.1, p.357; Tylor borrowed this example from Stanbridge in *Tr. Eth. Soc.*, Vol. i, pp.301-3).

Concluding the examination of several examples, Tylor noted:

"When we consider that the Australians who can invent such myths, and invent them with such fullness of meaning, are savages who put two and one together to make their numeral for three, we may judge how deep in the history of culture those conceptions lie, of which the relics are still represented in our star-maps…" (*Op. cit.*, p.358).

Can you really find humans or animals in the sky? A fair answer is *NO*. Groups of stars unified into constellations are, as a rule, unfit for the pictures "reflected" in their names. Outward appearances of constellations have nothing to do with their names. And for the purposes of this book, we shall thus consider it justified to insert the general presumption for the subsequent reconstruction: the names of constellations *WERE NOT* the result of wild and unorganized imagination; they were brought into existence with symbolic definitions.

Were Constellations Sky Pictures or Registry Marks?

What triggered the vision of the authors of new constellations such as, for example, the Giraffe, the Fly, or the Telescope? It is doubtful that anyone would argue that the creators were looking in the star groups for a visual similarity with their namesakes. All the creators were trying to achieve was to fill an empty stretch of sky and give the new constellations names that were stylish in their era and reflected the spirit thereof. Would this thought be true for the earlier constellations?

Abu'l-Hasayn al-Sūfī (903-986), a great authority on Islamic astronomy whose illustrious manuscript (MS Marsh 144) on constellations is a true pearl at the Bodleian Library, Oxford, UK, insisted that the constellations were formed and named from their outward natural appearance. And that was an aspect of a very old dispute: was it appearance or some other principle that stuck out in the minds of the first constellation-makers?

Of course, it is impossible to deny entirely that some ancient constellations with bright stars were established early on as very noteworthy stellar groups. Many people know the constellations that are distinguished in accordance with their configuration peculiarities, such as Ursa Major and some others. However, it is first of all the zodiacal constellations on the ecliptic that provide opposing examples.

In the sky, we distinguish stars with so called *stellar magnitudes*. The brightest of them we call stars of the 1st magnitude. Seven stars of Ursa Major are about 2nd magnitude. The dimmest stars visible to the naked eye are about 6th magnitude.

So, what do we have among the zodiacal constellations? The vast area of Pisces, for instance, contains no star brighter than magnitude 4, and Aquarius includes none brighter than magnitude 3. Nor are there any bright stars in Sagittarius. These facts testify that ancient observers wanted not only to unite bright starry groups into constellations as *starry pictures*, but sometimes also to put together certain important areas of the heaven as *celestial markers*.

Astrological Classifications of the Zodiac

A classification is the first mindstep of each and every scientific research. What do we know about the Zodiac in this respect?

Obviously, as a final stage, the zodiacal succession resulted in a set of 12 enigmatic images. It was elaborated into a rather confused polysemantic, semiotic complex, and many various classifications of its constituents appeared to be viable. Only a few authors were interested in the interpretation of the zodiacal symbolism, while it had a great significance for astrology.

Modern astrology is a subject of severe critique by scholars. In no way is it a science. Nevertheless, for millennia astrology had its share in shaping human culture. As such, in certain aspects it could be a key to better understanding many social and cultural issues.

Just as simple examples, let us think about the literal meanings of two ordinary words: the noun, *disaster*, and the verb, *to consider*. It is obvious that disaster has the same Greek root as astronomy; in the Greek language, *astron* means 'star' while *dis* is a prefix of negation. Disaster, which nowadays means a grave misfortune, originally was an astrological term for an unfavorable influence of a celestial body, i.e., an ill-starred event, or an event going on under an improper star.

To consider is a similar case. *Con* is a prefix for moving together in the same direction like in the words *conformist, concenter, concord*, etc.

Siderus is Latin for 'star'. The genuine meaning of the verb, to consider, was the astrological term to observe the stars carefully.

> "The roots of modern astrology reach very deep into our past and into the past of other world cultures… Old astrology dealt with decision making at the state as well as at the individual level. It was as much concerned with how to deal with the world and society as economics, sociology, and political theory are today…
>
> Astrology was not a mere appendage to history that stood in the way of scientific advancement. It was a vital part of the culture that spawned modern science. To attempt to skim it from the surface of science like some useless scum, or 'superstitious flotsam' as one historian of science once characterized it, does a disservice to history" (Aveni, 2002, pp.ix-x).

Traces of astrology in human culture are manifold and, in this book, sometimes we shall use astrology for purposes of clarification.

It comes as no surprise then, regardless of our current attitude toward astrology, that we are forced to follow astrological literature to glance at the deeper meaning of the zodiacal semiotic complex. The ultimate examples of various classifications of the Zodiac can be excerpted from the poetic opus of the Roman author, Marcus Manilius (the latest edition in the Loeb Classical Library with an English translation by G.P.Goold, 1977).

Marcus Manilius was a Roman astrologer and versifier, the author of *Astronomica*. If Aratus compiled a didactic poem concerning constellations in Greek, about three centuries later Manilius exercised the same genre to compile a protracted astrological encyclopedia of the period in Latin. It is the first surviving textbook of astrological views. Two manuscripts of *Astronomica* made in the 10th and 11th centuries lay hidden in monasteries, one at Gembloux in Brabant (now in Brussels) and another that has come to rest in the library at Leipzig. The unknown text was rediscovered by the humanist Bracciolini somewhere not very far from Constance during a break in the sessions of the Council of Constance that he was attending, in 1416 or 1417.

Nothing certain is known of Manilius' biography, but from the context of his own opus, it may be concluded that it was written during the last years of the "Golden Age" of the founder of the Roman Empire Octavianus Augustus (reigned as the sole ruler of the Roman world from 27 BCE to 14 CE) or the first years of the rule of Tiberius (14-31 CE). Both of them were contemporaries of Jesus Christ. The astrological treatise of Marcus Manilius considerably preceded the books of Claudius Ptolemy, who flourished in the 2nd century CE.

Manilius' *Astronomica* contains 5 books, ranging in length from 650 to nearly 1,000 lines for a total of about 4,500 lines. He counts the zodiacal signs anticlockwise, east-west direction, starting with the vernal equinox. So, for him Aries is the leader:

> "First Aries shining in his golden fleece,
> Wonders to see the back of Taurus rise,
> Taurus who calls, with lowered head, the Twins,
> Whom Cancer follows; Leo follows him,
> Then Virgo; Libra next, day equaling night,
> Draws on the Scorpion with its blazing star,
> Whose tail the Half-horse aims at with his bow,
> Ever about to loose his arrow swift.
> Then comes the narrow curve of Capricorn,
> And after him Aquarius pours from his urn
> Waters the following Fishes greedily use
> Which Aries touches, last of all the signs."

Manilius derived many different kinds of classifications for the zodiacal signs according to their positions on the ecliptic, names, "natures," and "qualities." For instance, Manilius considered signs to be masculine and feminine:

> "My song must first mark the different nature of the signs according to sex. For six are masculine, whilst as many, led by the Bull, are of the opposite sex: you see how he rises by his hind limbs when he reappears. They alternate their sex, changing one after another round the circle" (p.95).

The masculine signs are Aries, Gemini, Leo, Libra, Sagittarius, and Aquarius. As strange as it seems, the feminine ones are Taurus, Cancer, Virgo, Scorpio, Capricorn, and Pisces. As it is clear, for Manilius, a sign's gender is founded not on sex but on the Pythagorean judgment that odd numbers are male and even numbers are female. As a result, for Manilius a celestial Bull is a female sign.

> "You will also behold the human form in some, and the depositions they bestow are not out of keeping; some will produce the nature of cattle and beasts. Certain signs must with careful mind be noted as single, and these keep to an unshared estate. Now turn to the double signs; being doubled they will exert influences the power of which is tempered by a partner" (p.95).

Manilius classified the Lion, the Archer, and the Ram as running signs; the Virgin, the Twins, and the Waterman as standing erect with their limbs perfectly poised; the Bull, the Balance, and Capricorn as sitting fatigued and reflecting their weariness of mind, while the Crab, the Scorpion, and the Fishes as lying flat.

Another type of Manilius' classification comes from the way the signs rise: unlike the other signs, which rise in upright posture, Taurus, Gemini, and Cancer do so upside down:

> "… Three adjacent signs are at variance with the other nine and a kind of dissension takes hold on heaven. Observe that the Bull rises by his hind quarters, the Twins by their feet, the Crab by his shell, whereas all the others rise in upright posture" (p.99).

The Roman listed four signs – Scorpio, Taurus, Cancer, and Sagittarius – as "maimed" (diminished by the loss of some parts):

> "Now if you examine all the signs with keen attention, you will find some bereft of limbs which are lost. The Scorpion expends its arms on the Scales, the Bull sinks lame with leg doubled under it, the Crab lacks eyes, whilst of the Centaur's one survives and one is missing. Thus the sky assuages our misfortunes in its stars, and by example teaches us to undergo loss with fortitude, since the whole scheme of fortune depends upon heaven, and even constellations are fashioned with limbs deformed" (p.103).

There are numerous other classifications in the Manilius tractate. He described Aries, Taurus, Cancer, Leo, Libra, Scorpio, and Aquarius as the single signs, while the remainders are double. Of those, Gemini and Pisces are pairs, Sagittarius and Capricorn are composites, while Virgo demands classification as a double by belonging to the square, each of whose members effects a juncture of two seasons.

Manilius discusses the opposite signs of day and night (diurnal or nocturnal); aquatic, terrestrial, and amphibious; fertile and barren; seasonal signs which are by three allotted to each season; so called *trigons, tetragons, hexagons*, and so on.

Manilius' annotations are of a didactic value in that they show the various approaches to classifying the zodiacal signs. The Roman astrologer possessed a rich imagination when it came to interpreting the complicated semiotic assemblage of the Zodiac. This, however, does not imply that the various kinds of classification Manilius utilized can be of serious scientific value in establishing the origins of the Zodiac. His classifications are executed based either on the names of the constellations or on the images of the signs in their pictorial representations as Manilius knew them, which was retroactively, after the constellations had existed for a long time and were consistently depicted in accordance with certain visual canons. Classifications done so late after the fact cannot accurately reflect the guiding principles behind the constellations at the time of their inception.

What will prove truly useful in our investigation is the much more important classification imposed by the great astronomer, who was simultaneously the great astrologer, Claudius Ptolemy of Egyptian Alexandria. We have mentioned him in Chapter 2. His classification has a sensible structure and a deeper meaning. It is based on the location of constellations along the ecliptic in accordance with the influence of precession. To put it more simply, it is based on the correlation of zodiacal signs with the seasons. In the 2nd century CE, Ptolemy considered three key quartets (*tetragons*) of the Zodiac: *Cardinal* signs, *Fixed* signs, and *Mutable*, or *Common*, signs. This classification is identical to the concept of world-ages: in both cases we deal with the same four-strong sets of the zodiacal constellations.

The Scorpion/Eagle Equivalency: A Curios Detail

The odd pairing of the zodiacal Scorpio and the non-zodiacal Aquila (Eagle) has no precedent. This couple is unique: a zodiacal sign has a non-zodiacal backup.

A very old-standing astrological tradition declares that in the sky the ugly venomous arachnid, the Scorpion, and the airborne predator, the Eagle, are interchangeable and can stand in place of each other. When I first heard of this from a practicing astrologer in Moscow, I did not believe my ears because it was so absurd from an astronomical point of view. But it turned out to be true.

References to the Scorpion/Eagle equivalency do, indeed, exist in a number of old astrological treatises. The detailed account of this occurrence can be found in *The Oedipus Judaicus* (1811) by Sir William Drummond (c.1770-1828), a British diplomat, polyglot, and classicist.

Around 1786, Sir William Jones had made the pioneering (though, at the time, unappreciated) comparative study of Sanskrit, Greek, and Latin in the context of modern European languages. Sir Drummond utilized the same comparative method in respect to Biblical criticism. Analyzing the most ancient Hebrew religious texts, he found strong parallels between the twelve tribes of Israel and zodiacal symbolism, though in certain cases these parallels seem a far cry from obvious. Each tribe exhibited its own zodiacal symbol (or adjusted symbol) on its standard. There was only one exception: the tribe of Dan utilized either Scorpion or Eagle. Two centuries ago, for Sir Drummond, who followed in the steps of some other authors, there was not a shadow of a doubt regarding the Scorpion/Eagle equivalency.

The expert in the history of the Zodiac, Rupert Gleadow (1968), summarizes:

> "Astrologers, when they make the equation with the four fixed signs, used the eagle instead of Scorpio, and pretended that it represents the higher side of that maligned constellation" (p.126).

In the astrological literature, I was unable to find an explanation of this exclusive coupling. Scorpio is a zodiacal constellation. The constellation of Aquila is also located near the ecliptic and is even relatively close to Scorpio. But Aquila does not belong to the Zodiac. Based on its location alone, it cannot serve as a replacement for Scorpio. It is much more likely that the Scorpion and the Eagle go hand in hand not so much because of their physical proximity in the sky but due to some hidden metaphysical connection.

We have nothing better to do than to suppose that the astrological tradition reflects some ancient events that have been forgotten by the historians of culture but survived in the annals of astrology. We have a right to suggest that the old astrological tradition reflects a later substitution of the original celestial Scorpio with the more appropriate, noble, celestial Eagle. It seems that, for some reason, the Eagle was more appropriate and expressive for metaphorical purposes than the poisonous arachnid, the Scorpion. As a result, confusion ensued: in some cultural tokens and texts, history speaks of Scorpio, while in others the Scorpion was replaced with the Eagle.

Zodiacal Signs in Disarray

While visiting the *Glyptothek* museum in Munich, I could not, of course, pass by a floor mosaic with images of the zodiacal signs. This was a square artistic composition two meters on a side. It was discovered at the site of a villa in the Italian village of Sassoferrato near the ruins of the Roman city of Sentinum in Umbria north of Rome. The mosaic is dated to the first half of the 3rd century CE. In the center of the composition stands a young Sun god. In the foreground before him is a semi-reclining Mother Earth, surrounded by four children with the characteristic features of the four seasons of the year. In his right hand, the god holds a hoop with the twelve signs of the Zodiac (Gurshtein, 1994).

The signs are not represented evenly across the hoop, but with two separations, which were necessary for the artist because of the shape of the composition. The first sign – Aries – rises above the head of the summer-child. He leads a sector of four signs. Next follows a break above the god's head, allowing the artist to invert the hoop. Past the god's head are the other eight signs. The god's legs and the figures of the spring and summer forced the artist to make a second break here.

The symbolical meaning of the entire composition is not convoluted and can be read without any trouble. It is clearly talking about the light-giving Sun, which dictates the changing of the Earth's weather throughout the year: it consists of twelve months and four seasons. Archaeologists in other regions of the Roman world have discovered similar mosaics. A very similar mosaic originates from the ruins of Silin near Leptis Magna, one of three prosperous Roman cities – Leptis Magna, Sabratha, and Oea – on the site of which grew the modern capital of Lybia, Tripoli (Gundel, 1992, p.302). The mosaic from Munich is characterized, however, by one rare peculiarity. Usually, in artistic material, the signs of the Zodiac are shown in their widely known order, either clockwise or counter-clockwise. Their order on the Munich mosaic is scrambled.

H.G.Gundel in his introductory article to a catalogue of zodiacal images (1992) makes the obvious conclusion that the inaccuracy in the mosaic at the *Glyptothek* arose either from the lack of the author's knowledge or from the lack of knowledge of the restorer who renewed the mosaic some time after its creation. In his catalogue, Gundel gives several examples of incorrect ordering of the zodiacal signs in works of art. Arguably, such facts may be more widely interpreted than is done by Gundel.

The Zodiac was inherited by Greece, Hellenized Egypt, and Rome as one manifestation of the ancient oriental mysticism in a ready, fully formed shape. The people of this epoch did not and could not have known about the origin and evolution of the Zodiac in the ancient Near East. By the beginning of the Common Era, in the vast reaches of the Roman Empire the Zodiac maintained its meaning only for a narrow circle of specialists-astrologers. In the eyes of the general public it transformed into a comprehensive symbol of the calendric year and was commonly used as artistic décor. The signs of the Zodiac were regularly implemented alone or in small selections. Like today, laymen could remember all twelve signs, but did not bother to memorize the correct order. In this epoch, the original function of the Zodiac was forgotten, and it became difficult to find a knowing consultant on the subject even for the purpose of making expensive items. Due to this issue, it was possible for blatant errors in the portrayal of the Zodiac to arise. Incidentally, nothing of the kind is observed about the Chinese

Zodiac, in which the order of the symbols was always just as important as the symbols themselves.

For our investigation, the existence of a number of "erroneous" zodiacal images is important as proof of the loss of historical memory regarding the Western Zodiac by the time of the Romans. The problem of remembering and maintaining information about the Zodiac became increasingly difficult in subsequent epochs.

The Zodiac in Mithraism

There were some dead-ends in the Western astronomical tradition, Mithraism being one of the telling examples. Mithraism, a mysterious religious sect of the ancient Persian god Mithras, spread in the Hellenistic world in the 1st century BCE like wildfire; its original, remote roots are absolutely uncertain. It spread throughout the entire Roman Empire, from Parthia in the east to Caledonia (Scotland) in the west, and from the coast of the Black Sea in the north to the great Sahara Desert in the south, being especially favored by the Roman military. Indeed, in old times, Mithraism appeared to be the principal competitor for Christianity. As Ernst Renan, the eminent French historian of religions, assessed the situation: "If Christianity had been stopped at its birth by some mortal illness, the world would have become Mithraic." Even several Roman emperors are known to have advocated Mithraism.

No adequate written sources exist to clarify the meaning of the Mithraic Mysteries. Meanwhile, we can check out dozens of *Mithraea*, underground cave-type Mithraic shrines, scattered everywhere through the Roman dominions. They have been well preserved, placing Mithraism among the best-documented religious movements of Antiquity.

The main attribute of Mithraism is its blatant astronomical and astrological decor. Every Mithraic altar is embellished with zodiacal signs, and the majority of zodiacal images from Antiquity came to us from Mithraea. Notably, sometimes there are erroneous orders of the zodiacal constellations in Mithraic decorations, which means – as it was stated above - that not the order but the 12-strong integrity was of the greatest interest for the ministers and the worshippers. In every Mithraeum, the central altar image is Mithra slaughtering a bull, the so-called *tauroctone*. Many a baseless suggestion has been expressed on this issue.

But, seemingly, the issue was resolved in recent years. In his groundbreaking work, David Ulansey (1989) has convincingly proved that this Mithraic icon was initially motivated by the transition of the vernal equinox from the constellation of Taurus to the constellation of Aries. It was a salute of a sort to the new world-age of Aries.

With enthusiasm, I share Ulansey's persuasion that the main Mithraic icon manifested the end of the world-age of Taurus and the transition to that of Aries, about which we shall speak later.

Astronomers in Search of the Zodiacal Roots

A huge corpus of scientific publications, as well as many vagaries, is devoted to the history of the Zodiac and other ancient constellation images.

> "How and when did all those human, animal, and other figures come to be associated with particular groups of stars? The question is probably unanswerable. The stories told to account for the names of the constellations (in various sources such as the pseudo-Eratosthenic *Catasterismoi*, the *Astronomica* attributed to Hyginus, and Ovid's *Fasti*) provide no answer, since they are obviously mere mythological rationalizations of an already existing state of affairs" (Dicks, 1970, p.159).

This pessimistic author and very severe judge of extrinsic research concluded the passage cited with the resume that this is a "subject, about which a great deal of nonsense has been written." It is really unthinkable to trace all of the publications in the field, and I believe it will be enough to restrict us to some primary milestones only.

It was Marquis Pierre Simon de Laplace (1749-1827) of France, a great authority in celestial mechanics and theory of probability (and, by the way, the author of the methodological principle of World Determination), who at the beginning of the 19th century stated very thoughtfully:

"The names of the zodiacal constellations were not haphazard fancies. They reflected relationships that were the subjects of many inquiries or attempts at a systematic organization. It seems that some of the signs have to be connected with the motion of the Sun. For example, Cancer and Capricorn marked its return to the solstices while Libra symbolized a balance between day and night at the equinox. It seems that some others were forced by agriculture or the climatic conditions of people who had established the zodiac" (1796).

Unfortunately, these presumptions, which are certainly correct, were not realized in the strongly argued conclusions, and his subsequent considerations are in obvious discord with modern historical knowledge. Meanwhile, the same view belongs to Christian Ludwig Ideler (1766-1846) of Germany, who asserted that the constellations originated on the Euphrates as the "reduplications of simpler ideas connected with natural phenomena" (1809, 1815).

At the end of the 19th century, in his extensive survey, *Les étoiles et les curiosités du ciel* (1882), the acclaimed Camille Flammarion cited a dozen contributions to the problem and pointed out at last:

"A critical examination of these works doesn't reveal that there is something prompt and trustworthy neither for origination of the zodiacal names nor for a genesis of the Zodiac itself."

In 1894, a book of great stimulating significance was printed, *Dawn of Astronomy*, written by a prominent astronomer of that time, Sir Norman Lockyer (1836-1920). It brought attention to a close correlation between the history of ancient astronomy and problems of ancient cultural history. After seventy years, this almost forgotten book was brought back into print with a preface by Giorgio de Santillana (1902-1974), Professor of History and Philosophy of Science at M.I.T. Shortly thereafter, Prof. de Santillana, in collaboration with Prof. Hertha von Dechend (1915-2001) of Germany, published his own essay on myth and the frame of time - *Hamlet's Mill* (1969). The latter contains no serious astronomical considerations, but, in this author's mind, it does base on philosophical grounds some correct oracular revelations on the Zodiac.

In 1899, the first edition of the noteworthy guidebook, *Star-names and Their Meaning*, by Richard Hinckley Allen, appeared. He was very cautious in presenting his attitude toward the problem:

> "What were the dates of formation and places of origin of the earliest of the present sky figures are questions that have often been asked, but till recently impossible to be answered, and now only in part, and that tentatively. Greece and Rome, Egypt and Chaldaea, China, India, Aethiopia, and Phoenicia, and perhaps other countries, all lay claim to the honor, while history, theory, and tradition are all cited in proof; but we may safely agree with La Place that their forms and names have not been given them by chance" (Allen, 1963, p.16).

Concerning specifically the zodiacal constellations, Allen is a little bit more certain:

> "Many theories have been propounded for the birthplace and time of formation of this; but there now seems to be general agreement of opinion that it originated, mainly as we have it, in archaic Euphratean astronomy, possibly with only the six alternate signs, Taurus, Cancer, Virgo, Scorpio, Capricornus, and Pisces, and later divided because of the annual occurrence of twelve full moons in successive parts of it" (Ibid, p.1).

Some commentators have warned that, from a contemporary point of view, Allen's rich collection of data contains many factual inaccuracies and blunders, and one who intends to use this book has to be very considerate and cautious.

A Lame Duck: the Uniformist View

Concerning the genesis of the Western Zodiac as of today, the mainstream view is the Uniformist model. It enjoys a plethora of patrons due to its simplicity and appeal, which gives it a nice-looking aura of persuasion. This conception is not the product of specialized research, but rather formed spontaneously as if it was self-evident and is considered so obvious as not to require any proof (Lankford, 1997). To the backers, it seems secure from any kind of criticism.

The Uniformist view is derived exclusively from direct written sources that speak of the Zodiac as a fully formed 12-strong assemblage. Implicitly, it is supposed that the Western Zodiac popped up all at once (in a single moment) in one place and exactly at the time from which we have received randomly preserved scattered texts. The possibility that the Zodiac is simply not reflected in more ancient sources is not even considered within this conception. And the question of the possibility of the Zodiac's origin preceding written documentation is not only not considered, it is not even posed.

So far, the oldest mentions of the Zodiac have been unearthed in the written artifacts of the Land of the Two Rivers (Mesopotamia). A full list of the 12 zodiacal constellations first appears in the Babylonian texts of the so-called Persian and Seleucid periods, i.e. from the end of the 6th century BCE (Ungnad, 1944; Waerden, 1952-53; Gleadow, 1968; Emelianov, 1999). The earliest surviving astrological horoscope utilizing the twelve-sign zodiacal set was calculated for April 29, 410 BCE (Lankford, 1997, Astrology, p.44).

The most ancient copy of the famous astronomical text ^{mul}APIN dates back to 687 BCE and contains a list of 18 constellations on the Moon's path without singling out the zodiacal constellations. This gives serious grounds for van der Waerden to consider this text as a final stage in the development of Babylonian astronomy directly preceding the institution of the Zodiac (Waerden, 1966). All the cited data fashion the foundation of the Uniformist concept, which leads in the end to one unequivocal conclusion: the zodiacal system was consolidated historically late, namely in Mesopotamia in the 7th-6th centuries BCE.

The most vulnerable point of the Uniformist concept consists in the fact that no evidence of the fairness of the Uniformist approach itself exists. What do the written sources indicate? Strictly speaking, only that the Zodiac in its full form was already in use no later than the given period of time, nothing more. They tell neither how much earlier than the writing nor based on what internal logic did the process of the Zodiac's implementation take place. The writers making the Uniformist claim propose no explanations as to why the Zodiac would have been instituted at this certain time in this certain place. They do not fathom the possible evolution of the Zodiac from a simpler to a more complicated assemblage.

The vulnerability of the Uniformist approach is evident in the example that, in the 19th century, other ancient sources on the Zodiac were known in Greece that claimed it as a brainchild of the "Greek miracle". With the archeological discovery of Mesopotamia and cuneiform, researchers got their hands on Mesopotamian texts, and the nascence of the Zodiac was moved back in time and place to Mesopotamia. This historical precedent demonstrates that the methodological approach of the Uniformists is false: the absence of a written source does not prove at all the absence of existence.

Whether they are crediting the birth of the Zodiac to the Greeks or the Mesopotamians, the Uniformists do not even try to explain the peculiarities of the Zodiac. If it appeared all at once, then it should be not a collection of 12 random elements but a purposely designed and connected system, most likely a symbolical system. Meanwhile, the Uniformist view neither detects nor supposes any meaningful interconnections between the cognomens of the zodiacal constellations.

This leaves only the option that the creators of the Zodiac utilized without corrections and adjustments 12 previously existing accidental constellations on the Sun's pathway. But in this case, we stumble upon new questions without any coherent answers. For instance, it is commonly known that the Mesopotamians used a lunar-solar calendar since time immemorial. It is known that the 12 lunar months were over 11 days shorter overall than the solar year, which led, through a complicated intercalation, to approximately every third year or so having 13 lunar months instead of 12. Subsequently, the number 12 could not possibly have been special in Mesopotamia. So the question is, why institute the Zodiac, which contains 12 random elements?

What's more, the anonymous authors of the Zodiac saved in the Sun's pathway a 13th constellation, Ophiuchus, without including it among the zodiacal insignia, despite the Sun's presence in this constellation for two and a half weeks. In our opinion, the presence on the Sun's path of the extra constellation Ophiuchus, which, for some reason, was never added to the Zodiac, can signify only that already existing star groups were used for the Zodiac, yet the entire path of the

Sun was "marked" not all at once but through the course of successive transformations. By virtue of traditional conservatism, each new change preserved unharmed those already existing elements that had nothing to do with the current transformation.

In connection with this previous conclusion, it is important to reiterate a fact we have already discussed. Far from instantly, but rather much later did the Claws of the constellation Scorpio become dismembered in order to make room for the 12th zodiacal constellation of Libra. The name of this constellation held an allegorical connotation as well: in the epoch of its addition to the sky, Libra contained the autumnal equinox and allegorically symbolized the equilibrium of night and day. The question is then, why, given the already existing 12 constellations in the path of the Sun (I include Ophiuchus in this list), was it necessary to chop Scorpio into two parts?

There is one more striking element in the zodiacal strip. In each and every star map, in full accordance with the descriptions of early authors, the heavenly Taurus is represented not as an entire bull but only as its front half – the head and chest. It is the only image of its kind among the Zodiac: all the other figures are always pictured as complete entities. Unfortunately, we have no evidence regarding this oddity at our disposal. Nevertheless, this remarkable incident must have some rational explanation.

The Uniformist model supposes, without explication, that initially the 12 constellations on the Sun's path served as a celestial "mirror" for the 12 calendric months. But from an astronomical standpoint this is utterly misguided. First, as we have already mentioned, the Mesopotamian year regularly had 13 lunar months, not only 12. This is not, however, the most important point. The Sun travels across Scorpio (with amputated claws) for merely one week, whereas it travels in Virgo for six weeks. Plus, it spends two and a half weeks in Ophiuchus, which was for some reason not included in the Zodiac. Under these circumstances, there can be no discussion of a reasonable correlation between zodiacal constellations and calendric months. What then is the motivation for the introduction of the Zodiac?

The drifting of the Sun across the Zodiac is so uncoordinated with calendric months that this could not possibly have been the motivation for the Zodiac's inception. The claim that the Babylonians of 7th-6th centuries BCE enacted the 12 zodiacal constellations to correlate them with the 12 months of the solar calendar does not stand up to even the most basic scrutiny. The Zodiac is so unrelated to the counting of months that it is silly to suppose that it was instituted as a system rationally designed for this goal. For this goal, the *signs* of the Zodiac, instead of the *constellations*, were later instituted: an artificial division of the Sun's path into 12 even segments. So why, before that, implement 12 arguably poorly formed constellations?

Several more questions like the ones above can be posed about the formation of the Zodiac, and none of them can be answered unequivocally by the Uniformist concept. At best, in a discussion of such questions, the proponents of the concept will give second-hand *ad hoc* arguments. Within the Uniformist concept, all historical and astronomical circumstances related to the Zodiac's genesis, namely the specifics of the Sun's motion, the specifics of the motions of celestial luminosities within the zodiacal belt, the historical context for the Zodiac's implementation, its astronomical meaning, its practical usefulness, its initial role, its historic allusions, etc. are not analyzed in any way and are simply ignored.

It seems to this author that the fault of the Uniformist concept is rooted in its lack of historicity. The genesis of the Zodiac is examined without any historical context. The conception completely ignores the evolutionary tendency of historical processes and their dependence on the realities of man's surrounding world, in our case the motions of the celestial luminaries as they appeared to ancient man. Even at one glance, it is clear that such a fancy 12-strong conglomerate as the Zodiac cannot have a short pedigree. It had to be somehow developed from a simpler assemblage to a more elaborate one.

Rupert Seeley Gleadow in his *The Origin of the Zodiac* (1968, p.206) skillfully captured a pivotal point in the protracted evolutionary development of the Zodiac:

> "The origin of an idea is naturally hard to trace; it appears to spring full-grown like Athena from the head of Zeus. But when Athena was called on to create she produced an olive-tree out of the earth; and the study of human intuition shows that there is normally some soil in which the idea is grown.

Its genesis, like that of anything else, is by conflation: the meeting and mating of two old and known ideas produces one which is new.

The Zodiac grew up, and must have grown up, as a device for measuring time. Only later did it come to be used for divination, and later still for the analysis of character."

Gleadow's viewpoint was shared *in toto* by the modern connoisseur in the history of Western astrology, Jim Tester (1987, p.15). This very thought regarding the evolution of the Zodiac served for this author as Ariadne's thread during the development of an alternate conception for its creation.

The next Chapter will be the height of our investigation. Capitalizing on the above-collected findings and considerations, we shall elaborate an innovative approach in search for the lost pedigree of the Western Zodiac, a hypothesis of three zodiacal quartets. It has received the title of the Gradualist, or evolutionary, concept.

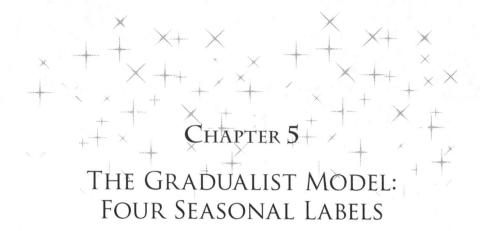

CHAPTER 5

THE GRADUALIST MODEL: FOUR SEASONAL LABELS

Summing up everything from the preceding Chapters, the author now offers to you his working hypothesis.

Some time between 6,000 and 4,300 BCE, ancient sky watchers labeled the path of the Sun with four star groups, which corresponded to the beginnings of the seasons - spring, summer, autumn, and winter. This was easy to do with regular observations of the sky since from year to year over hundreds of generations the seasons begin in practically the same places on the Sun's path among the stars. Such an event was easy to note, remember, and orally pass on for use from generation to generation. From an astronomical viewpoint, this period of time between 6,000 and 4,300 BCE was the world-age of Gemini.

Due to the effect of precession, a shift in the "seasonal dwellings" of the Sun arises from year to year, but it is so minuscule and accumulates so slowly that any real difference is only noticeable after many hundreds of years.

The four star groups selected during the above-mentioned epoch were the precursors for the modern constellations of Gemini, Virgo, Sagittarius, and Pisces. There is a good chance that some of these groups already existed in those locations. In that case, due to a subconscious desire to perpetuate tradition, the older preexisting configurations were disturbed as little as possible. We cannot, however, rule out the possibility that some groups were freshly arranged to serve specifically the purposes of plotting the Sun's path. This is probably most relevant for Pisces, which, despite its huge area, contains no noticeable bright stars and would be unlikely to have been among the earliest constellations, which tended to grow around bright stars.

If such a comparison pleases you, we could say the ancient sky watcher acted in the same manner as the road maintenance worker putting up orange cones to mark certain parts of the road; with meaningful names, the ancient astronomers designated certain parts of the Sun's path. The four designated areas on the path of the Sun became the visualized «clock face» for the solar calendar.

This was a tremendous intellectual breakthrough because after this conceptual innovation ancient astronomers' duties became easier: the need to observe regularly the length of the Sun's shadow or the position of the sunrises on the horizon vanished. The beginnings of yearly seasons could be determined at a glance (just like the beginnings of lunar months due to the changing outward appearance of the Moon before people's eyes).

If some starry groups already existed in the newly utilized locations, it is difficult to say what their names were. As to the names of all four of the newly acquired celestial emblems, they were adjusted and made interconnected in such a way that they could be seen as a unified symbolic entity. This was necessary to provide an appropriate way to remember the names and create a meaningful sequence that could be transmitted orally from generation to generation.

Since that ancient time, the locations of the four chosen constellations and their names – at least the symbolic substance of those names – have not undergone any major changes in the European tradition. For the sake of practical convenience, in the ensuing pages we shall call the four marker constellations of a given world-age a *quartet* and distinguish the quartets by naming them after the spring constellation. Thus, the marker constellations of the world-age of Gemini in our terminology are denoted as the *quartet of Gemini*.

From a practitioner's standpoint, even for ancient man, there was no trouble in locating the four distinct ecliptic areas for spring, summer, fall, and winter. According to our modern understanding, it was as easy as putting a vertical stick in the ground and measuring its shadow (Ruggles, 1999). In this context, the possibility that four markers on the path of the Sun could be instituted as early as the world-age of Gemini should not provoke any arguments.

An Everlasting Merry-go-round in the Sky

Due to the unceasing influence of precession, the displacements in the positions of the "seasonal dwellings" of the Sun on its yearly journey through the sky slowly but inevitably accumulated. By the start of the next world-age, which was that of Taurus (between 4,300 and 1,800 BCE), these positions shifted altogether like a rigid system into the modern constellations of Taurus, Leo, Scorpio, and Aquarius (the Taurus quartet). To recognize such a slow metamorphosis, ancient sky watchers needed a sufficiently long time, probably no less than several centuries. Nevertheless, sooner or later it became impossible to ignore the obvious fact that the previous four markers in the sky were no longer accurate. The "seasonal dwellings" of the Sun required new markers.

We can say the same about the four new symbolic groups of stars as we said about the previous four. Their function remained the same: to serve as the "clock face" of the solar calendar. As with the first quartet, there is a possibility that certain starry groups had already preexisted in the needed locations, but we cannot rule out that some of them were newly instituted. Their names were adjusted or introduced so as to create an interlocked symbolic succession reflecting the socio-cultural context of the era: intensification of agricultural economics.

It is important to note that through the power of conservation of traditions and the specificities of the transfer of knowledge, none of the ancient astronomers could have even contemplated erasing the previous four constellations on the Sun's path. Doubtless, the constellations of the previous quartet remained in their places, which brought the total number of meaningful groups on the path of the Sun to eight, although in all likelihood the overall number of starry groups on the ecliptic could have been even larger. One extra group, for instance, was the small but very characteristic stellar cluster the Pleiades, which was most likely included in the constellation of Taurus much later.

Lastly (already after the invention of writing during the world-age of Taurus), due to precession, the world-age of Aries (from about 1800 BCE to the brink of the Common Era) arrived. The positions of the "seasonal dwellings" had once again shifted, this time into the modern constellations of Aries, Cancer, Libra, and Capricorn (the Aries quartet). As far as this quartet goes, we know for certain that it was subject to modifications. First of all, there had previously been no constellation in the sky for the new autumnal position; the claws of Scorpio had occupied this place. They were dismembered so as to form a new independent starry group under the symbolic title of equilibrium – the Balance. Someone also conceived the idea of renaming the already existing Mesopotamian starry group, the Hireling (hired farm-hand), which was now located in the new spring position, into an appropriate spring symbol – the Ram (or the Lamb), a sacrificial spring animal (Gleadow, 1968).

Attentive astronomers long before me explained the mystery of depicting only the front half of Taurus (Wilson, 1913). The relatively small Aries is nestled where Taurus' hindquarters ought to be. So this must be the same case as Libra: half of the large area of Taurus was artificially hacked off to squeeze in a new constellation – a new emblem for the migrating vernal equinox. No other reasonable explanation is possible.

Groups of stars that did not directly interfere with the visualization of the solar calendar on the path of the Sun were left unharmed. Thus, Ophiuchus, the mighty Serpent-holder, was left untouched despite its sizeable area. With the addition of a third quartet, the total number of symbolic «seasonal» starry groups reached twelve – the same as the number of lunar months in a solar year. These twelve groups are in fact what we inherited as the set of the zodiacal constellations.

World-age Quartets: Meaningful and Senseless

From an astronomical standpoint, the zodiacal constellations form a complete circle in the sky with myriad possible quartets. Thus, we can also formally consider the quartets prior to the quartet of Gemini. These include, for example, the quartet of Cancer (8,000 – 6,000 BCE), the quartet of Leo (10,800 – 8,000 BCE), etc.

We should reiterate that the boundaries in time between the quartets are fuzzy. They depend on how we measure the spring's position: by its factual location in the real constellation or by its location in the corresponding geometrically regular zodiacal sign. Discrepancies can reach several centuries.

If the four constellations of each quartet served as seasonal labels to indicate four distinct points on the annual path of the Sun, they had to be used simultaneously as an interlocked ensemble. So, we can compile the data on quartets in a table, where every line reflects the quartet for marking the distinctive points in a certain period of time. (The table could be expanded both up and down).

THE ZODIACAL QUARTETS IN VARIOUS EPOCHS DUE TO PRECESSION

Approximate time	Spring	Summer	Autumn	Winter
....	......	......	......	....
10,800-8,000 BCE	Leo	Scorpio	Aquarius	Taurus
8,000-6,000 BCE	Cancer	Libra	Capricorn	Aries
6,000-4,300 BCE	**Gemini**	**Virgo**	**Sagittarius**	**Pisces**
4,300-1,800 BCE	**Taurus**	**Leo**	**Scorpio**	**Aquarius**
1,800 BCE-1 CE	**Aries**	**Cancer**	**Libra**	**Capricorn**
1 – 2,600 CE	Pisces	Gemini	Virgo	Sagittarius
2,600-4,500 CE	Aquarius	Taurus	Leo	Scorpio
....	....	....	......	....

One can object that the aforementioned zodiacal constellations did not even exist in the days we are talking about in the given table, and I would fully agree. For example, I am absolutely positive that Cancer and Libra did not exist in 6,000 BCE. What is necessary to remember, though, is that despite the non-existence of Cancer, the vernal equinox between 8,000 and 6,000 BCE was still located in the area which later became the constellation of Cancer.

So, does the Cancer quartet make sense? No, it is senseless like all the previous quartets. It is just a theoretical possibility that was not realized in human prehistory. We shall demonstrate that three and only three quartets (bold lines in the table) are recognizable as products of regular astronomical activities.

After the world-age of Aries, the verge of the Common Era also brought with it the start of the world-age of Pisces, which continues to the present day. As we have already mentioned, it will be replaced by the world-age of Aquarius. When to celebrate this event once again depends on how you determine the vernal equinox position. Most current astrologers believe the new world-age will arrive in just a few decades. In our account we depend on the actual position of spring in Aquarius, and as a result we estimate that the arrival of this world-age will happen around the year 2,600 and will last until about 4,500.

So, what is there to say about the quartets of Pisces and Aquarius? They are real as markers of seasonal solar points in appropriate eras but never have elements of these quartets represented a meaningful symbolic sequence. These quartets are just incidental byproducts of earlier-commissioned purposeful quartets.

After the world-age of Aries, the twelve-strong symbolism of the ecliptic was complete. No more symbols were put onto the ecliptic but a reverse process took place: celestial symbols started to be utilized for earthly purposes. Is it accidental that the new celestial symbol of the vernal equinox – Pisces, the fish – appeared as a symbol for the messiah of the emerging religious movement – Jesus Christ?

I have already drawn attention to the fact that highlighting the Sun on its annual path (ecliptic) requires a concurrent distinction of exactly four special points. So, further consideration requires a collective analysis of the ecliptic constellations within the limits (and only within the limits) of the quartets that are designated. In ancient times, when one world-age changed to another because of precession, sky-seers could empirically determine a new unity of four constellations for the seasonal markers of the ecliptic and also had the possibility of proposing new symbolic labels, which preserved the integrity of concept within the limits of the new quartet.

The changing quartets are the direct result of precession and the everlasting slow shift of the four "seasonal" points along the ecliptic, regardless of whether or not ancient observers comprehended the cause of the difference between their observations and those of their predecessors. Having no idea of precession, they might have thought that the difference between their observations and the canon of their predecessors derived either from the inaccuracy of their predecessors' data or from the will of the gods. Each time, the placement of the distinct points was determined by a purely empirical method.

The Sum and Substance of the Gradualist Model

So far, our working hypothesis – the Gradualist Model - has been based on astronomical considerations and deals with only three quartets. Its primary supposition consists of the idea that ancient stargazers utilized the quartets of "seasonal" constellations on the ecliptic as labels of the corresponding seasons of the solar year. Having already structured the sky with starry groups, they noticed that four of the constellations served as "dwellings" for the Sun on especially meaningful days of its travel across the sky now called the equinoxes and the solstices. Whether immediately or not, these four special constellations received cognomens infused with the symbolism of the seasons to which they belonged.

Through the influence of precession, approximately every two millennia the ancient skywatchers were faced with the task of changing the quartets. Due to the conservative cultural traditionalism common to ancient societies, the antiquated quartet was preserved while a new quartet was added to it, updated with current symbolism reflective of the change of the solar seasons. For our hypothesis, it does not matter whether the elements of the new quartet were named anew or if the observers restricted themselves to corrections and adjustments of preexisting names.

Our Gradualist Model suggests that the twelve-strong zodiacal necklace along the ecliptic was elaborated gradually in three stages. Each quartet of zodiacal constellations was the outcome of astronomical recognition of the behavior of the ancient celestial god - the deified Sun. Their necessity was determined by their value for calendric purposes. These constellations were heavenly "dwellings" - the icons to demarcate the certain celestial areas that included the vernal, summer, autumnal, and winter points. To fulfill this aim, not only bright but also faint stars were involved into the ecliptic groupings.

A key precept in our working hypothesis is that the cognomens of the constellations had absolutely nothing to do with their outward appearances. The appearances were incidental while the names were imbued with a deeper sense. They metaphorically mirrored prevailing views on the rhythmic cycles of natural events in context with the religious-mythological mentalities of the epochs when they served as labels. They mimicked such weighty metaphorical fourfold progressions as ascent – height – decline – depth, or morning – noon – evening – midnight. So, our working hypothesis focuses on the interpretation of the quartets' symbolism.

The Validity of Symbolism

Being a professional astronomer, I feel I must clarify my view on the issues that are distant from astronomy and are not evident to some of my colleagues, i.e., the problems of archaic symbology at large. In no way is this author the first among those who have paid attention to this significant problem. Throughout the 20th century this problem has been carefully investigated by many scholars; for example, by the prominent German philosopher and historian of ideas Ernst Cassirer (1874-1945) who formed his own school of thought in this respect (1923; 1925; 1929; 1944).

Cassirer saw that, while all animal species possess the receptor system and the effector system, man obtained a third link to the world that could be described as the symbolic system. According to Cassirer, the symbol is a clue to the nature of man and his behavioral conduct. It is man's outstanding characteristic and his distinguishing feature. Man discovers world step by step via his symbolizing activities. As a result, Cassirer claimed that human beings are, above all, **symbolizing animals**, and such a conclusion is probably very true in particular concerning the archaic mind of pre-written history.

In his own words, Ernst Cassirer recognized:

> "... In the human world we find a new characteristic which appears to be the distinctive mark of human life. The functional circle of man is not only quantitatively enlarged; it has also undergone a qualitative change. Man has, as it

were, discovered a new method of adapting himself to his environment. Between the receptor system and the effector system, which are to be found in all animal species, we find in man a third link which we may describe as the *symbolic system*. This new acquisition transforms the whole of human life. As compared with the other animals man lives not merely in a broader reality; he lives, so to speak, in a new dimension of reality" (1944, p.24).

Analyzing multiple retrospective instances, Cassirer convincingly demonstrates that the whole range of human achievements – language, mythology, religion, arts, science, history, political thoughts – was reached via the symbolical approach that formed man's attitude to the world and his experience within it.

The examination of symbols is by no means an easy task. A symbol is not merely a sound or a picture displayed on paper or carved on rock. Symbols are the condensed articulation of beliefs, aspirations, and abstract ideas in visible form. Symbols rarely reveal their full depth of meaning; rather, their destiny is to inspire the imagination. In the broadest sense, a symbol could be an agreed-upon graphic sign, a sound, a verbal formula, or even a gesture.

The essence of symbolism is much easier to elucidate through examples. If one looks, for instance, at the sketch of an ancient fibula, a clasp the Romans wore at the shoulder, its sense comes not through its functional use as a clothing item. Rather, its significance is revealed when one knows that to the Romans it represented virginity. Similarly, the eagle to us is so much more than a bird; it is a symbol of power, of the spirit, or of the principle of spirituality in general. An egg is an ancient cosmic symbol of potentiality and immortality. The sign of the arm stands for activity in general. The list goes on and on.

There is no conventional definition of symbolism. One can consider it to be the art of thinking in images. Another way of viewing it is as a more precise and crystallized mode of expression through indirect means. A rather observant consideration of symbolism belongs to Erwin Ramsdell Goodenough (1893-1965) who wrote (1988, p.40):

"A symbol is an image or design with a significance, to the one who uses it, quite beyond its manifest content. Or...

we may say that a symbol is an object or a pattern which, whatever the reason may be, operates upon men, and causes effect in them, beyond mere recognition of what is literally presented in the given form."

An important corollary to the definition of symbols is that they are never frozen in time. In fact, symbols are quite often polysemantic, possessing complex and richly multivalent significations. They can have multiple meanings with unforeseen transmutations in time, and decoding the meanings of symbols may be accomplished only in the frame of their associated epochs. In Clive Ruggles' words concerning the sky, "perceptions of the sky are culture-specific" (1999, p.147).

Though these terms sometimes trespass on one another's territory, symbols are different from allegory, with its various manifestations through parables, fables, folklore, and religious writing. A symbol is a distinctive and focused metaphor, a singular memorable image (or sound) while an allegory is a more complex form of an extended metaphor. Just like a symbol, an allegory is a representation of something through analogy, but in a more comprehensible and concrete form. Most often, an allegory expresses spiritual, emotional, or intellectual matters in terms close to those of material reality. It does force man into looking at the familiar in an unconventional way, but it cannot deliver as much punch through a single image as a symbol.

The flourishing of allegories, extensive and complex as they are, was contingent on the development of writing, when they became a widely utilized literary tool. Allegories were present throughout such examples of early literate masterpieces as the story of Gilgamesh, ancient epics, the Jewish Scriptures, and other religious texts.

It is vital for the research at hand that symbolism be recognized as a dominant part of ancient mentality.

In developing our working hypothesis, we need to demonstrate:

1) the differences in the symbolism of the three zodiacal quartets;
2) the interconnectedness of the symbols in each quartet which constitute a single meaningful corpus (simplegma);
3) the exactitude with which the symbols in each quartet correspond to the respective symbolic systems of the eras to which we date them using astronomical data (precession).

A Visit to a Neolithic Settlement: the Gemini Quartet

The quartet of Gemini was a functional calendric tool during the world-age of Gemini, which lasted from about 6,000 to 4,300 BCE. What peculiarities, one wonders, characterized the lifestyle and culture of the most advanced people of that time?

Looking at the Near East (Anatolia, Mesopotamia, Syro-Palestine, Egypt) and the adjacent so-called Old Europe (Aegean and Adriatic areas extending to the Czech Republic and Slovakia, southern Poland and western Ukraine), in line with modern archaeologists, we have to state that the era of nomadic hunters had already passed by this time in those areas. Hunting, of course, continued to take place but the populace of the indicated territories led primarily a settled way of life in villages reliant upon domesticated plants and animals. The inhabitants of these villages numbered in the hundreds. The new food-producing lifestyle manifested itself in the emergent artistic tradition of the Neolithic (Feder, 1995).

The transitory borderline between the food-consuming lifestyles of the Paleolithic and the Mesolithic and the newly established food-producing one received the name of the Neolithic revolution (Childe, 1942). In southeastern Europe, the Neolithic revolution occurred most likely in the 7th millennium BCE. In the region of the Near East, it happened millennia earlier. So, the world-age of Gemini certainly falls into the period of history after the Neolithic revolution when minor sedentary and matrilineal communities flourished (Fagan, 1996).

In his overview of archaeoastronomy in traditional areas of Eurasia, the Polish archaeologist, Stanislaw Iwaniszewski (1999) comes to conclusions that are very supportive to our own:

> "This Mesolithic-Neolithic transition appears to be a very interesting epoch of cultural transformations. Obviously, one can expect that a series of changes in traditional patterns of life, such as gradual acquisition of sedentarism (associated with the intensive exploration of maritime resources), and the development of social stratification and social division of labor could have resulted in more elaborate conceptions of temporal strategies and models. Obviously, if the substitution of lunar tallies with the solar calendars is proved, then the

implication is that around that time, the formal arithmetic and structural bases for calendars were transformed" (p.92).

Despite the introduction of numerous novelties by the Neolithic people, the settled population that skillfully domesticated plants and animals inherited many views and cultural traditions of its nomadic (Paleolithic) ancestors. One of the most influential and controversial archaeologists of the 20th century, Marija Gimbutas (1921-1994), helps to understand the state of affairs in its entirety (1982, p.11):

> "In art and mythical imagery it is not possible to draw a line between two eras, Palaeolithic and Neolithic, just as it is not possible to draw a line between wild and domestic plants and animals. Much of the symbolism of the early agriculturists was taken over from the hunters and fishers. Such images as the fish, snake, bird, or horns are not Neolithic creations; they have roots in Paleolithic times. And yet, the art and myths of the first farmers differed in inspiration and hence in form and content from those of the hunters and fishers."

Keeping in mind the remarks of both scholars, let us consider the Gemini quartet, which is comprised of Gemini (Spring), Virgo (Summer), Sagittarius (Fall), and Pisces (Winter). Of the three world-ages (Geminean, Taurean, and Ariean) that immediately antedate the oldest known record of the twelve-strong Zodiac, the Gemini quartet stands out because it contains three of the four existing anthropomorphic (humanlike) constellations (Gemini, Virgo, and Sagittarius), and thus actually constitutes a sort of Anthropodiac - a circle of human creatures. Of all the anthropomorphic figures of the Zodiac, only Aquarius remains outside this quartet. No other anthropomorphic personages exist in the Zodiac. Why are practically all of the humans, with only one exception, concentrated in a single quartet?

Anthropomorphic images are common among the artifacts of the Neolithic (and older) peoples, so it seems consistent that such images would be placed in the sky, as well. But in no way could the anthropomorphic constellations claim the name of the circle of animals because they pose a circle of human beings. It will be necessary to find an answer to this question.

Paired Deities Who Appear at Dawn

In analyzing the symbolism of the names of the Gemini quartet, we start with its head, Gemini. Would this duo have been known and significant in the Neolithic world? A breakthrough into understanding this problem was made by James Rendel Harris (1852-1941), the prolific English biblical scholar. Our current knowledge points to the fact that twins were one of the main cultic figures in Proto-Indo-European culture (Mallory, 1989).

Let us turn at first to comparatively recent history - to the first centuries CE, a time from which we have indexes of Christian saints and martyrs. It is remarkable how often one finds twins among them. Among the more famous are the twin brothers St. Florus and St. Laurus, who lived in the 2nd century CE (their feast day is August 18). Another well-known pair is St. Cosmas and St. Domian, who lived in the 3rd century (the feast day is September 26).

In the 5th century, St. Benedict had a twin sister, St. Scholastica (their feast day is July 11), but it is relatively rare that one finds a twin brother and sister among legendary twins. In the historical record one does read, though, that Cleopatra did have twins with Marc Anthony: Alexander and his twin sister, Cleopatra. The Greek Gods Apollo and Diana were also considered to be twins.

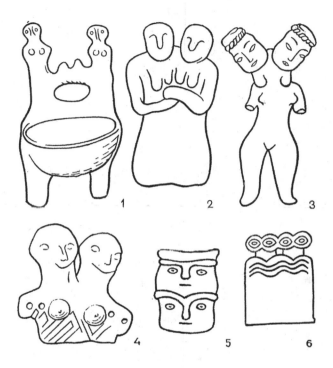

Fig. 2. Russian-born scholar Ariel Golan deserves a certain credit for his attentive study of the twin cult. A group of two-headed images (twins) collected by Ariel Golan, *Myth & Symbol,* Jerusalem-Moscow, 1994, ill. 293 (in Russian). # 1 from Ukraine, 4th millennium BCE; # 2 from Asia Minor, 7th millennium BCE; # 3 from Pre-Columbian America; # 4 from Romania, ca. 5,000 BCE; # 5 from Chechen-Ingushetija, Early Medieval Time; # 6 from Northern Mesopotamia, Neolithic. (Permitted for reproduction by Ariel Golan).

In the meantime, the majority of widely famous twins are brothers. To those who have already been mentioned from Christian sources, one can add the patron saints of Milan, St. Protasius and St. Gervasius (2nd century; June 19); the one-time Catholic patron saints of cobblers, tanners, and leather workers, martyrs Crispin and Crispinian (3rd century; October 25); St. Anthony (4th century; January 17) and his twin brother Atanas; St. Aizan (4th century; October 1) and his twin brother Sazan; and many others. J.R.Harris has written some books on the topic and adjacent subjects (1903; 1906; 1913).

Information on twins is hardly limited only to the lists of Christian saints and martyrs; one can trace them into a much deeper past. And while we do not have verifiable historical records from the earlier epochs, mythologies of various peoples teem with mentions of twins. The children of the biblical Isaac and Rebecca were the twins Esau and Jacob. As already mentioned, the Greek Gods Apollo and Diana were twins, as were the figures of Roman legends, Romulus and Remus and Castor and Pollux (in fact, the two brightest stars in Gemini are named Castor and Pollux in their honor).

Twin brothers include Hengist (Old English, meaning "stallion") and Horsa (Old English, meaning "horse") – the legendary leaders who conquered the first territories of England in the 5th century CE.

In Hindu mythology, one finds the twin children of Rama, Lava and Kusa; the biblical Cain and Abel are likely to have been twins; and in Christian eschatology there are references to yet another pair, Gog and Magog. Several pairs of twins appear in Egyptian mythology.

In accordance with modern viewpoints on prehistory, the images of mythological heroes typically have their origins at least in the Neolithic. This fact is at the crux of the question at hand: were twins treated in some sort of special fashion in Neolithic cultures?

As early as a century ago, in his book, *The Cult of the Heavenly Twins* (1906), J.R.Harris convincingly argued that the common origin of the Heavenly Twins, or Children of the Sky, as well as the cult of the Mother-Goddess, "can be carried back to the very bounds of the Aryan civilization" (p.5). He stated the cult of twins belongs (p.2)

> "to a period of human development which can only be called historical at all by a very liberal use of the term, and that their varied activities and philanthropies are a mirror in which we can read the evolution of the arts of human life as disclosed by the inventions of many aeons of progress. For this reason the Heavenly Twins are a peculiarly attractive study to the anthropologist, who can take us back in their company to the very dawn of civilization."

He continued,

"I propose to show that the explanation can be found at an earlier date than any known civilization" (p.5).

Today, a century after J.R.Harris' books, with a great degree of certainty we can say that, yes, along with gods and goddesses, twins held an important place in the pantheons of Neolithic agriculturists and herders, especially in the Mediterranean and so-called Old Europe, two regions for which the archaeological record is the most extensive.

In the first lines of his paper from 1986, the modern Italian author Cristiano Grottanelli insists:

"The bibliography on the "Indo-European (or "Divine") Heavenly Twins" is so rich and so well known that I have no need to introduce them" (p.125).

The twins seemed for ancient peoples to be a mystery of Mother Nature, and the image of twins was commonplace in the ancient world. Without a doubt, the Divine Twins were pagan gods. They played a significant role in many cultures and held a unique place. As it was mentioned, in a much later epoch, for instance, during the time of Homer, the twins' myth was presented in the form of a story about the Dioscuri. In Greek mythology, the Dioscuri were the two divine brothers, Castor and Polydeuces (Castor and Pollux in Roman mythology). This story, however, was not the only version of the myth, and, importantly, in other renditions, not both of the twins were boys.

Fig. 3. Did the cult of twins really exist at the time of the first zodiacal quartet? Are they in fact twins? Double-headed goddess from Gomolava on the river Sava, Vojvodina (modern Serbia). Vinča civilization, which belongs to the Central Balkan Neolithic Starčevo Culture. Mid-fifth millennium BCE. In 1997, this charming small terracotta figurine was even reproduced on a Yugoslavian postage stamp (Courtesy Anna Kharitonova).

In the study of folklore and mythology, it is conventional to distinguish two main categories of twins: those of like sex (parallel twins) and those of opposite sex (cross twins). Mythological traditions of both categories are very rich and remarkably similar throughout the world (Ward, 1968). Predating Homer, the Divine Twins were a recurrent theme of many religions. Such a theme was well known not only in the mythologies of Greeks and Romans but Indians, Mitanni, Persians, Armenians, Germans, Balts, Slavs, and many others. Especially rich data surfaced from Indo-European heritage.

In ancient India, twin deities, the *Asvins*, were the earliest bringers of light in the morning sky, the couple that prepared the way for the Dawn. They were thought to be the brothers of the Glorious Dawn (*Usha*) and children of the Sun (Bowker, 1997).

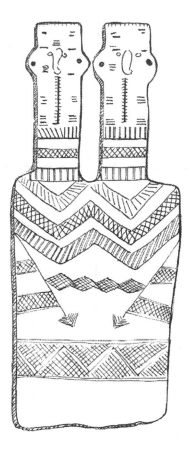

Fig. 4. Another excellent example of dualism is from another archaeological site - a crossroad of the ancient Mediterranean world. Plank-shaped idol of Red Polished Ware, dating to the third millennium BCE. From Dhenia, Cyprus (Nicosia), tomb I:6, height 30 cm, Cyprus Museum, inv. no. 1943/IV-13/4 (permission to publish this sketch has been granted by the Department of Antiquities, Cyprus).

In the ancient Indo-European pantheon, the Sun embodied the supreme God of Sky. The cult of the twins in this mythology goes back to a general Proto-Indo-European myth about the heavenly twin children of the Sun-god. This myth appears in all major ancient Indo-European traditions. In the book on this myth in Germanic tradition, Donald Ward sums up all the facts in following words (1968, p.28):

> "The evidence is too overwhelming to allow more than one conclusion: The Divine Twins, sons of the Sky God, brothers of the Sun Maiden, were well-defined deities in the Proto-Indo-European pantheon, and they were borne by the various migrating peoples to the new homelands, where the religious concept changed remarkably little through the centuries in the new environments."

There is another version of the twins' role. It suggests that the Proto-Indo-Europeans believed that the progenitors of mankind were *Man* and *Twin*, "the latter of which was sacrificed and carved up by his brother to produce mankind" (Mallory, 1989, p.140).

Since the idea of twins as progenitors of mankind was prevalent (and probably relatively new) roughly during the same time as the institution of the Gemini quartet, there is little wonder that we can find its traces not only on Earth, but in the Sky, as well. The constellation of Gemini was called the Great Twins in the Mesopotamian text *mul*APIN. As A.M.Zolotarev remarks, the twins-demiurges (demiurge = world creator) were the most archaic version of the cosmological myth (1984; for details see Bromley, 1988, Vol. 3, or Ivanov, 2008).

To make a long story short, numerous authors have scrupulously investigated the issue of the Divine Twins (see, for example, Golan, 1991). Most of them insist that the Divine Twins came into being much earlier than the Indo-European raids on the Near East and Old Europe. A worship of twins existed as early as at the dawn of the agricultural era, i.e. in the early Neolithic age, which is the subject of our concern.

Following J.R.Harris, we fully agree with his old conclusion:

> "In the history of Twins, the elevation to a Zodiacal peerage is almost the last honour that is conferred upon them" (1913, p. xv).

Based on everything said above, the role of twin symbolism for spring within the Gemini quartet is unquestionable. In spring, flora and fauna come alive. The birds chirp in the trees, plants blossom. It is spring that is the natural beginning of every annual cycle. Gemini, as the source of regenerated life in the mind of ancients, could be easily seen as a metaphor for the conception of life, the springtime renewal of nature. It is a very proper metaphor for the historic epoch in question.

In accordance with reputed scientific literature, the Divine Twins were firmly linked with the Great Goddess and horses. For example, the name of the twin Vedic deities, the *Asvins*, literally means "horse possessors"; they have strong parallels with the Greeks' Dioscuri as well as with Lettish and Lithuanian myths (Mallory, 1989; Meletinsky, 1991). Twins Hengist and Horsa are also named after horses. The above-mentioned Italian, Cristiano Grottanelli, wrote a detailed paper on the amazing linkage between horses, twins, and the powerful lady in various cultures of India, Greece, Ireland and elsewhere (1986). This is exactly the case we deal with in the zodiacal quartet of Gemini. Not only do all symbols of the Gemini quartet belong to the corresponding era, but three of them are strongly bound together into a unique bunch.

Virgo was not a Virgin

The second constituent within the Gemini quartet is Virgo, which corresponded to the summer solstice during this epoch. In the eyes of the Greeks, Virgo was a virgin, a vestal. It is not granted that the figure of a virgin could have ascended to the sky in more ancient times since back then the ideal of sexual innocence and purity was in no way considered a feminine virtue. Nevertheless, the roots of a feminine figure in the archaic sky can be interpreted without hesitation.

For ancient humans, birth giving was a miracle of Nature, and the woman's womb was the metaphor of fertility and productivity. Starting with the Paleolithic, a plenitude of female figurines have surfaced among archaeological finds. The figurines of naked, pregnant women and women giving birth are typical of the art from the Paleolithic to the early agricultural societies.

Fig. 5. More than 150 small figurines of naked females in very generalized forms were unearthed in various Paleolithic sites. Usually they are called *Paleolithic Venuses*. They are considered to be evidence that during the Paleolithic time the cult of a goddess was widespread and dominant. This was the time of the first proto-zodiacal quartet. In this file photo, Russian archaeologist L.M.Tarasov (1925-2010) of Saint-Petersburg with his find from Gagarino village (Carved from mammoth tusk, Gravettian period, Upper Paleolithic, height 12.7 cm). All in all, 14 such figurines were discovered at this site. (Courtesy S.A.Vasil'ev from the Institute for History of Material Culture, Saint-Petersburg, Russian Academy of Sciences).

James Mellaart, the great specialist on Asia before and during the Neolithic revolution, pointed to the finding of cult female statuettes practically in every house of Hacilar-6 (nearly 5,600 BCE). Mellaart (1965) proposed these figurines were designed for the performance of the rites of the fertility cult. They lacked sexual symbolism, and their exterior was primarily aimed at displaying pregnancy.

Another prolific scholar on the role of a woman during the Neolithic was Marija Gimbutas who viewed the culture of the time as being

> "characterized by a dominance of woman in society and worship of a Goddess incarnating the creative principle as Source and Giver of All" (1982, p.9).

In her publications, Gimbutas emphasized that goddess symbolism focuses on the enigma of birth and death and the renewal of life, not only human but all life on Earth and indeed in the whole cosmos. There was probably more than one female goddess in the Neolithic:

> "With the inception of agriculture, farming man began to observe the phenomena of the miraculous Earth more closely and more intensively than the previous hunter-fisher had done. A separate deity emerged, the Goddess of Vegetation, a symbol of the sacral nature of the seed and the sown field, whose ties with the Great Goddess are intimate" (Op. cit., p.237).

Gimbutas' approach is not without objections, and there are various interpretations of ancient female statuettes. Nevertheless, one conclusion is inevitable: they played an outstanding role.

Fig. 6. This so-called Venus of Laussel (with a lunar calendar in her hand) was discovered in 1911 in Dordogne, France. It was carved into a large block of limestone in a rock shelter (*abri de Laussel*). Its height is about 18 inches (43 cm). It is currently displayed in Bordeaux, France. This world-famous carving is associated with the Gravettian Upper Paleolithic culture (approximately 25,000 years old). It is evidence that a naked female figurine was an important symbol for a very prolonged period of time in prehistory. (Image is from Wikimedia).

Did the Greeks mislead us with the celestial name of Virgo? Is it possible the name originally stood for "young woman" and the connotations of sexual innocence were attached later to a figure who was meant to symbolize the fertility of youth and whose Greek/Latin name was descriptively neutral rather than actually misleading?

In agreement with Gimbutas and many other scholars, these are the avenues of searching for the roots of the insignia of the summer solstice. Virgo may be a symbol (or a mutated symbol) of summertime fertility. It would be reasonable to link the celestial Virgo with the cult of the Mother-goddess that was so widely spread in the Paleolithic and Neolithic times, including cultures of Proto- and Pre-Indo-Europeans.

There is also another meaningful key to the celestial Virgo. It is essential to underline Virgo in all the known ancient astronomical portrayals as being depicted with an ear of grain, which echoes the images of the terrestrial Goddesses and which should be seen as further emphasizing the link of the celestial figure to fertility. Thus, the choice of the Mother-goddess holding a spike as the symbol of fertility seems to be correct within the framework of Neolithic traditions.

Possibly, it was not until a certain time in Greece, where chastity was increasingly demanded of women and projected onto goddesses as class societies developed and where the attributes of the goddess were transformed, that a vestal Virgo appeared in the sky instead of a life-giving woman. But it does not matter for us: the fact is that such a personage as a goddess was of prime importance in the Neolithic.

In Mesopotamia, Virgo's place in the sky was occupied by the Furrow (Bobrova, Militarev, 1993). Strange? Not at all. This is just another version of a steady visualization of fertility. The conclusion is: the visualization of the summer solstice through Virgo during the epoch in question is quite reasonable.

A Horseback Archer and a Pair of Fishes

The autumnal constellation of the Gemini quartet is Sagittarius – a centaur, or simply a hunting archer on horseback with a bow in his hands. Was hunting yet another miracle of Mother Nature? Of course it was for the ancestors of the Neolithic people. Supporting their very existence, it was murder in the name of life.

The utilization of tamed or domesticated horses added another layer of symbolic meaning to hunting. As T.V.Gamkrelidze and V.V.Ivanov (1984; 1995) note, the Indo-Europeans distinguished horses as primarily domestic animals, the creatures that were ritually the closest to people. An indication of the ritual significance of horses is the tradition of burying kings together not only with their wives but also their horses.

Fig. 7. Sagittarius. Source: Photo from The Babylonian Expedition of the University of Pennsylvania, Series D: Researches and Treatises edited by H.V.Hilprecht, Vol. IV A New Boundary Stone of Nebuchadrezzar I from Nippur by William John Hinke, University of Pennsylvania, 1907, page 98. Original carved boundary stone of limestone (height 51 cm) is in the British Museum, No.90829. It was found in Sippar, some 60 km north of Babylon and 30 km southwest of Baghdad. Dates are 1,186-1,172 BCE.
This strange creature of various parts (chimera) served probably as a precursor for the modern Sagittarius (Archer). The image is from a Babylonian boundary stone (kudurru).

I have already had occasion to mention that A.Yu. Militarev (1995) insists that when they are read correctly, cuneiform texts of the Sumerian period refer to Sagittarius as «old man» or «elder kinsman». Militarev then asserts that we have no information as to the name of this constellation in the pre-Sumerian period. I cannot agree with this. After a mutation, the Sumerian name in fact evokes and preserves the original symbolic meaning of the constellation.

For early agriculturists, hunting and armed defense of their land remained a vital activity. No doubt the «elder kinsman» would deal directly with these duties, and in this context, semantically, «elder kinsman» and «archer» become closely related. The term «elder kinsman» not only does not exclude, but, rather, suggests the probability that he would own a horse, an expensive commodity, and would participate in activities requiring bow and arrows.

Sagittarius the hunter fully fits the autumnal symbolism. Hunting as an activity fits into the symbolic view of the world moving in a cyclical pattern, with life leading to death leading again to life. When a hunter took an animal's life, he perpetuated his own, and were an animal to kill him, the animal would be, by sustaining itself, also providing future sustenance for the hunter's progeny. Likewise, the Sun on its annual journey through autumn had to give less light and heat, symbolically to die (and take plants and hibernating animals with it), before its springtime resurrection. A celestial hunter, then, would be seen as an appropriate metaphor for man to mark the beginning of autumn. A hunter shoots at the Sun before the latter starts its descent into the Lower World.

Armed with a bow, Sagittarius can only be an archaic personage. In the epoch of the Gemini quartet, bows started to be replaced with more sophisticated types of weapons. Sagittarius' bow thus stands as a vestige of an older age and points to his earlier origin.

Now, please recollect that in mythology three ancient metaphors – Twins, the Great Goddess, and horses – were connected together as a single string through a number of mutual symbolical properties. Is this not evidence that all three celestial labels comprise a symbolical togetherness on the path of the Sun?

In winter, the Sun reaches its lowest midday position in the sky and appears to linger over the threshold of the Lower World, corresponding to Pisces, the fishes of the Gemini quartet.

The water medium as a very special milieu had a long pedigree within the paradigm of the primordial mind. When ancient men had no capacity to cross vast water bodies, it was water that served as a frontier of their landmass habitat - the darkness of the mournful Space Night, or a threshold of the Netherworld. Millennia before turning into the emblem of regeneration in the ceremony of baptism, in the ancient world water debuted as a symbol of death.

The 19th-century British ethnographer Sir Edward Burnet Tylor, the leader of the time in cultural evolutionism, and many others have illustrated the cross-cultural link between winter and the concept of a Lower World. Numerous rites in various cultures indicate that water has long been considered to be the primary element of the Lower World. With the rich ethnographic material, E.B.Tylor concluded:

> "It is by the simplest poetic adaptation of the Sun's daily life, typifying Man's life in drawing beauty, in mid-day glory, in evening death, that mythic fancy even fixed the belief in the religions of the world, that the land of Departed Souls lies in the Far West or the World Below. How deeply the myth of the sunset has entered into the doctrine of men concerning a Future State, how the West and the Under-World have become by mere imaginative analogy Religions of the Dead, how the quaint day-dreams of savage poets may pass into honored dogmas of classic sages and modern divines, - all this crowd of details here cited from the wide range of culture stand to prove" (1903, Vol. 2, pp. 48-49).

M.Eiade elucidates the same connection, as well (for example, 1949). The "Land of the Departed Souls" is situated in the Far West, beneath a watery boundary. Likewise, the River Styx of Greek mythology was considered to be an essential element of the Lower World. The waters of the Lower World had no anthropomorphic symbolism, and so a pair of fishes served the purpose. Marija Gimbutas repeatedly mentions fishes among the most important symbols of the Neolithic peoples (see also Baring, Cashford, 1991).

There is no doubt that bodies of water – vast and extremely specific ecosystems – seemed to the Neolithic people to be yet another marvel of Mother Nature. The symbol of water – fish – was elevated to godlike status, which is evidenced in archaeological finds.

In 1967, a well-preserved Mesolithic site, *Lepenski Vir*, was found on the Serbian bank of the Danube River in the region of the Iron Gates Gorge. The villages at this site flourished during the period of the first zodiacal quartet, 6000 to 4900 BCE. In front of several houses huge fish-human stone idols were unearthed. They obviously portrayed fish gods revered by the village occupants (Fagan, 1996).

Fig. 8. Gods in the shape of fishes. These fish-like stone heads without bodies were carved about 6,000 BCE. They are from a Mesolithic settled community of 59 houses on the right bank of the Danube river (Lepensky Vir, now in Serbia). It is great archaeological evidence that, at the time of the first zodiacal quartet, water creatures had indeed played the role of ranked deities (photo by Dragoslav Srejović).

The reconstruction of the symbolism of these four constellations, which we call the quartet of Gemini, seems logical and not difficult to fit within the frames of the general Neolithic religious-mythological mentality. Underlining the characteristics similar to all four symbols, we first note that all of them manifest the amazement of the Neolithic man before the unexplainable marvels of Mother Nature: the wonder of the birth of twins; the miracle of the reproductive process itself; and the marvel of supporting life through hunting and fishing.

Three of the four symbols are anthropomorphic. Since it was impossible to find an anthropomorphic symbol for water, the fourth symbol - aquatic - became the fishes. Altogether, the four symbols of the Gemini quartet form a "business card" of the Neolithic settlement.

Aside from the major specificities of the symbolism of the Gemini quartet, there exists also a less significant but more problematic detail - the dualism of the symbols in the Gemini quartet.

The Dualism of Archaic Symbolism

It is both curious and important that Marcus Manilius, the Roman astrologer, describes five of the zodiacal insignia – Gemini and Pisces (images of pairs), Sagittarius and Capricorn (composites), and Virgo - as doubled rather than singular images. Of these five, four belong to the quartet of Gemini. Ptolemy goes even further and directly refers to all four members of the Gemini quartet as bicorporal, i.e., having two distinct main parts. Is there a deeper meaning behind these references?

Considering the symbolism of the constellations on the Sun's track, we unwillingly again touch on the more complicated issue of archaic symbolism at large. Like modern mascots, symbols then were visualized ideas. Thinking through apparent images, i.e., symbolical mentality, was born with the making of human mentality itself and, as far as we can evaluate today, long before the Neolithic revolution.

Before they could domesticate plants and animals, primeval hunters/gatherers had to adjust their lifestyle to the environmental realities. In the absence of a developed oral vocabulary, associations, primarily graphic ones, better served this goal. Archaic symbolism is a gigantic tier of human culture based on the belief in the magical power of associations that served as tribal emblems, distinctions of property, were used for healing and for cult rites.

Ancient symbolism, which made itself known long before the birth of literature as a genre, had various levels of complexity. There are serious grounds to suppose that, echoing the specificities of human mentality, the earlier symbolism was in its core dualistic, or, if you prefer, binary. Behind this term is the fairly simple idea that primeval man obviously leaned towards thinking through binary oppositions.

Extrapolating to prewritten history, research of later sources shows such meaningful binary oppositions for ancient man could have been day and night, male and female, top and bottom, left and right, good and evil, etc. These oppositions are broadly reflected in ancient philosophies (Toporov, 1982). Mallory (1989) suggests that binary oppositions were the underlying structures of Indo-European and Proto-Indo-European ideology (p.140). V.V.Ivanov, of Russia, recently performed an exhaustive investigation of this problem (2008).

The best symbols must have been those that in themselves combined features of both opposites; for example, twenty four hours as a unity of daylight and nighttime, a dangerous hunting beast as a combination of good and evil, primeval chaos as a mixture of sky and earth (top and bottom). The latter – the unification of top and bottom – might also have been embodied by vertical slabs dug into the ground, along with the many other *axis mundi*, knowledge of which has been well preserved through oral tradition; from this practice came tombstones and later funerary kurgans (hills).

T.V.Gamkrelidze and V.V.Ivanov (*Op.cit.*, Part 2, pp.776) emphasize that

> "the dualism of the social organization of the ancient Indo-European society… greatly influences the nature of the spiritual life of ancient Indo-Europeans and determines the binary character of religious and mythological mentality as well as some features of the model of the real World."

In simplest terms, a dualist symbol is a composite created by combining at least two elements, each of which has a meaning attached to it. These elements typify different aspects of a whole. A dualism can be relative or absolute. It is said to be relative if one element is held to be subordinate to, derivative from, explicable by or in any way dependent upon the other. If the elements are independent and contrasting, then the dualism is absolute (see, for example, the entry "Dualism" in the *Encyclopaedia Britannica*).

With the proposed zodiacal quartets in our mind, it is amazing yet true that binary (dual) symbols are totally absent in the second quartet but are used in all four labels of the Gemini quartet. The absolute dualism of Gemini's symbol (twins) needs no prolonged explanation. Even having no knowledge of their exact meaning, two bodies are contrasting elements of the whole process of recreation of life. The second member of the Gemini quartet is the Mother-goddess. This image as the symbol of fertility in the fine arts, as I have mentioned, is doubled by another symbol of fertility – a relative one in respect to the woman - the ear of wheat. It fits the definition of relative dualism.

The duality of the symbol of a horse and a rider is indubitable, as well. The horse is an element to stress mobility of the whole, while the other element, the man, stands as characterization of successful hunting. The symbols rely on each other to create a meaning as a whole that is greater than the sum of its parts. Moreover, Sagittarius as a centaur, man and animal physically fused into one, appeared only in Antiquity. There is a much older picture of Sagittarius on a Babylonian boundary stone of the Kassite period (the second half of the second millennium BCE); it depicts a horse with a creature on its back having two heads, two tails, and two wings. This symbol is doubly dual (Waerden, 1966).

Lastly, all of the known pictures of the Pisces consist of not just one fish, but two of them facing in opposite directions. Once again, the presence of two complementary elements that constitute an absolute dualistic symbol in this emblem is unquestionable.

The fact that the majority of the zodiacal constellations with clearly expressed binary symbols turn out to be concentrated in the quartet of Gemini seems significant. Neither Cancer, nor Leo, Scorpio, Aries, or Taurus possess binary symbolism. Aquarius is the only constellation possessing this probable dual nature in the quartet of Taurus: in the ancient material, he often carries two vessels in his hands. Libra and Capricorn (two of the four constellations in the quartet of Aries) could be claimed to have a binary interpretation. Libra is certainly drawn with two cups, though it is a single symbol of the equilibrium, while Capricorn, which resembles a mermaid in the imitative material, is also a single creature; in this sense, it differs radically from the Babylonian version of Sagittarius which has two heads and two tails.

Dualism is a common visual and structural feature of all four symbols of the Gemini quartet. In my opinion, every common feature distinguishing one quartet from others is additional evidence that each quartet was designed and executed as a singular thematic entirety.

Thus, the coincidence of the symbolism of the Gemini quartet with the widespread Neolithic symbolism and the Indo-European myths, strong inner links between three elements of this quartet as well as its dualism are the evidence that these constellations belong to a single symbolic unity. We have enough reasons to suggest either a Pre-Indo-European or a Proto-Indo-European origin of this symbolism.

The problem of Pre-Indo-European culture was summarized by Winfred P. Lehmann (2002). This culture, defined as a result of linguistic, archaeological, and genetic research, is attributed mainly to the period between 8,000 and 5,000 BCE. Having preserved some characteristics of the preceding hunters/gatherers, Pre-Indo-Europeans led a settled way of life and practiced herding and agriculture. Socially connected groups were modest in size, and they had no central power that dominated any considerable territory. Pre-Indo-Europeans occupied small settlements. Each one was a family with a head who was master of his extended family. Tribal chiefs were basically independent of one another.

Being agriculturists, Pre-Indo-Europeans had a tendency towards expansionism. They easily moved from place to place with a highly developed sense of adaptability. In new surroundings, they quickly exchanged knowledge and spiritual views with the aborigines. Researchers believe the basis for this expansionism was the horse:

> "... The horse had been domesticated as early as the end of the sixth millennium, and was prominent in the assumed Indo-European community from the fifth. Used initially for food, the horse only later became the means for territorial expansion. Increasing evidence for it is found in the Moldau area and the Hungarian plains in the fourth and third millennia, which Meid associates with the expansion of the Indo-Europeans. This type of horse was the tarpan, in contrast with Przewalski type that was prominent among Asiatic people who later used it in their raids on Indo-European settlements" (Lehmann, 2002, pp.41-42).

The inheritors of the Pre-Indo-Europeans were the Proto-Indo-Europeans. On the basis of linguistics, J.P.Mallory stated:

> "... Proto-Indo-European language is commonly ascribed by linguists to the period ca. 4000-2500 B.C. with some room for debate concerning how much earlier one may set the existence of the protolanguage" (Fagan, 1996, p.347).

The homeland of Proto-Indo-Europeans is still unknown, so we can define the epoch but cannot define the territory where the first proto-zodiacal constellation-makers resided.

The constituents of the Gemini quartet were the earliest star groups fixed on the path of the Sun for the purpose of creating an agricultural solar calendar. We can call them the constellations of the *first* quartet, or the *first generation*.

Note that if we try to examine the quartet of Cancer (Cancer, Libra, Capricorn, and Aries), which precedes that of Gemini as far as its epoch is concerned, not a single assertion that we made above (the correspondence to the socio-cultural context of the epoch, the integrity of the quartet's symbolism as a circle of anthropomorphic gods, the links between symbols, the connection of the symbols with the corresponding seasons, the water symbol in winter, the dualism of all symbols) would suit it. The quartet of Cancer, and all others before it, are just formal astronomical constructs without any historic sense.

The quartet of Gemini is the first one that interconnects all its elements into a unique symbolic togetherness, which, in turn, fits into the historical period determined due to the phenomenon of precession (the Neolithic era).

Some years ago I discussed my concept with I.M.Diakonoff (1915-1999), an outstanding world authority on ancient history at St.Petersburg University in Russia. He pointed out that the period around 5,600 BCE was a special point in Near East pre-written history - a very important stage of the Neolithic revolution, with a sudden rise of agriculture and urban cultures. And so it came as no surprise that an interest in improving the solar calendar should appear at that time.

A Display of Power and Might: the Taurus Quartet

As the 4th millennium BCE approached, the precession of the Earth's axis moved the four distinct "seasonal" points westward along the ecliptic out of the "mascots" of the Gemini quartet. How might the ancient observers have reacted to this change? It seems likely that the tendency to retain cultural traditions would not have permitted the obliteration of icons of the Gemini quartet, but they lost their original metaphoric sense. To address the new loci of the seasonal points, it would have become necessary to mark new sectors of the path of the Sun. These sectors became the icons of the Taurus quartet: *Taurus* the bull, *Leo* the lion, *Scorpio* the scorpion, and *Aquarius* the water carrier. Thus, the astronomical *Age of Taurus* entered the historical scene. It lasted from about 4,300 to about 1,800 BCE, but its actual implementation surely started several centuries later than 4,300 BCE.

In this section, I shall collect arguments in favor of the claim that the quartet of Taurus is another symbolic unity that stands in contrast with the quartet of Gemini because they belong to entirely different historical epochs. If the quartet of Gemini mirrored the reverence of the Neolithic settlement before the pageants of Mother Nature, then the quartet of Taurus could only appear in an already socially stratified society with a distinct caste of rulers: warlords and cult-custodians. These power brokers maintained the symbolism of power and might. The celestial icons of the quartet of Taurus are the very same metaphors that manifested the strength of power for the chosen on Earth; they are a "business card" of the new epoch.

For the rulers of clans, the marvels of Mother Nature connected, for instance, with the birth of new life no longer presented any value. They considered themselves equal to gods and strove to highlight their superiority above others. In the new quartet, the symbols were not humans but primarily living creatures that in one way or another distinguished themselves through their power or dominance in the animal world: the mighty bull; the vicious lion; the menacing scorpion, whose deadly sting knows no mercy; and a custodian of cult water rituals.

The Age of Taurus comes about towards the end of the Neolithic; in a number of territories, it corresponds with the next major stage of human history, the Bronze Age. In the 4th or 3rd millennium BCE, when icons of the Taurus quartet were first clipped onto the new segments of the ecliptic, the economical and socio-cultural context of the ancient world had changed considerably in the 2,000 (or more) years since the Gemini quartet had been instituted. The former epoch saw the dawn of agriculture and urban societies; the latter beheld the advance of religious institutions that controlled the cult, the economy, and the rituals of the temples (Stearns, 2001).

Whereas the Neolithic populace often possessed small clay statuettes of anthropomorphic images, further development of agricultural civilizations led to the use of gold, silver, and stone for the fabrication of long-living standing idols in the form of animals. This transition in popular imagery is consistent with the application of animal metaphors for three of the four constellations of the Taurus quartet.

The region which the people who were involved in the elaboration of the four new ecliptic constellations of the *second* generation habituated may be quite different from the homeland of the first quartet. Nevertheless, within the framework of the known motifs of Sumerian, Assyrian, and Egyptian creative work, the metaphoric structure of the new symbolism is decoded without any difficulty.

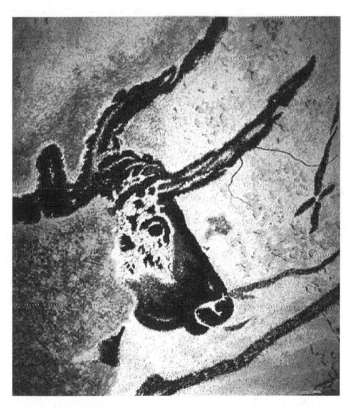

Fig. 9. Aurochs - wild bulls - due to their great energy attracted attention from people long before their domestication. They were depicted on many walls of Paleolithic, Mesolithic and Neolithic cave dwellings. This is one such example: a cave painting in Lascaux, France (Wikimedia).

The transition from the worship of a Mother-goddess (female) image to a male image at this time may account for the use of a bull, or its phallus (signifying masculine virility), as the symbol for the vernal revival. The image of a bull unquestionably belongs to the most ancient and imposing symbols. Apparently its account goes back to the Paleolithic rock paintings on the walls of caves. It is widely presented in various regions of the world. With time, the symbolical figure became a cult one. Bulls were present in the artwork of early farmers too, but, at that time, the bull was nothing more than a secondary cohort of the Great Goddess. This is only natural: everyone knows that female productivity is dependent on the act of male fertilization. Therefore, in the Neolithic, the bull played a subordinate role as a low-ranking assistant to the goddess (Rice, 1998).

In the specialized research, *The Power of the Bull*, one can find a lot of exciting specifics about this issue:

> "Of course, there are many other enduring cults detectable over the long span of time, judged in terms of human history at least, with which we are concerned. The moon is a constant object of veneration, mysterious and, sometimes in a literal sense, occult; the sun, too, though rather less frequently than might be thought, for it is a curiously late object of universal reverence. Divinity is immanent in streams, mountains, the storm and in many animal forms. None of such manifestations, however, seems to me to have the persistence nor the power of the bull in grasping and holding the imagination of men. From late Upper Paleolithic times to the end of antiquity the bull is always honoured as a divine creature, as the manifestation of a god or as the witness of a god's presence. For more than 15,000 years therefore this creature has seized the god-making imagination of men throughout the great band of territory which sweeps from the Atlantic to the borders of India, and south into Africa, in which most of the worthwhile advances of our species, as well as many of its more resounding disasters, were realized" (Rice, 1998, p.5).

Fig. 10. The Bull was a theophany for several solar gods of Ancient Egypt. Scholars know such sacred bulls as A'a-Nefer, Apis, Buchis, Mnevis. Here is Apis, a theophany of the Ptah-Sokar-Osiris cult at Memphis. His ceremonies date to the 1st Dynasty, i.e., earlier than the time of the Great Pyramids.

Destroying the golden calf and appearing with the ram's horns, Moses metaphorically demonstrated the end of the Age of Taurus and its replacement by the Age of Aries (drawing by Anna Kharitonova).

As for ancient Egypt, its inhabitants had a long-standing cattle-raising pedigree. And in their land the bull was royal and divine since the Neolithic revolution (*Ibid.*, p.121,123):

> "Egyptian recorded history begins with the recognition of the founder of the First Dynasty, Nar-Mer, as King of Upper and Lower Egypt, a title which was to be the most important in the royal titulary for the next 3,000 years. The most valuable 'document' from this time (though it has been suggested that its production is actually later in date than the First Dynasty) is the superb palette from the

so-called 'Main Hoard' at Hierakonpolis which portrays Nar-Mer presiding over his two kingships and enacting episodes in the course of the imposition of his family's rule over the Valley. In one episode the king is personified as the bull, destroying a city's wall. From this time onwards the representation of the bull proliferates, generally (but not invariably) in the context of the royal power. Several other important references survive from the very earliest time of the Egyptian kingship which commemorate the importance of the bull."

The Egyptians instituted the cult of the divine bull Apis, which in all probability was older than the Pyramids, with its roots in the pre-Dynastic past. Besides Apis, there were cults of the bulls Mnevis and Bochis. In many cases the king was hailed as a bull; he was, for example, 'Great Bull of his Mother', an epithet of considerable antiquity, which appears in the Pyramid Texts.

Under the new conditions of the Bronze Age, society makes a transition into a patrilineal mode, and the bull becomes a completely independent and even dominating deity. It serves as an important decoration of ancient oriental temples and has left a firm memory in the arts, establishing itself in the pages of the Old Testament under the name of the *Golden Calf*. Our name of 'wild bull'- or *taurus* - goes back to the Indo-European root and is reconstructed as *t(h) auro-*. T.V.Gamkrelidze and V.V.Ivanov (1984, Part 2, pp. 519-520) emphasize

> "the similarity of this Indo-European word with the general Semite *tawr-...testifies to the fact that these words are a reflection of a certain migrational Near East term designed to distinguish this animal which played a special cult role in the ancient cultures of the Eastern Mediterranean."

Bulls were one of the first animals to be domesticated and were widely used in the economic-transport activity. Bulls are also widely known as the most important worship animals of the Near East culture of the 7th-6th millennia BCE thanks to artifacts found during archaeological excavations. Numerous Assyrian and Egyptian statues, the Greek legend of the Minotaur, the mountain name Taur, the modern bull fight, and finally the Indian attitude toward cows as sacred animals are all remote echoes of the archaic cult of the Bull.

The spreading of the cult of the Bull all over the ancient Orient precludes this author from determining the territory where the possible creators of the name of the Taurus constellation lived. However, the correctness of this label in connection with the vernal revival of Nature is unlikely to be challenged.

The second image of the Taurus quartet — that of a lion — also played a meaningful role as a metaphor of supreme power, and this is consistent with its use during this epoch for the constellation Leo, which indicated the power of summertime, the Sun's highest point on its way along the ecliptic.

Fig. 11. Seen as the lord of the land, for many thousand years the lion stayed as a symbol for deathless courage, strength, fearlessness, and bravery. This photo pictures the so-called Guennol Lioness – the Mesopotamian figurine unearthed near modern Baghdad, Iraq by Sir Leonard Woolley on his 1924-34 dig (the collection was named Guennol after the Welsh word for martin, the bird). The small limestone artifact (8.3 cm) is believed to have been carved circa 3,000–2,800 BCE (Protoliterate Period). Experts consider it as approximately contemporaneous with the first known use of the wheel, the development of cuneiform writing, and the emergence of the first cities. It was at that time that a lion appeared as a novel symbol of might and the highest power (Courtesy Wikimedia). The symbolism of a lion has nothing in common with the first proto-zodiacal quartet.

The memory of the lion's symbolic role is reflected by such world-famous monuments as the lions over the gate of Mycenae. The mementos of Mycenaean Greece repeat the motives of the Hettic and Lubean imitative arts. An image of a goddess upon a lion's back is a regular subject in fine arts. A lion, as a sacred symbol of empowerment, is reflected in the Greek myth of Hercules, who kills the Nemean lion and puts its skin on. Today the lion still remains the King of Animals and an important heraldic sign.

Associations of the bull and the lion with the role of the king as well as with the nature of kingship are perceived in many cultures of the Bronze Age. Chikako Esther Watanabe of Osaka, Japan, probes the issue on the example of Mesopotamia from the 2nd millennium BCE:

> "In metaphors, Mesopotamian kings are identified with lions, the idea of which is observed in a personal name already in the Fara period, such as **Lugal-pirig** (the king is a lion) or in the UR III period, **Lugal-pirig-bànda** (the king is a fierce lion). Similarly, the king is also identified with the wild bull, another strong wild animal. The king Šulgi, for example, is described in royal epithets as "the wild bull of extraordinary vigour" (**am.á.pàd.da**) or "born to be the great wild bull" (**am.gal.šè.tu.da**), and Hammurabi described as "the goring wild bull who attacks enemies" (Watanabe in Prosecký, 1998).

Research by Willy Hartner (1965), which turned out to be a priceless stimulus toward the current reconstruction, contains an analysis of the motif of a Lion tearing a Bull. Such a motif is regularly found in ancient Eastern art starting from the 4th millennium BCE and going on through Sumerian art up to the late Persian miniatures.

Fig. 12. A lion as a concomitant (symbol) of mighty supreme power. Minoan seal of the Great Minoan goddess with a lion from the so-called Western Repository. C. 1,500 BCE. Crete.
Source: Photo from *The Palace of Minos at Knossos* by Sir Arthur Evans, Vol.1 *The Neolithic and Early and Middle Minoan Ages; Macmillan and Co., 1921, page 505.*

Willy Hartner suggested that the plot of the fight of the lion with the bull was of sacred astronomical meaning and marked the calendric event of transition from spring to summer. (Much later in 1999 V.V.Emel'yanov shared the same opinion). Agreeing with Hartner, I have to add that the problem he raised is much broader: before they were taken from the sky, Taurus and Leo, together with the two other symbols, were deliberately "elevated" into the sky as the mascots of the special positions of the Sun on its annual path.

The third mascot within the Taurus quartet is a scorpion, which is yet another familiar symbol from ancient Egyptian and Babylonian sources (Van Buren, 1937-39 and 1945; Aurigemma, 1976). It is repeatedly mentioned as an image in the Scriptures. The scorpion, like the bull and the lion, is a metaphor of fierceness, strength and power.

The presence of Scorpio at the point of autumn is self-evident. Sagittarius "wounded" the Sun with his arrow, causing it to begin its descent into the waters of the ocean; exactly the same symbolic function belongs to the stinging Scorpio, a night spider, which ends its existence in autumn after copulating and fulfilling its main physiological function. For different epochs with different symbolic tongues, both Sagittarius and Scorpio perfectly symbolize the substance of the same natural process - the autumnal decline of the world.

In this context, Aquarius, the performer of water rituals, who is the last mascot within the Taurus set, at first glance appears out of place. However, everything that has been mentioned above concerning the symbolic role of Pisces is applicable to the symbolism of the new winter constellation, as well. Aquarius, like Pisces, is evidently connected with water, which embodies the winter withdrawal of the Sun to the Lower World. Within another symbolic tongue, the role of Aquarius is exactly parallel to the functional role of Pisces. The main difference is: while the dual symbol of two fishes was taken from the natural world, the cult custodian of death is a personification of power and might. He is as much a part of the entourage of a royal court as a bull, a lion, and a scorpion.

I think that I have achieved my self-set goal. I have demonstrated that, just like in the Gemini quartet, all four metaphors in the second quartet are chained into a single thematic string, and altogether they fit in their corresponding historic era of the Bronze Age.

The symbolism of the Taurus quartet cannot yet provide clues to the territory of its origin. However, there seems little doubt of its direct connection with the ancient Oriental civilizations in the epoch of town growth and relatively developed religious and worship mentality, i.e., in the Bronze Age. At a glance, the symbolism of the quartet of Taurus is probably linked with the Mediterranean area.

As a byproduct, the contents of the second quartet immediately lead us to a suggestion on the genesis of the term Zodiac. The first quartet was patently a "circle of human beings." It was only the second one that could be dubbed a "circle of animals." Is it not possible that, later on, the byname of the second quartet was expanded to the entire twelve-strong ecliptic assemblage? The guess that sooner or later one element of a group can give its name to the entire group is not extravagant at all. Each and every language knows hundreds of such synecdoches.

In Russian, the name of the seven-day week is *nedelya,* which literally means *no work*. Originally, it was the name of only the weekend holiday. After Christianisation of the land, this special day got another name, *voskresenie*, which literally means *resurrection*. Nevertheless, the older term, nedelya, did not disappear and was expanded as a general term for the entire seven-day week. From a common-sense viewpoint, it is absurdity to designate the seven-day week as *no work*. But this is exactly the case in the Russian language.

In English, the term, *disaster,* contains two components: the negation *dis* and the Greek root for star. Originally, a disaster was an astrological term for an event occurring under an improper star. Later on, it became a general term for any adverse happening or misfortune. I want to stress that words die seldom but change their meanings often.

Following this linguistic logic, I posit that, after the origination of the second quartet on the path of the Sun, its name – the circle of animals – was transposed to the entire set of zodiacal constellations.

A perusal of the old astronomical cuneiform texts of the Babylonians (the *mul*APIN tablets) reveals that all names of the constellations in the Gemini and the Taurus quartets existed by about 700 BCE. This is not the case with some of the constellations of the next quartet, marked by the transition of the vernal equinox into Aries.

Agnus Dei at the Head: the Quartet of Aries

Due to precession, after c. 1,800 BCE, the labels of the Taurus quartet lost their roles as it had happened with the icons of the Gemini quartet about two millennia earlier. Just as in the previous case, it seems certain that the transition from the Taurus quartet to the quartet of Aries (Aries, Cancer, Libra, and Capricorn) continued for several centuries, until the discrepancy between the actual points of spring, summer, autumn, and winter on the path of the Sun and the outdated markers became evident. The Age of Aries lasted to the brink of our era. It falls mainly on the Iron Age of human history (Fagan, 1996).

In its makeup, the quartet of Aries would have been similar to the quartet of Cancer, had it existed around 8,000-6,000 BCE. However, there is an insurmountable rift between them. The symbols of the Cancer quartet in no way correspond to their historic era. In the period of 8,000-6,000 BCE, the images of Cancer, Libra, Capricorn, and Aries have not been archaeologically fixated; such metaphors did not exist in that remote time. Furthermore, the order of those symbols does not give any plausible reasons for their correspondence with the seasonal points. The Cancer quartet cannot be interpreted as a symbolic whole.

On the same grounds, the completely negative conclusion applies to all the other possible quartets prior to the Gemini quartet. Three, and only three, sequential zodiacal quartets of Gemini, Taurus, and Aries are exceptional. Only they can be interpreted within themselves as a symbolic togetherness through symbolism corresponding to their specific "working" epochs. This is precisely what speaks in favor of a certain spiritual endowment that was given them at birth.

The Aries quartet is the youngest. Rupert Gleadow (1968) was among the first to observe that Aries the ram was absent from the Babylonian sky of about 1000 BCE. Instead of the ram, it was a Hired Laborer, a hireling. Cancer the crab was also absent. The Akkadian name for the star pattern in Libra at this time means "horn of a scorpion," suggesting Libra did not exist but was part of Scorpio.

The symbolism of the Aries quartet is consistent with the wind of socio-cultural changes in the Near East of the time. The Old Testament warned against the idols and cult statues of Near Eastern temples when monotheism was on the verge of dominance. Artistic images and parables had become widespread in the literature of the era, and it is in this context that the names of the Aries quartet are allegorical, rather than merely symbolic representations. It has been remarked that the Age of Aries is associated with the story of Moses coming down from Mount Sinai as "two horned," or crowned with the ram's horns, while his flock disobediently insists on dancing around the golden calf, a metaphor for Taurus (de Santillana and von Dechend, 1969).

The significance of Ram-Aries basically comes from the great economic role of domesticated sheep, which provided the ancients with wool. Alongside horses and cows, sheep belong to the three main sacrificial animals. Just as a bull was always located near a sacrificial cow, a ram always stood near a sheep. In the Babylonian written evidence, we see that the name of the Ram is not of Babylonian origin but actually quite compatible with the traditions of the Indo-Europeans, Babylonians, and Egyptians. The symbolic significance of the ram is doubtless. The ram was strongly connected with ancient vernal rituals. In the 2nd millennium BCE, God changed the subject of Abraham's ritual sacrifice from a human being to a ram.

Cancer the crab, as the allegory of summer, can refer to the reversal of the Sun's motion as it passes the summit of the ecliptic. Even today, the most northerly latitude over which the Sun can shine directly overhead is named the Tropic of Cancer, suggesting that this term was first applied when Cancer marked the summer solstice point.

Libra, represented by the scales, no longer shoots the Sun as did the autumnal constellations of the Gemini and Taurus quartets, but, instead, it represents the night-and-day balance of the equinox.

Capricorn, the fanciful goat-fish, stands in this quartet for winter. The Goat's cult designation can be found in many ancient religions. In the mythology of ancient Iceland, the Goat is known as the animal harnessed to the Chariot of god.

> "The exclusive archaism of this image is proved by the similar evidence of some Indo-European traditions: the Baltic one, in which thunder-god Perkunas rides goats, the Slavonic, mythological heroes which are on goat-back, and especially the ancient Indian one, in which goats appear as means of transport used by gods" (Gamkrelidze and Ivanov, 1984, Pt 2, pp. 586-587).

The ritual mission of the carrier-goat is reflected in the Bible. The scapegoat liberates people from their moral burden, carrying away their sins; this motif undoubtedly has deep religious-mythological roots.

Celestial Capricorn is illustrated everywhere in ancient depictions as a goat with a fish's tail. The name Goat-fish, according to written sources, is of Sumerian origin. This means that Capricorn is actually the direct heir of water symbols used for the winter equinox both in the quartet of Gemini and of Taurus. Capricorn could be the carrier of the souls of the dead down to the Lower World.

I think once again I have fulfilled my promise, showing the inner unity of the Aries quartet and its accord with the historical epoch. In the quartet of the first generation, we encountered ancient binary symbols.

The second quartet, that of Taurus, contained primarily monosymbols, while the last quartet, Aries, appears to be allegorical.

The Three Quartets are Radically Different Sets

A few of my fellow astronomers, who by profession are distant from the problems of symbology, have perceived the indicated quartets as being "corrupted." Why do Pisces cripple the harmony of the anthropomorphic quartet of Gemini? How did Aquarius, a man, sneak his way into the zoomorphic quartet of Taurus? Would it not be more reasonable if the two switched places: Aquarius would take his place among humans, making the Gemini quartet completely anthropomorphic, while Pisces would enter into the circle of animals, making the Taurus quartet entirely zoomorphic? This consideration has sometimes served as an argument that my interpretation of the quartets is illusory and subject to doubt. Meanwhile, the inner integrity of the first and second quartets does not rely merely upon the formal distinction between anthropomorphism and zoomorphism. It lies considerably deeper.

As I have already noted, any symbolism is a brainchild of its epoch, an epitome of it that is specific to the societal peculiarities of a given era. These peculiarities lie in the buried chasms of human mentality. So, what social ethos does the Gemini quartet mirror?

This quartet was fashioned by the early agriculturists, who did not yet have any notion of statehood or social stratification. In jest, the society of the early agriculturists can be called an "equal opportunity company." The headmen of this society could rightly call themselves the first among equals, and they had not yet thought of raising themselves into the ranks of the chosen and the godlike.

The early agriculturists remained Nature's children. Their thoughts focused on their bodies, on the marvels and perils of the surrounding world, and on the magnificent occurrences of Nature. All their symbols, including fishes, were direct excerpts from natural facts and phenomena: the miracle of twins; the miracle of pregnancy and birth giving; the miracle of death that perpetuated life, i.e. hunting, which was among the basic preoccupations of their immediate ancestors; and the miracle of the water body, as represented by fish, which was a piece of a unique ecosystem and an important source of nutrition that appeared just before the Neolithic during the Mesolithic.

The four metaphors of the first quartet may serve as a sound illustration to the vivid characteristic of the making of the Neolithic Age that, for example, the authors Baring and Cashford (1991) advocate. These authors know nothing of the possible emergence of the Zodiac embryo during the Neolithic, but their words are adequate for our conclusions about the features of the Gemini quartet:

> "The Neolithic was the great age of discovery and the result was no less than a new relation to the universe. This was the time when humanity was released from the need to live in complete accord with what nature offered or withheld and now learned to participate in the mysterious processes of growing. With the realization that certain seeds changed into wheat and corn, which could be transformed into bread, and that certain animals would live close to the home and provide milk, eggs and meat, a new spirit of conscious co-operation between human beings and their world was born.
>
> The life of the cosmos became a story that included humanity as one of the characters… We know this not just from the evidence of agriculture and the domestication of animals, but from art, the oldest human record. The art of this time has a new and exciting sense of narrative: images weave together to tell a story, separate and rephrase in a continual act of exploring the relation between the different orders of creation. These stories have come down to us in the great legacy of fairytales all over the world… (pp.46-47).

The second quartet of the Bronze Age was instituted when the state (class) organization of society with its hierarchic structure had long since become an accepted factor of life. In order to get a very condensed characteristic of this time, we can once again turn to Baring and Cashford (1991) and excerpt just the titles of a number of sections from the chapter about the Bronze Age: The Separation from Nature; The Order of the Patriarchy; The Ritual of Sacrifice.

The symbolism of the second quartet, including Aquarius, tells us not of marvels of Nature but of the problems of upholding and strengthening the dominance of the emergent power brokers of a patrilineal society. The headman of an ancient state and his spiritual circle were concerned with self-affirmation. They practiced shaman-like communications with heavenly forces and sought ways to assert the lawfulness of the power granted to them through divine providence. Not fellow tribesmen, but only the ruler (the monarch, the pharaoh, the king) and the religious elite had a prerogative to perform sacrifices and other power-granting and fortune-telling acts. During this time, war had already become a professional business.

In the first quartet, a celestial pregnant woman epitomized the awe of reproduction, which was central for the matrilineal clan. In the patrilineal Bronze Age, metaphors in human likeness had outlived their time. Was it sufficient for a ruler of a new type who thought of himself as a mediator between mortals and gods to use a female productivity principle? The answer is no. He was not interested in hoisting another human being into the heavens; neither was he interested in maintaining the authority of a Mother-goddess, who stood for a cultural philosophy so contrary to his own.

Could the Mother-goddess maintain her authority among a new generation of symbols? Again, the answer is no. The archaic goddess, of course, survived multiple upheavals down to our days in images from the goddess Demeter to the Virgin Mary. Nevertheless, she lost her primacy. There are many examples in mythology reflecting the patrilineal trend to subvert the power of the goddess. We see this in the Gilgamesh epics when he murders Tiamat, we see it in the Greek pantheon, and in dozens of other cases. Who then was delegated to the sky in these new conditions of stratified social organization of the Bronze Age? They were symbols of power and might of the predominantly male rulers.

In the second quartet, the Mother-goddess was ousted by a sacred bull. The bull is not a secondary character anymore, a sidekick of the Mother-goddess. Now, the bull has the upper hand in the celestial cast of characters. It is the embodiment of the unworldly link of the ruler with the life-giving power of the gods. The lion, the king of beasts, clearly represents the uniqueness, dignity and hegemony of the ruler, and the potency of this symbol can be seen to this day in the heraldic paraphernalia of numerous monarchies. What about a scorpion? It is an embodiment of ruthless power. As Egyptologists claim, several early pharaohs bore the name of Scorpion. Is this not another symbol of power?

Finally, Aquarius is unquestionably connected with state-sponsored water rituals that were undeniably derivative of well-established state (and religious) systems.

Do you feel the principal distinction between the sets? If the first quartet can be called the quartet of "free villagers," then the second is the quartet of "mighty rulers." I insist that both Pisces and Aquarius have their proper places in these quartets. These symbols fit perfectly into the underlying connotations of their corresponding epochs.

In a theoretical consideration of symbolic conflicts, i.e., the transition from one set of symbolic inventories to another, a University of Ulster sociologist, Simon Harrison (1995), distinguished four basic features of various political or cultural symbolic inventories:

1) they are properties of certain interested groups;
2) they are status markers, ascribed with qualities broadly describable as sacredness or prestige value;
3) the control of symbols is a source of legitimacy and privileges;
4) the symbols are a focus of emotional attachment, loyalty, and identification, invested in their owners' sense of self.

In accordance with these, Harrison recognized four variations of conflicts in contests for dominance of certain symbolic inventories: valuation contest; proprietary contest; innovation contest; and expansionary contest. In Harrison's terms, the transition from the first ecliptic quartet to the second one could exemplify a typical *innovation contest*, which is so typical for the creation of new views.

As far as the third quartet and its allegories go, they are records of the advanced state of development of the church and religious doctrine of the Iron Age. During the Bronze Age, religion ossified into a powerful authoritative institution, the church, and the church is not the same as religion. The latter is about ideology while the former is about supremacy. As a rule, the church serves the interests of those in power, and, in this respect, it looks not to the elite but to the general population. And if at the dawn of the formation of religious views symbolism played the leading role, then in the everyday practice of the established church allegories emerged to take the lead. Allegories are the instrument of clerical prophecies; they are far more transparent and thus far more appealing to inexperienced minds. The third quartet seems to be a hallmark of the "well- established priesthood."

All three quartets carry with them the permanent marks of the epochs of their originations.

Credibility of the Gradualist Model

To evaluate the significance of the proposed Gradualist Model, it is worthwhile to digest the results that can be derived. Here they are.

■ The most arresting feature of the concept is its evolutionary nature. The formation of the Zodiac does not appear to have proceeded as an instantaneous epiphany by a single group of sages (Uniformist model). It grew and matured as a product of a gradual process; each step was separated by several millennia. The authors of each generation of symbols could not remember the spiritual aspiration of the antecedents. All the authors had only one creative imperative in common: the utilitarian role of each set of symbols as elements of the solar calendar.

Discussing the Gradualist Model, Russian archaeologist I.L.Kyzlasov rightfully noted (1995, pp.161-164):

> "In accordance with the law of its progress, during thousands of years the spiritual culture of mankind developed without negation but with absorption and reconsideration of the views of previous generations. Each result concerning the world view is historically multilayered and mixed, so it implicitly contains in itself a memory on its genesis and evolution... The concept of several stages of accumulation of proto-zodiacal constellations, a process in which observations of older astronomical facts were not turned down but were included into a new experience, is completely correspondent to the traditional attribute of a traditional view of world."

■ The utilitarian role of symbolic icons on the path of the Sun consisted in labeling four seasonal points in the solar yearly cycle and, thus, bringing into being an integrity of the solar calendar. The continuous value of the proto-Zodiacal quartets as a bedrock of the solar calendar was the anchor that held them in the historical retrospective of humankind for millennia. As time passed, the vivid ancient emblems became celestial fossils.

■ Due to precession, our reconstruction provides an option of dating the epoch of the first quartet of the proto-zodiacal constellations - the middle of the 6th millennium BCE, i.e., at least three thousand years before the invention of writing. Nonetheless, it is not surprising within the context of the history of mankind because historians agree that this particular period saw the greatest jump in the development of urban-type civilizations. It was a period of human history that persistently demanded the necessity of the solar calendar: it came into existence when it became an overbearing need for agricultural progress. The solar calendar was moved forward by agriculturists and not by hunters who had no need of the exact knowledge of seasons.

■ The date under discussion seems to be placed appropriately on the chronological scale of humanity's astronomical accomplishments. Many scholars have reasoned that a lunar month and a seven-day week were the products of the Upper Paleolithic. Owen Gingerich dated the codification of the constellations with characteristic bright patterns to the Ice Age. In this general context, it is not very surprising that constellations adjusted to mark distinct "seasonal" areas along the path of the Sun could have been established as far back as the 6th millennium BCE.

■ In the frame of the reconstruction, I interpreted constellation names for every generation in connection with the cultural background of the corresponding epochs. All three generations of celestial symbols are really in complete agreement with historical connotations.

■ I have demonstrated the meaningful arrangements of the four names within each generation, which are in total agreement with the corresponding mentalities of the epochs. Each of the three sets is not a random miscellany of occasional labels but an organized progression that mirrors a harmonic sequence of the same type as, for example, morning – noon – evening – midnight (or, vernal awakening – summertime upward flight – autumnal downfall – winter termination).

■ I established that the most ancient writings and other types of material artifacts may be used as verifications for the concept. Of course, the archaeological material is limited, and it is impossible to justify each and every step of this research with proper evidence. Nevertheless, archaeological findings on hand do not falsify but rather verify the conclusions of the proposed reconstruction.

■ I found an explanation to the origin of the term Zodiac as an antipode to the preceding set of symbols, which was the circle of humans.

■ The reconstruction reveals the "aquatic" portion of the quartets - three constellations with water symbolism, which, one after another, were used to personify the winter solstice. In my mind, this is a very solid argument in favor of the view of land as an island encircled by ocean, which was formed very early and continued to flourish for many millennia. The existence of the "aquatic" segment of the zodiacal quartets is hard to explain as just a coincidence.

We may consolidate and generalize everything said in this Chapter in a few simple words. The tale of the Zodiac is a story of the birth and development of the solar calendar. This latter growth was propelled by the introduction of the four seasonal "mascots" on the path of the Sun. The influence of precession forced sky watchers to renovate the quartets of the "mascots" every two thousand years. As a result, by the 1st millennium BCE the path of the Sun was gradually filled with the twelve-strong pagan zodiacal necklace. The Serpent-holder was not affiliated with the Zodiac. He remained behind on the ecliptic as a relic of the pre-zodiacal time.

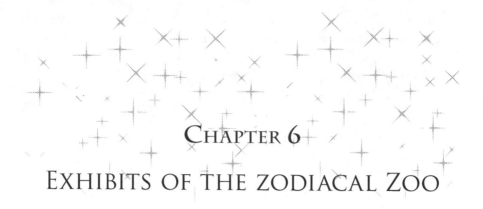

CHAPTER 6

EXHIBITS OF THE ZODIACAL ZOO

We have asserted and verified that the proposed hypothesis fits into the context of the time it encompasses and has no inner contradictions. To convert the hypothesis into an accomplished theory, we have to delve into historical artifacts and find evidence, written or material, which can serve as proof of the real existence of seasonal quartets.

The hardest to prove, of course, is the existence of the earliest (anthropomorphic) quartet of Gemini. Thus, we will endeavor to start with a simpler task – to find traces of the second (zoomorphic) seasonal quartet, that of Taurus. A crucial piece of evidence would be an elucidation of the symbolic connections that tie together all four of the quartet's labels in relation to each other as a solitary ensemble.

The French historian of religion and archaeologist Louis Charbonneau-Lassay (1871-1946) was in the process of realizing a grandiose plan of writing four reference books on Christian symbology: *The Bestiary of Christ, The Flowers of Christ, The Vulnerary of Christ,* and *The Lapidary of Christ.* Through great misfortune, the painstakingly prepared materials were destroyed in an air raid after the outbreak of WWII, and only one book of the series survived to see the light of day. The French edition of *The Bestiary of Christ* came out in 1940 and was translated into English half a century later (1991).

The Bestiary of Christ opens with "The Tetramorph" (p. 3):

> "In the series of living beings claimed by Christian symbolism to form the mysterious crown of Christ, a group of four animals is notable for the large place it held, and continues to hold, in sacred art and mystical literature. We see them

represented at times separately from one another and at times united, blended together in the form of a unique being that would be strange indeed and disconcerting to anyone ignorant of ecclesiastical symbolism."

The Tetramorph is the foursome comprised of a bull, a lion, an eagle, and a man, who in the modern world serve as the symbols of the four evangelists. The French author explains the meaning of such a group as the four being the noblest of all creatures and each one holding the title of "king" of a certain "kingdom." The bull – king among all sacrificial animals, the lion – king of all beasts, the eagle – king of the birds, and man – king of nature. There is no need to prove such an explanation was retroactive. The indicated tetrad entered contemporary culture out of the Holy Bible, where it is described twice: in the vision of Ezekiel, towards the end of the 7th century BCE, and the vision of St. John in the first years of the Church.

Let us immediately observe this tetrad is represented in the Bible quite widely. Historians of religion tie the tetrad with the *cherubim* mentioned in the Bible more than 90 times. There is no exact account of this creature in the Bible, but everything we know about it suggests the cherubim are a combination of a bull, a lion, an eagle, and a man.

However, the story of the intriguing tetrad is not limited to the Bible. Among archaeological finds in the Mediterranean area, one comes across many such images, and, characteristically, a great many of them are older than the vision of Ezekiel: we were able to find this tetrad united in a single image of two and a half millennia BCE. It represents a stunning example of longevity of a symbolical group. We can view this tetrad as a single entity, as pairs, or individually.

Jumping ahead, let us immediately say that this amazing foursome is in fact the second seasonal quartet previously separated out solely based on astronomical considerations. There is only one puzzling problem: why is there Scorpio within the second quartet while in the Biblical tetrad we have an eagle?

Egyptian Trace: The Sphinx and the "Scorpion" Mace-head

Long before the Greek man-bull Minotaur, Scandinavian tailed mermaids, the Indian multi-armed deity Shiva and other living hybrids, the Great Egyptian Sphinx was the first symbiotic emblem in world history.

The Great Egyptian Sphinx is unique. A contemporary of the Great Pyramids and their guardian, the Sphinx is one of the greatest mysteries in world history. It is about 5,000 years old, and the time of its creation falls in the world-age of Taurus. And the figure of the Sphinx with its *nemes* – the headdress worn only by the Egyptian kings – is so grand that it had to personify something of vital importance.

The Great Sphinx is a mixture of a lion's body with a human's head. As you can recall, in the second zodiacal quartet the images of a lion and a guardian of water rituals (water bearer) are present vis-à-vis the seasons of summer and winter. Has the human component of the Great Sphinx something to do with the celestial Water Bearer?

The response is not that easy, but I would like to recollect a curious polemic between professional and non-professional Egyptologists ignited years ago.

The Great Sphinx was sculpted in a deep bedrock enclosure. With time, the enclosure has been filled with sands of the desert. On a few occasions the enclosure was cleaned out, but sooner or later it has been filled with sands again. Authorities cleaned it out recently again and for the time being a visitor can check the results of centuries-long erosion of both the enclosure's walls and the Sphinx's body.

In a geological sense, horizontal layers of bedrock have different softness, and a picture of horizontal erosion of the hybrid's body and the enclosure's wall due to wind and sand is pretty typical. But there is another type of erosion clearly evident in a vertical direction, and competent geologists agree only falling water can activate its origination.

The likely existence of water erosion invigorated the free-lance author, John Anthony West (1979), who is an amateur in Egyptology. West guessed that the Sphinx was cut out of bedrock not concurrently with the Cheops' pyramid about 2,500 BCE, as mainstream scholars evaluate, but at least about five millennia earlier when there was rain in this area, not an arid plateau. Professional Egyptologists disgraced West's claim as a red herring. And they are right in all respects but one. Evidence of water erosion is persistent (Schoch, 1999), and nobody has proposed a realistic clarification of the issue.

Meanwhile, for our concept there is no hardship in this case at all. If the Sphinx's human visage has something to do with the symbolic Water Bearer, the water rites ought to take place beside it. If praying priests year-by-year poured water offerings on the same points of this consecrated territory, the corresponding traces would be like the imprints of water streams. That is a natural scientific explanation which can resolve the problem forever, isn't it?

An interesting artifact that could be evidence of the Sphinx's water mission is exhibited in the next figure. This is a lion in combination with a water carrier, who is basically a male human being. It has to be the summer/winter set and exemplify two of the four symbols that stand for the second zodiacal quartet.

Fig. 13. *Above.* The constellation of Aquarius, as it appears on the ceiling of the Egyptian temple of Hathor at Dendera. This image of a pharaoh with two water-pots from the late Hellenistic period was made at about 100 BCE, but surely reflects and reproduces an older tradition (after *Hinke*, A New Boundary Stone).

This blue faience sphinx with two water-pots in its hands is a sort of a water bearer like the Aquarius pictured above. The artifact portrays a pharaoh, Amenhotep III, who was the father of Akhenaten the heretic. The dating of the artifact is ca. 1390–1352 BCE. It is direct evidence that water rituals were an important component of the sphinx' mission and, originally, the Great Sphinx could have been a hybrid of the celestial Leo and Aquarius. The artifact in question is in New York, Metropolitan Museum of Art, accession number 1972.125 (in public domain).

At the same time in Egypt, where is the vernal/autumnal set? Are there two other symbols as a set: a bull and a scorpion?

In the halls of the Ashmolean Museum in Oxford, one can detect an artifact, which is of pretty much the same period as the Great Sphinx:

the so-called "Scorpion" mace-head. It depicts a pharaoh who is ready to perform a sacred ceremony. Whatever the ritual being performed, two features are absolutely clear: the pharaoh's ritual dress is decorated with a bull's tail, while a drawing of a scorpion is depicted right in front of him.

Fig. 14. This is a detail from the fragmented so-called "Scorpion" mace-head that was found in the temple of Horus at Hierakonpolis, Egypt. Now it is in the Ashmolean Museum of Art and Archaeology, Oxford, England (accession number AN1896-1908 E.3632). It measures 25 centimeters long, is made of limestone, and is attributed to a pharaoh soon after the unification of Egypt. The king is seen in full ritual dress with the ritual bull's tail hanging from the back of his belt. In front of the king's face there is a scorpion. In this artifact both vernal and autumnal symbols are depicted close to the pharaoh. An image of a scorpion is located together with a star, which underlines an astral meaning to the entire scene. The dating of this mace-head is 3,150 to 3,050 BCE, i.e., older than the Great Sphinx of Giza (reproduced courtesy of the Ashmolean Museum).

So far, it is clear that all four symbols of the second zodiacal quartet were familiar to the Egypt of the Great Pyramids. These symbols are sound and obviously played a substantial role in Egyptian sacred life. A probable objection is that in this case we have just pairs of symbols and not a single artifact with all four emblems together. Do not worry, we shall find them all together, as well.

A Vision from Mesopotamia

If we start to shop around for potential evidence, we shall discover that, within the period of the second zodiacal quartet's eminence, a lot of amalgams of its four symbols are scattered throughout the Mediterranean world. Among the most impressive ones is the vision of Ezekiel:

> "And out of the midst of it there was a likeness of four living creatures… And as for the likeness of their faces, the four of them had a man's face with a lion's face to the right, and the four of them had a bull's face on the left; the four of them also had an eagle's face…" (Ezekiel, 5, 10).

The thirty-year-old priest Ezekiel, son of Buzi, was born around 623 BCE in Jerusalem. He grew up in the most privileged Judean society and was educated in the scribal schools and priestly academies (Silberman, 1998). Within a few years after the battle near Har Megiddo (Armageddon), the Kingdom of Judea became a possession of the Babylonian Empire, and, as many others, Ezekiel was deported to Tell-abib on the River Chebar, a canal which ran from the Euphrates and passed through the large commercial city of Nippur. Like other exiles, Ezekiel was influenced by Babylonian culture. They adopted the Aramaic language and alphabet and the Mesopotamian calendar, and many people even took Babylonian names (Comay, Brownrigg, 1971).

For our cause, it is important to understand: who are those four mysterious creatures, the *cherubim* of Ezekiel? Rupert Gleadow (1968) commented "it was Zimmern who first suggested that the Cherubim in the first chapter of Ezekiel represent the cardinal constellations of the third and fourth millennium B.C." (p.126). [Zimmern's opinion is from Schrader, *Die Keilinschriften u. das alte Testament,* ed. Zimmern & Winckler, pp. 631 ff. (1903)]. Later on, the same four cherubim's faces occur in the fourth chapter of the *Revelation of St. John,* and are among the many supposedly astrological references in that exposure.

In his book, Gleadow proceeds with the example of the "winged bulls" from the British Museum which have a human head, the forefeet of a bull, the hind feet of a lion, and eagle's wings. In both cases of Ezekiel's vision and the "winged bulls" we are dealing with the second quartet, but why does the Eagle stand for Scorpion? The same Gleadow has an explanation (p.126):

> "Astrologers, when they make the equation with the four fixed
> signs, used the eagle instead of Scorpio, and pretended that
> it represents the higher side of that maligned constellation."

Recall that we have explained previously this very old-standing astrological tradition that the eagle and the scorpion are interchangeable. We have a right to suggest this old tradition reflects an earlier substitution of the original celestial Scorpio with the more appropriate, noble, celestial Eagle. It seems the Eagle is more fitting for the metaphorical sequence of Bull, Lion, and Man than the ugly arachnid.

It was Egypt that was surrounded with arid deserts. These deserts were a habitat for plenty of scorpions. Attacks of scorpions were great catastrophes. As a result, Scorpio could be an incarnation of the heavenly almighty that can cause great evil. It is not accidental that the Book of Revelation recollected scorpions as wicked evil:

> "And out of the smoke locusts came forth upon the earth;
> and authority was given them, the same authority as the
> scorpions of the earth have" (9:3).

The utilization of the scorpion as a celestial symbol was in line with a general Egyptian tendency. For example, as a powerful sacred symbol of the Sun they found nothing better than a scarab, which is nothing more than a dung beetle, certainly a lowly creature.

The marshland of Mesopotamia presented a stark contrast with Egyptian deserts. Scorpions lived in Mesopotamia as well as in Egypt, but under Mesopotamian conditions, their promotion to the rank of a celestial symbol was discreditable. That is why, hypothetically, it was in Mesopotamia that the ill-favored and unattractive Egyptian scorpion was substituted with the noble predator - the classical symbol of the Eagle.

Sent into exile, Ezekiel did not wax nostalgic for the past; he prophesied. And his prophecies were programmatic statements for future action, with the understanding of the "celestial structure" that Ezekiel gained during his forced stay in Mesopotamia.

Mesopotamian Smoking Gun

As it was stated, on many occasions, historians of religions tie the tetrad of Ezekiel's vision with the cherubim. Numerous details of this problem are described in a paper by Elie Borowski (1995).

Fig. 15. This cherub is a decorative detail of an object from the Bible Lands Museum, Jerusalem, collection—a bronze cult stand from the 12th century BCE. Only parts of two sides of this openwork stand have survived. The artifact is said to have come from Cyprus. Here all four legs of a composite creature end in lion's paws, but the hindquarters are clearly those of a bull. The tail of the creature sculpted in the bronze stand is that of a bull, not a lion; the tail rises and then falls straight down, like a bull's tail. The bronze figure thus combines the same four famous elements of the tetrad - man, eagle, lion, and bull (source: *Cherubim: God's Throne?* by Elie Borowski, Biblical Archaeology Review, v. 21, No. 4, p. 39, Jul-Aug 1995; sketch by Anna Kharitonova).

The link between the tetrad and the second zodiacal quartet is not more than a guess. Nevertheless, let me work out this guess as a possibility of a Mesopotamian version of the second quartet. In Ezekiel's vision, the Eagle stands instead of Scorpio. In this version, the symbols are Bull, Lion, Eagle, and Human. An important piece of corroborative evidence of the existence of the second quartet, and the validity of our hypothesis as a whole, will be the bas-relief from a Mesopotamian temple that shows the foursome of the symbols in the proper order they should occur if they represent the changing of seasons.

Ezekiel's prophecy postdates the quartet of Taurus by more than a millennium. This, however, cannot be used to deny that the Taurus quartet is what Ezekiel was describing. As we have already mentioned, used quartets that ceased to have an astronomical purpose continued to be in use during transitional times until the invention of newer ones and remained stored in cultural memory of humans forever.

In his exceptional publication of 1965, Willy Hartner noticed a combination of only two beasts: a lion tearing a bull. He suggested that these kinds of images represent not naturalistic scenes but rather a symbolic astral embodiment of the replacement of spring with summer. But Hartner did not notice that the motif of the lion that devours the bull is often a fragment of a picture that includes all four elements we are seeking: the bull, the lion, the eagle, and the human.

To find excellent examples for our cause, it will be enough to address just one artistic catalogue that contains hundreds of images. This catalogue – *Art of the First Cities* – was published by the Metropolitan Museum of Art and Yale University Press in conjunction with the exhibition held at the Metropolitan Museum, New York, from May 8 to August 17, 2003 (Joan Aruz with Ronald Wallenfels, 2003).

Let us start with a limestone block with sides 14 x 14 cm, which was part of the decorations from the Ninhursanga Temple. This temple was excavated at Tell al Ubaid; this is the modern name of a small hamlet six kilometers west of Ur. The main structure that was uncovered was a large temple complex dating from Early Dynastic III to Ur III.

Fig. 16. The second zodiacal quartet with all four symbols collected together. Plaque with a lion-headed eagle and human-headed bull or bison. Limestone, 14x14 cm. Mesopotamia, Tell al Ubaid. Early Dynastic IIIB, ca. 2,400-2,250 BCE. University of Pennsylvania Museum of Archaeology and Anthropology. Philadelphia B15606 (courtesy of the museum).

The relief-carved plaque depicts a lion-headed eagle biting into the hindquarters of a human-headed bull. An album text explains that the lion-headed eagle is called *Imdugud* and in later cuneiform tablets this creature is associated with the sun god Shamash and the human-headed bison, or the bull. The latter hybrid is called *kusarikkum*, and it is also connected with the god of the Sun, Shamash. The album informs us such subject matter was distributed throughout the entire Mesopotamian region and far beyond its borders, for example, in Syria.

What attracts our attention in this image? First of all, all four elements of the image create a ring. Moving clockwise along this ring from the bull, we observe consequently bull–lion–eagle–human - the exact sequence of elements that corresponds to the order of seasons within the second zodiacal quartet. Secondly, this limestone block is dated from 2,400-2,250 BCE, i.e., it is just a few centuries younger than the Sphinx and the second zodiacal quartet in its Egyptian form. Is this image a real smoking gun for the Taurus quartet or not?

Limestone Inlay from Syria

The limestone block from the Ninhursanga Temple is by no means alone. An image of the same type was excavated in Ebla, the ancient city in northern Syria. This image is pretty close to the previous one. It contains the same foursome in the same order. The age is almost the same, too: between 2,350 and 2,250 BCE (Early Bronze Age).

Fig. 17. Another variant of the second zodiacal quartet. A lion-headed bird over a human-headed bull. Limestone inlay. Height 13.8 cm. Syria, Ebla, Palace G. Early Bronze Age, ca. 2,350-2,250 BCE. Idlib Museum, Syria 3294 (courtesy of the University of Minnesota; digital ID 8004117).

The number of examples could be larger. In the Royal Cemetery of Ur, Leonard Wooley discovered the object he dubbed the "Standard of Ur." Now it is on display in the British Museum. Its dating is from

2,550 to 2,400 BCE. On its butt-end, there is exactly the same image of the foursome that we have observed in the two previous examples.

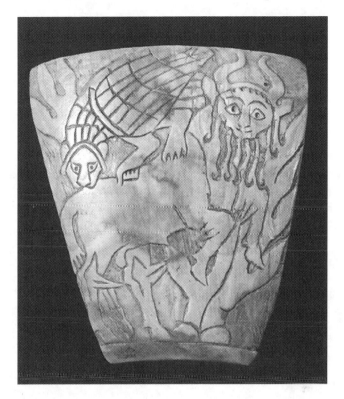

Fig.18. A find by Leonard Woolley in the Royal tombs of Ur. Carved shell inlay with a scene of combat: the lion-headed eagle, attacking a bull-man. Dating to the Early Dynastic IIIA (ca. 2,600-2,500 BCE). Size 5.89x5.31 cm. Metropolitan Museum, accession number 1984.77 (courtesy of the museum).

In Egypt, the Great Sphinx unified just two of the four elements of the second quartet. Could the same situation have taken place with the Mesopotamian version of the second quartet? The answer can be found in the same album of imitative art from the first cities. Aside from the images with all four elements of the second quartet, there are plenty of artifacts with just two elements combined in pairs: a human-headed bull and a lion-headed eagle.

As we have mentioned, the human-headed hybrid with a bull body had a special name, *kusarikkum*. Such a creature could be found over an immense territory. In our illustration, for example, there is a recumbent human-headed bull from Ebla. It is manufactured from wood, steatite, and gold. The time: Early Bronze Age (c. 2,350-2,250 BCE). The caption of the catalogue reads:

> "The use of gold for the body and head may be explained by the connection between the *kusarikkum* and the sun god. Ebla's links with Egypt provided access to one of the principal sources of the metal. The small size of the object suggests that it served as an amulet" (p.173).

A little younger, there is another recumbent human-headed bull from the Syrian Museum of Deir ez-Zor that was uncovered in the ancient city of Nagar (modern Tell Brak) and dates 2,300-2,159 BCE.

Fig. 19. Winter/spring symbols of the second zodiacal quartet bound together. Recumbent human-headed bull or bison. Limestone, shell, and bitumen. Height 28.2 cm. Syria, Nagar, Area SS. Ca. 2,300-2,159 BCE. Museum of Deir ez-Zor, Syria 11754. (GettyImages).

Bovines with human heads - two elements of the "Mesopotamian version" of the second quartet bound together - are found throughout the history of Mesopotamia everywhere. There is no problem to find also the two other elements: the lion and the eagle.

There is a mace-head dedicated to the ruler of Lagash, a certain Enannatum (c. 2,400-2,250 BCE). The center of the entire composition is *Imdugud*, a lion-headed eagle.

Fig. 20. An example of summer/autumnal symbols of the second zodiacal quartet bound together. Cuneiform limestone mace-head from Mesopotamia (probably from the city of Lagash). Height 12.7 cm. Early Dynastic IIIB, ca. 2,400-2,250 BCE. British Museum, BM 23287 (courtesy of the museum).

A beautiful pendant of a lion-headed eagle made of lapis lazuli, gold, bitumen, and copper alloy was uncovered among the "Treasures of Ur" and is now in the National Museum in Damascus, Syria. It is dated c. 2,400-2,250 BCE. The explanation to this artifact reads:

> "The lion-headed eagle, which combines the qualities of two fearsome predators, is first seen on a seal from the Late Uruk period. Over the course of the Early Dynastic period it took on a largely standardized appearance, with spread wings, wide tail feathers, and the head en face" (p.140).

Images of the lion-headed eagle are not always standardized. In the city of Nagar, Syria, in one hoard there were both standardized and non-standardized depictions. The latter one is a sheet-gold plaque depicting two crossed lions in relief with incised decorations. The lions' feet are represented as eagles' claws.

It seems the attentive reader will agree: a quantity of facts is obtaining a new quality. As a point for your attention, I defend a thesis that there were two traditions. The original tradition of the second celestial quartet was born in Egypt during the epoch of the Great Pyramids together with the emergence of the solar cult and the solar calendar. The Egyptian foursome included the Scorpio.

Just a few centuries later, the Egyptian quartet was borrowed in Mesopotamia and rectified by the replacement of the scorpion with the eagle. The Egyptians preferred to combine together emblems of opposite seasons, such as summer and winter. The Mesopotamians chose to combine neighboring seasons, such as spring and summer.

Being younger, the symbols of the Mesopotamian version of the quartet were distributed wider than those of the older Egyptian version. In Egypt, these symbols were very sacred and served only pharaohs and their entourage. In Mesopotamia, these symbols were foreign, and their users had no obligation to protect the secrecy. The area of the second celestial quartet in its Mesopotamian version, bull – lion – eagle – human, was much broader than just Mesopotamia itself.

Evidence of the Nippurian Calendar

Today, not a single modern historian has any doubt whatsoever of the important role the Sumers played in the 3rd millennium BCE in the making of human culture. In many respects, they were the ancestors of the antique culture of ancient Greece. Nevertheless, contemporary knowledge of early Sumerian history suffers from serious gaps.

How the Sumerians, or Blackheads as they named themselves, appeared in Lower Mesopotamia remains totally unclear (Kramer, 1963; Diakonoff, 1983). Indisputable proof that the population of Lower Mesopotamia was Sumerian belongs to the transition from the 4th to the 3rd millennium BCE when their writing appeared, most of which can be read today, although archaeological materials allow for even earlier dates. Overall, the Sumerian period of the history of Mesopotamia covers the 3rd millennium BCE. During this time, they were the main characters on the historical scene of the Near East. They invented their own writing, perfected the lunar calendar, and formed the foundation for school-based education.

In the early stages of their farming history, the technological advancements of the Sumerians was somewhat lacking compared to their powerful neighbor – ancient Egypt. The root of the problem stemmed from the Sumerians settling in the highly boggy environment of the lower reaches of Tigris and Euphrates, an area extremely poor in natural resources. They formed a net of inter-competing and fairly small city-states. On the other hand, Egypt, unlike the Sumers, united early on in the much friendlier valley of the Nile as a single rich agricultural empire under the sovereign rule of a pharaoh, harnessing possibilities unheard of by the Sumerians. By the time of the Great Egyptian Pyramids, the Blackheads could still build nothing of the sort.

Each coin, however, has two sides. Just like later on in Greece, the hostile conditions of Lower Mesopotamia and the competitiveness between cities stimulated an accelerated development of the Sumerian civilization compared to the Egyptian due to the dependence of creative potential in the latter on a solitary ruler and his court.

Among the city-states of the dawn of Sumerian history one of the more important to cultural developments was Nippur (today the settlement Niffer in Iraq). There in the 3rd millennium BCE a local lunisolar calendar was in use – one of dozens of local calendars. Suddenly, in the beginning of the 2nd millennium BCE for reasons unclear today, the Nippurian calendar entered widespread use as the universally accepted calendar in all of Babylonia, the cultural heir of Sumer. Later, the Nippurian calendar served as the model for the Jewish, Syrian, and some other calendars. Since the start of the 3rd millennium BCE, the Nippurian calendar practically did not change.

In 1999 in Saint Petersburg, Russia, a monograph was published by V.V.Emeljanov entitled "The Nippurian Calendar and the Early History of the Zodiac." Addressing many interesting issues that shed light on the particulars of the Nippurian calendar, this monograph contains a number of valuable conclusions important to our investigation. Let us briefly summarize them for our cause.

Starting with the earliest texts regarding the Nippurian calendar, it appears to be a well-developed system of lunar months, reflecting the specificities of agriculture throughout the year in the conditions of Lower Mesopotamia.

> "The names of the months and their explanations (including uses in astrological predictions) represent a special symbolical system, which is used to aid the expression of ancient man's psychophysiological reaction to the changes of natural phenomena and the seasons" (Emeljanov, 1999, p.243).

The names of the months in and of themselves are connected to rituals and have no direct link to the Zodiac. Nevertheless, using the words of Emeljanov (p. 241),

> "the main astronomical decision during the creation of the calendar in Nippur was the correlation of the observations of lunar phase changes with the observations of the Sun's yearly progress…"

In another place in the book the thought is expressed even more clearly:

> "The main rituals of Nippur are tied to the cult of the Sun as the keeper of world order" (p. 162).

According to Emeljanov, the Nippurian calendar was divided into two half-years beginning on the vernal and autumnal equinoxes. After this division, another one existed separating the months into four seasons. In the mind of the Sumerians, the spring and fall months were associated with the Bull, the summer belonged to the Lion, and the symbolism of winter was tied to Water and Fish (1999, p.46).

Let us extrapolate the indicated conclusions to our hypothesis. By the dawn of Sumerian written history, the Nippurian lunisolar calendar is already totally formed and its roots are lost "behind the horizon"; the written sources are not applicable to the analysis of the prehistory of the Nippurian calendar, which was formed before the beginning of the 3rd millennium (before 3,000 BCE).

In its original format, the Nippurian calendar was lunar, i.e., simpler than an agricultural solar calendar. Shoving the lunar months into the four solar seasons perfected it. The symbols of seasons were, as proven by Emeljanov, the Bull (spring), the Lion (summer), and the Fish (winter); the symbol of autumn duplicated the symbol of spring. The absence of an individual well-established autumnal symbol is in favor of our case for the interchange between a scorpion and an eagle.

In all the facts presented and interpreted by Emeljanov we can see a direct tie to the second quartet, which according to our chronological scale consistently gained popularity some centuries after 4,000 BCE. The ancient designers of the Nippurian calendar had a clear understanding of the four seasons of the solar year and used the symbolism of the Bull for spring and the Lion for summer. At this time the second zodiacal quartet had not yet fully formed for them.

Using the symbol of the horseback Archer for autumn was not convenient for the farmers of Sumer, but around 3,000 BCE they did not yet possess a new separate symbol (either the Scorpion or the Eagle), although in his private communication Emeljanov has informed me that the constellation of Scorpio was known in a certain form as early as the end of the 3rd millennium BCE. Nor did the Sumerians of the beginning of the 3rd millennium have a new symbol for winter (the Water Bearer), although hints of it can be found in the holidays and rituals of certain months.

In its finished form with four seasonal symbols, the second quartet will find itself in the Near East only in the second half of the 2nd millennium BCE, i.e., after the disappearance of Sumer from the historical scene. In later Chapters, we will argue that the birthplace of symbols from the second quartet was not Mesopotamia but Egypt.

Concluding overall, Emeljanov's monograph utilizes a rich factual database I can use to support the concept of the second quartet, which appears in Nippur in an incomplete form. Emeljanov's historical facts chronologically fall entirely in the time frame, calculated by us using precession. I would like here to thank V.V.Emeljanov personally for an interesting discussion of the results exhibited in his book.

A Mirror from Cyprus

The geography of the finds of the symbols of the second quartet represented as a single entity would seem to be much broader than simply the land between the Tigris and the Euphrates. Let me direct you to an example of ivory carving excavated from the city of Enkomi on the Eastern coast of the island of Cyprus (Christopoulos, 1974; Courtois, Lagarce, Lagarce, 1986). It is in the British Museum under the number GR 1897.4-1.872.

Ivory carving was an art practiced by Cypriot artisans in the Late Bronze Age (1550-1050 BCE). The great number and individuality of ivory products shows they were made in native workshops.

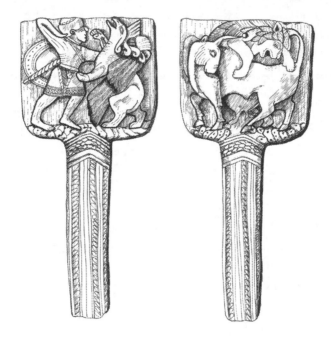

Fig. 21. An example of Cypriot ivory carving: a mirror handle from Enkomi, a city on the Eastern coast of the island of Cyprus. Ivory carving was an art practiced by Cypriot artists in the Late Bronze Age (1,550-1,050 BCE). On this handle there are carved decorations on both faces; one side depicts a lion attacking a bull, the other depicts a warrior slaying a griffin. The British Museum, No. 1897,0401.872 (Courtesy of the British Museum; sketch by Anna Kharitonova).

Cyprus became a most vigorous outpost of Hellenism in the Eastern Mediterranean after the volcano Thera supposedly terminated the Minoan civilization on Crete.

The artifact I am talking about is a mirror handle dated to about 1200-1100 BCE. In ancient times, a mirror was considered in a close relation with the Universe, and it doesn't come as a surprise that a mirror's handle could embody the issues of the world's structure. In our case, on one side of the handle we watch a lion crushing a bull and, on the other side, a male warrior is in combat with a griffin. The latter is a combination of an eagle with a lion, the same one as the hybrids on the previous artifacts but in the reciprocal order (the top part of the body is an eagle, while the lower part is a lion).

Following the avenue of our deliberation, the symbolism of those images is not hard to decode. The traditional scene of the lion fighting the bull, as Willy Hartner (1965) had noticed a long time ago, is a seasonal shift to summer after spring, while the man killing the eagle is a seasonal shift to winter after autumn; the symbolism is absolutely the same as in Ezekiel's vision, which supposedly dates several centuries later than the ivory handle from Enkomi.

In no way is the ivory mirror handle the only archaeological find of our interest from Enkomi. There are several vases with images of foursome hybrid monsters of the same type as all other cherubim.

Fig. 22. This krater from Enkomi, Cyprus, is dated to 1,250-1,200 BCE. Among its decorations is the usual second-quartet monster of four elements. Height: 41 cm; diameter: 36.6 cm; width: 40.5 cm; weight: 3 kg. Excavated from tomb 89. Now this artifact is in the British Museum (Courtesy of the British Museum).

A roster of these examples could be further enlarged, but the conclusion is inevitable: during the period of our interest in Egypt and its Mediterranean surroundings, the fine arts widely reflected the four symbols of the second celestial quartet combined together as a single intermixture. It is not senseless to suppose the second (mainly zoomorphic) quartet appeared in Egypt at the time we calculated for this event. It could easily be an Egyptian innovative brainchild as part of a movement that promoted the Great Pyramid Age.

Here is a condensed finale. As a result of systematic astronomical observations, in addition to the four archaic constellations of the first quartet, the Egyptians added onto the ecliptic four more symbolically named for the seasons' succession. These constellations became a base to check the solar movement for the new civil calendar and, moreover, a prognosis of the weather. In this function, they stimulated the nascence of constellation astrology. At the same time, because of the advantageous conditions of economic prosperity, the raising of the Great Pyramids as sanctuaries commemorating these great god-given events began. The number eight became sacred in Egypt.

The Royal Stars of the Ancient Persian Sky

In talking of the second quartet, one cannot circumvent the so-called Four Guardians of Heaven, or Royal Stars. They are known from Persian sources and, therefore, are often attributed to Persia (modern-day Iran), even though it is not necessarily so. It is possible the Royal Stars may have an earlier origin connected with India.

A documented history of the Persians goes back to the 9th century BCE when their predecessor Indo-European tribe settled to the south of Susa. By the 6th century BCE, the Persians had conquered all of their neighbors and created a powerful empire. Under Cyrus the Great they took over all of the Babylonian Empire. The origins of Persian history, however, and presumably those of the Royal Stars lie much deeper.

The Royal stars of Persia are four very bright stars, which are among the brightest stars in the sky. In the Persian sources they have names that require decoding and identification against a modern celestial map (Allen, 1963, p.256). The original names of these stars are *Tascheter* (marking the cardinal point of the East), *Venant* (the South), *Satevis* (the West), and *Hastorang* (the North).

Literature identifies these four with modern stars as follows: the star Aldebaran (of Taurus), the star Regulus (of Leo), the star Antares (of Scorpio), and the star Fomalhaut from the constellation of Pisces Austrinus (the Southern Fish). The brightest of the Royal Stars, Aldebaran, holds 13th place in the list of the sky's brightest stars; the dimmest, Regulus, holds 21st place; Antares and Fomalhaut hold 15th and 18th places respectively (Burnham, 1978).

Three of the four Royal Stars are contained within the zodiacal constellations of our easily recognizable second quartet. The fourth in this group should have been Aquarius, but it does not contain any bright stars. The two brightest stars in Aquarius hold only the 123rd and 126th places in the sky. This, presumably, was the reason why Fomalhaut, a bright star closest to the place on the ecliptic that needed marking, was selected as the fourth Royal Star.

The idea behind the Royal Stars is that they are evenly distributed along the path of the Sun and fix four seasonal points. An astronomical dating of a time when these stars could have served their desired function produces an unequivocal result. Since the vernal equinox at that time was in Taurus, the Royal Stars could only have been used as significant markers during the world-age of Taurus, namely after 4,300 BCE through the middle of the 2nd millennium BCE.

None of the historians question the fact that the first references to the Royal Stars occur in connection with the astral religion of Zarathustra, the Iranian prophet and founder of the Parsee religion that bears his name. In Greek form, the name of this prophet is Zoroaster, which literally means "star worshiper."

Attempts to determine the time of his life have led to intense debates. The Greeks thought him to have lived c. 3,000 BCE, but modern historians have dated his life and work to c. 600 BCE. This dating, however, has been subjected to harsh criticism, with the newest dating at c. 1,200 BCE (Bowker, 1997). Given the purpose of the Royal Stars, which are historically connected with Zarathustra, from an astronomical viewpoint, the last date is vastly preferable.

Contemporary historiography tends to view Zarathustra as a historical person. As a leader of chieftains, he carried on a struggle for a holy agricultural state against Turanian and Vedic aggressors. Stars played a huge role in Zoroastrianism and thus it is not surprising that Zarathustra's name is connected with the Royal Stars. In the context of our hypothesis it seems undeniable the Royal Stars of Persia fixed the equinoxes and solstices on the path of the Sun during the time when the quartet of Taurus was used for the same purpose.

The literature about the Royal Stars is full of guesses and analogies. One can find suggestions, for example, that they were connected from an early time in India with the legends concerning the four Maharajas (regents of the cardinal points), and have come down to us in connection with Hebrew and Semitic writings as the archangels Uriel, Gabriel, Michael, and Raphael. Another possible point of connection with the Hebrew tradition is the fact that Aldebaran, the principal star of Taurus, which marks the spring, symbolizes the Hebrew aleph (the first letter of the Hebrew alphabet, or figure one).

The unique aspect of the Royal Stars as astronomical markers is that they were used singly as stars, without being attached to larger areas that could make up constellations. This, however, does not affect the similarities between the larger meaning and purpose of the celestial quartets and the Royal Stars. The early constellations were formed, by and large, around bright stars as enclosed areas that simplified observations; it is somewhat easier to observe the position of the Sun relative to a certain area of the sky rather than a single star, though the latter may in some ways be seen as more obvious, even though it does lead to reduced accuracy of observations.

Either way, the Royal Stars of Persia serve as yet another weighty testimony in favor of the proposed working hypothesis, supporting the argument that four labels were placed consistently along the Sun's path in the sky to mark the advent of the four solar seasons.

The Eight-strong Proto-Zodiac

One of the conclusions that necessarily flows out of the proposed working hypothesis is that after the introduction of the four constellations of the Taurus quartet, the total number of the "divine houses" on the path of the Sun rose from four to eight. Only after the introduction of four more constellations of the quartet of Aries did the eight-strong proto-Zodiac become the full-fledged twelve-strong entity we know today. Such a historical fact is quite significant, and the transition from an ecliptic with eight meaningful signs on it to an ecliptic with twelve meaningful signs may well have been imprinted on the historical memory of the priests who witnessed it.

Indeed, the traces of a system with eight elements can be clearly found in several kinds of sources, the most important of which is ancient astrology. In older astrological doctrine, the circle of the ecliptic was subdivided not into twelve, but into eight sections, and "an account of the older division of the zodiac into eight *loci,* the *octatopos*" (Tester, 1987, p.46) was soundly preserved in a number of ancient sources and artifacts. In his detailed history of Western astrology, Tester informs us the astrological system of "houses" evolved from a primitive and natural four elements "through the *octatopos* to the twelve-house system" (p.239).

The Greek term *octatopos* – meaning literally "eight places" - is used in astrology in reference to horoscopes with eight "houses." Not only Jim Tester, but many others, as well, write about them (see Fagan, Firebrace, 1950). Ancient Greeks named their horoscope system *Dodekotopos*, i.e. the Twelve pieces (places). But this term Dodekotopos came about initially from the hermetical writings by Hermes Trismegest, which were Hellenistic reminiscences of the Egyptian prototype. As to the prototype, it was described in the Greek Michigan Papyrus # 149, probably written by Pseudo-Manetho (c. 80 CE) and translated into English by R.Gleadow (American Astrology, September and October, 1950). A hint on the same original Egyptian scheme, the *Octotopos*, is contained in *Astronomicon* by Manilius.

The Octotopos contained not twelve, but only eight places (watches) clockwise. This scheme was not connected with the Zodiacal signs counted from the vernal equinox but served for measuring time along fixed constellations. It seems this information supports my position very strongly: before being twelve-segment-strong, the older proto-Zodiac had only eight structural elements.

Since all events occurring in the sky were considered by the ancients to have divine origins, it seems reasonable for us to make a foray into the numerical symbolism of ancient Egypt. In regard to this aspect of the Egyptian rituals, we have a few random remarks made by Herodotus (circa 485-425 BCE), the Father of History. In Book II of his *Histories,* Euterpe, devoted to Egypt, we find the following dicta:

- "The Egyptians, they said, were the first to discover the solar year, and to portion out its course into twelve parts. They obtained this knowledge from the stars... The Egyptians, they went on to affirm, first brought into use the names of the twelve gods, which the Greeks adopted from them" (Book Two, 4).

- "The Greeks regard Heracles, Dionysus, and Pan as the youngest of the gods. With the Egyptians, contrariwise, Pan is exceedingly ancient, and belongs to those whom they call 'the eight gods', who existed before the rest. Heracles is one of the gods of the second order, who are known as 'the twelve'; and Dionysus belongs to the gods of the third order, whom the twelve produced" (Book Two, 145).

• "Seventeen thousand years before the reign of Amasis, the twelve gods were, they affirm, produced from the eight" (Book Two, 43).

Let us leave aside Herodotus' chronological claim of 17,000 years, which is absurd. The "Father of History" is regularly inaccurate in his dating. Modern historians feel no doubt that dynastic Egypt is not much older than 3,000 years BCE; there is absolutely no sense in 17,000 at all. The notion is a fairy tale, and it is well known that Herodotus had no worthy information on the chronological framework of ancient Egyptian history. At the same time, it is unlikely that his qualitative narration about the order of events is as bad.

The memory of eight primeval deities was reflected in the name of the town in Middle Egypt called *Khemenu*:

"The name of this town was derived from the ancient Egyptian word for eight, *Omn*, and means 'the Town of the Eight Gods'; and its modern name, el-Eshmunein, is derived from the Arabic word for eight. The Greeks named the town Hermopolis after another of its deities, Thoth, the god of wisdom and scribe of the gods, whom they identified with Hermes; and referred to the eight deities as the Ogdoad of Hermopolis" (Watterson, 1997, p.135-136).

Thus, much evidence exists that at first, there were the eight gods in Egypt, but in a later historical period, the number jumped to twelve. Is there something new in this message? Not at all, because this fact is known to modern historians from different sources. Ancient Egypt praised two particular numbers: 8 and 9. The number of homogeneous elements was eight plus the whole entity of them, which upgraded the holy number to nine. A similar situation flourished in ancient Chinese philosophy, where the special number of homogeneous elements was four. The addition of the whole entity of them (the center) elevated the perfect holy number to five.

A crucial challenge for this part of our investigation is when in ancient Egypt was the traditional holy number eight substituted by the number twelve? Right now, I do not see any serious historical grounds to answer this question with certainty. The reader, however, might grasp that I cannot keep myself from the temptation of corresponding the transit from eight traditional Egyptian gods to twelve with the transit from eight of the Sun's residences on the ecliptic to twelve. Being speculative, this interpretation, nevertheless, is very logical.

Peripeteias with Scythian Gold

The European world first heard about the Scythians from the Greeks who had started to develop the Northern Coast of the Black Sea and met these skilled riders there. The "father of history" Herodotus, who visited those places personally, dedicated to the Scythians almost the whole book, <u>Melpomene</u>, in his *Histories*.

In earlier times, nomadic tribes related to Scythians in language and culture occupied a vast territory in the steppe zone from the river Don to Lake Baikal, including foothills and mountain valleys of the Tien Shan, Pamir, Hindu Kush, Altai Mountains, and Sayan Mountains. Typically Scythian artifacts were oftentimes found in the remote regions of China, in Iran and Anatolia. These nomads got the name of the *Asian Scythians* though in Greek, Iranian and Chinese texts they were called "Massagetae", "Saka", "Seh". They kept in touch with their neighbors to the South as far as Mesopotamia. Among numerous finds in the burials of European Scythia, together with subjects with elements of Greek and ancient oriental traditions, one can see the "purely" Scythian manner with the same stylistic peculiarities as on artifacts found in Central Asia and Southern Siberia.

Due to a confluence of historical events, forced out of the parts of Central Asia they settled in an earlier invasion, in the 8-7th centuries BCE, some nomadic tribes of Indo-European origins invaded the steppes of modern-day southern Russia and populated areas along the Kuban river. Under the name "the Royal Scythians," they left here numerous burial sites, the so-called *kurgans*, containing the richest of wares and arms, which have been found in the course of numerous archaeological digs. Inside the Scythian kurgans, a significant number of golden objects was found, which is why in literature there is frequent mention of the generic "Scythian Gold."

One of the most expert Russian specialists in Scythian history, the late Dmitry S. Raevsky (1941-2004), pointed out to me two remarkable gold artifacts belonging to the early period of the Scythian settlement along the Kuban. The two objects are a gold scabbard from the so-called *Litaya mogila* burial site and a gold sword in a gold scabbard from the kurgan near the village of Kelermes (7-6th centuries BCE). The two objects look very similar and do not warrant individual descriptions (Grakov, 1971, Plates XXIV and XXV).

On both objects, a chain of fantastical animal hybrids is depicted along the length of the scabbards. There is absolutely no doubt that the hybrids are composed out of the zodiacal animal symbols and only of them – the images contain no other extraneous symbolic elements. The bodies of the hybrids are either those of a bull or of a lion; the heads are those of an eagle, ram, or human; the tails belong either to a bull or a scorpion; and each carries on its back, where regularly a set of wings would be, a pair of fishes. The majority of the figures have stretched out in front of them a bow, carried in position that is well-known from traditional depictions of Sagittarius.

Fig. 23. Fantastic creatures on golden Scythian scabbards are mixed from the constituent elements of the first and the second zodiacal quartets (original photos courtesy Prof. D.S.Raevsky; drawings by Anna Kharitonova).

I cannot propose a guess as to the significance of the order in which the creatures are depicted and leave that to the experts on Scythia. One thing, though, becomes very clear in looking at the images: the Scythians knew the importance of this symbolism even before the appearance of the twelve-strong Zodiac in its final form. Swords made of gold were far too precious and far too soft to serve as real armor for the bellicose Scythians; these swords were ceremonial. And on the scabbards of the ritual swords, the "Royal Scythians" stamped out two of the four symbols from the oldest Gemini quartet (Sagittarius and Pisces), all four of the symbols from the Taurus quartet (Taurus, Leo, Scorpio/Eagle, and Man), and only one of the symbols from the oncoming Aries quartet (Aries itself).

The obvious conclusion is that the Scythians had preserved a material artifact from a time when the oldest quartet was no longer functional, the second quartet was still in use, and the third quartet had not yet been fully formed, though the spring had already moved into Aries. The Scythians preserved a memory from the same period when the second quartet was in usage as the Persians did through their four Royal Stars. Is this not yet another serious argument in favor of the idea of the gradual formation of the twelve-strong Zodiac?

Evidence from a Cuneiform Text

So far, the oldest written evidence of regular astronomical activity is found in Babylonian cuneiform texts, the earliest of which date as far back as the turn from the 2nd to the 1st millennium BCE. The number of astronomical texts discovered by archaeologists is now considerable. Unfortunately, most of them have not yet been carefully interpreted, so we are forced to wait for new materials in this avenue.

It was B.L.Van der Waerden who dedicated many works to the problem of analyzing the emblems of the Zodiac by investigations of ancient sources. He is also the author of the summary of results available in regards to this problem (1953; 1974). The identification of the Babylonian asterisms in comparison with the modern constellations is based on the star catalogue of the famous astronomical text ^{mul}APIN, along with more ancient astronomical texts, known under the general name of astrolabes.

The text of ^{mul}APIN is an encyclopedia of the Babylonians' astronomical knowledge accumulated by 700 BCE (the date when the most ancient tablet was made). However, the description of the visual conditions for the observations of planets and constellations in ^{mul}APIN gives grounds for earlier dating of practical observations used in this encyclopedia. Van der Waerden originally dated the period of the accumulation of information for ^{mul}APIN from 1400 to 900 BCE. Later, the revision of the identification of some stars made by W.Papke (1978) influenced him to date the ^{mul}APIN's observation epoch as 2300 BCE; Van der Waerden (1984) agrees with W.Papke's arguments.

Many constellations in the ^{mul}APIN tablets are reliably identified with the modern ones, in some cases even having the same names. When applied to our problem, it is most relevant to consider the section of the ^{mul}APIN which states that the path of the Moon on the sky, also

used by the Sun and five planets, goes through the 18 "houses of gods."
Here is their complete list.

1) *mul*MUL, which corresponds to the Akkad word *zappu* (translated as the hair brush) = the present Pleiades;
2) *mul*GUD.AN.NA, which means the bull of the god Anu = Taurus;
3) *mul*SIBA.ZI.AN.NA - the true shepherd of the god Anu = Orion;
4) *mul*SHU.GI, which corresponds to the Akkad word *shibu* meaning an old man = Perseus;
5) *mul*GAM - sickle sword = Auriga;
6) *mul*MASH.TAB.BA.GAL.GAL - the great twins = Gemini;
7) *mul*AL.LUL - there is something to clear up = Cancer + the star called Procyon;
8) *mul*UR.GU.LA - a lion, or a lioness = Leo;
9) *mul*AB.SIN - a furrow or, according to later decoding, a wheat ear of the goddess Shala = Virgo;
10) *mul*ZI-BA-NI-TUM - an Akkadian word for the scales = Libra;
11) *mul*GIR.TAB - a scorpion = Scorpio;
12) *mul*PA.BIL.SAG - an archer, or the mythical hero with two heads, armed with a bow = Sagittarius;
13) *mul*SUHUR.MASH - a goat with a fish tail = Capricorn;
14) *mul*GU.LA - a giant(?) = Aquarius;
15) *mul*ZIBBATImesh - fish tails = Pisces;
16) *mul*SHIM.MAH - a great swallow = the southwestern part of Pisces + Pegasus;
17) *mul*A-NU-NI-TUM - the Akkadian goddess, known to the priests of the 3rd millennium BCE as ANUNIT = the north-eastern part of Pisces + the middle part of the constellation Andromeda;
18) *mul*LU.HUN.GA - the Akkadian equivalent of agru, the hireling = Aries.

This list is primarily evidence that the main ecliptic constellations in that epoch had already been elaborated, though their quantity exceeded twelve. As Van der Waerden notes, the 12 signs - not constellations, but zodiacal signs - had appeared for the first time in the texts of the 5th century BCE. The names of the signs are the names of the corresponding constellations; it is remarkable that one and the same sign in this period is marked by the names of several related constellations. Thus, the sign of Taurus in this and future texts can be named *mul*CUD.AN.NA - the bull of the sky god Anu, but it also could be named *mul*MUL - the Pleiades, or one could use the Akkadian word mulis-li-e - a bull yoke.

This is proof that ancient names of the nearest constellations were applied to define the signs. As follows from *mul*APIN and more ancient documents, the list of ecliptic constellations begins with Taurus, which strongly suggests the epoch of their first use - the epoch of the Taurus quartet (between 4,300 and 1,800 BCE).

In the *mul*APIN list, our attention is drawn to the completely formed names of the quartet of Gemini. The only peculiarity of this quartet is that some parts of Pisces are included in two other constellations, listed above in #16 and #17. Comparing the Greek names of the zodiacal belt with their Babylonian prototypes, Van der Waerden (1953) notes that the original sense of the name *mul*AB.SIN was a furrow, though in another place of *mul*APIN it is asserted that *mul*AB.SIN is the wheat ear of the goddess Shala. In the picture of *mul*AB.SIN in the text AO 6448 there is an image of the goddess with a wheat ear in her hands.

The meaning of the name *mul*PA.BIL.SAG from the cuneiform texts is not clear, though the Greeks graphically displayed it as a centaur. However, in this case, our examination is supported by the pictures on Babylonian boundary stones, where this constellation is presented in the image of a mythological creature with a horse body and two heads, two tails and two wings (Van der Waerden, *Op.cit.*).

Thus, in accordance with the *mul*APIN, the Gemini quartet in that epoch had been completely formed, and we have no counterproof not to consider it as coming from the 6th millennium BCE.

The Taurus quartet corresponds to the observation base of the *mul*APIN text and actually is represented with only two peculiarities. First, besides the bull of the sky god Anu = Taurus, there was also the *mul*MUL group = Pleiades, which existed separately because of their unusual appearance. Second, the meaning of the name of the constellation *mul*GA.LA is not yet clear, though it is considered to be identical with the Greek Aquarius: on a Babylonian boundary stone, this constellation is depicted as of a god pouring water from two vessels (Van der Waerden, 1974).

The most interesting point, however, is that, as could be expected from the timing of ^{mul}APIN's composition, the Aries quartet is far from being completed. Instead of Aries, a man, a hireling, is found in that spot. It is only in the Greek Zodiac that the Ram (Aries) appears there, and the origin of its name is not yet sufficiently clear. The meaning of the ideogram ^{mul}AL.LUL of the text ^{mul}APIN, which resided in the place of the Greek Cancer, is also unclear. It suggests that Cancer, together with Aries, has no Babylonian origin.

It seems also that a metamorphosis happened to the Babylonian Balance. For the early Greeks, it was the Claws of the Scorpion, while later they switched to the alternative name, the Balance. The Goat-fish of the Babylonians, as clearly proved by the picture on the boundary stone, was probably the carrier of the dead to the Lower World. In the Greek Zodiac it turned out to be Capricorn. So, as it follows from the ^{mul}APIN tablets, the quartet of Aries was far from having its present shape. This entity belongs to the last foursome of the zodiacal labels and was formed only in the second half of the 1st millennium BCE.

A Testimony of a Later Epoch: Mithraism and the Aries Quartet

The Aries quartet belongs to that late period when the identification of its images as a four-strong symbolic entity did not raise questions for anyone who had any knowledge regarding it. We have already quoted Marcus Manilius as writing on the meaning of the four fixed seasonal points on the ecliptic (3, 666-668),

> "for as they mark the changing seasons, so do they alter this issue of affairs or that, suffering naught to persist in its initial state."

One can find very similar sentiments in the writings of Ptolemy, as well as in those of other authoritative astronomical writers. Since the situation with the Aries quartet is more evident than that with other two, we shall limit ourselves to but one striking example.

Fig. 24. The white marble monster, the Leontocephalus (one of many) is from the mysterious cult of Mithras. 2nd century CE, Roman Empire. This one is from *Corpus Inscriptionum et Monumentorum Religionis Mithriacae* (CIMRM) No. 545 (in the public domain). Height is 1.55 m. CIMRM indicated that the sculpture was formerly located in the Villa Albani; in 1780 it was purchased for the Vatican Museums. In the Vatican Museums (Museo Gregoriano Profano), it was near the entrance of the former Library (inv. No. MV_67900_0_0). Only the torso of the monster with four zodiacal signs is genuine; the remainder is a modern restoration. I hesitate to speculate on interpretation of this puzzling artifact, but it has an arresting peculiarity: the front of the Leontocephalus' torso features zodiacal symbols which are constituents of the third quartet. The upper line is a ram and a scale-holder (spring/fall) while the lower line is a cancer and a capricorn (summer/winter); it is an obvious exhibition of the third zodiacal quartet as an entity. By the way, the monster himself combines four symbols: a man, a lion, an eagle, and a serpent, three of them being constituents of the second zodiacal quartet (sketch by Anna Kharitonova).

The marble monster, the Leontocephalus, is from the mystery cult of Mithras. He shows an important highlight: the front of his torso features only four zodiacal symbols, which are the elements of the quartet of Aries. The upper line is a ram and a scale-holder (spring/fall) while the lower line is a cancer and a capricorn (summer/winter). The 1.5-meter figure was sculpted in the 3rd century CE in the Roman Empire and is now in the Vatican (CIMRM 545).

With this artifact, we have direct evidence of the Aries quartet as a single symbolical entity separate from the other zodiacal labels. What I have not yet found in archaic iconography is the first quartet as a unit appearing anywhere from the 6th millennium BCE onward. This task will continue to be a goal for future research.

A Hint from Archaic China

As it was explained in Chapter 3, the unique case of the Chinese sky appeared to be entirely different than the case of the sky in the Mediterranean region because, in the centuries before the Common Era, the sky of the "Empire beneath the Heavens" was mercilessly reshuffled. The novel celestial pileup was propagated by all Chinese royal astronomical institutions of later times. The previous celestial repertoire was utterly abandoned.

Meanwhile, research of the archaic, pre-Han, Chinese sky would be of great importance. Results could be reached through purely astronomical considerations, archaic images, linguistics, and, last of all, probably through mythology. My knowledge of Chinese mythology, of course, is not complete. So far, I only know of one attempt to analyze some issues connected with it. A question posed by two Russian researchers is whether any correlation exists between early Chinese mythology and the symbolism reflected in the names of the first zodiacal quartet. Is it possible to recognize archetypes for *Gemini*, *Virgo*, *Sagittarius*, and *Pisces* among the mythological characters of archaic China during the era that was synchronous or, at least, reasonably close to the institution of the first quartet?

The attempt in question was carried out by two Russian scholars: T.V.Stepugina, a Russian historian of Chinese culture, and E.N.Kaurov, a beginner in archaeoastronomy. Their task was rather restricted, and their sources were solely mythological. They aimed to research Chinese mythology for the purpose of determining whether the early features of Chinese mythological narration could be interpreted as derived from the same archetypes as the figures of the earliest zodiacal quartet. The title of their short presentation was *Ancient Chinese Myth and Mythological Grounds of Zodiacal Constellations*, and it was published as a part of a discussion in the *Herald of Ancient History*, a magazine of the Russian Academy of Sciences (1995, No.1, pp.172-175). Their conclusions were positive.

Concerning the idea of twins, as a Chinese analogy to this metaphor they suggest a pair of early Chinese deities: a male, *Fuxi*, and a divine ruler of the world, a female named *Nuwa* (Lady Wa). It is evident that alternative transliterations of original Chinese names were possible. For example, *Fuxi* could be spelt as *Fu-hsi*; *Paoxi*; *Fu-Xsing*; *Pho-hsi*; *Pi-hsi*; and so on. The same is true in respect of *Nuwa*.

Who are these mythological characters? The goddess, *Nuwa*, was either a sister or a bride to *Fuxi*. A later tradition ascribes to them demiurgic activities: this divine couple administered order out of primordial chaos, they designed the world, and they configured human beings with a capacity to create their own sons and daughters. That is absolutely the same idea that was behind the symbolism of *Gemini* in the European tradition.

For an analogy to the Mother Goddess – an archetype for the constellation of *Virgo* – the above-mentioned authors consider the same Chinese goddess, Lady *Wa*, who played a pivotal role in early Chinese mythology and at times was depicted with the body of a fish. The latter peculiarity stresses strong aquatic elements in Chinese mythology that could be easily linked with the symbolism of water seen behind the zodiacal constellation of *Pisces*.

Finally, the fourth metaphor within the first quartet, *Sagittarius*, was seen to be represented in early Chinese mythology by the Great Archer, *Yi*, who also has strong astral connotations. This legendary archer saved the earth from death by shooting down nine of ten suns that originally were brought into being.

Stepugina and Kaurov's paper strongly argues in favor of a conclusion that suggests it can reasonably be argued that early Chinese mythology and zodiacal symbolism of the earliest quartet could possess the very same archetypes.

I am citing this research chiefly as an example of queries into the Chinese sky that are relevant to my own archaeoastronomical queries. As with many other scholars, I consider archaic Chinese data as crucial to the verification or falsification of the hypothesis on zodiacal development: they could be very instrumental in cracking the puzzles of genesis and development of the archaic constellations that took place before recorded history.

A Test of Sizes

Last but not least, we have to put the most unusual evidence on the table. In Chapter 3, we have shown that when a single line of development is preserved in historical memory and practice without revolutionary changes, the most ancient constellations statistically have the largest sizes. That is to say that as the nomenclature of constellations expands and new members are fitted into the overall conservative tradition, the individual additions tend to get smaller the younger they are. If the rule "larger implies older", or the *size criterion,* is trustworthy, we should see consistent results once we apply it to the three generations of the zodiacal quartets.

The principal parameter for characterizing the size of a constellation will be its area, though this parameter alone could lead to error. Two other parameters can also be used: the general length of the constellation (its maximum length projected to the ecliptic), as well as the length of the constellation along the ecliptic line expressed in the duration of the Sun's presence within that constellation. Because we can assume that the position of the ecliptic among the stars has varied little in the past 10 thousand years, the above-mentioned parameters do not depend on precession and should remain invariant with time.

There is no need to determine with high precision the dimensions of the constellations, so the modern constellation boundaries may be used. It could be shown that, in comparison with the ancient constellation boundaries (for example, those of Ptolemy), the errors in our statistical results will be negligible. The required data is given in the table.

The first column of the table includes the names of the zodiacal constellations; the second one gives the constellation areas in square degrees; the third one gives the maximum length of the constellations projected onto the ecliptic (in hours); the fourth one gives the duration of the Sun's presence in the given constellation (in days). The explanation of the quartets' timing will come in the next section.

The Sun makes one full revolution along the ecliptic in approximately 365 days (column 4); however, a part of the ecliptic is located within the boundaries of Ophiuchus, which, as you remember, is not included in the set of the zodiacal constellations. Because of this, Scorpio is illustrated by two different figures. The sum of the lengths of the constellations, projected to the ecliptic, amounts to more than 24 hours, because the constellations "intrude" on each other.

APPLICATION OF THE SIZE CRITERION

Names	Area (square degrees)	Maximum lengths (hours)	Duration of the Sun's presence (days)

Quartet of Gemini (could be after 6,000 BCE)

Gemini	514	2.4	30
Virgo	1,290	3.5	44
Sagittarius	867	2.7	34
Pisces	889	3.0	38
Average	**890**	**2.9**	**36.5**

Quartet of Taurus (could be after 4,300 BCE)

Taurus	797	2.7	38
Leo	947	2.6	27
Scorpio	497	2.1	37 (21)
Aquarius	980	3.7	24
Average	**805**	**2.8**	**31.5 (27.5)**

Quartet of Aries (could be after 1,800 BCE)

Aries	441	1.7	25
Cancer	506	1.3	21
Libra	538	1.6	23
Capricorn	414	1.9	24
Average	**475**	**1.6**	**23**

The table confirms that on average, according to all parameters, the constellations of the quartet of Gemini are greater than the quartet of Taurus, and the latter in their turn are much greater than the constellations of the quartet of Aries. The differences in all parameters are much larger than errors due to uncertainties in boundaries. If we agree with the correctness of the size criterion, it will provide a quite independent and singular acknowledgment of the fact that the constellations of the Gemini quartet should, indeed, be attributed to the first generation, the constellations of the Taurus quartet to the second generation, and the constellations of the Aries quartet to the third generation.

We have collected facts that provide evidence in favor of our hypothesis of the origin of the twelve-strong Zodiac through the gradual accumulation of symbols for four distinct points on the track of the Sun. The most indisputable evidence applies to the Taurus quartet.

Let us draw a parallel. Imagine a written work in three autonomous volumes. In order to reconstruct the creative process at a later time, one would have to know whether the three parts were published separately in three volumes or together in one volume. If we discover a book containing only the second part of the work, it will definitely mean that both the first and third parts were published separately, as well.

I hope you catch the gist of the analogy. If we have substantial proof of the existence of the second (Taurus) quartet, we can make with certainty the conclusion that the first quartet also existed and was used as a separate entity. Finally, with the birth of the third quartet, all twelve elements of the modern Zodiac were put in their permanent places.

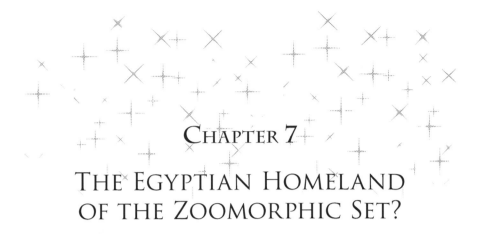

CHAPTER 7

THE EGYPTIAN HOMELAND OF THE ZOOMORPHIC SET?

The oldest artifact with an image of the second (zoomorphic) quartet as a single entity came from Mesopotamia, and nobody could condemn us if we designate Mesopotamia as the homeland of this quartet. The difficulty, however, persists in that the known facts do not allow for considering the scattered city-states of the Land of Two Rivers in the historical context as the cradle of the second zodiacal quartet. Meanwhile, in ancient Egypt, as far as we know the history today, such a context practically casts itself before our eyes.

Five strong arguments in the view of this author tilt the scales in favor of ancient Egypt as the territory where the second zodiacal quartet gained its power.

1. The proper timing. The appearance of the second quartet correlates in time to the unification of Egypt and the Age of the Great Pyramids when this agricultural civilization reached the peak of its ascent.
2. The proper background. In ancient Egypt, the Sun was the supreme god and the focal point of all religious rituals. It was Egypt where

   "the sun appeared from remote ages as the essential manifestation, the visible face, the "Eye" of the One and only God. The whole mythology of Egypt, at the period of its complete development, had ended by becoming, to borrow an expression of M. Paul Pierret, a solar drama" (D'Alviella, 1956, p.218).

3. The proper cultural context. Since the second quartet is zoomorphic, one cannot help but think that it could only receive wide use in a region where animals played the most significant role in religious practices: Egypt was first and foremost among such regions.
4. The argument from economics. In socio-economic terms, unlike the divided Mesopotamian city-states that varied in deities worshiped and religious practices, Egypt after its unification obtained sufficient economic and political means to ensure that people all across its territory held the same religious beliefs.
5. Since the very beginning of this book, I underlined that the three-quartet concept can be and has to be interpreted as a development of the solar calendar. Only one among the greatest ancient civilizations created the solar calendar in its pure form. It was Egypt.

Could Egypt have indeed served as the incubator for the nascent mostly zoomorphic second zodiacal quartet? To start with, one primary question needs to be resolved. A zodiacal quartet could only have been promoted by a people that have had interest in astronomy and its practical applications for a long time. Were the Egyptians that kind of people?

Egyptian Astronomy in the Age of the Great Pyramids

Concerning ancient Egyptian astronomy, the preeminent historian of science, Otto Neugebauer (1899-1980), can be considered as both the doyen and the superior judge in this field of research. His sentence for Egypt was utterly merciless (1957, p.80):

> "Egyptian astronomy remained through all its history on an exceedingly crude level which had practically no relations to the rapidly growing mathematical astronomy of the Hellenistic age."

At his kindest, Neugebauer wrote of the "extreme inaccuracy of all aspects of Egyptian astronomy" (1975, 2, p.561). Proselytes of his school shared the same position, some of the finer points of which were discussed in a very protracted essay by Robert Palter (see, Lefkowitz, MacLean, 1996).

I have no intention to question Neugebauer's authority and see no need to argue with him or his followers since all of them only discuss *mathematical* aspects of astronomical prognostications, tracing the origins of *mathematical astronomy* to the Babylonian "zigzag functions" used for astronomical computations.

Probably, the harsh judgment is true as long as astronomy is specified by the term *mathematical*. Mathematics is the language of modern science, especially exact sciences such as physics and astronomy. But who said that even exact sciences were born from the beginning as quantitative undertakings? Could they be qualitative? Surely, despite being essentially quantitative, they started as qualitative efforts.

It is true that we have knowledge of mathematical astronomy from younger Mesopotamian cuneiform texts. It is true that we have nothing of the sort from Egypt. Does this mean that Egyptian qualitative astronomy did not exist before Mesopotamian texts?

Without a doubt, mathematical astronomy was a logical – and higher – step of development of astronomy and one that may not have been reached in Egypt or reached very late. Probably it is correct that Mesopotamia has to be credited for the development of mathematical astronomy. Multifaceted ancient astronomical activity, however, cannot be reduced only to mathematical astronomy.

Unfortunately, Neugebauer's scientific school grew too influential, and followers of the "grand old man of the history of science" discarded ancient Egyptian astronomy in its totality, forgetting the limitation of the word *mathematical*. The heated debate was focused on texts that are absent in Egypt. I want to focus your attention on evidence other than texts.

Egyptian Astronomy in the Age of the Great Pyramids: Material Evidence

The first evidence: the forerunner in world history, ancient Egypt instituted the solar calendar. I argue this event was an achievement of extraordinary rank, and it demanded long skillful observations that could be not quantitative but merely qualitative. The solar calendar was the greatest astronomical accomplishment of the 3rd millennium BCE.

Prior to the birth of mathematical astronomy, there did exist an extensive practice of astronomical observations, which over the course of several tens of thousands of years before the Common Era led to the introduction of the lunar month, the designation of constellations, the determination of seasons, the recognition of cardinal points of the horizon, and so on. Did this practice exist in ancient Egypt? The answer is unequivocally *yes* since at least two momentous astronomical accomplishments – the introduction of the solar year and the precise orientation of the gigantic Great Pyramids – were achieved in Egypt.

The implementation of the lunar calendar occurred most likely no later than 30,000 years ago (with a huge margin of error, which does not lessen the significance of this dating). It was a gigantic step on the path of man away from his instinct-based animal past. It displayed a conceptual breakthrough in time reckoning, spread throughout the entire inhabited Earth, and is still used even now in the form of the year's division into months and weeks. Meanwhile, this event had absolutely nothing to do with *mathematical* astronomy, being entirely *observational*.

There is the next interesting question: was the radical perfection of time reckoning by rejection of the lunar and adoption of a purely solar calendar a significant astronomical achievement? In the eyes of this author, it undoubtedly was. It became possible only as a result of a clear understanding of the Sun's role and the specificities of its visible travel both in relation to the horizon and along the ecliptic. Is it possible to imagine that such a success was reached by people who had not already collected a rich body of knowledge about observations of the celestial luminaries and their motions? I cannot imagine such a thing. Yet among historians of science there is no dissent that the solar calendar was instituted in Egypt no later than the Great Pyramid Age.

However, even the creation of the solar calendar, inherited by Julius Caesar and the majority of the countries of the modern world, is not the most arresting triumph of ancient Egyptian astronomy. For a long time now historians have known the facets of the pyramids were aligned with the cardinal points of the horizon with amazing accuracy. And this is the second evidence of advanced Egyptian astronomy: the fantastic orientation of the Great Pyramids (± 2-4 arc-minutes).

I have read on the Internet how some critics deny the great accuracy of those orientations. As for me, I have no grounds to disbelieve the results received by archaeologists and published in all corresponding monographs and textbooks. Let us use the official data. According to reliable surveys, the errors in orientations are as follows (Edwards, 1993, p. 256; see also Atiya, 2004, p.87):

Maidum Pyramid - 0° 24' 25" ;
Bent Pyramid - 0° 9' 12" ;
The Great Cheops Pyramid - 0° 2' 28" (North side) ;
- 0° 1' 57" (South side) ;
- 0° 5' 30" (East side) ;
- 0° 2' 30" (West side) ;
Pyramid of Chephren - 0° 5' 26" (mean error of East and West sides) ;
Pyramid of Mycerinus - 0° 14' 03".

For those who are not familiar enough with the problems of angular measurements and orientation, I will remind you that the angular diameter of the Moon in the sky is very close to 30'. This means the orientation of the Pyramid of Cheops with respect to the cardinal points of the horizon was performed with an accuracy of about one tenth of the Moon's disk. Even if this is not evident for modern man, I will further remind you that orientation with respect to the cardinal points of the horizon could only have been performed as a result of angular astronomical observations. Other methods in the pre-space epoch (without navigational satellites) did not exist. Astronomical measurements are the only tool for finding the cardinal points of the horizon and orientation on the Earth's surface.

Is it easy to achieve an accuracy of orientation of several angular minutes without an optical device? Topographers and astronomers-practitioners know. The greatest mastery of astronomical observations in the pre-telescope age was achieved by the elder contemporary of Galileo and Kepler, the Dane Tycho Brahe (1546-1601). The accuracy of his angular measurements with the naked eye was the pinnacle of astronomical art of the 16th century, praised by his contemporaries and analyzed numerous times by historians of science. It reached several angular minutes, i.e., Tycho Brahe without a telescope did not manage to overcome the margin of error that was reached 4.5 millennia before him by the Egyptian skygazers.

Let me stress that, with regard to the orientation of the Great Pyramids, the comparison with Tycho Brahe means that measurements for the Pyramids' orientation were performed with the highest possible accuracy for the naked eye. Without exception, all astronomers – both contemporaries of Tycho Brahe and subsequent generations – extolled his feats and had no doubts that he had attained the highest peaks in the art of astronomy. So, were his results in the 16th century a scientific accomplishment, or were they completely unworthy of their praise?

Ill-wishers of ancient Egyptian astronomy have long defended their position with the thesis that the orientation of the Pyramids is not in any way related to true science, but is a mere engineering problem. Is this so? This author is ready to personally speak up in a public dispute in defense of the greatness of ancient Egyptian astronomy.

Just for example. Close to the equinoxes, the change of the Sun's declination (a solar coordinate with respect to the celestial equator) from morning to evening is more than 15'. If you determine the north-south line as an average between the sunrise and the sunset during these seasons, the accuracy of this line will be no better than tens of minutes. To achieve an accuracy of ± 2-4', the determination of the orientation due to the Sun has to be performed only near the days of the solstices when the change of declination is minimal.

I am afraid not all readers understand what I am talking about. These are nuances of so-called astrometry – the branch of astronomy dealing with precise astronomical measurements of celestial positions. Being a mathematician, Otto Neugebauer as well as his followers did not realize how to do astronomical measurements in their reality. They did not perform a single precise measurement in their life. It is truthful to say they were ignorant in this field.

In accordance with my background training, it so happens that I am an expert in astrometry, and I carried out a lot of exact astronomical measurements in my life. I insist that the determination of the Pyramids' orientation with an accuracy of a few arc-minutes could be performed only by a "champion among champions" who knew details of astronomical determinations exceedingly well on the basis of rich previous practice.

There is extra evidence: astronomy related to the Nabta Playa Ceremonial Complex. This archaeological site is located in the Egyptian Sahara, about 100 kilometers due west of Abu Simbel. It was excavated and thoroughly investigated by the Combined Prehistoric Expedition since its inception in 1962. The basic results of the Expedition were published in two voluminous books under the general title *Holocene Settlement of the Egyptian Sahara* by Kluwer Academic/Plenum Publishers. The first volume, prepared by Fred Wendorf, Romuald Schild, and associates, is subtitled *The Archaeology of Nabta Playa* (2001). It contains two sections on ancient astronomy: Section 14, *Site E-92-9: A Possible Late Neolithic Solar Calendar* (by Alex Applegate and Nieves Zedeño) and Section 16, *The Megalithic Alignments* (by Fred Wendorf and J.McKim Malville).

The verdict those archaeologists have reached is very sound. They uncovered indications of protracted astronomical activities by Nabta Playa inhabitants at such a remote time as at least 4,000 BCE, a millennium before the emergence of the great civilization of the Nile.

"Site E-92-9, a collection of small Nubia Sandstone slabs within a 49 m² area, most probably functioned as a calendar that marked the position of the rising sun at the summer solstice around 6000 years ago. Although many circular megalithic sites have been reported, only one other site also has been defined as a celestial calendar. The site may date to the Late or Final Neolithic...

Given the larger amounts of labor that went into building the other features of the Nabta Megalithic Complex, a much smaller labor investment, perhaps just one person or a small group, was needed for the construction of the calendar circle. All that was required was the astronomical knowledge" (p.467).

The conclusion to Section 16 (p.502):

> "Our evidence of attention to the prominent stars, Sirius, Dubhe, and those of the belt of Orion, coupled with the recurrent symbolism of cattle on the earth and in the sky, suggests cultural connections across both space and time in southern Egypt. The astronomical traditions of Nabta may have been part of the inheritance of the nomadic cultures that was passed to populations of the Nile Valley."

So how did it come about that ancient Egyptian astronomy was brought into disrepute by historians of science (mostly humanitarians) and even declared as non-existent? The answer is simple: it is a consequence of preference for written sources and a lack of attention to material monuments. In Mesopotamia, a long lasting material – clay – was used for writing, and thus the most ancient written texts fell into the hands of historians. We are easily susceptible to the charms of these ancient texts, not wanting to take into account, for instance, that Egyptian monuments are thousands of years older than Mesopotamian writings, yet these monuments are unaccompanied by any texts that could clarify their significance or the methods of their erection. Naturally, a circumstantial decoding of the Egyptians' knowledge based on the analysis of their monuments is much more complicated and uncertain that a direct reading of Mesopotamian texts. The result: a rough underestimation of the scientific achievements of ancient Egypt compared to the neighboring Mesopotamia. The Egyptian choice of papyrus for a writing medium, all of which has long crumbled into dust, condemns them to being misunderstood down the ages.

The unequivocal conclusion that follows: the demotion of the role of Egyptian astronomy is utterly unfair. Well-honed astronomical practice existed in ancient Egypt. Egyptian astronomy possessed in stock millennia of development and outstanding accomplishments. And observational Egyptian astronomy was considerably older than the Mesopotamian "mathematical" astronomy of cuneiform texts.

Ancient Egyptian astronomers had by the time of the Great Pyramid Age gathered enough intellectual potential to implement the second zodiacal quartet as a way of registering the seasons of the solar year.

There is, however, a tremendous difference between the two statements: could implement or did indeed implement?

"Gift of the Nile": a Background Check

In the Holy Scripture, a kindhearted portrayal of the Egyptian lifestyle like the words "all the wisdom of Egyptians" in the New Testament is exceptional. Ultimately, the Old Testament in particular provides a darkened view of Egypt as a sort of "evil empire": a nation infected by despotism, hubris, sorcery, animal-worship, and idolatry.

Such an adversary vision of Egypt lasted until the Renaissance, when sources other than the Holy Bible and writings of the Church Fathers gradually seeped into human minds. At this very time, confidence in the authority of the Bible as a reliable historical report was undermined, and Egyptophilia emerged.

Egyptophilia, a.k.a. Egyptomania, culminated during the 1798-99 Egyptian campaign by Napoleon, whose troops were accompanied by French savants. They recovered a true grandeur of mute Egyptian antiquities. Two decades later, large-scale excavations began and, soon after, hieroglyphs were deciphered by Jean François Champollion (1790-1832), who established the study of early Egyptian history and culture onto firm footing.

Naturally, various times accented different priorities in historical studies. Thus, the end of the 19th century produced Pan-Babylonians. Egyptology reentered the limelight thanks to the sensational discovery of Tutankhamen's tomb in 1922. But very soon the fortune of Egypt was eclipsed after notable excavations in Mesopotamia. At that time, the Mesopotamian culture, not the Egyptian one, appeared to be the immediate ancestor of the classical world of the Greeks.

To this day, the comparative roles of consecutive Mesopotamian cultures and ancient Egypt in forming the modern Western-type civilization are a far cry from being clear. Through Greece and Rome, modern civilization has inherited the achievements of both of them. In this Chapter, we do not, of course, make our goal to answer which of these cultures made a greater contribution to modern civilization. Our task is much more limited: to show that the contribution of Egypt was great enough.

The Origin of the Egyptian Civil Calendar

In 1996, the newest source book in the genre, *A Chronicle of Pre-telescopic Astronomy* by B.Hetherington, was published in Great Britain. It makes known that the so-called Egyptian civil calendar - a precursor of the modern solar calendric system - with 12 equal months of 30 days each plus 5 additional days at the end of the year was initiated in Egypt in 4,241 BCE. After this entry, a corroborating reference is mentioned, and it is a matter of fact that there are many publications that claim this very date. For example, under the entry CALENDAR: WESTERN, Garland's *Encyclopedia of Time* (1994) shares a similar stance: "The Egyptian calendar might have been in use as early as 4242 B.C." [A one year difference may occur because historians have no zero year in their chronology, even though it is astronomically appropriate; they count 1st BCE (i.e. -1st year) directly before 1st CE].

Isn't it too ambitious a goal to determine such an old dating within the accuracy of a single year, and how was it proved, if right?

These claims are based on misinterpretation of historical evidence and use of imprecise astronomical data. It is accepted worldwide that the protodynastic Egyptians, like all ancients, used a lunar calendar. A solar calendar of 365 days (Clagett, Vol.2, 1995, p.1)

> "was securely in place by the time of the Old Kingdom. An investigation of the origins of this calendar is fraught with uncertainty and difficulty, but such an investigation will be most useful for anyone attempting to understand the steps taken in Pharaonic times to organize society and express its religious culture in a satisfying, efficient and productive way."

This comment is from an up-to-date source book on ancient Egyptian science. All details concerning the problem of the remarkable Egyptian solar calendar may be found in the works of R.Parker (1950, 1974 and later on in a summary of his studies titled *Egyptian Astronomy, Astrology and Calendrical Reckoning* in: C.C.Gillispie (ed.) *Dictionary of Scientific Biographies* **15**, 1978, pp.706-727).

From Frere (1758), a fundamental conclusion was reached: the Egyptian solar calendar remained essentially unchanged from the time of its inception, having New Year's Day (the first day of the month of

Thoth) at the heliacal rising of Sirius, which was called *wp rnpt* (Opener of the Year), throughout the whole Pharaonic period and was accorded the same number of days - equal to 365 (Bickermann, 1968).

Actually, such a civil solar year was a little shorter than the natural period between successive risings of Sirius (for Egyptians, the star of Sothis) by about 1/4 of a day. As a result, New Year's Day in the Egyptian civil calendar was about one day earlier after 4 years, and, doing the math, 1461 Egyptian civil years = 1460 natural (or Sothic) years. Due to this peculiarity, making a detour through all the seasons, New Year's Day of the Egyptian solar calendar would return back to its initial position every 1460 Sothic (in modern terms, Julian) years.

The crucial information on this issue came from a preserved manuscript by a certain Roman author, Censorinus, who opined that in 139 CE the Egyptian New Year's Day did return back to its original starting point (Clagett, 1995, pp. 334-335).

Censorinus' tip is strongly confirmed by the fact that around 139 CE the Roman emperor Titus Aelius Antoninus Pius (the successor to the emperor Hadrian; born 86, ruled 138-161 CE) minted coins with the word AIΩN meaning ERA (literally, *eon*) (Dattari, 1901, Pl. xxxii, No.2428). It was the celebration of the date of the Phoenix Era, or the Birth of the Phoenix, in other words the return of the Egyptian New Year's Day to its starting position. (Don't forget that after 30 BCE Ptolemaic Egypt became a Roman administrative division).

In all, here are the data for computation. If one were to work backward from Censorinus' 139 CE, and use the period of 1460 years, the dates of the coincidence of New Year's Day (1st day of the month of Thoth) with the heliacal rising of Sirius produce the likely dates for the inauguration of the civil calendar:

..... 4,241 BCE .... 2,781 BCE ..... 1,321 BCE .....

Since the 19th century, scholars have vacillated between 1,321 BCE and 2,781 BCE as the starting year of the Egyptian calendar (Ideler, 1825-26). In 1904, Eduard Meyer (1855-1930) moved the date back to 4,241 BCE as the starting year. He believed 2,781 BCE was too late for the establishment of the Egyptian civil calendar, and so he adopted an earlier date. His writings are the primary reference to the date cited in so many presentations (Meyer, 1904; 1908).

However, with the promotion of the so named "short chronology" of Egyptian history, it appears to be evident that in the 5th millennium BCE Egyptian society was at an undeveloped level, and Egypt was not a unified state. Thus, Otto Neugebauer criticized Meyer's evaluation (see, his presentation of 1938 as well as of 1942; both of them were reprinted in a collection of his papers from 1983), and I believe he was right.

In turn, R.Parker opposed O.Neugebauer; in Parker's mind, the civil calendar was introduced between 2,937 and 2,821 BCE (see in Gillispie, *Dictionary of Scientific Biographies,* **15**, pp. 706-727). Parker's conclusions have been disputed by R.K.Krauss (1981) and some others without any substantial progress.

M.Clagett in his very concentrated and up-to-date monograph, *Ancient Egyptian Science,* vol.2 (1995), stated cautiously that the Egyptian civil calendar originated c. 3,000 BCE.

At that remote time the sky-seers could not perform measurements on the starry dome of the sky, and they preferred measuring along the line of the horizon only. Systematic observations of luminaries' risings and settings took place, partially in comparison with each other, and one may fairly identify that time as an *epoch of astronomy on the horizon*. As a result of systematic observations, an occasional coincidence of Sirius' heliacal rising with the Nile flooding was discovered. It seems to be the Pharaoh's counselor Imhotep who created a new calendric system and simultaneously introduced the Sothic Era, c. 2,781 BCE, as calculated above.

So far, all the facts in hand from the Old Egypt Kingdom confirm the period and likely the very person who was responsible for this innovation of the greatest importance: the solar (civil) calendar.

How Accurate are the Dates in early Egyptian History?

My attention in the present and the next Chapter will be concentrated primarily on two periods of Egyptian history, nicknamed the Great Pyramid Age and the Amarna Age (the reign of Amenhotep IV a.k.a. Akhenaten, of the XVIII Dynasty). How accurate are chronological dates for these historic periods?

In terms of relative chronology, historians have no troubles with dating the Great Pyramid Age. Surely, it dawned with Djoser (Zoser), the founder of the III Dynasty. It was the Pharaoh's vizier Imhotep who designed for him the first large edifice of hewn stone - the Step Pyramid.

Nevertheless, despite the voluminous data, in terms of absolute chronology the dating of the Pyramid Age is a troublesome issue. A contemporary overview of the Great Pyramid Age, by I.E.S.Edwards (1909-1996), opens with the clear-cut statement (1993, p.1):

> "One of the first questions which occur to the mind of anyone looking at an ancient monument is its date. In the case of Egyptian monuments it is often difficult, and sometimes impossible, to answer the question in terms of years before the beginning of the Christian era, because our knowledge of Egyptian chronology, especially in the early periods, is still very incomplete. We know the main sequence of events, and frequently the relationship to one another, but, except in rare instances, an exact chronology will not be possible until the discovery of material of a different and more precisely datable character than anything found hitherto."

Another prominent modern scholar echoes this statement:

> "Egyptian chronology and the dates of dynasties and pharaohs are still the subject of scholarly debate, with different systems proposed" (Lehner, 1997, p.8).

Unfortunately, the cited is a bitter truth. The chronology of ancient Egypt is short of perfection.

The first stable absolute chronology for Egypt emerged as a byproduct of the successful archaeological excavations on the verge of the 19th and 20th centuries, mainly due to the efforts of James Henry Breasted (1865-1935) and Eduard Meyer. Today it is dubbed *long* or *high chronology*. For the founder of the III Dynasty, the Pharaoh Djoser, this chronology gives something like 3,000 BCE.

Lowering the dates has prevailed through the 20th century:

> "The disputes were generally between the adherents of a so-called "long" chronology, based on a fairly unscientific

207

use of textual sources, and those who proposed a "short" chronology, based on a less romantic and more archaeological view of history. Now, however, virtually all scholars adhere to the "short" chronology" (Grimal, English translation of 1997 from the French of 1988).

In the *short chronology*, Djoser's reign took place 3 centuries later than in the long one, i.e., something like 2,700 BCE with an essential margin bar of uncertainty. Various authors have published this date in short chronology with variants differing in an interval of ± 50 years. As a result of the disputes, the *middle chronology* emerged.

Margins of Uncertainties

The conventional wisdom of Egyptologists was scandalized by the eminent British archaeologist James Mellaart who published the alarming article "Egyptian and Near Eastern chronology: a dilemma?" (1979). On the grounds of contemporary radiocarbon dating, Mellaart argued to discard the short chronology and called for retrieving the long one. His concerns were immediately attacked and discredited by some opponents. Meanwhile, more new radiocarbon analysis of organic samples from the pyramids ignited an extension of the dispute. Many peripeteias of the controversy may be found in Bernal (1991, Vol.2, pp.206-211), who himself is a fierce advocate of the long chronology.

Many valuable data on the current chronological problems were deliberated recently in three volumes of the *Acts of an International Colloquium on Absolute Chronology Held at the University of Gothenburg 20th-22nd August 1987* (Åström, 1987-1989). To characterize the general situation in the field, let me cite the title of the first presentation opening the *Acts* and written by Peter J.Huber, of Harvard University. It reads *Astronomical Evidence for the Long and against the Middle and Short Chronologies.*

All in all to this day, alas, the uncertainty of the beginning of the Great Pyramid Age remains unresolved within a period of 300-500 years.

Unlike the Great Pyramid Age, the datings within the 2nd millennium BCE in the Near East are actually more reliable, although in this period we deal with noticeable uncertainties, as well. Because of some common events in chronologies for adjacent nations, it is possible to conjoin those chronologies into a single network and perform corresponding adjustments. But even in this advanced case, the whole system remains very shaky, and it looks like a house of cards. If you push it in one place, the whole Near East chronology could be ruined at once.

What are the real margins? In respect to Egypt, the time of the XVIII Dynasty and the Amarna Age are pinpointed in the absolute time scale with a margin bar of uncertainty that is still not less than a few decades. Here are the figures for Amenhotep IV's reign from some modern authoritative sources:

Author	Reign started (BCE)	Reign finished (BCE)
J.H.Breasted (1905)	1375	1358
D.Redford (1984)	1377, January	1359, summer
D.Redford (1999)	1374	1356
W.Helck (1987)	1340	1324
V.Hankey (1987) *Radiocarbon dating*	1402	1385
K.Kitchen (1989)	1353	1337
M.Bernal (1991)	1381	1364
P.Clayton (1994)	1350	1334
S.Ikram, A.Dobson (1998)	1360	1343
B.Watterson (1999) *In accordance with Aström (1987)*	1353	1337
I.Shaw (2000)	1352	1336

The day-exact reliable chronology of Egypt counts its beginning only after 664 BCE (Depuydt, 2005, p.31).

In the subsequent research, we will be forced to determine the coincidence of various historical occurrences. To this end, we will need chronological margin bars characteristic for the corresponding epochs. It is important to remember that exact coincidences of events with a low accuracy of determining their chronological dates are, naturally, impossible. To state that a coincidence of two or more events has occurred will only be possible under the condition that according to available historical data the differences in dates do not exceed the margins of error. For the exact same goal, we will also need to estimate the potential accuracy of the Egyptians' determination of the duration of their Cycle of Eternity.

The Cycle of Eternity and its Duration

This calendric problem of Egyptian history has been investigated for decades. In my publication of 1997, I stated that the Sothic period, or the Great Cycle of the Egyptian calendar (Cycle of Eternity), was equal to 1460 years, but it was an approximation without adjustment due to the phenomenon of precession.

Checking my claims, astrophysicist Bradley E.Schaefer, then of Yale University, undertook the most sophisticated state-of-the-art digital modeling (2000a). He calculated with a high precision that the Great Cycle length is equal to 1457 years. As a result, his conclusion was as follows:

> "For a Great Cycle that has one start date in A.D. 139, the previous cycle started in 1319 ± 20 B.C." (p.152).

I would like to stress the special importance of the fact that Schaefer was the first to evaluate the margin bar of the figure announced. His evaluation of ± 20-years is the formal so-called *one-sigma* error. In real life, there is an essential probability that the error may easily be larger and even reach the amount of *three-sigma*. For our situation, that would be over a half of a century.

Thus, the consequent dates of coincidences of New Year's Days of the Egyptian civil calendar with heliacal risings of Sirius may be:

.... 4,233 BCE .... 2,776 BCE .... 1,319 BCE ....

In my mind, to the best of modern knowledge, the Egyptian civil calendar was really instituted in 2,776 BCE with an uncertainty of several decades only. Let us go ahead with this reasonable date.

Quite recently practically the same dating was independently and credibly confirmed by Roman A.Orekhov (2014) of Russia. His claim is 2,767 BCE.

A Carnival of Coincidences

In c. 280 BCE, Manetho, a high-ranking Egyptian priest of Ptolemaic Alexandria under Ptolemy I Soter (reigned 304-285 BCE) and Ptolemy II Philadelphus (285-246 BCE), drafted a history of his motherland in Greek for current Greek rulers to exhibit lengthy Egyptian glory. His manuscript vanished, but fragments of the clergyman's narration have been preserved in citations of later authors, and now they are a unique valuable source (Depuydt, 2005, p.33).

Manetho the priest credited one Imhotep with having been the inventor of the art of building in hewn stone. And that does not come as a surprise. Imhotep's accomplishments were proclaimed in some stone inscriptions and became legendary among the later generations of Egyptians, who regarded him not only as an architect but also as a sculptor, a magician, a healer who was the father of medicine and, finally, an astronomer. His official title as a Sun-god priest was the "Overseer of the Observers." Imhotep seems to be the preeminent genius and innovator of the entire Old Kingdom. In about 1,200 BCE Imhotep was deified, and Egyptians built cult temples to honor him.

There is no doubt that Imhotep, the vizier to the Egyptian pharaoh Djoser, was the designer of the huge edifice of stone at Saqqara called the Step Pyramid, the first in the world. This was the overture for the Great Pyramid Age.

A critical item in our investigation is the calculation of the time when Djoser and Imhotep flourished. There is no single opinion on the accuracy of the dates of their lifetimes; however, an approximation of about 2,900-2,700 BCE seems preferable for many. (To be honest, for this period of Egyptian history uncertainties are estimated to reach more than just 200 years). In other words, within the accuracy of dating, Imhotep's lifetime is likely to be pretty close to the inaugural epoch of the Egyptian civil calendar, which is considered above as being 2,776 BCE. Moreover, Imhotep is the only historical individual of the period with credentials to be a developer of the forward-looking Egyptian calendar. This would be the first amazing happenstance.

Another suspicious coincidence is due to the basic outcome of my previous research, which claims that about 2,700 BCE (with an uncertainty ± 250 years) the anthropomorphic constellations of the first zodiacal quartet were substituted with a new zoomorphic foursome. In contrast to the belt of human beings, the names of the constellations for this new tetrad were mainly from the animal (faunal) kingdom. That is the most likely reason that the term "Zodiac" (a circle of animals) was later branded and perpetuated.

Once again, within the accuracy of its determination, the second zodiacal quartet was installed at the same time as the Egyptian civil calendar was, and the first light of the Great Pyramid Age took place. So far, which nation could have created all these together?

The Chronological Framework

After all, three is a pattern and, as a result of our considerations, three coincident innovations are suspiciously close in time to each other: the erection of the Great Pyramids, the introduction of the Egyptian solar calendar, and the institution of the second zodiacal quartet. Can all three be linked by their genesis on Egyptian soil?

Unfortunately, the Great Pyramids of Egypt have been subjected to fantasy; Egyptologists used to joke about *pyramidiotic* speculations in many works during the last centuries, a rush of pyramidology being urged on by the three-volume treatise of the second Astronomer Royal for Scotland, Charles Piazzi Smyth (1867; for many details of his life and works check H.A.Bruck & M.T.Bruck, 1988).

For a professional scientist, nowadays it is very embarrassing to be dubbed a pyramidologist. Meanwhile, today Egyptologists and historians of astronomy don't hesitate to consider the Great Pyramids as having some astronomical, mainly solar, significance. In a textbook on the history of astronomy by John North (1994) we read:

"For all their outward simplicity, there seems to have been a relationship of sorts between the pyramids and the Sun and stars."

The hard problem is to determine what exactly that relationship is. It is doubtful anyone really knows the exact answer at the moment. I shall attempt to establish grounds for a novel approach to this problem.

With an uncertainty of 150-250 years, not a relative but an absolute chronology of our interest may be compiled as follows.

- About **3,200** or **3,100** BCE. Two separate lands of Upper and Lower Egypt are united under a single crown by the Pharaoh Menes. At first a king of Upper Egypt only, he is reported to be the earliest human being in history whose name we know for sure. The Egyptians were to become the world's first consolidated nation and, together with Sumer, ancient China, and ancient India, to take the eventual step from archaic obscurity into the light of history, becoming the most advanced stable civilizations. The unification of Egypt was to be a launching pad for the forthcoming economic power of the state, and a vast agricultural empire was created.
- **3,100-2,700** BCE. Early Dynastic Period (I-II Dynasties).
- C. **2,700** BCE. The beginning of the OLD KINGDOM (2,700 - 2,150 BCE), or the Great Pyramid Age, originated with the Third Dynasty. As an improvement over the regular flat-topped tombs built of sun-baked mud-brick (the Mastabas - an Arabic word meaning a bench), the first large structure of stone, called the Step Pyramid at Saqqara, was erected in about three decades for the founder of the Third Dynasty, the Pharaoh Djoser (c. 2,700-2,650 BCE), by his vizier Imhotep. The absolute dating by historians is uncertain. For the Step Pyramid, D.Roberts in *National Geographic* (January 1995) mentioned 2,630 BCE; that date is in disagreement with other sources. No single opinion exists on the time of Djoser and Imhotep; for example, in *World History: A Chronological Dictionary of Dates*, by Rodney Castleden (1994), Djoser's reign is at 2,900-2,870 BCE.

Imhotep's Step Pyramid was not merely the symbol of a stairway to heaven but was an actual one with seven levels, by which the soul of the dead pharaoh might climb to the sky, joining the gods in immortality. On the north side of this Pyramid there is a small stone cubicle, canted toward the north, with a pair of tiny holes in its façade, likely for astronomical observations by the dead pharaoh.

• C. **2,600** BCE. The Fourth Dynasty started with the Pharaoh Snefru (I.E.S.Edwards prefers spelling *Seneferu*). At this time important progress in the design of the royal tomb occurred: the Step Pyramid was replaced by a true pyramid. Egyptologists are fortunate to be able to trace this progression in the unfinished and badly damaged Pyramid at Maidum and the Bent Pyramid of Snefru.

Snefru's son and successor, Khufu (better known by his Greek name *Cheops*), beginning c. 2,550 BCE (according to other valuations about 2,675 BCE) in 23 years erected the greatest stone monument in the world on the plateau of Giza (Gizeh). The official name of his Great Pyramid was "Khufu is one belonging to the horizon."

Two latter kings of the 4th Dynasty, Khaef-Rë (Khufu's son) and Men-kau-Rë (Khufu's grandson), in Greek called *Chephren* and *Mycerinus*, followed Khufu by building their gigantic pyramids on the same plateau. East of his pyramid, facing the rising Sun behind the Nile, the colossal Sphinx, being probably the king's portrait, was sculpted within a bedrock enclosure by Chephren's order. The Greek word, sphinx, means "to bind closely together" (Rawlinson, 1912). Many centuries after its construction, during the Greeks' travels throughout Egypt, the Egyptians considered the Sphinx - a hybrid creature - to be an embodiment of Harmakhis, another manifestation of their Sun-god. The official name of Chephren's pyramid is "Great is Khaef-Rë" and that of Mycerinus is "Men-kau-Rë is divine." The best present-day compendiums on the Pyramids are *The Complete Pyramids*, by Mark Lehner (1997) and *The world of pyramid builders,* by Roman Orekhov (2014).

The reasons for building the Great Pyramids remain a mystery that is open to debate to this day:

"Even though Greek and Roman authors unanimously claimed that the Pyramids were the tombs of kings, many people did not believe (and some do not believe even now) that this is indeed the case. The Pyramids were taken for temples, venues of secret rites, buildings for housekeeping needs, structures designed to observe celestial bodies, barriers against the sands of the desert, and even nature's frivolity" (G.M.Bongard-Levin, 1988).

All together, the three Great Pyramids and the Sphinx constitute possibly the most celebrated group of monuments in the world created, by the way, in a very short period of time, about a single century.

The Cult of the Sun-god

Although direct documentary records are lacking, there are many indications that at this very time it was the first pyramid-maker pharaohs who promoted the cult of the Sun-god Rë to the position of the official state religion. The cult was derived from a more primitive cult of a temple located a short distance to the north of Memphis at the City of On. This city was specifically mentioned by the same name in the *Book of Genesis*, where Potipherach is described as a priest of On. The sanctum within the temple was the **benben**, a conically shaped stone structure that later was depicted on a sacred image of the Sun-god Rë-Atum in the form of an obelisk; some scholars think the benben may have had an obelisk form originally.

The Sun-god was worshiped in multiple forms; for example, Horakhti - meaning "Horus of the Horizon." Later the Greeks called "the City of the Sun-god" in their spelling Heliopolis. After Imhotep, the title "Chief of the Observers" was recognized as a permanent title of the High Priest of Heliopolis.

All three successors of Cheops - sons Djedef-Rë and Khaef-Rë (Chephren), and the grandson Men-kau-Rë (Mycerinus) - proclaimed their recognition of the Sun-god Rë by forming their names of compounds with his name. There is also some strong evidence that Chephren and Mycerinus adopted the title "Son of Rë", a royal title, which became routine from the 5th Dynasty onwards.

- C. **2,500** BCE. The dawn of the 5th Dynasty. According to a legend from a papyrus in the Berlin Museum, the first three pharaohs of the 5th Dynasty were triplets begotten of Rë and born of the wife of a priest of Rë. Each of these three kings and three of their successors erected peculiar Sun-temples in honor of Rë, in which the principal feature was a rectangular podium built to support a squat obelisk as the sacred symbol of the Sun-god. The pyramid building process now became much more modest; pyramids suddenly became less important. At this time the Iron Age in the Middle East began.

- C. **2,350** BCE. The ebb of the 5th Dynasty. In the late 5th and 6th Dynasties, the earliest corpus of hieroglyphic inscriptions, which are known as the Pyramid Texts, were carved on the walls of the chambers and corridors of pyramids. These do not form a continuous narrative, but consist of spells assembled in no fixed order. The Pyramid Texts were meant to secure a happy after-life. They usually reproduce the rituals, which the priest used to recite every day. It seems certain, in view of the constant appeals to the solar cult, that the Texts were arranged by the "Observers," the priesthood of Heliopolis.

   Written in hieroglyphs, the Texts include many representations of living creatures. Such images not only possessed the value of a particular hieroglyphic sign, but also, through the power of magic, became actual embodiments of the creatures represented. The lion, for instance, was simultaneously both a phonogram with the value of *ru* and the living animal itself. Meanwhile, one important creature (with a single exception) that never appeared in the burial-chambers was the **fish**. This was a result of a belief that the fish, although innocuous to living people, would defile a dead body (Edwards, *Ibid*., p. 194).

   During the MIDDLE KINGDOM (2,133-1,786 BCE), instead of the Pyramid Texts, modified inscriptions appeared on the interior surfaces of the wooden coffins, appropriately named the Coffin Texts. During the NEW KINGDOM (1,570-1,070 BCE), the texts were written on papyri, and were called the "Book of the Dead."

The Enigmas of the Great Pyramids

Hieroglyphic writing has recently been traced back to 3,200 BCE, but during the Old Kingdom script was used for titularies, epithets, and bureaucratic records. There was no literature, no glimpse into the human side of the epoch, and no explanation for the meaning of pyramids. Under these circumstances, Egyptologists are forced to answer the questions by mental reconstructions, and many of the basic questions about the Great Pyramids have remained unanswered.

Among unanswered questions is what is the meaning of the precise astronomical orientations of the Great Pyramids? There is another pressing question associated with the previous one. All the artifacts which exist are indicative that there was a solar cult in Egypt of the Great Pyramid Age. Meanwhile,

> "...turning again to the Pyramid texts, it may be seen that the dead king was frequently considered to have ascended to the stars, and particularly to the circumpolar stars, the so-called "Indestructibles"... On the ground of internal evidence alone it has been deduced that the Pyramid texts which refer to the stars had an independent origin from the solar spells and that eventually they were merged into the Heliopolitan doctrine... Here therefore may be the difference between the underlying purpose of the true and the step Pyramid, the latter being a product of the stellar cult and intended to enable the king to reach the astral heaven" (Edwards, *Ibid.*, p. 292).

This is the problem: how to combine the solar cult with the astral one at the same time? There is a question about the meaning of the accurate geometrical true-pyramid form for tombs. J.H.Breasted (1912), analyzing the problem, stated:

> "The pyramidal form of the king's tomb was of the most sacred significance. The king was buried under the very symbol of the Sun-god which stood in the holy of holies in the Sun-temple at Heliopolis...And when in mountainous proportions the Pyramid rose above the king's sepulcher, dominating the royal city below and the valley beyond for

many miles, it was the loftiest object which greeted the Sun-god in all the land…" (p.72).

I.E.S.Edwards continues the query:

> "Although it now seems probable that the stone symbol of the Sun-god at Heliopolis, the benben, was conical and not pyramidal in shape, Breasted was undoubtedly right in associating it with the true Pyramid… What did the benben and its architectural derivative, the true Pyramid, represent? Only one answer suggests itself: the rays of the sun shining down on earth…" (*Ibid.*, p. 291).

In the middle of the fifth century BCE Herodotus traveled throughout Egypt and reported many features of the pyramids (Rawlinson, 1912). According to Herodotus, the pyramids were not built by slaves but by free Egyptians; worship was postponed in the temples during this work. That is autonomous evidence that in the Old Kingdom people really believed in the great importance of building a pyramid: worship could be postponed only if the act of working itself was another way to worship the same god. Herodotus informs that the kings, builders of the Great Pyramids, were contemptuous of the old gods of ancient Egypt, with the exception only of the Sun-god.

It is well-known by archaeologists that the Great Pyramids were built with copper and even some partially stone tools. It was a very old technology for the time, and obviously the building of the Pyramids may be considered not as a result of some technological progress but a result of ideological ambitions only.

It is puzzling that the Great Pyramids were not the result of a long evolutionary process. Moreover, these greatest monuments were constructed first, but after their erection the whole process was downgraded. The building of the Great Pyramids took just about one century. On the historical background of millennia, it was not a process but only a short-lived flash of lightning, so to speak. And one more puzzle: in the whole history of mankind there are only rare examples of such a great construction being created in honor of a dead ruler. Money usually was spent for living rulers for palaces, temples, festivals, ceremonies, etc. Orekhov (2014) explains: the Great Pyramids were not burial places, they were dwellings for the middle men between their nation and their God.

In Search of Answers

At this time, we can expose preliminary conclusions. For a long time before its unification, fragmented Egypt had an astral (starry) cult that was replaced with a solar one after unification. Says Edwards (*Ibid.*):

> "Seneferu, by deciding to be buried in a true pyramid rather than in a step pyramid, gave visible evidence that solar ideas of the after-life had prevailed over the older astral concepts, which, however, had not been entirely discarded. It is significant that the high priest of the center of the sun-cult at Heliopolis bore the title 'Chief of the Astronomers' and was represented wearing a mantle adorned with stars. The process of solarization continued under Cheops, but he had probably been on the throne for some years before putting into effect two innovations, which were clearly influenced by the solar creed. One of these innovations was to confer on his son Djedefrë the title of 'Son of Rë'; the other was to include a stone sarcophagus in his pyramid" (p.286).

So, we have collected some intriguing features of the pyramids and some unanswered questions. Meanwhile, all these questions will be cut like the Gordian knot if we assume that the occurrence during the same period of time of the Great Pyramid construction and the initiation of the second ecliptic quartet was not "coincidental."

Let's assume that it was the Egyptians during the time of Imhotep - and probably Imhotep himself - who discovered the misalignment between the real track of the Sun and its "theoretical" positions marked by the old anthropomorphic quartet, and such an assumption provides adequate explanations for all the above mentioned uncertainties.

The establishing of the new, Egyptian-born, zoomorphic quartet for the Sun-god's behavior explains completely why the Sun-god was chosen as a main natural god among others and why this event became a stimulus for the new cult of the Sun. It explains why the pharaohs declared themselves the sons of the Sun-Rë and why they included the Sun's name Rë as part of their titularies.

In accordance with this approach, there is no trouble in answering the question about the Egyptian religion: was it solar or stellar? It was an evident combination of both. In ancient Egypt, the Sun was undoubtedly the dominant god, but its natural movements were observed on the starry background. The constellations that the Sun's motion referred to were the forms of the gods as well, eight of them plus the whole thing as a ninth: and so the Egyptian religion contained both solar and stellar elements together.

Historians unanimously agree that the Pyramids were associated with the names of kings. However, it was during the construction of the Great Pyramids that the kings' names underwent a serious metamorphosis. The name of preceding pharaohs was *Horus*, which meant God, followed by a characteristic such as Outstretching, Wholehearted, Viscerally Friendly, High-Handed, Shining with Staff, etc. The situation changed radically as the erection of the Pyramids began. The kings seem to have been completely convinced of their kinship with the Sun. Khufu, as well as a prevailing majority of the subsequent kings, had names composed in honor of the Sun. All of them were the sons of the Sun. Thus, the close kinship of the pharaohs with the Sun was established only in the epoch of the Great Pyramids.

Herodotus reported that the kings who built the Great Pyramids began to treat with disdain all the gods of Egypt except the Sun-god. Investigators refuted this evidence because the Egyptian gods were honored in later times as well. However, the information provided by Herodotus is extra evidence that the Sun took on a special status precisely in the epoch of the Great Pyramids.

In addition to the Pyramids, the Egyptians built majestic memorial temples that glorified the life-giving force of the Sun. In the courtyard of each temple, a squat peaked column in the form of an obelisk, the idol of the Sun, was erected. A stone column of the same type was set up to embody the Sun in the Sun's city of Heliopolis. One can believe the Egyptian obelisks to be indicators to cast shadows on sundials.

Under these conditions, the Great Pyramids were not ordinary tombs but the eternal dwellings of the Sun-god passing on the starry background, sanctuaries to pronounce and glorify the Sun's almighty.

Dead pharaohs wanted to be in close touch with this greatest power; that is why they wanted to be buried under the pyramids as the Popes were buried underneath St.Peter's Basilica in Rome.

With many astronomical questions being answered by the Sun's shadow, the pyramids remained in the shape of the device for solar observations - an obelisk - with the slopes being a mimicry of the Sun's rays. The orientation of the Pyramids, consistent with the cardinal points of the horizon, is one more reminder of the Sun's glory.

Observing the Sun coordinated its position on the starry background. That is why elements of the sun cult were mixed with elements of the older astral cult. Tracking the Sun resulted in the establishment of four distinct points for the seasons. That is why the four-sloped form of the true pyramid was the best for worshiping the Sun. From this viewpoint, the Great Pyramids were a hymn to the Sun.

The fact the discovery described was an Egyptian one is reflected in the purely Egyptian symbolism of the newly introduced quartet: a bull, a lion, a scorpion, and a male related with the after-life, i.e., with water. This symbolism was doubled in the Sphinx by a combination of the labels for the extreme - highest and lowest - positions of the Sun. It was really a guard of the Sun's track among the stars.

Back to the Puzzle: Eagle *vs* Scorpion

We have at our disposal, it seems, key evidence, i.e., two variants of the second seasonal quartet: one with a scorpion in the lineup, another with an eagle. Might not this serve as a basis for localizing their places of origin?

In the 2001 publication *An Egyptian Bestiary: Animals in Life and Religion in the Land of Pharaohs*, Philippe Germond and Jacques Livet gathered in one place all the known images of animals in ancient Egypt. Here is their complete list:

Baboon	Frog	Ram
Bull, cow	Hippopotamus	Scarab
Cat	Ibis	Scorpion
Crocodile	Ichneumon (mongoose)	Serpent

Eel	Jackal	Swallow
Fabulous animal	Kite	Uraeus (cobra)
Falcon, female falcon	Lion, lioness	Vulture
Fish (Nile Perch)	Nile goose	Wild dog

Our attention is, naturally, attracted by the fact that this list contains all the animals of the second quartet. There are, of course, among Egyptian artistic material, also images of a priest with water (Aquarius = Water Bearer). What is missing is an eagle, although Egyptian material is not lacking in birds of prey. The conclusion: the quartet with the eagle had its origin outside of Egypt.

The artistic material of prehistoric Mesopotamia has been thoroughly researched in the seminal work of Beatrice Goff (1963). Here all the characters of our zoomorphic quartet are presented as well. Interestingly enough, unlike Egypt, the Mesopotamian artistic sources contain quite a few eagles and only a relatively small number of scorpions. The conclusion: it is preferable to attribute the variant of the second quartet with the eagle to Mesopotamia, not to Egypt.

Admittedly, the presented arguments are not convincing enough, and the question of where the zoomorphic quartet was born – Egypt or Mesopotamia – cannot honestly be resolved based solely on these considerations. The only obvious fact is that European culture absorbed the variant of the quartet with the scorpion, but whether it came from Egypt or Mesopotamia might be decided only by further research. In any case let us repeat that, taking into consideration all the researched facts, the author leans towards the Egyptian origin over the Mesopotamian origin of the second zodiacal quartet.

The summary of the author's claims is as simple. From time immemorial, the Sun disk was the ultimate divine Lord of Egypt. It protected and commanded Egyptian agriculture dependent on the Nile's inundation. Pinpointing the Sun's movement through the sky on the starry background, Egyptian priesthood secured a breakthrough in understanding calendric laws. As a result, for the first time in world history, they instituted an advanced solar (civil) calendar with a constant duration of a year 365 days long. For this cause, they installed four new starry "houses" of the Sun, increasing the number of them from the archaic 4 that composed an anthropomorphic circle to 8. From then on, this number became sacred to the Egyptians of the time.

For the Egyptian priesthood, the new chain of the starry "houses" became known as a circle of beasts (Zodiac). That is the missing link between the old solar cult and old star observations.

Anthony Spalinger (in Lippincott, 1999, p.269) stressed that

> "the regularized system of timekeeping was the natural outcome of the political centralization of the Nile Valley. The emerging bureaucracy required an efficient dating system and the growing treasury needed an easy method of bookkeeping. The old-lunar-based calendar, which had been in use before the creation of a civil calendar, was then discarded so that the state could preserve and date its records more efficiently."

Honoring the Sun – the Lord and the calendric wizard – Egyptian leadership erected colossal pyramidal houses of god, precisely oriented to all four corners of the world as directed by such an omnipotent deity. In their totality, the set of events – the erection of the Great Pyramids, the installation of the second zodiacal quartet with Egyptian animal symbolism, and the institution of the Egyptian civil calendar – are strictly interconnected in their genesis. It seems logical to ascribe all these events to the Great Pyramid Age and adjust its dating due to the starting point of the civil calendar as about 2,800 BCE.

After the emergence of the second seasonal quartet with its original Egyptian subjects, the same quartet in an alternate version arose in Mesopotamia, the malignant scorpion being substituted with the noble predator, the eagle.

CHAPTER 8

SAGA OF THE "HERETIC" PHARAOH

About one and a half millennia after the solar calendar's implementation in Egypt, once it completed its first full cycle, the drifting Egyptian New Year's Day came "home" to its initial position within the year. By all accounts, this had to prompt the utmost festivity on Egyptian soil. Pharaohs of several generations supposedly masterminded the preparations decades beforehand. And it was under the young Pharaoh Akhenaten that the glorious celebration took place. It echoed an epic glory with many ancient rituals specially unearthed for the occasion. Is such a mental picture well-grounded? Let us cross-examine this hypothetical scenario.

Amenhotep IV a.k.a. Akhenaten

The above scenario appeared in one of my early papers on the Zodiac. There I foresaw the emergence of Amenhotep IV (in Greek literature, Amenophis IV) as a true believer in the Sun, influenced by astronomical motivation (1992, p.61). In that paper I had no room to argue the idea, but now it is appropriate to support it with well-established facts.

The so-called Old Kingdom of Egypt was followed by the Middle Kingdom (2,133-1,786 BCE) and later on by the New Kingdom (1,570-1,070 BCE). For chronology of the New Kingdom, I often use a contribution by Edward F.Wente and Charles C.Van Siclen III (*Studies in Ancient Oriental Civilization*, No.39, 1976).

The Egyptian New Kingdom was basically the decline of the great agricultural empire. New peoples were entering onto the historical scene: the Mesopotamians, the Mycenaeans, who from 1,600 to 1,200 BCE spread from mainland Greece to the shores of Asia Minor, the Habiru-Hebrews, the Chinese under the Shang Dynasty, the Hittites, who masterminded the technique of ironwork, and some others.

Meanwhile, in Egypt under Amenhotep III, likely 1,391-1,354 BCE, as considered by J.Fletcher (2000), the 18th Dynasty reached its peak. Egypt was at peace, and trade was in its heyday. The Pharaoh was at work on an enormous building program - a court, colossal statues, a funeral temple for himself and other temples throughout the land.

Then came his son, Amenhotep IV, the teenage "heretic," who allegedly undertook to revolutionize Egypt's religion and to administer monotheism. He failed. No current historians have an explanation for his rebellion. They know only an outline of events.

The following is a portrait of this Pharaoh (Watterson, 1999):

> "Amenhotep IV (1353-1337 BC) was destined to become in modern times the most discussed monarch ever to rule Egypt. He has been the subject of countless academic studies, the hero of many novels, and, sung by a countertenor, the protagonist in an opera. He has even inspired a play, *Akhnaten,* written, in departure from her normal genre, detective fiction, by Agatha Christie in a style that is pastiche Noel Coward! No other king in the 3000-year-long history of ancient Egypt has aroused such passions, many of them contradictory, in those studying his reign. He has been admired as a visionary who made a valiant attempt to wean the ancient Egyptians away from their traditional polytheism in favor of an enlightened monotheism, in pursuit of which he instigated a revolutionary and much admired new style of art; and was condemned as a king who neglected to fulfill his traditional duties and brought Egypt to the brink of ruin. His 17-year-long reign, known today as the Amarna Age, is undoubtedly one of the most fascinating eras in Egyptian history" (p.45).

Historians guess that Amenhotep IV tried to overthrow the polytheistic accretion of centuries. In particular, he wanted to replace the traditional god Amon with Aten (or Aton), conceived as a single universal god of the whole world, the source of all life, and represented by the Sun's disc with its life-giving rays. The Pharaoh changed his own name from Amenhotep, which meant "Amon is content, the god ruler of Thebes", to Akhenaten (Akhenaton, Ikhnaton, Akhanyati), meaning "Pleasing-to-the-Aten," or "Serviceable-to-the-Aten," or "Beneficial for the Aten" - the name by which he entered history.

As a rule, at the thirtieth year of their reign, the pharaohs arranged the so-called *sed*-festival to rejuvenate their divine power. Akhenaten didn't wait for 30 years. He orchestrated his *sed*-festival three years after his ascension to the throne. But the Pharaoh announced this festival was not just his own: it was devoted jointly to the king and his heavenly lord, the Sun-disk Aten. From that moment, the name of Aten was enclosed into two cartouches, as though it were a part of a royal titulary; see, for example, Hornung (1999, p.34).

In the eighth regnal year, the heretical Pharaoh moved the capital into the midpoint of Egypt, about 200 miles south of what is now Cairo. This was near the modern site of Tell-el-Amarna, where the Sun disc, Aten, was elevated to the rank of the single true god. The capital was furnished with Sun-inspired art of a new style. He called his new capital Akhetaten, "the Horizon of Aten." He instructed his aides to destroy the old name and image of Amon from all temples and tombs.

When the Pharaoh erected his own tomb at Tell-el-Amarna, all corridors and rooms leading up to the burial chamber, in violation of a tradition of his forebears, were aligned along a single axis directed from south-east to north-west (solar rising direction at the solstices).

The leading idea for Akhenaten (and his wife Nefertiti) was focused on truth and the natural. The revolutionary Akhenaten tried to redirect the canons of art and literature as he did the tenets of religion. No artist's subject was ever better fitted for naturalistic treatment than Akhenaten himself, for he was a strange-looking person with a protruding jaw, scrawny neck, a pear-shaped torso with pendulous breasts, long, sinewy arms, bloated belly, fatty thighs, thin, unmuscular legs, and a soft, sensitive mouth.

An inscription on a rock at Aswan says Bek, Akhenaten's royal sculptor, was taught his craft by His Majesty himself. It was something of a novel trend in art, the so-called Amarna style. That is why we have a charming, life-like bust of Nefertiti now in the Berlin Museum. But historians have no idea concerning what was the Truth in Akhenaten's new worship of the Sun.

Originally Amon and Rë had been two distinct Sun-gods. We know that during the Great Pyramid Age the Egyptians merged them and worshiped Amon-Rë as the king of the gods. Besides Amon-Rë, the Egyptians honored such other deities as Osiris, Osiris' wife, Isis, his son, Horus, and many others. Egyptian religion had room for many gods and an easy tolerance for new gods. Akhenaten destroyed the welfare of many priests. On the grounds of self-interest, the priesthood had to oppose the Pharaoh and defeat him. But, as strange as it seems, they were silent for Akhenaten's entire life. The Pharaoh died in peace.

Akhenaten's reign is well-documented because of the protracted surviving archives from Tell-el-Amarna, which were inscribed in cuneiform, not hieroglyphics. Babylonian cuneiform, like French in the 19th century, was the diplomatic medium of the time, and the tablets came from the files of the Pharaoh's foreign office. The *Amarna letters* preserved much of the international correspondence under Akhenaten.

So, Akhenaten launched a "heretical revolt" against the great god Amon, the principal deity of the time, and sought to impose upon Egypt a new truthful god and a new form of worship. He was a truth-maker who was not in tune with his time. He seemed to be engaged in a life-and-death struggle with the bureaucracy and the priesthood. He displaced the clergy and destroyed the gods the clergy served. But his religious reformation, owing to the opposition of the priests of Amon-Rë at Thebes, didn't survive him. His "revolution" failed. After Akhenaten died in his middle age, under his very young son Tutankhamen (1,338-1,329 BCE), the Egyptians fell back to old ways.

The historians fall short of grasping Akhenaten's motives, but they may be clarified if we remember that Akhenaten took the crown about 1,353 BCE, right before the end of the Great Cycle of the Egyptian solar calendar, which, as it was stated above, according to Censorinus' and Schaefer's evaluation, had to happen in 1,319 BCE.

For our narrative, it is extremely important that both events are concurrent with the shaping of the third seasonal quartet, as well. Having knowledge of all the oddities of his reign, one must conclude precisely that AKHENATEN WAS CELEBRATING THE RETURN

OF THE NEW YEAR'S DAY ONTO ITS INITIAL POSITION. Is there solid evidence for such an idea?

Was Akhenaten a Radical Rebel or a Dedicated Doer?

First of all, let me declare with full emphasis: Akhenaten was not the progenitor in the Sun cult's ascension. In that pursuit he followed in the footsteps of his immediate ancestors.

A long time ago, Sir Wallis Budge (1857-1934), the Keeper of the Egyptian and Assyrian Antiquities at the British Museum, pointed out that Akhenaten was not at all a reformer. If we examine his teaching, we shall find there is hardly a single presumption in it that is not borrowed from the older Egyptian religious books. "Modern writers describe him as a 'reformer' but he reformed nothing," says Sir Budge. He didn't create a new god, Aten, but revived "an old, perhaps THE OLDEST, solar god, whose cult had been dead for centuries" (Wallis Budge, *Tutankhamen*). "Having appointed himself High Priest," the author continues, "he, curiously enough, adopted the old title of the High Priest of Heliopolis and called himself 'Ur-maa,' i.e., the 'Great Seer'."

One more proof that the Pharaoh moved back to the original older tradition is that his portrait as a SPHINX is on a palace decoration: the honor was repeated after Khafre, who produced the first Great Sphinx in his own likeness. Another fact: soon after Akhenaten's "revolt," Imhotep, the designer of the first pyramid, was deified.

In the solar temple of Rë, Akhenaten declined the contemporary style and, once again, restored the tradition of the Great Pyramid Age: to build the temple as a simple open courtyard which allowed the Sun to shine down on the worship of the faithful (Tyldesley, 1999, p.76).

In our context, it is very intriguing that Akhenaten's "revolution" was drafted partially by his father, Amenhotep III, and his grandfather, Tuthmosis IV, and even his great-grandfather. In the British Museum, there is a scarab (a holy beetle) of Tuthmosis IV with a text that mentions the Sun-disc Aten. Moreover, Tuthmosis IV undertook an enormous project to clear away the sand engulfing the enclosure of the Great Sphinx and to fix its damaged limestone body. It was the first architectural restoration in world history. What are all these facts telling us?

This is an overall characterization of Akhenaten by Wallis Budge:

> "This king was described as a reformer, an individualist, and an idealist and a pacifist; but he was a reformer who initiated no permanent reform, an individualist who diverted the revenues of the gods of his country to his own uses, an idealist who followed the cult of the material, and a pacifist who lost Egypt's Asiatic Empire" (*Ibid.*, p. xiv).

The present-day writers think the same:

> "Volumes written about Akhenaten credited him with being a revolutionary in religion and art when in fact his father had led the way years before" (Fletcher, 2000, p.163).

Meanwhile, these words are only a part of the story. The entire truth is that Akhenaten's avenue was paved not only by his preeminent father but both his short-lived grandfather and his great-grandfather, as well.

Here I would like to expose that, in truth, Akhenaten was not a heretic or a revolutionary. He was just a devoted executor who headed the commemoration of the greatest solar anniversary in the entire Egyptian history: the groundwork for such a grandiose all-Egyptian festival had to be laid a long time in advance of the teenage Pharaoh.

The indications of preparations have to be traced within the historical annals of Akhenaten's predecessors. Of course, the task of identifying specifics in Egyptian history is too hard for me, the astronomer. Fortunately, Dr. Joann Fletcher, Honorary Visiting Professor in the Department of Archaeology at the University of York and Consultant Egyptologist for Harrogate Museums and Arts, has performed it in her book, *Chronicle of a Pharaoh: The intimate life of Amenhotep III* (2000). This book is an up-to-date review of Akhenaten's predecessors' reigns. I am going forward guided by Dr. J. Fletcher.

- Amenhotep II was the great-grandfather of Akhenaten. His rule started c. 1427 BCE and lasted up to c. 1401 BCE.

> "Amenhotep II had built a temple dedicated to the Sphinx as Horemakhet (a form of the sun god) and had set up a stela to honor the Old Kingdom monarchs Khafre and

Khufu. Amenhotep II also created what is probably the first representation of the Aten disc (the sun disk worshiped as a god) as a human-armed sun-disk...

Amenhotep II also erected a great statue of himself between the paws of the Sphinx...

He had paid particular attention to the ancient site of Giza and its mighty Sphinx... Both Amenhotep II and his son Prince Tuthmosis (father of the future Amenhotep III) had venerated the Sphinx as the mighty sun god Ra combined with Horakhty (or "Horus in the horizon")" (p.15-16).

And one more important peculiarity (p.20):

"... Following Amenhotep II, subsequent pharaohs visited the Sphinx at Giza after their coronation to confirm their position. By making offerings to this massive representative of the sun god, each monarch played the part of Horus the dutiful son as he undertook the transference of royal power from his predecessors."

- Tuthmosis IV was the grandfather of Akhenaten. He was enthroned as a child, maybe only 15 years old. This boy honored the Sun god Rë with a limestone shrine at Giza plateau. He began work

  "in the Karnak temple complex of Egypt's state god Amun, who had by now merged with the sun god to form the supreme deity Amun-Ra" (p.22).

Tuthmosis had a very special relationship with the Sphinx, and it is absolutely amazing that this youngster performed the first renewal in Egyptian history of this symbolic embodiment of the Sun:

"Prince Tuthmosis dutifully cleared away the sand and undertook the restoration of the Sphinx's paws and chest. Modern excavations have revealed the mudbrick retaining walls the prince ordered to be built to protect the great monument from further sand encroachment" (p.15).

Tuthmosis died only in his tenth year of reigning, but his son inherited commitment to the Sun, too.

- <u>Amenhotep III</u> was the father of Akhenaten. He started his rule c. 1391 BCE, being 12 years old, because his older brother and the heir to the throne died in an untimely manner.

  "Shortly after his coronation the king would have followed in the footsteps of his father and grandfather by paying homage before the Sphinx – the embodiment of the sun god – thus undertaking the transference of royal power and confirming his authority under the great creature's watchful eye" (p.34).

Amenhotep III did more for hailing the Sun (p.43):

"During the earlier part of his reign, Amenhotep also built a limestone temple at the sun god's great cult center Heliopolis ("Iunu") in Lower Egypt. *(This cult center was older than the Great Pyramids. – A.G.).* This project formed part of the king's systematic transformation of Egypt's religious policy: he envisaged a great complex of new ritual temples in which Amun of Thebes would be worshiped as the sun god Amun-Ra in appropriately magnificent surroundings. As the other deities were absorbed into the sun cult, their relevant solar epithets were emphasized and Amenhotep himself was portrayed as their representative on earth."

But that was only the start. Fletcher writes:

"In a continuation of his father's policy, Amenhotep focused the religious ideology of his court increasingly on solar worship. The period in which the state god Amun was united with the sun god to create Egypt's ultimate deity, Amun-Ra, saw the solar image achieve ever-greater prominence in the form of the Aten (the sun disk that was now worshiped as a god).

The Aten was first referred to during the Middle Kingdom ca. 1950 BCE, and the living king was likened to the Aten as early as the first years of the Eighteen Dynasty. The Aten's

231

earliest representation in its familiar form of a disk adorned with the royal uraeus serpent, and rays ending in small hands holding out the *ankh* sign, appeared on a stela erected at Giza by Amenhotep II, Amenhotep III's grandfather. Amenhotep II's son, Tuthmosis IV, was identified in his inscriptions as "lord of what the Aten encircles"…, and it was the Aten, rather than god Amun, that appeared in one of the inscriptions referring to Tuthmosis's military conquests. Throughout his reign Tuthmosis stressed his allegiance to the sun god rather than solely to Amun – a religious policy later developed and pursued by his son Amenhotep III.

Through his choice of names and epithets, Amenhotep III publicly announced his solar allegiance, proudly and repeatedly confirming that he was the sun god's chosen one and the one made in that god's image… During Amenhotep's reign, moreover, there appeared the first evidence of an actual cult of the Aten, which was based at Heliopolis in Lower Egypt…" (pp.60-61).

Fletcher additionally underlines the situation in a special box named *Cult of the sun king*:

"Amenhotep III's reign saw great emphasis on the sun in all its aspects… For the first time, the Aten was provided with its own priesthood and its own temple built in the traditional solar capital of Heliopolis, and throughout the reign there were countless references to this "new" god. The king's own favorite epithet was *Aten-tjehen*, "dazzling Aten".

Amenhotep II and his son Tuthmosis IV had begun the process of regenerating the ancient solar cult that had existed 1,000 years before under the pyramid-building monarchy of the Old Kingdom. The steps Tuthmosis had taken… were taken much further by Amenhotep III, who skillfully manipulated the Amun cult for his own ends while promoting the sun god Ra in the form of the Aten" (p.162).

Within his mortuary temple marked with the so-called Colossi of Memnon, Amenhotep III designed an extended alley of sphinxes. It was a return to the beliefs of remote predecessors, a revival of the past. J.Fletcher deliberately stresses this feature:

"According to an inscription in the tomb of Kheruef, "generations of men since the time of the ancestors had not celebrated *sed*-festival rites, but it was commanded for Amenhotep, son of Amun… his majesty did this in accordance with the ancient writings." In reviving the *sed*-festival Amenhotep recreated ancient ceremonies not seen on such a scale in Egypt since the pyramid age.

The pharaoh researched the traditional festivities with great care. While his leading official… checked temple archives, other royal scribes were sent out to visit the ancient sites and report back on the reliefs and inscriptions they saw there…

Amenhotep ordered that many of the ancient sites be restored to their former glory" (p.139).

Joann Fletcher scrupulously describes the facts established by current-day historians and archaeologists. What an amazing picture appears! All above-mentioned facts match my hypothesis perfectly. In no way was Akhenaten a revolutionary. He was a devoted executor who completed the celebration gradually prepared by his forefathers. He and his precursors hailed the greatest accomplishments of their illustrious royal predecessors from the Pyramid Age.

It is impossible to express the fact that the Sun's disk was in jubilee in clearer words than Akhenaten declared himself:

"May the good god live who takes pleasure in Truth, Lord of all that the Aten encompasses, Lord of Heaven, Lord of earth, Aten, the living, the great, who illuminates the two lands, may the father live: Re-Harakhty appearing on the horizon in his name of Shu who is Aten, who is given life for ever and ever, Aten, the Living, the Great, *WHO IS IN JUBILEE*, who dwells in the temple of Aten in Akhetaten" (Tyldesley, 1999, p.90).

The latter author does not stop short with the obvious conclusion:

"Indeed, it would appear that Akhenaten's Theban jubilee was to be considered to belong as much to the Aten as to the king" (*Ibid.*, p.91).

The same specification that the Aten is in his jubilee is persistently included in the god's original name and his titulary. It was the Sun (and observable peculiarities of its movement) that served as a focal point of the epoch.

Akhenaten and the Timing of the Festivity

Brad Schaefer, of Yale (2000), examined this problem painstakingly. By determining the margin bars of uncertainties, he conclusively brought all confrontations to an end:

> "In recent years, the exact date of the heliacal rise [of Sirius] from Egypt has become critical in several areas of inquiry. Gurshtein has made a key point in his broad reconstruction of the history of the zodiac based on the dates on which the heliacal rising of Sirius starts its Great Cycle. At the Oxford VI conference in La Laguna, several questioners tried to refute Gurshtein's thesis by arguing that his dates of the heliacal rising of Sirius were wrong since there should also be the effects of precession... This paper targets the question of the dates of Sirius' heliacal rise from ancient Egypt with the full power of modern astronomy...
>
> In all, the difference between my calculated cycle start date and the canonical reign years of Akhenaten are small enough that this difference cannot be used to reject Gurshtein's claim. Rather, Gurshtein's historical evidence of an anomalous jubilee celebration by Akhenaten is now the critical element in deciding the validity of Gurshtein's claim" (p.149 and 153).

In the critical round of a fight with challengers, I put on the table a heavyweight rationale. I have used this way of reasoning a few times against doubtful-minded Egyptologists and not once have I heard a convincing rebuttal. It is as follows.

Let me agree for a moment that Akhenaten was not engaged in the greatest celebration in Egyptian history. In this case such a celebration ought to take place in another time, either before Akhenaten or after him. Do you really propose that the Egyptians missed their proclaimed festivity that was observed even by a Roman emperor 1.5 millennia later? Such a thought is utterly inconceivable. But when did the celebration take place? We have absolutely no indications on this issue, neither centuries before Akhenaten nor centuries after him. There is only one reasonable conclusion *a contrario*: it was Akhenaten who observed this great happening himself.

His behavior as well as the pattern of behavior of his predecessors correspond to all the possible earmarks of the great commemorative Sun-god festival and fully support my idea. No other known event of Egyptian records matches this long-awaited festival. So, I shall base further premises on this conclusion.

Let me suggest the Pharaoh Akhenaten knew – and it was his duty to know – the circumstances connecting the establishment of the solar Egyptian calendar and the new celestial quartet as well as the reasons for the construction of the Great Pyramids by his prominent forefathers. Meanwhile, his rule began a short time before an extremely inspiring moment – the first returning of the drifting New Year's Day into its starting point as during Imhotep's time. Of course, it was of the utmost importance for Akhenaten.

In this connection, the Pharaoh may have asked the priesthood: "Is the issue in order nowadays? Do our native Egyptian constellations mark four distinctive "houses" of the Sun god during its annual track throughout the sky adequately?" And an honest-minded priesthood reaction had to be: "No, we don't know why, but the god no longer resides in its ancient "houses" on its most important days. To mark four distinctive "houses" of the Sun god properly, it is necessary to establish four new constellations on its track."

Under such circumstances, it is not hard to believe that this was the issue that Akhenaten had in mind in his desire to struggle for the Truth. This may be his supreme Truth – the real observations of the Sun god! Such a strong motivation certainly would have been enough for him to act boldly and resolutely in spite of the priesthood's protests.

During the Pyramid Age, the Pharaohs introduced original Egyptian constellations in the sky instead of ancient ones with unknown roots. This time, Akhenaten proposed to replace the Egyptians' own traditional symbols with new ones, likely causing disastrous consequences for the clergy. Undoubtedly the clergy, stuck in its dogmatic ways, tried as vigorously as it could to block the Pharaoh's actions.

Of course, one may speculate in a different way as we have no direct evidence. But once more we have found a startlingly crucial and meaningful coincidence of three events:

1. the finale of the Great Cycle of Eternity for the Egyptian calendar and the New Year's Day homecoming back to its starting point;
2. the solar turnout by Akhenaten; and
3. the previously calculated astronomical fact that the third quartet for the Sun's track labels originated at the very same time.

Moreover, via the Great Cycle of the Egyptian calendar, these three events are interconnected with three other events investigated earlier; all six historical occurrences constitute a single pattern.

Did Akhenaten propose the names for the constellations of the new quartet? I think not because, in my mind, these names - Aries, Cancer, Libra, and Capricorn - most likely are not of Egyptian origin and seem to belong to another symbolical stratum.

After 3,000 BCE, in unified Egypt, due to the annual fertilizing of land with the Nile's mud, a great civilization emerged. Today, a strange historical controversy is developing concerning this civilization: while the Egyptian achievements in agriculture, stonework, craftsmanship, architecture, art, and management of huge projects are still in place, a majority of scholars are emphatically denying the presence of science and, particularly, the knowledge of astronomy.

R.Gleadow has some interesting reservations (1968):

> "The ancient Greeks, and after them the Romans, had great respect for the wisdom of the Egyptians; but modern professors have almost no idea in what that wisdom consisted. This is because learning is static and consists largely of information, while wisdom is dynamic and requires mastery of the art of life. Wisdom therefore is not the same as the ability to reason, and in any case the Greeks did not learn that from Egypt. Genuine wisdom cannot be written, nor congealed into aphorisms and avuncular advice... Man

is always trying to get life under control, and among his methods of doing so are system, rule, legislation, dogma, and punishment. But the wise man does not try to get life under control; he adapts himself and swims with the stream instead of angrily trying to dam it.

Where wisdom and knowledge meet is in the solving of problems; and one problem for which the Egyptians alone of the ancient nations had found a reliable solution was the organization of the calendar" (p.175).

The Egyptians were all alone with their advanced, excellently organized solar calendar amidst neighbors who used outdated lunar calendars from the Paleolithic Age. The fundamental problem is that we have no written documents on this issue, nor do we have documents on a lot of real events throughout world history including, for example, technology for Pyramid building, features of Solomon's Temple, Mithraistic mysteries, etc. *ad infinitum*. The case is that ancient Egyptian astronomy grew up under another kind of social memory, which existed either in the absence of regular written texts or in texts that have since decayed and vanished. As a result, it is hard for astronomical and other scientific activities to be reconstructed.

A stimulating and controversial book, *Black Athena: The Afroasiatic Roots of Classical Civilization*, by Martin Bernal (1937-2013), has to be mentioned here. In its three volumes first published in 1987, 1991, and 2006 respectively Bernal claims the great Western cultural, philosophical, and scientific traditions have to be derived not from the Greeks but originally from the Egyptians, who are deemed to be the Greeks' elder educators. Because of the existence of such strong political opponents as Afrocentrism versus Eurocentrism and Hellenomania, the outrageous conflicts occurring in connection with this publication, partially, concern the problem of Egyptian science.

In the huge anti-Bernal collection of papers, *Black Athena Revisited* (1996), you may find a 60-page opus written by R.Palter, who reiterated many old arguments by O.Neugebauer and other ill-wishers of Egyptian science in the attempt to specify that in ancient Egypt, contrary to Babylonia and Greece, science did not happen at all. I hope I have unmasked those baseless attacks.

Right here is not the place to arbitrate Bernal's great conceptual alternative: out of Egypt or not. But I hail Bernal's approach and realize my findings in Egyptian history are supportive of the vitality of great Egyptian astronomy.

For sure, Egyptian astronomy is not lost without a trace. It will be brought to light by a young devoted researcher. I have a dream that there will one day soon be a young, curious, adventurous Indiana Jones-type explorer who will find definitive evidence of a widespread deep astronomical understanding among the ancient Egyptians. Another ^{mul}APIN, a Rosetta Stone, or a lost Pharaonic tomb lies in the dust in some obscure corner yet to be discovered. Not by completely denying ancient Egyptian astronomy, but by seeing innovative steps in the proper direction will it be truly appreciated.

The Egyptian priesthood of Akhenaten's reign restrained itself out of a necessity to celebrate the Sun's jubilee as a very important happening, but they did not greet Akhenaten's religious innovations that infringed upon the entrenched interests of many of them. After Akhenaten's peaceful death, all of his incentives were gradually ignored. The priesthood under the juvenile Tutankhamen eliminated innovations and returned the capital from the new Sun-City of Akhetaten (Tell-el-Amarna) back to Thebes.

Were members of the entourage of Akhenaten the authors of the third starry quartet on the path of the Sun? To be candid, so far, we have no direct proofs at our disposal. But all indirect data amassed above are enough to hypothesize that the Egyptian leadership of that epoch was involved into unveiling the oddities of their main god - the Sun. And if they were contributors to the process, they were not alone.

World history recognizes an intellectual who had an inside understanding of those events, opposed the Egyptian traditions, and had strong grounds to support the innovations which the Egyptian priesthood had objected to.

"His education was probably gained in the priestly circle of Heliopolis, where the complex motifs of the cult of Re would form the background of his instruction... [He] was probably familiar with... the institution of solar monotheism by Ikhnaton and its overthrow under Tutankhamon, and the wide range of priestcraft that would be included in

the education of one who came from the royal household"
(Harrison, 1974, p.124).

This testimony is about Moses, the great religious reformer, who lived only some decades after Akhenaten's overturn, according to the Holy Bible (Exodus, Ch.1), at the time of the pharaohs Pithem and Raamses; historically they are identified more probably with Seti I (1,292-1,279 BCE) and Ramesses II the Great who reigned for 67 years (September 1,279 - July 1,212 BCE). During this very time, c. 1,275 BCE, the captive Israelites left Egypt to begin migrations that eventually led them to Canaan (the Exodus for the Promised Land).

As usual, there is a plenitude of contradictions around the dates mentioned. Some modern archaeologists believe that in absolute chronology Moses headed the Exodus as early as 1,470 BCE (Bimson, 1981). There are many other viewpoints, too. But let us not confuse a relative and an absolute chronological scale. At this moment, only a relative order of events is of interest for us, and if Moses was a real religious activist, he stepped out from Egypt to Canaan shortly after Akhenaten's reign. I wish to continue the dive deeper into the hypothesis we started to build up step by step. Therefore, in the next Chapter I am forced to pay attention to such an extremely debatable subject as Moses' deeds and acts. It will be a highly questionable and peculiar scenario.

CHAPTER 9

MOSES AND THE TWELVE-STRONG GROUP SYMBOLISM

Historical processes are governed and directed by the collective passions of ethnicities (peoples, tribes, nations) led by their spiritual or secular leaders, kings, presidents, policy-makers, or military commanders, who very often act behind the scenes. Besides this, history also produces over-exaggerated symbols of epochs, legendary heroes whose real historical role may be often controversial, minimal, or even fictitious. As symbols, however, they have a sound meaning. Because of this matter, judgments passed on such metaphorical people by subsequent generations are not based on obscure real-life facts but on the blossoming folklore developed through word of mouth.

A lack of an actual historical identity between a human being of flesh and bone and his/her legendary image often becomes the subject of *belles-lettres*. The examples that immediately come to mind are such characters as King Arthur or Joan of Arc.

At the dawn of Biblical times, a persona of immense legendary scale named Moses appeared. Whether we want to or not, we ought to dwell on the manifold Mosaic problem while analyzing the features of our hypothesis on the Zodiacal genesis. In keeping with the rest of this book, the present Chapter will expose the author's logic with two particular provisions. In accordance with the previous considerations, we shall take them for granted. These provisions are:

1) The second quartet of the seasonal constellations (Taurus, Leo, Scorpio, and Aquarius) was a product of Egyptian cultural

advances at the time of the Great Pyramid Age. This foursome reflected the standard Egyptian religious symbolism, the general Greek term *Zodiac* having surfaced later, due to the creatures comprising a symplegma.

2) The time of the installation of the third seasonal quartet (Aries, Cancer, Libra, and Capricorn) has been judged to be suspiciously close to the reign of the "heretical" Egyptian Pharaoh, Akhenaten. This coincidence enables us to assume the third quartet also to be originally a byproduct of Egyptian cultural developments at the Pharaoh's court.

This Chapter is devoted to a hypothetical scenario. We shall analyze the potential conclusions resulting from the above-mentioned provisions. The question is whether it is possible to incorporate both provisions into known historical contexts. The obstacles to furthering these provisions arise from the destruction of Akhenaten's entire legacy soon after his death. There is little hope of recovering any valuable information on this issue from Egyptian sources.

Is it possible that Akhenaten's newborn third seasonal quartet leading to the final form of the twelve-piece Zodiac might have been preserved for the future not by the Egyptians themselves, but by some other intermediaries somehow linked with them?

To guess at this point is to walk on shaky ground, but we cannot ignore the fascinating link between Akhenaten's time and that of the legendary Moses that was sensed, for example, by Sigmund Freud. The central point that has to draw our attention right now is whether Moses potentially could be a middleman between the Egyptians and the Jews. Was he capable of infusing the sacred astronomical lore accumulated by Akhenaten's court to the forthcoming generations and, as a result, installing this secret knowledge into the religion and the surrounding culture that became known as Judaism?

Historically, Moses' lifetime is actually coincidental with the transition period between the astronomical Age of Taurus and the Age of Aries. And we have established that Akhenaten could have been instrumental in shaping this transition by adding four new "gods' houses" to the path of the Sun. Meanwhile, this single fact, of course, is not enough. We have to answer a number of additional tough queries:

could Moses have known about the sacred knowledge of the Egyptian court under Akhenaten? Are there motives for Moses to have utilized this knowledge for Judaism? Was Moses interested in astronomy? And last: did Moses exist at all?

While the historicity of Akhenaten is manifest, nothing is reliable about the historicity of Moses, which is extremely questionable, and, thus, we find ourselves in the crossfire of bitter historical disputes. I shall do my best, however, to navigate through the mishmash of confusing conflicts and historical controversies.

"Something is rotten in the State of Denmark"

Of course, this aphorism is from *Act I, Scene IV* of *Hamlet*; the catch phrase belongs to the brave Danish officer Marcellus. Meanwhile, Thomas E. Levy sarcastically echoes it with respect to the book *The Mythic Past: Biblical Archaeology and the Myth of Israel*, by the Copenhagen-based Thomas L. Thompson (1999). Levy's derogatory review of this book appeared in the prestigious *Science* (2000).

Amazingly, today, it is Copenhagen of Denmark that harbors a small but vocal and zealous group of authors labeled as *revisionists* (or *minimalists*), who are eager to destroy many traditional Biblical truths. They have challenged the historicity of almost everything written in the Hebrew Bible. T. Thompson, the American transplanted to Copenhagen, is among their chieftains, and according to him,

> "We can now say with considerable confidence that the Bible is not a history of anyone's past. The story of the chosen and rejected Israel that it presents is a philosophical metaphor of a mankind that has lost its way."

According to Thompson, King David of the Hebrew Bible is a myth absolutely of the same nature as King Arthur of the Brits. What's there even to be said about the historicity of Moses?

Each scholar who explores a complex, multi-faceted, historical motif has his own primary approach and chooses aspects from his own perspective. Another Scandinavian, the Swedish scholar Gösta W. Ahlström (1918-1992), did so in his renowned general survey, *The*

History of Ancient Palestine (1993), when he determined that the "Exodus story is a literary construction" (p.418). He denied that there existed any reasonable grounds to support the historicity of Moses, and it was his inherent right as a scholar to maintain such a viewpoint. His very authoritative history of Palestine contained practically nothing with respect to the Exodus and the Mosaic problem.

There is a more specific and even more competent collection of papers entitled *Exodus: The Egyptian Evidence* (1997). Edited by Ernst S. Frerichs and Leonard H. Lesko, this book is the outcome of an international conference that convened in Providence, RI, in 1992, under the auspices of Brown University's Department of Egyptology. The opinion of the scholars from the USA, Canada, and Israel, who took the floor at the conference, was very skeptical:

> "Despite many differences between the perspectives of the conference participants, there is considerable agreement on the difficulties, and for some participants the impossibilities, of using Egyptian evidence to establish the historicity of the Exodus" (p.13).

The finale of the gathering seemed to be even more intolerant:

> "There is no Egyptian evidence that offers direct testimony to the Exodus as described in the Old Testament" (Summary and Conclusions, by William A. Ward, p.105).

Later, James K. Hoffmeier (1999) attempted to strengthen the Exodus with more Egyptian evidence. He collected together all the pieces and discussed all the possible clues, no matter how minute or contradictory. His evidence could probably satisfy believers that there was a historical Exodus, but unconvinced skeptics remain adamant.

To be honest, there is nothing new or extraordinary in denying the historicity of biblical stories. Advocating freedom of thought and the application of the historical method to the interpretation of the biblical narrative, the great Benedictus (Baruch) de Spinoza (1632-1677) was among the forerunners of Bible criticism.

In the middle of the 19th century, strong doubts again resurfaced regarding the historical value of the Bible. In Germany, this drive resulted in a school called the *Higher Criticism*, whose apologists considered the constituents of the Bible, both the Old and the New Testaments, an amalgam of historically insignificant fables pasted together to incarnate a more or less continuous scenario.

Alas, the biblical hypercriticism that was so typical decades ago is still alive in its postmodern formulas and continues to fight not only against the Exodus, but against even much more apparent issues, as well. Today, many examples of this position can be extracted, for instance, from a collection of short articles in the magazine, *Science* (Vol.287, No.5450, January 7, 2000, pp.28-35). As I have mentioned, a group of European biblical scholars eagerly attacks practically every piece of the Bible as a reliable historical source. Unfortunately, the bitter fight for history is politically motivated, and many political aspects of the battle can be found in the cover paper of *U.S. News & World Report* by Jeffery Sheler (2001).

Polemics on Ancient Israel

In 1992, the influential book by Philip Davies, *In Search of "Ancient Israel,"* gave a new impetus to a deliberate movement within biblical studies that was masked under various euphemisms: The Copenhagen School, Biblical Revisionists, Biblical Minimalists, or even Biblical Nihilists. An opponent, William G. Dever (2000), outlines:

> "The fundamental propositions of the revisionist historians, even if the "school" is not entirely monolithic, may be summarized as follows:

- The Hebrew Bible is a product of the religious and cultural "identity crisis" of Judaism in the Hellenistic era, *not* the story of an actual historical Israel in the long-gone Iron Age.
- The Hebrew Bible thus constitutes a *literary* tradition, not a historical document; it is a "social construct" that reflects the religious interests and propaganda of a late, elitist theocratic party within Judaism. It reveals *their* history, if any.
- It follows that "Biblical" and "ancient" Israel are fictitious – myths invented by the Biblical writers, not historical realities. Even if a "historical Israel" in the Iron Age could be reconstructed, it would

consist of a very brief outline of a handful of later kings and a few skeletal political events, corroborated mainly by extra-Biblical texts. Archaeology may be a putative source of history writing, but in practice it is largely "mute" owing to scant data and methodological impression", *etc.* (p.28-29).

A direct example of such a nihilistic approach is the book, *The Israelites in History and Tradition*, by N.P.Lemche (1998), another of Copenhagen's biblical revisionists. In this book, the author, a professor at the University of Copenhagen, argues that using surviving sources, it is impossible to prove not only the Exodus, but to locate historical Israel itself. Lemche declares that the followers of Judaism

> "constructed their own origin myth as a program for taking over a country which they reclaimed for themselves in spite of the inhabitants who already lived there."

W.G. Dever (2000) vigorously objects to biblical revisionists that the archaeological record is not at all silent, only that some historians are deaf. Thanks to unquestionable archaeological findings, it has been shown that biblical writings concerning the ancient Jewish state are the product of neither Jewish nationalistic ideology nor a Zionist myth of the late Second Temple period, but are historical facts.

The archaeological evidence demonstrates conclusively that there was an early Israel present in Canaan just before 1200 BCE. Of course, this historical Israel does not correspond in details with the panorama portrayed in the Hebrew Bible, but ancient Israel (and why not Moses?) is a firm historical actuality. A curious reader will enjoy following a furious polemic between opponents on this hot topic. As examples of the uncompromising dispute, see the program publications of sorts in the specialized magazine, *Biblical Archaeological Review* (Vol.26, No.2, March/April 2000) by Philip Davies and William G. Dever.

As with the evidence of the Exodus, the same kind of skepticism is usually applied to the legendary Moses. Was he a real, charismatic hero of many faces: oracular, law-giving, executive, and military? The skeptical approach to the Exodus inevitably results in doubts of whether there existed a historical Moses (see, Van Seters, 1994).

Moses' proponents, however, are not dormant either. On the pages of the *Biblical Archaeological Review* one may find the promotion of the book *The Mountain of Moses* by the Wall Street millionaire Larry Williams (see, for example, *BAR*, March-April 1999, Vol.25, No.2, p.67). The author claims to have determined the route of the Exodus and the locale of Mount Sinai in Saudi Arabia (Jabal al Lawz).

The presumably new discovery of Mount Sinai is advertised by Howard Blum in the book *The Gold of Exodus: Discovery of the True Mount Sinai* (1998). In turn, the book by H. Blum has been ironically mocked by Ronald Hendel (*Biblical Archaeological Review*, Vol.25, No.4, July/August 1999, pp.54-55; arguments on this issue continued in *BAR*, Vol.25, No.6, November/December 1999, pp.66-67).

Timing of the Exodus

Of course, the problems connected with Moses are not restricted to geographical identifications. Some of them are related to the epoch during which the biblical events of the Moses legend supposedly took place. Mainstream conventional wisdom tells us Moses flourished in the 13th century BCE (Comay and Brownrigg, 1993). If we turn to an investigation by David M.Rohl (1995), however, we find a different and offbeat opinion: Moses' epoch should be shifted at least 400 years back in the chronology of mainstream biblical scholarship.

Naturally, addressing the issues connected with Moses and the Holy Bible, we face the same type of severe questioning of the sources' reliability that Ahlström (1993) has stressed:

> "With what kind of material are we dealing? Who wrote it? For whom was it written, and for what purpose? Can the text be trusted? Is it biased? Does it pretend to relate a divine promise, or is it written for a special purpose, as are, for instance, a law code, a sales contract, a treaty text, a letter, a genealogy, a king-list, a chronicle, an apology, or a piece glorifying a person, a myth, a story about a folk-hero? Are we dealing with a form of political-religious advocacy or doctrines? with an etiology? with telescoping or a distortion of events? Or nothing other than fiction written as a fairytale?

Is a particular text built upon another source and therefore, whether intentionally or not, altering it?" (p.26).

All these questions can be rightfully applied to the Moses problem as well. I clearly realize that, in considering the contemporary situation concerning the Mosaic problem in scientific literature, there can be found a counter-argument undermining virtually any other argument.

Opposing the negation of Moses' historicity is the fact that such a respected ancient historian as the Roman P. Cornelius Tacitus (c.55 – c.117 CE) mentioned this man for sure. About two millennia ago, Tacitus (see, Great Books of the Western World, Vol.15, Encyclopedia Britannica, 1952) wrote very certainly:

> "The people, who had been collected after diligent search, finding themselves left in a desert, sat for the most part in a stupor of grief, till one of the exiles, Moyses by name, warned them not to look for any relief from God or man, forsaken as they were of both, but to trust to themselves, taking for their heaven-sent leader that man who should first help them to be quit of their present misery... Moyses, wishing to secure for the future his authority over the nation, gave them a novel form of worship, opposed to all that is practiced by other men," (p.295), *etc.*

Is this not a crucial argument? In no way, critics parry. The same Tacitus with the same inspiration wrote of Romulus, the founder of Rome, and many other imaginary characters that are no doubt legendary from a modern point of view.

While the archaeological situation concerning the Moses problem still remains uncertain, the reality is that, in general, biblical nihilism has seen itself under heavy fire in recent decades. Now and then, archaeological bombshells recover material evidence of the contested biblical facts that have been marginalized for centuries by aggressive skepticism.

An Israeli scientist once opined that the story of Moses is irrelevant to my Zodiac case. Even if he lived and acted, he was nothing more than a personality of local importance, while the problem of the Zodiac passes well beyond the history of individual tribes. I do not consider such a remark correct.

Regardless of whether Moses existed or not, during the post-Mosaic era, the Hebrew settlers of Canaan integrated a very specific bulk of cultural features, which manifested itself in Judaism. This cultural nucleus dominated only in the minds of local tribesmen. Later, however, through Hellenistic, Roman, and Christian cultures, it became one of the major components of world heritage. That is why the significance of the legendary Moses exceeds greatly his real historical role as a local tribe chieftain.

All of the above is there to demonstrate that the author realizes the complexities of the many current controversies around the Mosaic legend. Yet, despite them, it is the said legend considered in its totality of opposites that appears to be the motivating drive behind the events described in this Chapter.

I need to emphasize once more that the ideas expressed here are probably the most hypothetical among other hypotheses presented in this book. But I am engaged in this speculation because the dating of the third zodiacal quartet due to precession can most certainly be placed in the reign of Akhenaten. And if Akhenaten was, indeed, involved in the development of the modern twelve-strong Zodiac, then, with his passing away, it also was erased and forgotten, as were all of his other innovations. Who, then, recovered his legacy of solar observations?

Only one individual of the period, Moses the lawgiver, is reasonably worthy of discussion in this context, despite all the numerous contradictions that accompany the Mosaic problem.

In the minds and souls of the adherents of Christianity, Moses is the most majestic protagonist in the Old Testament. He is the greatest visionary and lawgiver. His exemplary seeds and (if he lived) posthumous impact were so profound that the Pentateuch (the first five books of the Holy Bible) has been called the Five Books of Moses, and the code of the moral religious commandments, the Law of Moses. The founding father of the nation, for Jews he is the Father of Israel's basic institutions: the priesthood, the sacred shrine, and the Covenant. He commissioned the structural features of the tribal union. For Jews, Moses is, and will stay forever, a savior of the Jewish people from Egyptian slavery and "Moses, Our Teacher."

One significant feature of Moses' life deserves our special intense attention: his close attachment to Egypt. From the New Testament (Acts, 7:20-22), it is well-known:

> "In that particular time Moses was born, and he was divinely beautiful. And he was nursed three months in [his] father's home. But when he was exposed, the daughter of Phar'aoh picked him up and brought him up as her own son. Consequently Moses was instructed in all the wisdom of the Egyptians. In fact, he was powerful in his words and deeds."

The Egyptian link is emphatically addressed in Moses' legendary biography, and in the 21st century, we have obtained much reliable evidence. For example, it is certain that the Egyptian vocabulary is sprinkled throughout the Pentateuch. Careful investigations confirm that the narrator (or narrators) of the Book of Exodus had first-hand knowledge of Egyptian customs and beliefs. Moreover, sometimes the Pentateuch demonstrates a polemical play with the Egyptian life-style.

Many aspects of the Exodus account maintain direct linguistic and thematic affinities with Egyptian magical practice (see, for instance, Noegel, 1996). It was not theologians alone who always scrutinized the Moses legend, but scholars in many various fields of cultural history, as well. An example of the impact of Moses on modern culture can be found in an argumentative treatise of Sigmund Freud (1856-1939).

Moses and Monotheism, by Sigmund Freud

The father of psychoanalysis, Freud in his old age attracted a modern current of controversial attention to Moses' legendary life story. Before he fled as a refugee from Vienna to England at the threshold of the Nazi Anschluss, in 1937 Freud published in the journal *Imago*, which he had founded and edited, two essays on Moses. In London, while suffering from cancer and knowing that his days were numbered, Freud continued to analyze the subject of his long-lasting interest. He was not daunted by friends' warnings that his manuscript in the Dark Age of Hitler's anti-Semitic attacks could prove detrimental to the Jewish cause. Despite all deterrence, Freud successfully completed the opus on

Moses with a third essay. All three were immediately translated from German into English and published together as a compact separate pamphlet, *Moses and Monotheism* (Freud, 1939).

In his swan-song booklet, the father of *libido* ventured into fields hitherto unexplored, and his latest challenge to the public was viewed by contemporaries as another tremendous breakthrough. Freud proclaimed the close ties between Moses' religious message and the Egyptian religion under Akhenaten, the heretic.

It is well established today that the Egyptian traces of Moses' legacy begin with his own name. Starting with J.H. Breasted (1905), it has been clearly determined that the name of Mose(s) is a derivation from an Egyptian word, *ms*, meaning *a child*, or *a son* (Griffiths, 1953). It is a regular component of compound Egyptian names, formed with a name of a god, such as *Amenmesses* (Amon-mose, a son of the god, Amon), or *Tuthmosis* (Thut-mose, a son of the god, Thoth) or great *Ramesses* (Rä-mose, a son of the god, Rä). Not only his Egyptian name but a large cluster of legends links Moses to the Egyptian Pharaoh's court, the features of his birth and education being spotlighted in the Bible.

Of course, Moses is not so much a figure of history, but of legend, and the majority of the features of his biography are likely to be legendary. For example, Freud himself had commented that the story of a basket in a water stream is commonplace for many other historical and legendary heroes. In practically the same words, the founder of Babylon, king Sargon of Agade, described his babyhood as early as the beginning of the 3rd millennium BCE, almost 15 centuries before Moses. Common biographical features can easily be found in the oral tradition for the life histories of Cyrus, Romulus, and many other notable personages.

Freud followed some prominent biblical scholars in mentioning such a strange correspondence as, for instance, the close resemblance of divine names: the Egyptian's name *Aton*, the Hebrew's *Adonai,* and the Syrian's *Adonis*. Freud's booklet also contains a number of other points of interest.

All in all, in 1939 Sigmund Freud had been eagerly insisting on the Egyptian backdrop of Moses' religious doctrine. And, of course, there were a lot of foes to such a nontrivial conclusion.

Moses as Featured by Jan Assmann

Being aged and fatally ailing, Sigmund Freud failed to undertake an exhaustive historical search of the Akhenaten/Moses scenario. As a psychologist of the highest rank, he insightfully grasped the problem by mere intuitive feeling. The difference was made by one of the eminent Egyptologists of our time, Prof. Jan Assmann, of Heidelberg University in Germany. In the treatise, *Moses the Egyptian: The Memory of Egypt in Western Monotheism* (1997*)*, he painstakingly advanced, broadened, and strengthened Freud's findings by taking into account many novel, thorough results in the field. As the reviewer for *Biblical Archaeology Review* R. Hendel has stated (**24**, 2, 1998, p.68):

> "In this remarkable book, Assmann takes the very essence of Western religion – the principle of monotheism – as his topic, tracing its effects by looking at its counter-image in the Western imagination – the memory of Egypt."

We have no need to touch any but limited aspects of this outstanding masterpiece of research. First of all, Assmann has masterfully eliminated the need for a discourse on Moses' historicity. He calls his form of historical investigation "mnemohistory"(pp.8-10):

> "Unlike history proper, mnemohistory is concerned not with the past as such, but only with the past as it is remembered… Mnemohistory is not the opposite of history, but rather is one of its branches or subdisciplines, such as intellectual history, social history, the history of mentalities, or the history of ideas… It concentrates exclusively on those aspects of significance and relevance which are the product of memory that is, of a recourse to a past – and which appear only in the light of later readings… The past is not simply "received" by the present. The present is "haunted" by the past and the past is modeled, invented, reinvented, and reconstructed by the present…
>
> The aim of a mnemohistorical study is not to ascertain the possible truth of traditions such as the traditions about Moses but to study these traditions as phenomena of collective memory. Memories may be false, distorted,

> invented, or implanted… Memory cannot be validated as a historical source without being checked against "objective" evidence… But for a historian of memory, the "truth" of a given memory lies not so much in its "factuality" as in its "actuality". Events tend to be forgotten unless they live on in collective memory… Mnemohistory analyzes the importance which a present ascribes to the past. The task of historical positivism consists in separating the historical from the mythical elements in memory and distinguishing the elements which retain the past from those which shape the present…The task of mnemohistory consists in analyzing the mythical elements in tradition and discovering their hidden agenda."

Thus, from this viewpoint, it does not matter whether or not Moses was a figure of history. For us, as for Prof. Assmann, Moses is a figure of a special branch of history, mnemohistory, and in this role he is the subject of the investigation using special mnemohistoric methods. Such an approach is of great value for my cause because so many problems of archaeoastronomy lie entirely in the area of mnemohistory.

Assmann has ruled out any discussion of the emotional issue of Moses' nationality: whether or not Moses was a Hebrew national or an Egyptian national. It is a matter of fact that being the subject of mnemohistory, Moses belonged entirely to the Egyptian court culture.

Finally, Assmann has brilliantly demonstrated that in Moses' claim for a new religious teaching, the mnemohistoric lawgiver used a counter-image of the Egyptian religion, or, in more sophisticated terminology, he exercised *normative inversion*. This method consists of inverting the abominations of one cultural medium into the obligations of another, and vice versa. It is a well-known process in human history: so often the items that are prohibited by predecessors become obligatory for new generations, and those new generations forbid all that has been prescribed earlier.

Prof. Assmann illuminates the simplest cases:

> "When this principle is applied on the alimentary level, the eating of pork, for example, would be commanded, not because it is cheap or tasty or nutritious, but only because it visibly demonstrates the fact that one does not belong

to a community that abominates this food. Inversely, the consumption of meat together with dairy products would be prohibited, not because the combination of meat and milk is unbecoming or unsavory, but because keeping them apart demonstrates separation from a society where consuming this combination is customary, perhaps even obligatory" (p.31).

Many such examples occurred in the 20th century after the 1917 Bolshevik revolution in Russia, and the next wave of normative inversions surfaced after the collapse of the Soviet Union.

Neither Sigmund Freud nor Assmann were the first to spot the links of early Judaism and Egyptian religion. Approximately the same idea was promoted by the French scholar, Joseph Ernest Renan (1823-1897). In the bestseller of the 19th century, *The Life of Jesus* (first edition of 1863), speaking on ancient Israelites, Renan claimed that their ancient relationships with Egypt, from which much was borrowed, even though the extent of the borrowing cannot be exactly determined, did strengthen the Israelites' scorn of idolatry.

Alex A. Gurshtein

What does Moses' *Normative Inversion* Mean?

To illustrate the significance of Moses' normative inversion, following Prof. Assmann's understanding of it, I present some fundamental facts collected in a single table.

NORMATIVE INVERSION, in the case of Moses

ANCIENT EGYPTIAN SYMBOLISM versus
        JUDEO-CHRISTIAN RELIGIOUS SYMBOLISM

Ideological basis:	*Ideological basis:*
SYSTEM FOR POWERFUL RULERS OF A POWERFUL SUPERSTATE	"ENCLAVE CULTURE" FOR A THREATENED MINORITY
CULT OF POWER	CLAIM FOR A TRUTHFUL (or SPIRITUAL) LIFE
GOLDEN CALF (Sacred APIS)	SACRIFICIAL RAM
GODS ARE PATRONS OF A PHARAOH	GOD IS FOR EVERYONE
GODS ARE IN NATURE	GOD IS SUPERNATURAL
POLYTHEISM	MONOTHEISM
ZOOMORPHIC GODS	ANTHROPOMORPHIC GOD
WORSHIP OF IMAGES	PROHIBITION OF IDOLATRY
WATER IS A SYMBOL FOR DEAD SOULS	WATER OF LIFE
UNDERWORLD IS AQUATIC	UNDERWORLD IS SUBTERRANEAN
CULT OF CELESTIAL LUMINARIES	NO DIRECT ASTRONOMICAL CONNOTATIONS
ASTROLOGY (FORECAST OF THE FUTURE)	TOTAL DENOUNCIATION OF ASTROLOGY (HUMAN'S RESPONSIBILITY FOR HIS/HER OWN FUTURE)
MAGIC	NO MAGICIANS
THE NUMBER EIGHT	THE NUMBER TWELVE

Normative inversion is the missing link that chained Egypt with the following spiritual-life events that appeared in the persona of Moses. He had an insightful understanding of the Amarna Age events, opposed the Egyptian traditions, and had strong grounds to support the innovations that the Egyptian priesthood had rejected so categorically.

If I am accurate in my claims, it was the "heretic" Pharaoh Akhenaten who was the first to attempt establishing the number-of-twelve as a meaningful sacred number of the *gods*, or the *gods' residences*, on the path of the Sun. His attempt was doomed to fail, as was everything associated with this king; soon after his reign, his innovations were completely disregarded. The introduction of the more complicated structure of twelve gods was out of the priesthood's realm and did not have any motivation for its further realization.

But Akhenaten's innovations could not be wiped out of memory entirely, and later on they appeared to be useful because of their practicality: it was very practical to correspond the twelve-strong subdivision of the year (an Egyptian regular month) with the twelve-strong subdivision of the ecliptic. Thus, each month had its reflection in one-twelfth of the ecliptic, which became a zodiacal label.

Moses was that very person who was interested in innovations, and who was especially interested in adopting all the new features that the Egyptian priesthood opposed. So, for me, Moses' normative inversion used to create a new religious symbolism is a good reason to speculate that Moses, who might have known about the new constellation quartet proposed by Akhenaten, took this fresh idea into consideration. It was after Moses that the number-of-TWELVE itself - the total number of the twelve-strong structure of the ecliptic and the number of months in the Egyptian calendar - became a meaningful and sacred symbol.

Crucial Evidence for the Number Twelve

A few times in literature on irrational fears, I have stumbled upon a word of Greek origin, *triskaidekaphobia*. This awkward coinage denotes a superstitious fear of a "baker's dozen," the number thirteen. There is a foggy guess that such a phobia is the result of the betrayal of Jesus by the thirteenth attendee at the Last Supper, Judas. But it seems more realistic that *triskaidekaphobia* is closely linked to a much older tendency, for which I am coining another Greek-derived clumsy term, *dodecamania*, i.e., devotion to the fortuitous number twelve.

I believe no one can deny that the European cultural tradition recognizes two very special and consecrated numerals: seven and twelve. There are a lot of speculations about these very special numbers, including the ideas regarding their divine genesis, purely mathematical origin, or any sort of numerological mystique. Meanwhile, the present author's stand is that these numbers are not a result either of any kind of divine revelation or of numerological mysticism, but are derivations from natural causes, which seem to have been of great significance to the people who introduced them. In this book, I shall not discuss the number seven, but this is the time to pay attention to the number twelve. Let us collect some of the examples in a comprehensive table.

THE NUMBER TWELVE
DODECANARY SYMBOLIC GROUPS IN HISTORY

The twelve months in a solar year (starting with the Egyptian civil calendar);
The twelve signs of the Zodiac (starting in the first millennium BCE);
The twelve hours of a day and the twelve hours of a night (Egyptian innovation);
The twelve main gods of Egypt;
The twelve sons of Jacob, or the twelve tribes of Israel;
The twelve gates of celestial Jerusalem;
The twelve precious stones of the rational, or the ornament worn
                by the high-priest of the Jews (starting with Aaron);
Dodecanese, literally a group of twelve islands, administrative unit of ancient Greece;
The four tribes of Athens, subdivided into three "fratries";
The twelve wards of the city, of which Plato conceived the plan;
The altar of Twelve Gods in Athens;
The six male and six female principal Greek gods;
The twelve labors of Hercules;
The twelve cantons of the Etruscan league;
The confederation of the twelve cities of Jonia, and that of Eolia;
The twelve altars of Janus;
The twelve Tcheu into which Chun divided China;

The twelve regions into which the natives of Korea divided the World;
The twelve Apostles;
The city of the twelve gates in the Apocalypse;
The twelve governors in the Manichean system;
The twelve asses of the Scandinavians;

etc.

Could the number twelve have acquired its status as a special symbol before it became the epitome of an important natural event? I see serious arguments against such a suggestion. Meanwhile, there are strong grounds to believe the number twelve has gained its high profile because of the number of months within a solar year. If this is correct, there is an interesting deduction. While the ancient lunar calendar reigned everywhere in the whole world, the number of lunar months within a solar year was either 12 or 13. The number twelve could not be outstanding and sacred under such a condition.

The first time in world history that twelve became the permanent number of months within the solar year was in the Egyptian civil calendar. Of course, at the beginning, this solution had to be seen as a formal, kind of bureaucratic trick. A long period of time had to pass before the number twelve deserved to be considered as very special. And the Egyptian Amarna Age is a proper candidate for the period when twelve obtained its very special status. Meanwhile, we remember that few Egyptian cultural traditions had a direct impact on the features of European life. So it is unlikely that the number twelve entered our common European usage through Egyptian cultural taxonomic formation, but, it seems likelier, through some other, and the best candidate for such a formation is Judaism.

This is not the first time that *Twelveness* has been claimed to be of Hebrew origin. As cited by R.H. Allen (1899), Rear Admiral William Henry Smyth (1788-1865) wrote in his *Cycle of Celestial Objects*:

> "Hebrew antiquaries have long recognized Enoch as inventor of the Dodecatemory divisions" (p.2).

To refresh the reader's memory, Enoch, a biblical personage, is associated with the very beginnings of Hebrew mnemohistory. R.H. Allen has added more information on the same subject:

> "The Jewish historian Flavius Josephus, followed by Saint Clement of Alexandria, A.D. 200, surmised that the twelve stones in the breastplate of the high priest might refer to the twelve zodiacal constellations" (p.2).

There is no doubt that the number twelve was in recurring usage in ancient Jewish tradition. It was a holy number for Israel, its greatest cosmic symbol. Charlalee B. Sedgwick (1976) collected many interesting facts on this issue in his MA thesis:

> "There are the Twelve Tribes of Israel, according to the twelve sons of Jacob (Gen. 29:31 ff), 49; Numbers 1,26; Deuteronomy 33); the twelve wells the Israelites found in their wanderings through the desert in Elim (Ex. 15,27); the twelve stones Joshua took out of the river Jordan to set up at Gilgal (Jos. 4); the twelve precious stones of the breastplate of the High Priest (Ex. 28, 17 ff); the twelve oxen that support the Brazen Sea in the Temple (I Kings 7,25); the twelve harnesses that Elisa used in his plowing, when he was called (I Kings, 19, 19)" (p.41-42).

Sedgwick reminds us that Philo of Alexandria (c.20 BCE – c.50 CE) also equated the twelve stones on the High Priest's breastplate with the Zodiac:

> "The twelve gems are figures of the twelve animals of the zodiac. This is the symbol of the twelve patriarchs, for their names are engraved on the stones, with the object of making them stars and as it were giving each its own constellation. More than that, each patriarch himself becomes a Constellation…" (p.43).

The number twelve appeared in the synagogue rituals, too, due to the Twelve Princes, twelve "Leaders of the Soul," twelve silver dishes, twelve bowls, twelve golden spoons, twelve lambs, twelve rams, twelve goats, and so on.

From my perspective, a decisive argument, the rule of contraries, favoring the status of the number twelve as originating in Egypt, being handled by Moses, and finally catapulting into Western culture thanks to Christian symbolism, can be excerpted from a treatise by the Roman author, Macrobius. This author compiled an extensive Commentary on the so-called Dream of Scipio, by Cicero, which contains a brief account of the Roman's beliefs.

As is usual for the time, little has come down to us on Macrobius, who flourished at the end of the 4th and the beginning of the 5th centuries CE. His writings testify that he was in favor of the leading adversaries of Christendom, such as the orator Quintus Aurelius Symmachus (c.340-402 CE), or Praetextatus, the praetorian prefect. No mention of Christians or Christianity exists in Macrobius' books, but he demonstrated a very broad knowledge in different areas and, specifically, a profound interest in pagan deities.

In his Commentary (see, for example, the edition by Columbia University Press, 1952 or 1990), Macrobius devotes a lot of pages to numerology, i.e., the interpretation of the hidden symbolic meanings of various numerals. Thus, the number seven is discussed in several dozen examples. Many other numerals are explained by Macrobius in great detail, while the discussion of the number twelve is conspicuously lacking. Macrobius knows nothing interesting about this number and points out only that the Zodiac is divided into twelve parts. Like many others, he states, regarding the Egyptian origin of the Zodiac:

> "The early Egyptians, acknowledged to be the first men who
> dared to search and measure the sky…" (p. 177).

One can see a very sound parallel in Macrobius' Commentary: the author doesn't know Christian symbolism and, therefore, finds no place in his treatise for the sacred number, twelve. This *argumentum a contrario* seems very profound to me.

Alex A. Gurshtein

Moses and the Celestial Symbol of Aries the Ram

In their pioneering book *Hamlet's Mill* (1969), de Santillana and von Dechend stress that the epoch of Aries is associated with the biblical narrative of Moses coming down from Mount Sinai as "two horned," or crowned with ram's horns, while his flock disobediently kept dancing around the golden calf, a metaphor for Taurus the bull.

The bull being the superior Egyptian divine symbol of that time, the opposition of the ram to the bull is the proper allegoric contraposition of a new Age of Aries to the old one of Taurus. The two-horned Moses is particularly illustrative, because it was in such a visage that the lawgiver was immortalized as the central figure of the grandiose tomb monument to Pope Julius II in Rome by the chisel of Michelangelo (1545). Before the latter, Claus Sluter created another masterful sculpture of the two-horned Moses (1395-1403); it is on the Well of Moses in Chartreuse de Champmol at Dijon, France. There are a number of other masterpieces featuring Moses with ram's horns.

I cited the note from *Hamlet's Mill* in a paper in *American Scientist* (1997) and was mercilessly attacked by Dr. M.L. Wolbarsht, of Duke University (Letters to the Editor, *Am. Sci.*, 1997, Vol.85, No.6, November-December, p.500). According to Wolbarsht's own investigation (Wolbarsht and Lichtenberg, 1961), the ram's horns of Moses are a relatively late concept derived from a mistranslation of the biblical Hebrew for "shining face." The adversaries of *Hamlet's Mill*'s claim that depictions of a horned Moses in art are based on the erroneous Vulgate translation by St. Jerome in the 4th century CE and are a Catholic concept rather than a pagan or Hebrew tradition.

In reality, there are several questionable interpretations of the "two-horned" Moses. For example, to a current-day layman, horns are an indication at best of cuckoldry and at worst of Satanism. Contrary to this, in the ancient Near East, horns were an unequivocal sign of divinity and were analogous to the Christian halo. Powerful kings, who claimed godhood, including Alexander the Great, might have been accordingly shown horned (Propp, 1988). It is also not by chance that horns served as honorary decor among medieval knights.

In the beginning of the 19th century, the Right Honorable Sir William Drummond writes on the meaning of the Paschal lamb:

"Thus the Sun at the vernal equinox passed from the sign of *Taurus* to that of *Aries*...It was probably not quite so easy to make the ignorant and superstitious people comprehend, why the principal symbol of their principal God should be changed from a bull, or calf, to a ram, or lamb.

It is to this source, that I am inclined to attribute the adoration, which was peculiarly offered up to bulls and calves, as principal symbols of the Sun, long after *Taurus* had ceased to be the first of the signs. The astronomers of Thebes in Egypt seem to have been the first, who obtained from the multitude that veneration for sheep, which is so remarkably noticed by Herodotus. In other regions, the Bull continued, through the lapse of ages, to maintain an unjust pre-eminence over the Ram, or Lamb, which had become the first of the signs" (1811, p.367).

Sir Drummond concludes:

"When, indeed, we find that this feast of the passover, or transit, was instituted at the time when the Jewish lawgiver altered the Calendar, and when he made the first month of the year that very month, in which the equinoctial Sun passed into *Aries*, it seems difficult to imagine that the Paschal lamb had nothing to do with the astronomical ram. But this opinion, which I submit to the judgment of my readers, becomes strongly confirmed by the customs and practices of the Egyptians, from whom the Jews copied many of their ceremonies, and obtained the greater part of their knowledge" (1811, p.380-1).

Let us recall that in his research on the origin of the Zodiac, Rupert Gleadow (1968) was perplexed by the presence of Aries, the name lacking in the Egyptian and Mesopotamian sources.

The logical question arises: could the ram, or the lamb, be appropriate as a meaningful divine symbol in agricultural domains? The response has to be, of course, *NO*. Both Mesopotamians and Egyptians were acquainted with domesticated sheep, but the animals' presence was not dominant in their lifestyles. It was the nomadic shepherds and sheep-breeders who were dependent on sheep, and from a very ancient age the ram has played a dominant metaphoric role for nomadic ancestors of the children of Israel.

For a long time the ram was connected with ancient vernal rituals. In the 2nd millennium BCE in the biblical narrative, the patriarch Abraham was forced to change the ritual sacrifice from that of a human to a ram. The next appearance in the Bible of the image of this creature is in connection with Moses, who marked the Israelites' doors with the blood of a lamb as God slew the Egyptian firstborn males. Soon after, the symbol of a ram took deep root in Hellenistic culture, Zeus being portrayed with ram's horns regularly. And, finally, the same symbol entered Christendom, Jesus Christ being distinguished as the "Lamb of God" (Fideler, 1993, pp.161-163).

The ram was a commonplace symbol for the Judeo-Christian and Hellenistic cultures. And being concerned with the chronology of these cultures, we have to ascribe the offspring of the ram, Aries the celestial symbol, basically to Moses. It is a matter of fact that Moses flourished during the transition period from the world-age of Taurus to the world-age of Ram (Aries). It is also a fact that the symbolism Moses used was consistent with the images of this transition period.

Moses the Astronomer?

Educated at the Egyptian court and initiated into all the wisdom of Egypt, Moses undoubtedly had to be knowledgeable about Egyptian astronomy. There are grounds to believe, however, his astronomical background was much more extensive than mere schoolboy learning.

According to the Scripture, Moses was an intellectual who backed the ideas of Abraham and the other Patriarchs. Importantly to this investigation, the Patriarchs, besides having many other merits, were experts in astronomical observations. Some colorful details on the subject were collected in a dissertation by Maurice D. Heatly (1971).

According to the assertion of the Alexandrian Jew, Philo, "Terah, the father of Abraham... had much studied astronomy, and taught it to Abraham" (Seiss, 1882). Josephus corroborates the fact that Abraham knew the stars, and that it was this knowledge of astronomy which led him to believe in one God (Josephus Flavius, 1963). The historian, Berossus (flourished c. 260 BCE), referring to Abraham said, "in the tenth generation after the flood, there was among the children a man righteous and great, and skillful in the celestial science" (Heatly, 1971, p.13).

Whatever can be said of the veracity of those statements, the ancient Jewish oral tradition regarded Abraham as an astronomer of the first rank while he was still in Ur of the Chaldees c. 1700 BCE.

Thus, astronomy was likely of importance for the ancient Hebrews, as well as for the ancient Egyptians and all other tribes. But the Old Testament was written in particular as a rejection of Egyptian religious polytheism and other beliefs of the former oppressors, including astronomy. Is this the reason that, to negate the concerns of the Egyptians in accordance with normative inversion, all astronomical interests of Moses were essentially erased from the Pentateuch?

There are only a few references to the constellations in the Holy Bible. The most famous fragment is from the Book of Job (38: 31-33):

"Canst thou bind the cluster of the Pleiades,
Or loose the bands of Orion?
Canst thou lead forth the Mazzaroth in their season?
Or canst thou guide the Bear with her sons?
Knowest thou the ordinances of the heavens?
Canst thou establish the dominion thereof in the earth?"

In Job's six-line stanza, there is a significant astronomical term, the MAZZAROTH. Only one more time in the Holy Bible is there a reference to the same term, but with a somewhat different spelling - the MAZZALOTH (II Kings, 23:5). Linguists believe the Mazzaroth to be an original word as far as the Mazzaloth is concerned, and probably synonymous with the latter, the sound "r" being softened to "l" in later Hebrew (Heatly, 1971, p.22). The most sophisticated decoding of this term reveals its meaning as an element of the zodiacal constellations.

Robert Brown (1900, Vol.2, pp.1-4) cited the fifth tablet of the Creation Legend compiled c. 650 BCE for Ashurbanipal (in Greek *Sardanapalos*), the king of Assyria who was a patron of the arts and letters and assembled a great library of cuneiform tablets at Nineveh. In this Legend some divine personage,

"Prepared the mansions of the great gods;
He fixed the stars, even the *Lumasi*, to correspond to them;
He ordained the year, appointing the *Mizrata yumazzir*
over it,
For each of the twelve months he fixed three stars."

In Semitic Babylonian there is a term *Matstsarati*. Both *Mizrata yumazzir* and *Matstsarati* seem to be connected with the Hebrew *Mazzaroth*; R. Brown interpreted it as the elements of the Zodiac.

In my mind, this could be true only partially. In accordance with all previous considerations, the Mazzaroth has to be the zodiacal constellations before they were adopted in their final form, i.e., only the first or the second quartet, or both of them together. That is why this term is so unusual and did not have a long life.

The problem of Egypt's astronomical legacy is huge, and it is awaiting a devoted investigator. We have to understand that in the 2nd-1st millennium BCE mental development went, at minimum, in three different directions. The Babylonians were mainly interested in mystic applications and they improved astrology. The Hebrews concentrated on moral relationships between human beings, as well as between people and God. The Greeks focused on the rational cognition of Nature and they advanced that type of knowledge, which today we identify as science. For all of them, the Egyptian astronomical legacy was of great importance, but it was reflected in different ways according to the needs of the user.

Returning to our point, in spite of certain difficulties, we possess reliable information on the astronomical (cosmic) symbolism of the Jewish culture, even as far back as Solomon's Temple. According to the prolific commentator and philosopher of the largest Jewish cultural center, Philo of Alexandria (c. 20 BCE – c. 50 CE), the altar in the Temple represented the four elements of Nature, while the table stood for the animate world and the Menorah - for the celestial sphere. A little bit later in Rome, the same issue was addressed by Flavius Josephus (Joseph ben Matthias, c. 35-100 CE) in his *The Antiquities of the Jews*. He wrote that objects of celestial symbolism in Solomon's Temple included the veil, on which the starry panorama was revealed, as well as the Menorah.

If it is hard to trace the history of astronomical decorations in the earliest Jewish cult buildings in more detail, we have a lot of reliable archaeological evidence starting with the third century CE. While one of the Decalogue (Ten Commandments) strongly prohibited the presence of any images, zodiacal pictures are found as a regular decorative motif on the mosaic floors of synagogues (Ness, 1999).

The first synagogue mosaic of any sort was uncovered in a dramatic way by a Turkish shell in 1918. This site is at Ein Duk, the ancient Naaran, close to Jericho. In accordance with recent research, the dating of the synagogue goes back to the 5th or 6th century CE. For our cause, the most intriguing feature of this building is the presence of the mosaic floor where, side by side with classical Jewish symbols, there is a zodiacal panel – a large mosaic square, four meters on a side.

Another synagogue was discovered, also accidentally and also with a mosaic floor, in 1928 at Beth Alpha. The second mosaic floor likewise contains images of the 12 signs of the Zodiac. So far, it is the best preserved, and, as a result, it has become the most famous. The Beth Alpha synagogue was probably erected in the later 5th century CE.

Nowadays, many more ancient synagogues with the Zodiac are known: in Husifa, which is on Mount Carmel, about 12 km from Haifa; at Hammath-Tiberias; at Khirbet Susiya, near Hebron; etc.

Several exotic guesses were voiced to explain this oddity; the problem, however, persists. How is it possible that the designers of synagogues considered the pagan Zodiac signs to be elements of symbolic decorations of the same value as traditional Jewish emblems? Only one point is clear: as a result of thorough investigation, it was demonstrated that those zodiacal ornaments were not the fruits of Jewish heretics, but were made in the full light of Jewish orthodoxy (Sedgwick, 1976).

As the reader has likely already guessed, our explanation makes itself obvious: the twelve-strong Zodiac appeared in synagogues because it counts its genesis from Moses. If this is indeed so, then the use of the Zodiac as a decoration in synagogues seems totally natural. The twelve-strong Zodiac is by no means the inheritance of the pagan world, but the legacy of an earlier stage of Judaism itself.

The general conclusion seems to emerge that it is not absurd for mnemohistoric Moses to be considered as a wise man knowledgeable in the science of astronomy. And, thus, the question mark in the title of this section can be removed.

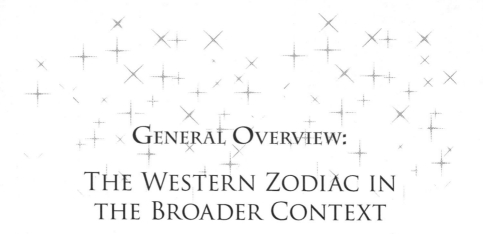

General Overview:

The Western Zodiac in the Broader Context

Animals have no predisposition to dominate the world. They undertake no efforts to impose their will on it. Humans are different. On the vast landmass of Eurasia, having weathered the Ice Age, they crawled out onto the broad expanse of history. They topped every regional food chain. In the course of the Neolithic revolution, having domesticated plants and animals, people broke the bonds of nature and managed the premises for taking their destiny into their own hands. They ceased eating "hand to mouth." They secured provisions beforehand: food supplies began to thrive and graze near their dwellings. Forever looming at the hunter's threshold, the ghost of fierce famine took a step back. *Homo sapiens* filed a bid to become the sovereign of nature.

Before the leap to their special status on the face of the planet, the most ancient people had to integrate themselves into the context of animate and inanimate nature. Huddled in caverns, hungry and cold, they had to regularize their habits and naïve beliefs for everyday practical and spiritual needs. Thus, human culture entered the stage. Some of its ancient rites are still present in our superstitions and prejudices.

The behavior of man is governed mostly by biological instincts. Culture – fragile and ever-changing from era to era - is a unique non-biological burden carried on the back of the human biological carcass. It is culture alone that gives humankind its true human dimension.

Before the Neolithic Revolution

Remaining a part of nature while comprehending neither its organization nor its driving forces, fighting for self-recognition and leverage over fellow tribesmen, the most ancient people, in contrast to animals, had already created a cultural superstructure upon a biological framework at a very early stage of their debut. They acquired articulate speech as a means of interaction - the social memory of the human community. They acquired primeval fine arts and utilized graphic notations, these in the absence of writing - the other advanced means of social memory. The studies of languages and rock paintings serve today as "time machines," rare time capsules filled with the brainchildren of our archaic forefathers.

Having made themselves familiar with language and fine arts, the would-be sovereigns of nature mixed "religion" into the picture. They peopled the globe with specters and superhuman beings – deities. They elevated these phantoms above themselves, figuratively and literally, registering them in the sky.

The formation of a cultural superstructure also included protoscience. From its embryonic stage, the cognition of nature was a utilitarian tool for survival. All this greatly predated the Neolithic revolution. It was a prelude to the subsequent adaptation of plants and animals. For the purposes of this book, it suffices to say that the domestication of plants and animals was preceded by the "domestication" of the landscape and sky.

The Roots of Astronomical Practice

There is no paradise on the Earth. Volcanoes erupt, breathing fire, and the ground ceases to be a solid support during earthquakes. On land, tropical hurricanes and landslides sweep through the terrain. Floodwaters devastate flatlands. Was it within primeval man's scope of mental ability to tie together such an assortment of natural phenomena into a manageable, logical system? Could he have forecast them?

The occurrences in the heavens were not as troublesome because, with rare exceptions, many of them possess consistency. The repetition of day and night, the phases of the Moon, the relationship between the picture of the sky and the rhythm of the seasons, all could be compactly generalized and recollected. Given the lack of written records, the sky became the "eye-pleasing diary." The rhythms of celestial phenomena lent themselves to predictions and could be foretold.

Ancient science was engendered not so much by the experience on the turbulent Earth as by the harvesting of knowledge about the sky. Of all the sciences, astronomy is the most deep-rooted in time. From its emergence, it secured two functions: a pragmatic one, for the sake of staying alive (topographic navigation and reckoning of time), and a worldview one (visualization of collected knowledge).

The sky guided the nomadic food-seekers of the Upper Paleolithic in time and space to track herds over long distances in the wilderness of the ice fields, the forests, and the deserts. The wax and wane of the Moon developed into an odometer for days and nights.

Modern man does not treat the calendar with much thought because he is burdened with excess information about it at every step. For primeval man, however, it was among the overlords of life. It was the conductor of all the living beats in the symphony of life.

The domestication of the sky for ancients became an inseparable component of the domestication of the landscape. The sky functioned for man as the guidebook for the cognition of nature. No alternative existed for this guidebook. On whichever continent of the Earth the ancients resided, they all lived under the same celestial vault, read this common guidebook, and matured in the same ways.

The common astronomical guidebook molded the archaic view of things. It pointed out to the most ancient starwatchers that the world has four corners or, if you wish, it is erected on four pillars, located at the astronomically determined directions of north, south, east, and west. Such a novelty opened more ways for orientation and became a cornerstone in the domestication of the environment. In burials, the deceased were aligned by the cardinal points.

As an additional important element of the sky's adaptation, the first constellations were administered.

Reconstructing Chronology

The emergence of modern humans, or Moderns, on the historical arena occurred approximately 40,000-35,000 years ago as a transition from the Middle to the Upper Paleolithic, accompanied by fundamental human cognitive changes. Despite the appearance of the anatomically modern humans at that time, certain aspects of the transition from Ancients to Moderns in various regions took at least 15,000-20,000 years more to be achieved. It is likely the transition in question took place in Eurasia, but, in truth, it remains unclear whether it happened in one specific area or if human advancement was polycentric.

An extinct human species that inhabited Europe and Western Asia about 150,000 to 35,000 years ago is called Neanderthal. Neanderthal's flake-based stone working technique is labeled as a Mousterian-type. From the time of the emergence of anatomically modern humans onward, we have a chronology of their further progress based upon the material artifacts unearthed in Europe, most of them coming from the Franco-Cantabrian region. No consensus exists, either on the exact absolute chronology itself, or on the possibility of applying it to the study of locales other than Southern Europe. Nevertheless, the basic stratigraphy of human progress from the Upper Paleolithic on appears to be well established as the following sequence of periods:

- Aurignacian began about 40,000 years ago in Eastern Europe and lasted until about 28,000 years ago (the population of the time is known as Cro-Magnon);
- Gravettian lasted from about 28,000 to about 22,000 years ago in the western part of Europe and was eye-catching for the production of magnificent "Venus" figurines;
- Solutrean occurred between 22,000 and 18,000 years ago, but is not recognized everywhere in Europe;
- and Magdalenian, which took place about 18,000-10,000 years ago, especially notable for its artistic accomplishments (18,000 years ago the last glaciation was at its peak and sea levels were 100-130 meters lower than today).

The behavioral contrasts between the Neanderthals (Mousterian culture) and the Cro-Magnons (Aurignacian culture) were very notable. The Neanderthals built shelters and buried the dead. The Cro-Magnons buried the dead elaborately; introduced body ornamentation; used multiple materials for tools from distant sources; developed subtle tool-making; applied complex hunting methods and started fishing; began use of fire; advanced decoration of objects (a kind of art); invented musical instruments and notation, including symbolism. The sky was part and parcel of the new symbolic mentality.

Some students in pre-written history remain strongly in favor of a sort of astronomical practice performed by early Upper Paleolithic (Aurignacian) people, maybe even Middle Paleolithic (Mousterian) people. The basic evidence comes from burials and various kinds of Paleolithic notations. Starting in the Mousterian, primordial burials were arranged deliberately to "orient" or align bodies along the cardinal points of the horizon. This tradition continued firmly through the Aurignacian. Meanwhile, the determination of the cardinal points of the horizon is achievable only by using astronomical positioning of the Sun, the Moon, the planets, and the stars. So, the conclusion is inevitable that the roots of astronomical practice, as simple as it was, can be traced back at least to the Aurignacian.

The First Marker Constellations for the Solar Calendar

The Neolithic revolution was the transition from food collection to food production: humans were no longer chained to the wild plants and animals; their food was in their backyards. As the secondary output, hierarchical-governing societies arose and the urban culture emanated en masse with more economic innovations. The Neolithic revolution supposedly dawned in the ancient Near East and extended from c. 8,300/8,000 to 3,700/3,500 BCE (B.Fagan, 1996, p.491-492).

Having turned to farming and herding cattle, man found himself in dependency on the seasons. Under the new circumstances, the lunar calendar turned out to be obsolete for agriculturists. The new lifestyle demanded that the priest-watchers delve into querying the annual travel of the Sun against the starry background. The development of the solar agricultural calendar was put on the agenda.

Establishing the annual track of the Sun among the starry patterns turned out to be possible by introducing four labels (constellations) that functioned like icons on a computer screen. These icons had to mark the days of solstices and equinoxes (four seasonal pointers). The configurations of previously existing constellations were not altered without good reason and, most likely, already existing ancient star groups were adjusted as markers. We shall call the four icon constellations of the first generation by the name of the vernal symbol, the quartet of Gemini.

The names of the four marker constellations either remained as the vestiges of earlier millennia or were "edited" in order to match seasons metaphorically. The second option is more likely under analysis of the names in the context of the entire quartet as a symbolic entity.

The fact is that all the symbols in the Gemini quartet are dual and three of them are anthropomorphic; this speaks in favor of the second option, as well. Anyhow, with the coming of the astronomical Age of Gemini, the milestones of the Sun in its track were set up in the constellations now defined as Gemini, Virgo, Sagittarius, and Pisces. At the time under consideration, the metaphors used in naming the constellations of the Gemini quartet were already aged and well settled in the minds of the populace.

All symbols of the Gemini quartet are reflections of marvels of Mother Nature, and as such, they are characteristic for a society before its noticeable social stratification. Dating, based on the sky's appearance due to precession, indicates the debut of the Gemini quartet in the 5th millennium BCE. This period was special in Near East pre-written history - a sudden rise of agriculture and urban cultures. So, it comes as no surprise that an interest in administrating the solar calendar should appear at that very time.

The First Great Agricultural Empire

The apotheosis of the triumphant march of farming in the Mediterranean was the emergence of the "gift of the Nile" – the immense agricultural civilization of ancient Egypt. The breakthrough occurred at the beginning of the 3rd millennium BCE as a result of the unification of Upper and Lower Egypt under a single power.

A solar cult existed in Egypt far earlier than its unification. The main cultic center of the Sun was located in the city of *On* in the Bible (and in Coptic), or *Heliopolis* for the ancient Greeks. The Sun idol represented a standing stone, or a *pillar* that served to symbolize the Sun. The old native Egyptian name of this Sun's city was *Iunu*, i.e., the city of the pillar. Somehow, this older emblem was transferred into an obelisk. The shadow cast by an obelisk was meaningful for the determination of solar azimuths.

Soon after unification, the Egyptian Solar Cult obtained a firm and authoritative form as the Cult of Rä. The exact date of its start is hard to determine, but, surely, the opener of the Great Pyramid Age, the Step Pyramid of Djoser, was dedicated to the Sun god, Rä. And there is no doubt that the Great Sphinx was a homage to the Sun, as well. At last, starting with the 5th Dynasty, the pharaohs typically erected Solar temples with the Sun depicted as squat two-sectioned obelisks and simultaneously improved their titularies with a fifth name as the sons of Rä. Being cautious, it is correct to say that the Cult of Rä appears to have been a newfangled idea of the Great Pyramid Age.

Older Egyptian chieftains could govern their small land parcels on their own. The newborn, great agricultural empire of unified Egypt demanded an extended bureaucratic system. In its turn, such a complex bureaucratic system demanded a single calendar for time reckoning. And it was quickly developed and introduced based on solar observations.

Instituted in the Pyramid Age, the Egyptian solar calendar contained 365 days while, in reality, the solar year is a quarter of a day longer. In the aftermath, the New Year day was not static in the Egyptian calendar, as it is in ours, but wandered: every four years, the New Year holiday moved one day and, thus, eventually passed through all seasons. This was the Great Cycle of Eternity of the Egyptian solar (civil) calendar, lasting about 1,460 years.

Meanwhile, from the time of the first quartet of seasonal markers to the unification of Egypt nearly 3 thousand years transpired, and precession had had enough time to squeeze the four seasonal pointers past the markers of the Gemini quartet, thus sapping the latter of practical and symbolic meaning. The troubleshooting was executed by the Egyptian monarchs and their entourage during the shaping of their vast agricultural empire. The Egyptians arranged the path of the Sun into a new fitting visual display.

Several mutually chained events avalanched virtually at the same period in Egypt at the beginning of the 3rd millennium BCE. The Sun, on which the entire country's welfare depended, was officially pronounced the supreme deity of unified Egypt. Thanks to systematic observations of the brightest star of the sky, Sirius, the duration of the solar year was measured with remarkable accuracy, and, for the first time in human history, a solar calendar with 12 equivalent months of 30 days each (+ 5 additional days) was officially implemented throughout the vast country. These events were forever imprinted in stone with the erection of three astronomically oriented sanctuaries – the Great Pyramids.

At this very time the annual track of the divine Sun on the sky was visualized by four new metaphoric markers with a characteristic Near Eastern tenor, mainly bestial: the Bull, the Lion, the Scorpion, and the Water Bearer (the Taurus quartet). The new celestial metaphors were not about the marvels of Mother Nature and natural human properties. This time they reflected ideas on the power of rulers and their priesthood.

Aside from the Pyramids, a pompous magic manifestation of the Egyptian innovations was the mammoth Sphinx, the imaginative mix of both new astronomical "mascots" for the solstices: the Water Bearer and the Lion. This fictional creature became the first hybrid in history to be visualized, exemplifying the human ability to invent such entertaining phantasms. There are solid grounds to suspect that the promoter of most of the mentioned novelties was the pharaoh Djoser's vizier Imhotep, later deified. Thus, the astronomical Age of Taurus strode onto the Earth and expressed itself in ancient Egypt.

The Egyptian zoo later gave the reason to call the marker constellations the Zodiac – the circle of animals. However, due to the conservatism of customs, the Egyptians did not annihilate the previous icons with which they initiated cultivation of the Nile Valley. Together with the new quartet, the four previous special star groups led to the religious perception of eight divine "celestial residences."

Egyptian innovations had the ultimate purpose of predicting floods of the Nile and spans of farming seasons as accurately as needed. Agricultural predictions as a result of astronomical activity proved to be a great success and could have ignited the misleading interpretation of astronomy as capable of predictions in a much wider area concerning various issues of kingly life. Thus, ancient Egypt could have become the womb of astrology and a number of other occult concepts.

It is astrology that explained the story of Scorpio. Outside Egypt, no consensus on the symbolism of the arachnid existed. Sometimes it was considered inadequate and the nearby celestial Eagle replaced it as an insignia. Due to this interchange, two metaphorical strings coexisted: Taurus – Leo – Scorpio – Aquarius and Taurus – Leo – Aquila – Aquarius. The latter string is known from multiple historic sources, including rich artistic representations.

The archaic astronomy practitioners could not pinpoint accurate positions for the moving luminaries on the two-dimensional orb of heaven. Meanwhile, those stargazers were advanced enough to discover the simple fact that, at a certain locale of observation, the tracks of the luminaries throughout the two-dimensional sky are directly bounded by the azimuths of their rising and setting on the horizon. That is why the long-standing practice of azimuthal astronomical positioning on the horizon took place, the world-famous Stonehenge and many other similar megaliths then being ordinary structures used as devices for astronomical alignments. Sometimes natural landmarks on the horizon were also used to register alignments (Ruggles, 1999).

Thanks to astronomical alignments, which were firmly fixed with landmarks and slabs, the priesthood performed their miraculous cosmic predictions — the foundation of their supreme authority seemed to have been gifted by the superhuman heavenly deities.

Akhenaten's Enigma Revisited

The millennia-long history of ancient Egypt witnessed the ebb and flow of successes and defeats, including foreign tyranny by the Asiatics (the Hyksos). Near the end of the 2nd millennium BCE, during the so-called Eighteenth Dynasty, the nation rose to its feet and once again took over the leading role in the Mediterranean. Two astronomical problems chronologically coincided with this period of economical and political stabilization.

The first problem was the ending of the first Great Cycle of Eternity. The second – the apparent escape of the four seasonal markers on the path of the Sun from their "dwellings" built up fifteen centuries before in the Pyramid Age with the star groups of the "circle of animals."

The Egyptian monarchy in a period of economic and political boom could not have missed such an important and incredibly rare occurrence as the first ever return of the New Year holiday to its original birthplace within the calendar. The date of the anniversary was predicted long beforehand and several pharaohs of the Eighteenth Dynasty relayed the baton of anticipation for the jubilee. The Sphinx, a momentous calendric idol, was dug up from the desert sand, cleaned up, and carefully repaired; it was the first restoration of a monument in history. The cult of the Sun regained its importance. Extraordinary steps were taken to get acquainted with the temple records of that remote epoch when the calendar was introduced, etc.

The grand occurrence was triumphantly celebrated early in the reign of the pharaoh Akhenaten, who called it the Jubilee of the Sun, his divine progenitor.

The second astronomical problem was that, in the aftermath of precession, the four seasonal points were once again squeezed out of their markers that had been figured out specifically for this purpose one and a half millennia earlier.

All circumstantial evidence favors the idea that Akhenaten, fanatically devoted to the "truth of the Sun," was the one who intended to indicate the Sun's track with four new marker constellations. The idea was attractive in that the total number of "divine dwellings" would amass to 12, so that every month of the solar year obtained its own patron sign (a god). And we know from Herodotus that at some point in Egyptian history the number of gods was actually increased from eight to twelve. The Greeks borrowed this number of primary gods – twelve – from the Egyptians. It is a matter of historical fact that the Greeks did indeed worship six primary Olympic gods and six goddesses.

In the bygone epoch of the Great Pyramids, the institution of the "circle of animals" – a genuinely Egyptian accomplishment – was the driving force of progress that elevated and cemented the power of the priesthood in the upstart empire. One and a half thousand years later, under Akhenaten, the situation was quite different. The Pharaoh's novelties tore down and redistributed the age-old settled power of the priests of certain temples and required a radical rearrangement of religious priorities.

The Most Fantastic Scenario

Akhenaten's innovations met with resistance and were pushed out of existence altogether after his death. Meanwhile, the concept of 12 superhuman beings might have flourished after Akhenaten's reign. Soon after this Pharaoh, a new energetic mover arrived onto the historical proscenium – the culture of Judaism.

Whether it was the lawgiver Moses himself, if he existed at all, or whether it was a think-tank of individuals under the collective cap of Moses who formed the dogma of a new religious worldview, but someone in Canaan took advantage of the impudent priestly proscriptions of Akhenaten's court. The fact remains that Judaism was not formed on an empty spot from a blank sheet. Its framers, well acquainted with the religious practices of Egypt, went the way of *normative inversion*. They tailored their conduct to Egyptian religious practice, reversing it inside out. Under such circumstances, the new starry markers discarded after Akhenaten's death suited them well.

In the archaic period of pre-written history, while the duration of the year fluctuated between twelve and thirteen lunar months, the number of 12 could not have been emphasized and sacred. The number of 12 was emphasized for the first time in the Egyptian civil calendar, which consistently contained twelve months. Later, the Egyptians had utilized a similar division for the day. Both daylight and nighttime were split into twelve fractions. Meanwhile, as magical and sacred, the number of 12 first popped up only in Judaism.

The name of Moses is directly related to many arresting twelve-strong symbols. We have no choice but to relate his name to the twelve-strong Zodiac. A circumstantial yet substantial affirmation of the link between Judaism and the formation of the Zodiac is that its icons, despite the taboo on images of animate life throughout Judaism, surfaced in the floor mosaics of the most ancient known synagogues.

Astronomical dating with precession of the third zodiacal quartet – the Aries quartet – gives its start after 1800 BCE. It covers both the reign of Akhenaten and the supposed Exodus of Jews from Egypt.

It seems that the transitional period from the Age of Taurus to the Age of Aries left a lasting trace of itself in the Old Testament. Moses forbids his tribesmen to dance around the Bull while returning from Mount Sinai with Ram's horns on his head.

The previous Egyptian quartet of Taurus was concealed by its authors, and, most likely, became known to the world by word of mouth through Egypt's next-door neighbors, the Mesopotamians. The same situation must have taken place again. Cabalistic Judaism was not to be disseminated amid the non-initiates, but snippets of news about the consecrated teaching leaked drop by drop to the neighboring peoples who capitalized on it but did not consider it their duty to keep quiet. Due to this process of information leakage, it is not surprising that the earliest written mentions of the twelve-strong Zodiac appear not in connection with Judaic artifacts, but in the cuneiform tablets of Mesopotamia.

The details of the stellar map testify that with the coming of the Age of Aries, it was not easy to cram markers of the last zodiacal quartet onto the ecliptic. All four star groups of this quartet – Aries, Cancer, Libra, and Capricorn – are tiny and lack bright stars. Based on this, none of them can be categorized as old constellations. They had to be shoved in amidst the existing constellations.

The metaphors of the last quartet of the Zodiac differ from its two predecessors. It is not a Neolithic "circle of humans," nor is it an Egyptian zoo. The last quartet of the Zodiac includes allegories, echoing, in part, Biblical parables. It seems that the markers of the third quartet were never intended to be handled separately from all the others. It is most likely that they were from the start installed as a part of a twelve-strong celestial god-packed belt.

The given facts testify that skywatchers tried not to modify the inherited ancestral pattern of constellations without good reason. An outstanding example is *Ophiuchus,* who was already standing on the ecliptic with his snakes, and is still standing there, even though he was never incorporated in the 12 marker constellations of the Zodiac. No one was brave enough to kick him out of there.

The allegorical names of the last zodiacal quartet, like its predecessors, correlate precisely with the metaphorical artistic imagery of their epoch. In the archaeological material of, say, the 6th or 5th millennium BCE, there is nothing whatsoever of a ram, a crab, a balance, or a goat with a fish tail. Such allusions could not have appeared in either the first or the second zodiacal quartet. But these metaphors surfaced in many areas and numerous historic documents of the epoch of the third quartet.

The Sky and Mythology

The cognomens of constellations came into the European tradition through the mediation of the colorful Greek mythology. Celestial myths of the Greeks overlapped terrestrial mythological subjects, and the mainstream belief is that the Greek sky mirrored earthly archetypes. Is this correct?

In his brief synopsis of the Nostratic language, Aharon Dolgopolsky (1998) comments:

> "Once I was asked by a journalist: 'Is there a Nostratic word for God?' I had to disappoint the gentleman: in the Nostratic lexical stock this concept has not been detected. The words for gods in the descendant languages usually go back to the name of a natural phenomenon associated with a deity in question" (p.95).

Dolgopolsky explains that within the Indo-European family, the supreme god's name goes back to an adjective meaning "that of the daylight." In their origins, for example, the Greek name *Zeus* or the Latin term *Deus* are relatives to the English *day*. Within the Finno-Ugrian family, the name of the supreme deity originally meant "heaven" or "sky."

It is no stretch that originally all supernatural divinities were connected with natural and, particularly, celestial phenomena. At the cradle of religion stood the sky with its luminaries, their regular occurrences and terrifying omens: the sky served as a mythology incubator. Only later, around the border of the Bronze Age, did people shift to forming a special pantheon of gods.

> "The old agricultural symbols of the Neolithic Age, especially the female deities associated with fertility and the earth, gradually gave way to a more masculine mythology, more consonant with the new reign of minerals and metals" (Mohen and Fluère, 2000, p.86).

The pedigree of the new pantheon became developed in full detail and was mirrored in the new "scholarly" genre of the Bronze Age – mythology. Starting in the 19th century, scientific investigation of myths convincingly demonstrated that they have nothing to do with regular legends and epics. Myths are very special lays of gods and their consorts. While fables and tales were "false and fictional stories," myths were considered to be "true and genuine stories." They narrated a sacred history; they related the events that had taken place in primordial times and told how out of the supernatural reality came into existence. Myths are always stories of "creation." They show how something was produced. Myths are orderly entities of data that generalized for ancient man his views of the world in which he resided and the forces that governed this world (Takho-Godi, 1989).

The cognizance of reality through sensory generalization, which is called mythological, is characteristic of a tribal system. When applied to Greece, this period is limited to the first third of the 1st millennium BCE, but its origins go much deeper.

The characteristics of those times include: life in lineage units; lack of private property; no clear distinction between the rich and the poor; and absence of societal hierarchy, when the land and tools belonged to the community. The ancient Greeks carried over these ideas into their perception of Nature. The cosmic unity was a single family that enveloped the earth, the sky, the sea, and the underworld. The Greeks personified them, turning occurrences into divinities.

A.A.Takho-Godi (1989) writes,

"Mythology is neither the product of simply immature and primitive thinking, nor the result of conscious and deliberate creation by the ancient man. It can be understood only through understanding the specific nature of the familial relations of a primitive community, being one of the forms of the community's exploration of the world" (p.10).

When applied to the astronomical issues, there is no doubt Greek mythology is intimately connected with the sky; but where is the start and where is the finish? Did the mythology basically reflect celestial events or earthly ones?

It is conventionally believed the Greeks pasted onto the sky their myths, which were born from earthly events. There is a Russian book titled *Myths of the Earth Reflected in the Sky*. Yet our entire investigation concludes the opposite. The behavior of mythological characters mimicked the behavior of the celestial bodies to which they were dedicated. As time went on, layers of details covered the original meaning, but the essence stayed the same. Greek mythology had basically celestial origins. This is important to realize in order to understand astronomy's place in the formation of human culture.

Astronomy played a role during the Paleolithic, the Mesolithic, and the Neolithic. And it continued to play a part in the later times of the tribal system. Greek mythology reflected precisely that. Vivid Greek mythological stories had their origins in Near Eastern astral myths like those of the Mesopotamian *Epic of Creation.*

The celestial map inherited by the Greeks from the older cultures was an essential factor of their world outlook. Thus, the pre-existing celestial tapestry affected Greek myths and not the other way around. The Greeks acquired foreign celestial personages and clothed them appropriately in Greek tunics. Still, it was fundamentally the same production as the one that had been staged long before them.

The role of Rome in the further development of the stellar map seems to be disappointing. Although brilliant as engineers, the Romans followed in the Greek view of the world. Their beliefs were eclectic, and in the touchy issues of philosophy they understood less than their teachers, the Greeks. Once they started proclaiming their deceased emperors gods, they took their religion to absurdity.

Unlike Rome, which did not greatly augment the cultural heritage of Greece, a truly explosive and creative intermixture arose after a brother-in-arms of Alexander the Great, a son of Lagus, and Alexander's most trusted general, known in history as Ptolemy I Soter, moved the Greek genius to the ancient soil of Egypt. Hellenistic Egypt, with its capital in Alexandria, became the soul of western culture. Here, for the first time, the seventy-two Jewish elders translated the Hebrew Bible into Greek. The Alexandrine Museum – the temple of the nine Muses – was the workplace of the greatest mathematician of all time, Euclid. The Alexandrine astronomer, Sosigenus, advised Julius Caesar on his calendar reform, implanting the European calendar for millennia to come. In the 2nd century CE, the grand-master of astronomy and astrology, Claudius Ptolemy, also flourished in Alexandria.

Besides classical Greece and Hellenistic Egypt, ancient astronomical lore found refuge in Persia and a string of other Oriental tyrannies, taking on the form, for example, of such an astral cult as Zoroastrianism. The spiritual descendants of the Orient were probably the Scythians, in whose fine arts, surprising as it may seem, there are a few mysterious zodiacal allusions.

The European astronomical tradition had a stroke of luck in that neither the lawgiver Moses nor any other social and religious leaders specifically tried to obliterate star lore from the minds of their adepts.

Astral Symbolism of Early Christianity

During the very brief historic time of three centuries – starting with the lifetime of Jesus of Nazareth and ending with the first ecumenical council at Niceae – a small group arose and claimed the position of the most powerful world religion. It matured and gained strength due to internal turmoil and external persecutions in the multinational melting pot of the deteriorating Roman Empire. It begot its martyrs and saints, cemented its creeds and canon. Withering, scrapped, the multiracial Empire needed a sort of ideological glue, and Christianity cemented many nations together for centuries to come.

Christianity acted as the tough antagonist to Mithraism, an enigmatic oriental religion originated centuries earlier, probably in Persia. The ancient images of the Western Zodiac came out mostly of Mithraic shrines. D.Ulancey (1989) claimed Mithraists' cryptic doctrines were a *celestial code*, and that the cult began as a religious response to a startling astronomical discovery: the ending of the astronomical Age of Taurus. As to the relationship between Christianity and Mithraism, the principle of *normative inversion* again comes to mind. Mithraism was an astral cult. An open address to celestial links by Mithraism forced the competitors, the founding fathers of Christianity, to do everything they could to eliminate from Christianity its astral rootstock. They succeeded, but not entirely. Some astronomical recollections lingered in early Christianity.

In early Christianity, Jesus Christ was recognized as the *Lamb of God*, "The next day he beheld Jesus coming towards him, and he said 'See the Lamb of God that takes away the sin of world!'…" (John

1:29). Another basic symbol in early Christian iconography was a fish. E.Ferguson (Ferguson *et al.*, 1990) under the entry FISH states:

> "The various uses of the fish symbolism are united by the identification of the fish with Christ... This identification is expressed most clearly in the acrostic on the word 'fish.' The letters of the Greek word for fish (*ichthus*) formed the first letters of the words in the phrase 'Jesus Christ, God's Son, Savior'... The fish was one of the emblems considered suitable on seals for Christians" (p. 351-352).

Christ's coming to the Earth occurred at the very special transition period when the vernal equinox moved out of the constellation of Aries (Ram, or Lamb) into the constellation of Pisces (Fishes). Many times various authors have put forth a guess that those emblems came from astral considerations. The first, Christ as a lamb, was left over from the outgoing astronomical Age of Aries, while the second, Christ as a fish, was a tribute to the oncoming Age of Pisces.

The given example is not unique in the Scripture. Astronomical realities can be found in accounts of the Moon having been created for the reckoning of time, in the "horns" of Moses, in the dances of idolatrous worshippers around a Golden Calf, in the Book of Ezekiel, and in some other Biblical citations. Victorious Christianity had time to eliminate the astronomical legacy of the ancestors; defeated Mithraism carried the secrets of the ancient Zodiac with it to its grave.

With the beginning of the Common Era, Christianity launched a full-scale offensive against astrology, but failed. Astrology remained a viable component of Medieval European culture, and it is astrology that brought to our understanding something from the celestial heritage that was foreign to the Christian credo.

Time flowed and the Middle Ages in Europe were replaced by an era of great seafarers. Sailing overseas opened a passage to the ascent of new constellations in the Southern sky. It was also an impulse for a refurbishing of the northern celestial hemisphere. Old solid reasons for constellation-making and constellation-naming were by this time long lost, and new cognomens frequently made no sense except for the desire to please the patrons of the authors. The tapestry of the sky became even more jumbled and jammed. The supreme goal of astronomy for millennia – the Zodiac as a herald of a reliable solar farmer-herder calendar – was abandoned.

Just like a handful of loose fossils can secure a reconstruction of the entire skeleton of a dinosaur, the loose footprints of former magnificence in the heavens helped us to undertake the reconstruction of the history of the sky. The facts that provide the launching pad for the present reconstruction were mainly borrowed from historical artifacts of the last four-five millennia. But this does not mean that the events they mirror have the same age. Oftentimes, archaeological and historical artifacts are backed by events a far cry older than the artifacts themselves. The underwater portion of the astronomical iceberg submerges into the depths of pre-written history.

The main feature of this study, in the author's mind, is that the derived results, in the terminology of Karl Popper, can be falsified, i.e., confirmed or dismissed with new factual finds. This corresponds to the basic qualifications of a scientific study: the hypothesis proposed here can be checked. The future will arbitrate and put everything in its appropriate place.

A characteristic trait of scientific activity is that one cannot disregard new scientific ideas simply because one does not like them. Ideas in science can only be discredited by better, more perfected ideas. Before our working hypothesis – the Gradualist model - we had not the slightest clue as to how the Zodiac originated. Now we have acquired a springboard of sorts.

ACKNOWLEDGMENTS

For years, I have been lucky to share the benevolent friendship of many colleagues and disciples, and I appreciate their persistent and sincere spiritual endorsement through essential and stimulating discussions of various stances presented on the pages of this book. Age, profession, or nationality does not limit those friends of mine. Fortunately, they are incredibly diverse and, among them, there are established and prolific scholars, publishers, younger post-docs, Russians, Americans, British, French, Germans, Spaniards, representatives of hard sciences as well as students in humanities. Their constructive criticisms and consultations have always proven to be advantageous and contributive. Being, of course, the only person responsible for any downfalls and misinterpretation within this book, it is the author's duty and great pleasure to exhibit his cordial gratitude to all of them.

Especially, I would like to convey my deepest thanks explicitly to such eminent colleagues as Profs. Owen Gingerich (Harvard Smithsonian Center for Astrophysics, Harvard University), the late Boris A. Frolov (Institute for Ethnology, Russian Academy of Sciences), the late Albert P. Gulyaev (Moscow University) and the late Igor M. Diakonoff (St.Petersburg, Russian Academy of Sciences), Vladimir A. Lefebvre (University of California, Irvine), Stephen C. McCluskey (West Virginia University), the late Alexander Marshack (Peabody Museum of Archaeology and Ethnology, Harvard University), Igor L. Kyzlasov (Institute for Archaeology), the late Dmitry S. Raevsky (Institute for Eastern Studies) and the late Vladimir N. Toporov (Institute for Slavic and Balkan Studies), the last three all of the Russian Academy of Sciences, Archie E. Roy (University of Glasgow, Scotland), and Brian Warner (University of Cape Town, South Africa). Some very interesting talks took place with the great person, the late Academician Boris V.

Rauschenbach (Russia), and I am very proud to have been acquainted with him for decades.

Very productive was my three-month long scholarship at *Deutsches Museum* in Munich, Germany.

This book came to light during my enjoyable and fruitful stay at Mesa State College (Colorado, USA), where I had the benefit of using its library and other facilities. For the invitation and extraordinary hospitality that conditioned this productive atmosphere I am cordially obliged to the former Vice-President of the College, Prof. James P. Rybak, and Mrs. Linda Rybak. Today, the college has been re-christened as Colorado Mesa University.

My work on US soil was generously supported by Drs. Fr. George V. Coyne, S.J. (Vatican Observatory), Michael J. Crowe (University of Notre Dame), Steven Dick (then US Naval Observatory), Roslyn M. Frank (University of Iowa), Samuel Gingerich (Mesa State College), Roger Launius (then NASA Headquarters), the late Donald E. Osterbrock (University of California, Santa Cruz).

Professor Robert Anderson, originally of Arizona University, volunteered to do me a priceless favor by putting on his shoulders the massive task of correcting the English of the draft. This book could not have been successfully completed without continuous backing by Mrs. Jane Heitman, the librarian, who very efficiently took care of my literary needs. All members of my family, Olga, Ksenya, and Michael, were patient, supportive, and very instrumental in heated discussions and improving my English, which is not my native language.

A number of scholars assisted me through their consulting and editing of several pieces of the text. For these, my special thanks go to Sara L. Gardner (then University of Arizona), Bradley E. Schaefer (then Yale University), and Michael Szpir (then *American Scientist*).

My sincere acknowledgements also go to Mr. Peter Beer, then Editor of *Vistas in Astronomy*, with whom I shared some remarkable hours of talks. Our correspondence was exhilarating, too.

Some scientists kindly replied to my requests and I used the privileges of their recommendations and advice. In this connection, first of all I would like to thank Drs. Marsha Levine (McDonald Institute for Archaeological Research, Cambridge University) and Marek Zvelebil (Sheffield University).

Many dozens of names are not mentioned here, but once again I take this opportunity to express due respect and gratefulness to all truthful friends and supporters. Not all of those mentioned agree with my scientific visions in their completeness and I am forced to repeat that, if even some of my results are seen to a fierce skeptic to be erroneous or misguided, I alone am responsible for all the aftermath.

SELECTED BIBLIOGRAPHY

Aaboe, Asger, 1991: Babylonian Mathematics, Astrology, and Astronomy. In: *Cambridge Ancient History*, III/2: 276-292.

Ahlström, Gösta Werner, 1994: *The history of ancient Palestine.* - Minneapolis, MN: Fortress Press.

Aitken, M.J., 1990: *Science-based Dating in Archaeology.* - London & New York: Longman.

Aitken, M.J.,C.B.Stringer, and P.A.Mellars, 1992: *The Origin of Modern Humans and the Impact of Chronometric Dating. -* Princeton, NJ: Princeton University Press.

Aldred, Cyril, 1984: *The Egyptians* (revised and enlarged edition). - London & New York: Thames and Hudson.

Aldred, Cyril, 1988: *Akhenaton, King of Egypt* (revised edition). - London & New York: Thames and Hudson.

Allen, James P., 1999: Monotheism - The Egyptian Roots, *Archaeology Odyssey*, **2**, 3 (July/August): 44-54.

Allen, Richard Hinkley, 1963: *Star names: Their Lore and Meaning. -* New York: Dover; 1st edition – *Star Names and Their Meanings*, New York, 1899 by G.E.Stechert.

Al Sufi, Abd al-Rahman b. Umar [10th century CE]: *Book of Fixes Stars. -* Bodleian Library, Oxford. - Manuscript Marsh 144.

Anthony, David W., 2007: *The Horse, the Wheel, and Language: How Bronze-Age Riders from the Eurasian Steppes Shaped the Modern World.* - Princeton University Press.

Anthony, David W. (editor) with Jennifer Y. Chi, 2010: *The Lost World of Old Europe. The Danube Valley, 5000 – 3500 BC.* – New York: Institute for the Study of the Ancient World and Princeton University Press.

Aratus, [c. 275 BCE], 2004: *Phaenomena*. – Cambridge, MA: Cambridge University Press.

Arnold, D., 1991: *Building in Egypt: Pharaonic Stone Masonry*. - New York, NY: Oxford University Press.

Aruz, Joan with Ronald Wallenfels (Eds.), 2003: *Art of the First Cities: The Third Millennium B.C. from the Mediterranean to the Indus*. - New York: The Metropolitan Museum of Art and Yale University Press.

Assmann, Jan, 1997: *Moses the Egyptian. The memory of Egypt in Western monotheism*. - Cambridge, MA & London: Harvard University Press.

Assmann, Jan, 2006: *Religion and Cultural Memory-Ten Studies*. – Stanford: Stanford University Press.

Assmann, Jan, 2011: *Cultural Memory and Early Civilization: Writing, Remembrance, and Political Imagination* (translation from German 1992 volume *Das kulturelle Gedächtnis: Schrift, Erinnerung und politische Identität in frühen Hochkulturen* - Munich: C.H.Beck). – Cambridge, UK: Cambridge University Press.

Åström, Paul (Ed.), 1987-89: *High, middle or low: Acts of an International Colloquium on Absolute Chronology*. 3 pts. - Gothenburg, Sweden: Paul Åström's Förlag.

Atiya, Farid, 2004: *Pyramids of the Fourth Dynasty*. - Cairo: Farid Atiya.

Atkinson, R.J.C., 1975: Megalithic astronomy - a pre-historian's comments, *Journal for the History of Astronomy*, 6: 42-52.

Aurigemma, Luigi, 1976: *Le Signe Zodiacal du Scorpion*. - Paris: Mouton.

Aveni, Anthony F. (Ed.), 1989: *World Archaeoastronomy*. - Cambridge, MA: Cambridge University Press.

Aveni, Anthony F., 1993: *Ancient astronomers*. - Washington: Smithsonian.

Aveni, Anthony F., 1997: *Stairways to the stars: Skywatching in three great ancient cultures*. - New York, NY: John Wiley & Sons.

Aveni, Anthony F., 2002: *Conversing with the Planets: How Science and Myth invented the Cosmos* (revised edition). - Boulder, CO: University Press of Colorado.

Bahn, Paul G. (Ed.), 1996: *Archaeology* (Cambridge Illustrated History). - Cambridge, UK: Cambridge University Press.

Baines, John and Jaromír Málek, 2000: *Cultural Atlas of Ancient Egypt*. - New York, NY: Facts on File.

Ball, Sir Robert Stawell, 1886: *The Story of the Heavens*. – London: Cassell.

Bard, Kathryn A. (Ed.; with S.B.Shubert), 1998: *Encyclopedia of the archaeology of ancient Egypt*. - New York: Routledge.

Baring, Anne & Jules Cashford, 1991: *The Myth of the Goddess: Evolution of an Image*. - London: Viking Arkana.

Barocius, Franciscus, 1585: *Cosmographia in quatuor libros distributa summo ordine, miraque facilitate, ac brevitate ad magnam Ptolemaei mathematicam constructionem, ad universamque astrologiam institutens*. – Venetiae.

Barton, Tamsyn, 1994: *Ancient astrology* (Sciences in antiquity). - London, New York: Routledge.

Bayer, Johannes, 1603: *Uranometria…* - Augsburg.

Becker, U., 1992: Babylonische Sternbilder and Sternnamen, Teil I. *Wissenschaft und Fortschritt*, 42: 235-237 (In German).

Bede (the Venerable; 673-735), 1999: *The Reckoning of Time*. - Liverpool: Liverpool University Press.

Belmonte Avilés, Juan Antonio, 1999: *Las leyes del cielo: Astronomia y civilizaciones antiguas*. – Madrid (In Spanish).

Belmonte Avilés, Juan Antonio and Michael Hoskin, 2002: *Reflejo del cosmos: atlas de arqueoastronomía en el Mediterráneo antiguo*. - Madrid : Equipo Sirius (In Spanish).

Bernal, John Desmond, 1954: *Science in History*. - London: C.A.Watts & Co. (The 3rd edition in four volumes started from 1965).

Bernal, Martin 1987: *Black Athena. The Afroasiatic Roots of Classical Civilization*. Vol. 1: *The Fabrication of Ancient Greece 1785-1985*. - New Brunswick, NJ: Rutgers University.

Bernal, Martin, 1991: *Black Athena*. Vol. 2: *The Archaeological and Documentary Evidence*. - New Brunswick, NJ: Rutgers University.

Bernal, Martin, 1992: Animadversions on the Origins of Western Science, *Isis*, **83**, 4 (December): 596-607.

Bernal, Martin, 2001: *Black Athena Writes Back. Martin Bernal responds to his critics*. - Durham, NC & London: Duke University Press.

Bickermann, Elias J., 1968: *Chronology of the Ancient World*. - London: Thames and Hudson. (The 2nd edition by various publishers in 1980).

Bimson, J. J., 1981: *Redating the Exodus and Conquest*. - Sheffield: Almond.

Blaauw, Adriaan, 1994: *History of the IAU: The Birth and First Half-Century of the International Astronomical Union*. - Dordrecht: Kluwer.

Black, Jeremy and Anthony Green, 1992: *Gods, Demons and Symbols of Ancient Mesopotamia. An Illustrated Dictionary*. - Austin: University of Texas (in cooperation with British Museum Press).

Blum, Howard, 1998: *The Gold of Exodus: Discovery of the True Mount Sinai*. - New York, NY: Simon & Schuster.

Bobrova L., Militarev A., 1993: From Mesopotamia to Greece: to the Origin of Semitic and Greek Star Names. – In: *Die Rolle der Astronomie in den Kulturen Mesopotamiens*, ed. Galter (Grazer Morgenländische Studien, 3). - Graz.

Bogucki, Peter, 1996: The Spread of Early Farming in Europe, *American Scientist*, **84**, 3: 242-253.

Bongard-Levin, Grigory Maksimovich (Ed.), 1988a: *History of the Ancient East*. - Moscow: Nauka (In Russian).

Bongard-Levin, Grigory Maksimovich (Ed.), 1988b: *Inception of the most ancient class societies... Part 2: Near East. Egypt*. - Moscow: Main Publishing Office for Oriental Literature (In Russian).

Borowski, Elie, 1995: Cherubim: God's Throne? *Biblical Archaeology Review*, **21**, 4: 36-42.

Bowker, John, 1997: *The Oxford Dictionary of World Religions*. - Oxford: Oxford University Press.

Boyce, M., 1989: *A History of Zoroastrianism. The Early Period* (Revised ed.). - Leiden: Brill.

Brace, C. Loving, 1991: *The Stages of Human Evolution*, 4th ed. - Engelwood Cliffs, NJ: Prentice-Hall.

Breasted, James Henry, 1905: *A History of Egypt from the Earliest Time to the Persian Conquest*. - New York: Charles Scribner's Sons.

Breasted, James Henry, 1906-1907: *Ancient Records of Egypt*, 5 vols. - Chicago.

Breasted, James Henry, 1912: *The Development of Religion and Thought*. - New York: Charles Scribner's Sons.

Breasted, James Henry, 1933: *The Dawn of Conscience*. - New York: Charles Scribner's Sons.

Brecher, Kenneth and Feirtag, Michael (Ed.), 1979: *Astronomy of the Ancients*. - Cambridge, MA: MIT Press.

Bromley, Yu.V. (Ed.), 1988: *The History of Primeval Society: The Epoch of Class Formation*. - Moscow: Nauka. - (In Russian; the 3rd volume of a series).

Brown, Basil, 1932: *Astronomical Atlases, Maps and Charts: A Historical & General Guide*. – London: Dawsons of Pall Mall.

Brown, P.L., 1979: *Megaliths and masterminds*. - London: Robert Hale.

Brown, Robert, 1899-1900: *Researches into the Origin of the Primitive Constellations of the Greeks, Phoenicians and Babylonians*. Two vol. - London: William & Norgate.

Bruck, H.A. & M.T.Bruck, 1988: *The Peripatetic Astronomer: The Life of Charles Piazzi Smyth*. - Bristol & Philadelphia: Adam Hilger.

Bryan, B.M., 1991: *The Reign of Thutmose IV*. - Baltimore: John Hopkins University Press.

Bud, Robert and Warner, Deborah, 1998: *Instruments of Science: A Historical Encyclopedia*. - London/Washington, DC/New York: Garland.

Budge, Ernest Alfred Wallis, 1925: *Egypt*. - New York: Holt.

Budge, Ernest Alfred Wallis, 1926: *Cleopatra's Needles and Other Egyptian Obelisks*. - London: The Religious Tract Society.

Budge, Ernest Alfred Wallis, 1991 (reprint): *Tutankhamen: Amenism, Atenism, and Egyptian Monotheism*. - New York: Dover.

Bunson, Margaret, 1995: *Dictionary of ancient Egypt*. - New York: Oxford University Press.

Bunson, Margaret, 1999: *Encyclopedia of ancient Egypt*. - New York: Grammercy Book.

Buren, Elizabeth Douglas van, 1937-39: The Scorpion in Mesopotamian Art and Religion, *Archiv fur Orientforschung*, **12**.

Buren, Elizabeth Douglas van, 1939: The Fauna of Ancient Mesopotamia as represented in Art, *Analecta Orientalia*, Rome, **18**.

Buren, Elizabeth Douglas van, 1945: *Symbols of the Gods in Mesopotamian Art*. – Roma: Pontificium institutum biblicum.

Buren, Elizabeth Douglas van, 1980: *Clay Figurines of Babylonia and Assyria*. - New York: AMS Press.

Burkert, Walter, 1987: *Ancient Mystery Cults*. - Cambridge, MA: Harvard University Press.

Burnham, Robert, Jr., 1978: *Burnham's Celestial Handbook. An Observer's Guide*, 3 vols. - New York: Dover.

Bush, Sherida, 1976: Ancient Astronomer - Fact or Fancy? *Psychology Today*, **10**, 7 (December): 100.

Campbell, Joseph, 1974: *The Mythic Image* (Bollingen Series C). - Princeton, NJ: Princeton University Press.

Campion, Nicholas, 2009: *A History of Western Astrology. Vol.1: The Ancient World (first published as The Dawn of Astrology). Vol.2: The Medieval and Modern Worlds.* – London: Continuum.

Campion, Nicholas, 2012: *Astrology and Cosmology in the World's Religions.* - New York, NY: New York University Press.

Cassirer, Ernst, 1923: *Philosophie der symbolischen Formen: Die Sprache.* - Berlin: Bruno Cassirer. Translation: *The Philosophy of Symbolic Forms*, vol. 1: *Language.* - New Haven: Yale University Press, 1953.

Cassirer, Ernst, 1925: *Philosophie der symbolischen Formen: Das mythische Denken.* - Berlin: Bruno Cassirer. Translation: *The Philosophy of Symbolic Forms*, vol. 2: *Mythical Thought.* - New Haven: Yale University Press, 1955.

Cassirer, Ernst, 1929: *Philosophie der symbolischen Formen: Phänomenologie der Erkenntnis.* - Berlin: Bruno Cassirer. - Translation: *The Philosophy of Symbolic Forms*, vol. 3: *The Phenomenology of Knowledge.* - New Haven: Yale University Press, 1957.

Cassirer, Ernst, 1944: *An Essay on Man: An Introduction to a Philosophy of Human Culture.* - New Haven and London: Yale University Press.

Cellarius, Andreas, 1661: *Atlas Coelestis, seu Harmonica Macrocosmica.* – Amsterdam: Johannes Janssonius.

Censorinus [238 CE], 2007: *The birthday book.* – Chicago & London: University of Chicago Press.

Chambers, George F., 1895: *The Story of the Stars.* - New York: Appleton.

Chapman-Rietschi, P.A.L., 1997: Astronomical Conceptions in Mithraic Iconography, *Journal of the Royal Astronomical Society of Canada*, **91**, 6: 133-134.

Charbonneau-Lassay, Louis, 1991: *The Bestiary of Christ*. - New York: Arkana.

Chase, P.G. & Dibble, H.L., 1992: Scientific archaeology and the origins of symbolism: a reply to Bednarik, *Cambridge Archaeological Journal*, **2**: 43-51.

Childe, Vere Gordon, 1925: *The Dawn of European Civilization*. - London: Routledge and Kegan Paul.

Childe, Vere Gordon, 1936: *Man makes himself* (Library of Science & Culture). - London: Watts.

Childe, Vere Gordon, 1942: *What Happened in History*. - Harmondsworth and New York: A Pelican Book by Penguin.

Childe, Vere Gordon, 1958: *The Prehistory of European Society*. - Harmondsworth and New York: Penguin.

Christopoulos, George A. (Ed.), 1974: *History of the Hellenic World: Prehistory and Protohistory*. – Athens, Greece: Ekdotike Athenon.

Cirlot, Juan-Eduardo, 1958: *Diccionario de simbolos tradicionales*. - Madrid. - Translation: Cirlot,J.E., *A Dictionary of Symbols* (2nd edition).- New York: Barnes and Noble, 1995.

Clagett, Marshall, 1955: *Greek Science in Antiquity*. - London: Collier Books.

Clagett, Marshall, 1995: *Ancient Egyptian Science*, vol. 2 (Memoirs of the American Philosophical Society, **214**). - Philadelphia: Am. Phil. Soc.

Clark, John Grahame Douglas, 1939: *Archaeology and Society*. – London: Methuen.

Clark, John Grahame Douglas, 1961: *World Prehistory*. – 3rd edition (1977). - Cambridge: Cambridge University Press.

Clark, John Grahame Douglas, 1977: *World Prehistory in New Perspective*. - Cambridge: Cambridge University Press.

Clark, John Grahame Douglas, 1980: *Symbols of excellence: Precious materials as expressions of status*. - Cambridge: Cambridge University Press.

Clark, John Grahame Douglas, 1980: *Mesolithic Prelude: The Paleolithic-Neolithic Transition in Old World Prehistory*. - Edinburgh: University Press.

Clark, John Grahame Douglas, 1992: *Space, Time and Man: a Prehistorian's View*. - Cambridge: Cambridge University Press.

Clark, Robert Thomas Rundle, 1959: *Myth and Symbol in Ancient Egypt*. – London: Thames and Hudson.

Clayton, Peter A., 1994: *Chronicle of the Pharaohs. The Reign-by-Reign Record of the Rulers and Dynasties of Ancient Egypt*. - London: Thames and Hudson.

Clutton-Brock, J., 1981: *Domesticated Animals from Early Times*. - Austin: University of Texas Press; London: British Museum.

Cocks, Elijah E. & Josiah C. Cocks, 1995: *Who's Who on the Moon: A Biographical Dictionary*. - Greensboro, NC: Tudor Publishers.

Cohen, I. Bernard, 1983: Éloge. Willy Hartner, 22 January 1905 – 16 May 1981, *Isis*, 74: 86-87.

Cohen, Mark E., 1993: *The Cultic Calendars of the Ancient Near East*. - Bethesda, MD: CDL Press.

Colson, F.H., 1926: *The Week: An Essay on the Origin & Development of the Seven-Day Cycle*. - London: Cambridge University Press.

Comay, Joan and Ronald Brownrigg, 1971: *Who's Who in the Bible*. Two vols in one. - Later edition (1993) by Wings Books.

Condos, Theony, 1997: *Star Myths of the Greeks and Romans. A Sourcebook*. - Grand Rapids, MI: Phanes Press.

Cornell, James, 1981: *The first stargazers*. - Old Tappan, NJ: Scribner.

Courtois, Jacques-Claude and Jacques and Elisabeth Lagarce, 1986: *Enkomi et le Bronze Récent à Chypre*. - Nicosia: Imprimerie Zavallis.

Crommelin, A.C.D., 1923: The Ancient Constellation Figures. In: *Hutchinson's Splendour of the Heavens*, (Ed. by T.E.R. Phillips and W.H.Steavenson), **2**, XVII: 640-669. - London: Hutchinson.

Cui, Shizhu, 1997: Astronomy and Culture in China. In: *Oriental Astronomy from Guo Shoujing to King Sejong*, ed. by Nha Il-Seong and F.Richard Stephenson: 29-43. - Seoul, Republic of Korea.

Cumont, Franz, 1956: *The Mysteries of Mithra*. - New York: Dover.

Cumont, Franz, 1960: *Astrology and Religion among the Greeks and Romans*. - New York: Dover.

Currid, J., 1991: An Examination of the Egyptian Background of the Genesis Cosmology, *Biblische Zeitschrift*, 35: 18-40.

Dashevsky, G., 1988: Preface to the translation *Celestial Phenomena after Aratus*. - In: *Research in History of Astronomy*, **20**: 336-345. – Moscow: Nauka (In Russian).

David, Rosalie and David A.E., 1991: *Biographical Dictionary of Ancient Egypt*. – London: Routledge.

Davies, Philip, 1992: *In Search of "Ancient Israel"*. - Sheffield: JSOT.

Davies, Philip, 2000: What Separates a Minimalist from a Maximalist? Not Much. - *Biblical Archaeological Review*, **26**, 2: 24-27 and 72-73.

Davis, George A., 1959: The Origin of the Constellations, *Sky & Telescope*, **18**, 8: 424-427.

Dekker, Elly, 1987a: Early Explorations of the Southern Celestial Sky. - *Annals of Science*, **44:** 439-470.

Dekker, Elly, 1987b: On the Dispersal of Knowledge of the Southern Celestial Sky. - *Der Globusfreund*, 35-37: 211-230.

Dekker, Elly, 1992: Der Himmelsglobus - Eine Welt für sich. - In: *Focus Behaim Globus*. - Nürnberg: Germanischen Nationalmuseums, **1**: 89-100.

Delporte, Eugène Joseph, 1930: *Délimitation scientifique des constellations: (tables et cartes)*. Report of Commission 3 of the International astronomical union. - Cambridge, UK: Cambridge University Press.

Depuydt, Leo, 1997: *Civil calendar and Lunar calendar in Ancient Egypt* (Orientalia Lovaniensia Analecta, 77).- Leuven, Belgium: Uitgeverij Peeters en Departement Oosterse Studies.

Desmond, A., 1982: *Archetypes and Ancestors*. - Chicago: University of Chicago Press.

Dever, William G., 2000: Save Us from Postmodern Malarkey. - *Biblical Archaeological Review*, **26**, 2: 28-35 and 68-69.

Diakonoff, Igor Mikhailovich (Ed.), 1983: *Inception of the most ancient class societies...* Part 1: *Mesopotamia*. - Moscow: Main Publishing Office for Oriental Literature (In Russian).

Diakonoff, Igor Mikhailovich, 1999: *The paths of history*. - Cambridge, UK: Cambridge University Press.

Dicks, D.R., 1970: *Early Greek Astronomy to Aristotle*. - Bristol: Thames and Hudson.

Diel, P., 1952: *Le Symbolisme dans la mythologie grecque*. – Paris (In French).

Dodson, Aidan Mark, 1995: *Monarchs of the Nile*. - London: Rubicon Press.

Dolgopolsky, Aharon, 1998: *The Nostratic Macrofamily and Linguistic Paleontology*. - Cambridge, UK: The McDonald Institute for Archaeological Research.

Drummond, Sir William, 1811: *The Oedipus Judaicus*. - Reprint by Research Into Lost Knowledge Organization via R.I.L.K.O.Books, Orpington, UK, 1986.

Duncan, David Ewing, 1998: *Calendar: Humanity's Epic Struggle to Determine a True and Accurate Year*. - New York: Avon Books.

Dupui, Charles François, 1781: *Memoire sur l'origine des constellations et sur l'explication de la fable pour le moyen de l'astronomie*. - Paris: V.Desaint (In French).

Dupui, Charles François, 1795: *Origine de tous les Cultes, ou Religion Universelle*, 12 vols. - Paris: H.Agasse. - Abridged translation 1984: *The Origin of all Religious Worship*. - New York: Garland.

Dupui, Charles François, 1806: *Memoire explicatif du zodiaque chronologique et mythologique*. – Paris (In French).

Edwards, Iorwerth Elddon Stephen, 1993: *The Pyramids of Egypt (With new material)*. - Revised Ed. - Harmondsworth and New York: Penguin.

Eliade, Mirca, 1949: *Le Mythe de l'eternal retour: Archetypes et repetition*. - Paris: Librairie Gallimard. First English translation in 1954 by Pantheon Books under the title *The Myth of the Eternal Return*.

Eliade, Mirca, 1952: *Images et Symboles*. – Paris (In French).

Eliade, Mircea, 1959: *The Sacred and the Profane*. - New York: Harcourt, Brace, and World.

Eliade, Mircea, 1967: *Gods, Goddesses, and Myths of Creation*. – New York.

Eliade, Mircea, 1974: *Patterns in Comparative Religion*. - New York: Meridian.

Eliade, Mirca, 1978: *A History of Religious Ideas: from the Stone Age to the Eleusian Mysteries*, vol. 1. - Chicago: University of Chicago Press.

Eliade, Mirca, 1992: Myths, dreams, and mysteries: the encounter between contemporary faiths and archaic realities. - Magnolia, MA: Smyth.

El-Sabban, Sherif, 1992: The Temple Calendars of Ancient Egypt. – *Dissertation*: University of Liverpool.

Elst, Koenraad, 1999: *Update on The Aryan Invasion Debate*. - New Delhi: Aditya Prakashah.

Emel'yanov, Vladimir Vladimirovich, 1999: *Nippur calendar and the early history of the Zodiac*. - Saint-Petersburg: Peterburgskoe Vostokove-denie (In Russian).

Evans, James, 1998: *The History and Practice of Ancient Astronomy*. - Oxford, UK: Oxford University Press.

Fagan, Brian M. (Ed.), 1996: *The Oxford Companion to Archaeology*. - New York, Oxford: Oxford University Press.

Fagan, Cyril, 1971: *Astrological Origins*. - St. Paul, MN: Llewellyn.

Fagan, Cyril and Firebrace, R.C., 1950: *Zodiacs Old and New*. - St.Paul, MN: Llewellyn.

Fagan, Cyril & Firebrace, R.C., 1971: Primer of Sideral Astrology.

Feder, Kenneth L., 1996: *The Past in Perspective: An Introduction to Human Prehistory*. - Mountain View, CA: Mayfield.

Ferguson, Everett (Ed.), 1990: *Encyclopedia of Early Christianity*. - New York & London: Garland.

Ferguson, George W., 1954: *Signs and Symbols in Christian Art*. – New York: Oxford University Press.

Fideler, David, 1993: *Jesus Christ, Sun of God. Ancient Cosmology and Early Christian Symbolism*. - Wheaton, 1L: Quest Books.

Finkelstein, Israel and Neil Asher Silberman, 2001: *The Bible Unearthed: Archaeolgy's New Vision of Ancient Israel and the Origin of Its Sacred Texts*. - New York: The Free Press.

Firmicus Maternus, Julius [IV century CE], 1975: *Mathesis. Ancient Astrology: theory and practice* (Noyes classical studies). - Park Ridge, NJ: Noyes Press.

Fishof, Iris (with A.Cohen and M.Idel), 2001. *Written in the Stars. Art and Symbolism of the Zodiac*. - Jerusalem: The Israel Museum.

Flammarion, Camille, 1872: *Histoire du Ciel.* - Paris: J.Hetzel (In French).

Flammarion, Camille, 1880: *L'Astronomie populaire.* - Paris: C.Marpon et E.Flammarion. Translation: *The Flammarion book of astronomy.* - New York: Simon & Schuster, 1964.

Flannery, K.V., 1972: The cultural evolution of civilizations, *Annual Review of Ecology and Systematics*, 3: 399-426.

Fletcher, Joann, 2000: Chronicle of a pharaoh: The intimate life of Amenhotep III. - New York: Oxford University Press.

Foxvog, D., 1993: Astral Dumuzi. In: *Near Eastern Studies in Honour of W.W.Hallo.* – Bethesda: 103-108.

Frankfort, Henry, 1948: *Ancient Egyptian Religion: An Interpretation.* - New York: Harper & Row.

Frankfort, Henry, Frankfort, H.A., Wilson, J.A., Jacobsen Thorkild, and Irwin, William A., 1977: *The Intellectual Adventure of Ancient Man. An Essay on Speculative Thought in the Ancient Near East.* - Chicago & London: The University of Chicago Press.

Frazer, Sir James G., 1890-15: The Golden Bough. A study in magic and religion, 12 vols. - London. The author's own abridgment in one volume was first published in 1922.

Freed, Rita E., Yvonne J. Markowitz and Sue H. D'Auria (Eds.), 1999: *Pharaohs of the Sun: Akhenaten, Nefertiti, Tutankhamen.* - Boston: Museum of Fine Arts, in association with Bulfinch Press/Little, Brown and Company.

Frere, N., 1784-1793: Observations generales sur l'origine et sur l'ancienne histoire des premiers habitants de la Grece Academie des Inscriptions, 47 (published 1809), Memoire de Litterature: 1-149.

Frerichs, Ernst S., Lesko, Leonard H. (Eds.), 1997: *Exodus: The Egyptian Evidence.* - Winona Lake, IN: Eisenbrauns.

Freud, Sigmund, 1939: *Moses and Monotheism.* Translation - New York: Vintage (Vintage works of science and psychology, **14**).

Frolov, Boris Alexeevich, 1972: The "magic seven", *Priroda*, 5: 52-59. (In Russian).

Frolov, Boris Alexeevich, 1974: *Numbers in Paleolithic graphics.* - Novosibirsk: Nauka (In Russian).

Frolov, Boris Alexeevich, 1977: Back to the sources of primordial astronomy, *Priroda*, 8 (In Russian).

Frolov, Boris Alexeevich, 1977-79: Numbers in Paleolithic graphic art and the Initial Stages of Development of Mathematics, Part 1. *Soviet Anthropology and Archeology* (1977-78), **16**, 3-4: 142-166; Part 2 (1978), **17**, 1: 73-93; Part 3 (1979), **17**, 3: 41-74; Part 4 (1979), **17**, 4: 61-113 [Translation of the Russian book of 1974].

Frolov, Boris Alexeevich, 1981: On astronomy in the Stone Age, *Current anthropology*, **22**, 5: 585.

Frolov, Boris Alexeevich, 1992: *Primordial graphics of Europe.* - Moscow: Nauka (In Russian).

Gamble, Clive, 1994: *Timewalkers: The Prehistory of Global Colonization.* - Cambridge, MA: Harvard University Press.

Gamkrelidze Thomas V. and Vjacheslav V. Ivanov, 1984: *Indo-European and the Indo-Europeans. A reconstruction and historical typological analysis of a proto-language and a proto-culture.* In two parts. - Tbilisi (In Russian).

Gamkrelidze Thomas V. and Vjacheslav V. Ivanov, 1990: The early history of Indo-European languages, *Scientific American,* 262, 3: 110-116.

Gamkrelidze Thomas V. and Vjacheslav V. Ivanov, 1995: *Indo-European and the Indo-Europeans: A reconstruction and historical analysis of a proto-language and a proto-culture* (Trends in Linguistics. Studies and Monographs). – Berlin, New York: Mouton de Gruyter.

Garin, Eugenio, 1983: *Astrology in the Renaissance: The Zodiac of Life.* - London: Routledge & Kegan Paul.

Gee, Emma, 2000: *Ovid, Aratus and Augustus: astronomy in Ovid's Fasti.* - Cambridge, MA: Cambridge University Press.

Germond, Philippe and Jacques Livet, 2001: *An Egyptian Bestiary: Animals in Life and Religion in the Land of Pharaohs.* - London: Thames & Hudson.

Gillispie, Charles Coulston (Ed.), 1970-74: *Dictionary of scientific biography*, 15 vols. - New York: Charles Scribner's Sons.

Gimbutas, Marija Alseikaite, 1982: *The Goddesses and Gods of Old Europe, 6500-3500 BC: Myths and Cult Images.* New and updated edition. - Berkley and Los Angeles, CA: University of California Press.

Gingerich, Owen, 1992: *The Great Copernicus Chase and other adventures in astronomical history*. - Cambridge, MA: Sky Publishing Company & Cambridge University Press.

Godwin, Joscelyn, 1981: *Mystery Religions in the Ancient World*. - London: Thames & Hudson.

Goff, Beatrice Laura, 1963: *Symbols of Prehistoric Mesopotamia*. - New Haven and London: Yale University Press.

Golan, Ariel, 1991: *Myth and Symbol. Symbolism in Prehistoric Religions*. - Jerusalem: Rubin Mass.

Goldstein, Bernard R., 1985: *Theory and observation in ancient and medieval astronomy*. - London: Variorum Reprints.

Gleadow, Rupert, 1968: *The Origin of the Zodiac*. - London: Jonathan Cape.

Goblet d'Alviella, Eugene, 1956: *The Migration of Symbols*. - New York: University Books.

Goodenough, Erwin Ramsdell, 1988: *Jewish symbols in the Greco-Roman period*. (Bollingen series). - Princeton, NJ: Princeton University.

Gössmann P., 1950: Planetarium Babylonicum. In: *Sumerisches Lexikon*, ed. P. Anton Deimel, **2**, IV. - Rome, Pap stl. Bibel-instituts.

Grakov, Boris Nikolaevich, 1971: *The Scythians*. - Moscow: Moscow University (In Russian).

Griffiths, J. Gwyn, 1953: The Egyptian Name Of Moses, *Journal of Near Eastern Studies*, **12**: 225-231.

Grimal, Nicolas, 1997: *A History of Ancient Egypt*. - Barnes & Noble Books.

Grimaldi, Alexander Beaufort, 1905: *Catalogue of Zodiacs and Planispheres: Ancient and Modern*. - London: Gall and Inglis.

Grottanelli, Cristiano, 1986: Yoked Horses, Twins, and the Powerful Lady: India, Greece, Ireland and Elsewhere, *Journal of Indo-European studies*, **14**: 125-152.

Gundel, Hans Georg, 1992: *Zodiakos: Tierkreisbilder im Altertum* (Kulturgeschichte der Antiken Welt, Band 54). - Mainz am Rhein: Philipp von Zabern (In German).

Gurshtein, A.A., 1991: Reconstruction of Zodiacal Constellation's Origin. In: *Advance Towards Cognition of the Universe* (Research in the History of Astronomy, **23**). - Moscow: Nauka: 19-62 (In Russian).

Gurshtein, A.A., 1993a: On the Origin of the Zodiacal Constellations, *Vistas in Astronomy*, **36**, part 2: 171-190.

Gurshtein, A.A., 1993b: The Zodiac and the Roots of European Civilization, *preprint for the International Archaeoastronomical Conference Oxford-4*. – Bulgaria: Stara Zagora.

Gurshtein, A.A., 1994a: Dating the Origin of Constellations by Precession, *Physics-Doklady* (Translation of the Russian Academy of Sciences Transactions), **39**, 8: 575-578.

Gurshtein, A.A., 1994b: Signs of the Zodiac: at the Dawn of Culture, *Science in Russia*, 5 (October): 28-33.

Gurshtein, A.A., 1994c: Problems mit Widder und Waage. Tierkreis-Sternbilder in der Antike, *Kultur und Technik*, 2: 28-29 (In German).

Gurshtein, A.A., 1995a: Prehistory of Zodiac Dating: Three Strata of Upper Paleolithic Constellations, *Vistas in Astronomy*, **39**: 347-362.

Gurshtein, A.A., 1995b: When the Zodiac Climbed into the Sky? *Sky & Telescope*, **90**, 4: 28-33.

Gurshtein, A.A., 1995c: Discovery of Prehistoric Skies, *Bulletin of the American Astronomical Society*, **27**, 4, abstract 27.01.

Gurshtein, A.A., 1996a: The Great Pyramids of Egypt as Sanctuaries Commemorating the Origin of the Zodiac: An Analysis of Astronomical Evidence, *Physics-Doklady*, **41**, 5: 228-232.

Gurshtein, A.A., 1996b: The Evolution of the Zodiac in the context of ancient Egyptian history, *Abstracts for Oxford-5 Conference*. - Santa Fe, New Mexico.

Gurshtein, A.A., 1996c: Past Civilizations as Imprinted in the Zodiac. In: Magisterium. - Moscow: 43-54.

Gurshtein, A.A., 1997a: The portrays of the archaic constellations: seven was their number, *Bulletin of the AAS*, **29**, 5, abstract 35.04.

Gurshtein, A.A., 1997b: Origins of Constellations and Their Egyptian Links (abstract for invited lecture), *Third Biennial History of Astronomy Workshop*. - University of Notre Dame.

Gurshtein, A.A., 1997c: The Origins of Constellations, *American Scientist*, **85**, 3: 264-273.

Gurshtein, A.A., 1997d: In Search of the First Constellations, *Sky & Telescope*, **93**, 6: 46-50.

Gurshtein, A.A., 1997e: Ursa Major and the Number Seven, *Sky & Telescope*, **93**, 6: 50.

Gurshtein, A.A., 1998: The Evolution of the Zodiac in the Context of Ancient Oriental History, *Vistas in Astronomy*, **41**, 4: 507-525.

Gurshtein, A.A., 2004: Relevant queries in respect to the archaic Chinese sky. In: *Astronomical Instruments and Archives from the Asia-Pacific Region* (edited by Orchiston, Stephenson, Débarbat, and Nha). - Seoul, Republic of Korea: Yonsei University Press: 75-79.

Gurshtein, A.A., 2005: Did the Pre-Indo-Europeans Influence the Formation of the Western Zodiac? *Journal of Indo-European Studies*, **33**, 1/2: 103-150.

Gurshtein, A.A., 2006: L'età della mappa celeste, *Prometeo*, **24**, 93: 76-83 (In Italian).

Gurshtein, A.A., 2017: Pietre Miliari Dell'Astronomia Premoderna, *Prometeo*, **36**, 138: 39-45 (In Italian).

Haak Wolfgang, Iosif Lazaridis, Nick Patterson, et al., 2015: Massive migration from the steppe was a source for Indo-European languages in Europe, *Nature*, **522**: 207–211 (11 June).

Hall, Manly P., 1927: *An encyclopedic outline of Masonic, Germetic, Qabbalistic and Rosirrurian Symbolical Philosophy*. - San Francisco: H.S.Crocker.

Hamp, Eric P., 1974: The Principal (?) Indo-European Constellations. In: *Proceedings of the Eleventh International Congress of Linguists*, **II**. - Bologna: Societa editrice il Mulino.

Harris, James Rendel, 1903: *The Dioscuri in the Christian Legends*. - London: C.J.Clay and sons.

Harris, James Rendel, 1906: *The Cult of the Heavenly Twins*. – Cambridge, UK: The University Press.

Harris, James Rendel, 1913: *Boanerges*. – Cambridge, UK: The University Press.

Harris, Marvin, 1968: *The Rise of Anthropological Theory: A History of Theories of Culture*. - New York: Thomas Y. Crowell.

Harrison, Simon, 1995: Four types of symbolic conflicts, *Journal of the Royal Anthropological Institute*, **1**, 2: 255-72.

Hart, George, 1986: *A Dictionary of Egyptian Gods and Goddesses.* - Boston: Routledge & Kegan Paul.

Hartner, Willy, 1965: The earliest history of the Constellations in the Near East and the motif of the Lion-Bull combat, *Journal of Near Eastern Studies*, **24**, 1-2: 1-16.

Hawass, Zahi A., 1990: *The Pyramids of Ancient Egypt.* - Pittsburgh: Carnegie Museum of Natural History.

Haywood, John with Brian Catchpole, Simon Hall, and Edward Barratt, 1997: *Atlas of World History.* - New York: Barnes & Noble.

Heatly, Maurice D., 1971: The Message of the Mazzaroth, *A Thesis Presented to the Faculty of the Department of Bible Exposition*, Dallas Theological Seminary.

Heggie, D.C.(Ed.), 1982: *Archaeoastronomy in the Old World.* Cambridge, MA: Cambridge University Press.

Herodotus [5th century BCE], 1996: *Histories.* - Ware, Hertfordshire: Wordsworth Classics.

Hesiod [8th century BCE], 1936: *Works and Days.* - In: *Hesiod, Homeric Hymns, Epic Cycle, Homerica.* - Cambridge, MA.

Hetherington, Barry, 1996: *A Chronicle of Pre-telescopic Astronomy.* - Chichester: John Wiley.

Hetherington, Norriss S., 1987: *Ancient Astronomy and Civilization* (History of astronomy series, 6). – Tucson, AZ: Pachart.

Heuter, Gwyneth, 1986: Star Names - Origins and Misconceptions, *Vistas in Astronomy*, **29**: 237-251.

Hinze, Oscar Marcel, 1966: Studien zum Verstandnis der archaischen Astronomie, *Symbolon*, **5**: 162-219 (In German).

Ho, Ping-Ti, 1975: *The Cradle of the East.* - Hong Kong: Chinese University.

Hodder, I., 1982a: *Symbols in Action: ethnoarchaeological studies of material culture.* - Cambridge: Cambridge University Press.

Hodder, I., 1982b: *The Present Past.* - London: Bastford.

Hodder, I., 1986: *Reading the Past.* - Cambridge: Cambridge University.

Hodder, I., 1990: *Domestication of Europe.* - Oxford: Blackwell.

Hoffman, M.A., 1991: *Egypt before the Pharaohs.* Rev. & updated ed. - Austin: University of Texas.

Hoffmeier, James K., 1999: *Israel in Egypt: The Evidence for the Authencity of the Exodus Tradition*. - New York and Oxford: Oxford University.

Holocene Settlement of the Egyptian Sahara, 2001-2002. – Vol. 1. *The Archaeology of Nabta Playa*, by Fred Wendorf, Romuald Schild, and Associates. Vol. 2. *The Pottery of Nabta Playa*, by Kit Nelson and Associates. - New York: Kluwer/Plenum.

Homer [9th century BCE], 1952: The Iliad; The Odyssey (Great Books of the Western World, 4). – Chicago: Encyclopedia Britannica (Benton).

Hornung, Eric, 1999: *Akhenaten and the Relgion of Light* (Translation from German of 1995). - Ithaca & London: Cornell University.

Horowitz, Wayne, 1998: Mesopotamian Cosmic Geography *(Mesopotamian Civilizations, 8)*. – Winona Lake, Indiana: Eisenbrauns.

Hornung, Eric; Rolf Krauss and David A.Warburton (Eds.), 2005: *Ancient Egyptian Chronology (Handbook of Oriental Studies)*. – Brill.

Hoskin, Michael (Ed.), 1997: *Astronomy* (Cambridge Illustrated History). – Cambridge, UK: Cambridge University Press.

Hucker, Charles O, 1975: *China's Imperial Past: An Introduction to Chinese History and Culture*. - Stanford, CA: Stanford University Press.

Hunger, Hermann, 1992: *Astrological Reports to Assyrian Kings* (State Archives of Assyria, 8). – Helsinki: Helsinki University Press.

Hunger, Hermann and David Pingree, 1989: MUL.APIN (An Astronomical Compendium in Cuneiform), *Archiv fur Orientforschung*, 24.

Hunger, Hermann and David Pingree, 1999: *Astral science in Mesopotamia*. (Handbook of Oriental Studies. The Near and Middle East, 44). - Leiden: Brill.

Hurry, Jamieson Boyd, 1978: *Imhotep. The Vizier and Physician of King Zoser and afterwards the Egyptian God of Medicine* (Reprint from the 2nd revised edition of 1928). - New York: AMS.

Hyginus, Gaius Julius [1st century CE], 1482: *Poeticon Astronomicon*. - Venice: Ratdolt. Translation: 1985, Greenbrae, CA: Allen.

Ideler, Christian Ludwig, 1806: *Historische Untersuchungen über die astromischen Beobachtungen der Alten.* - Berlin: Quien (In German).

Ideler, Christian Ludwig, 1809: *Untersuchungen über der Ursprung und die Bedeutung der Sternnamen.* - Berlin: J.F.Weiss (In German).

Ideler, Christian Ludwig, 1815: *Sternkunde der Chaldaer.* – Berlin (In German).

Ideler, Christian Ludwig, 1825-1826: *Handbuch der mathematischen und technischen Chronologie,* 2 vols. - Berlin: Rucker (In German).

Ideler, Christian Ludwig, 1931: *Lehrbuch der Chronologie.* - Berlin: Rucker (In German).

Ivanov, Vaycheslav Vsevolodovich, 2008: *Dual structures in anthropology.* – Moscow: Russian State Humanitarian University (In Russian).

Iwaniszewski, Stanislaw, 1999: Archaeoastronomy in Traditional Areas of Eurasia, *Archaeoastronomy,* **XIV**, 2: 87-127.

Jones S., R. Martin, and D. Pilbeam (Eds.), 1992: *The Cambridge Encyclopedia of Human Evolution.* - Cambridge, MA: Cambridge University Press.

Josephus Flavius [1st century CE], 1963: *Complete works.* - London: Pickering & Inglis.

Judge, Michael, 2004: *The Dance of Time. The Origins of the Calendar.* - New York: Arcade.

Kak, Subhash, 1997: Archaeoastronomy and literature, *Current Science,* 73: 624-627.

Kak, Subhash, 1998: Astronomy and its role in Vedic culture. In: *Science and Civilization in India,* vol. 1, *The Dawn of Indian civilization,* Part 1, (ed. G.C.Pande): 507-524. - Oxford: Oxford University Press.

Kanas, Nick, 2007: *Star Maps: History, Artistry, and Cartography.* – Chichister, UK: Praxis.

Karpenko, Yu.A., 1981: *The Names of the Starry Sky.* - Moscow: Nauka (In Russian).

Kelley, David H. and Eugene F. Milone, 2005 (2nd edition 2011): *Exploring Ancient Skies: An Encyclopedic Survey of Archaeoastronomy.* – New York: Springer.

Kendall, D.G., Piggott, S., King-Hele, D.G., Edwards, I.E.S. (orgs.), Hodson, E.R. (Ed.), 1974: *The Place of Astronomy in the Ancient*

World, A Joint Symposium of the Royal Society and the British Academy. - Oxford: Oxford University Press.

Kerns, John C., 1985: *Indo-European Prehistory*.- Cambridge: Heffer & Sons.

King, Henry C., 1957: *The Background of Astronomy*. – New York: Braziller.

Kitson, Annabella (Ed.), 1989: *History and Astrology; Clio and Urania confer*. - London: Unwin.

Klein, Richard G., 1999: *The Human Career: Human Biological and Cultural Origins*. - Chicago and London: University of Chicago Press.

Koch-Westenholz, Ulla, 1995: *Mesopotamian astrology. An Introduction to Babylonian and Assyrian celestial divination* (The Carsten Niebuhr Institute of Near Eastern Studies, **19**). - Copenhagen: Museum Tusculanum Press.

Kohen, I. Bernard, 1983: Éloge: Willy Hartner (1905-1981), *Isis*, **74**: 86.

Kottak, Conrad P., 2005: *Window on Humanity: A Concise Introduction to Anthropology*. - Boston: McGraw-Hill.

Koyré, Alexander, 1985: *Essays on the History of Philosophical Thought*. - Moscow: Progress (In Russian).

Koyré, Alexander, 1992: The astronomical revolution: Copernicus, Kepler, Borelli. - New York: Dover.

Kramer, Samuel Noah, 1944: *Sumerian Mythology: A Study of Spiritual and Literary Achievements in the Third Millennium B.C.* – Philadelphia: American Philosophical Society.

Kramer, Samuel Noah, 1956: *From the tablets of Sumer*. - Indian Hills, CO: Falcon's Wing. - Under the title *History begins in Sumer* published in 1959: Doubleday, Anchor Book.

Kramer, Samuel Noah, 1963: *The Sumerians: Their History, Culture and Character*. – Chicago: University of Chicago.

Krauss, Rolf K., 1981: Probleme des altaegyptischen Kalenders und der Chronologie des mittlern und neuen Reiches in Aegypten. - *Dissertation*. – Berlin (In German).

Krauss, Rolf K., 1997: Astronomische Konzepte und Jenseitsvorstellungen in den Pyramidentexten. – Wiesbaden: Harrassowitz (In German).

Kripke, Saul A., 1980: *Naming and Necessity.* – Cambridge, MA: Harvard University Press.

Krupp, E.C. (Ed.), 1978: *In search of ancient astronomies.* - Garden City, NY: Doubleday.

Krupp, E.C., 1983: *Echoes of the Ancient Skies.* - New York: Harper & Row.

Krupp, E.C., 1984: *Archaeoastronomy and the Roots of Science.* - Boulder, CO/Washington, DC: Westview Press/AAAS.

Krupp, E.C., 1991: *Beyond the Blue Horizon: Myths and Legends of the Sun, Moon, Stars, and Planets.* - New York: HarperCollins.

Krupp, E.C., 1997: *Skywatchers, Shamans & Kings: Astronomy and the Archaeology of Power.* - New York: John Wiley & Sons.

Krupp, E.C., 2000: Night Gallery: The Function, Origin, and Evolution of Constellations, *Archaeoastronomy,* **XV**: 43-63.

Kugler, F.X., 1907-35: *Sternkunde und Sterndienst in Babel.* Assyriologische, astronomische und astralmythologische Untersuchungen von Franz Xaver Kugler S.J. – Muenster (In German).

Kunitzsch, Paul, 1989: *The Arabs and the stars: texts and traditions on the fixed stars, and their influence in medieval Europe.* - Northampton, UK: Variorum Reprints.

Kurtik, Gennady Evseevich, 2007: *The Star Heaven of ancient Mesopotamia: the Sumero-Akkadian Names of Constellations and Other Heavenly Bodies.* - St.Petersburg: Aletheia (In Russian).

Kyzlasov, Igor Leonidovich, 1995: History of the Zodiac: General Approaches and Problems, *Vestnik Drevnei Istorii (The Herald of Ancient History)*, 1 (212): 161-164 (In Russian).

Landes, D.S., 1983: *Revolution in time.*- Cambridge, MA: Harvard University.

Langdon, Stephen Herbert, 1935: *Babylonian Menologies and the Semitic Calendars.* - Oxford, UK: Oxford University Press.

Lankford, John (Ed.), 1997: *History of Astronomy: An Encyclopedia.* - New York & London: Garland.

Laplace, Pierre Simon, marquis de, 1796: *Exposition du systême du Monde.* - Paris: De l'imprimerie du Cercle-Social. Translation: *The system of the world.* - Dublin, 1830.

Lawler, Andrew, 2001: Writing Gets a Rewrite, *Science,* **292**, 5526: 2418-20.

Lefkowitz, Mary R. and Rogers, Guy MacLean (Eds.), 1996: *Black Athena Revisited.* - Chapel Hill: University of North Carolina.

Lehmann, Winfred P., 2002: *Pre-Indo-Europeans* (Journal of Indo-European Studies Monograph Series, 41). - Washington, D.C.

Lehner, Mark, 1997: *The Complete Pyramids.* - London: Thames and Hudson.

Lehner, Mark and other participants of the David H. Koch Pyramids Radiocarbon Project, 1999: Dating the Pyramid, *Archaeology,* **52**, 5: 26-33.

Leitz, Christian, 1989: *Studien zur agyptischen Astronomie* (Agyptologische Abhandlungen, 49). - Wiesbaden: Harrassowitz (In German).

Lemche, Niels Peter, 1998: *The Israelites in History and Tradition.* - London: SPCK; Louisville: Westminster John Knox.

Lévêque, Pierre, 1969: *Le Monde Hellénnistique.* - Paris: Armand Colin (In French).

Lévi-Strauss, Claude, 1966: *The Savage Mind.* - Chicago: The University of Chicago Press.

Levy, Thomas E., 2000: Remember Marcellus's Warning, *Science,* **289**, 5482: 1145-46.

Lewis, G.C., 1862: *A Historical Survey of the Astronomy of the Ancients.* - London: Parker, Son, and Bourn, West Strand.

Lindly, J.M. & G.A.Clark, 1990: Symbolism and modern human origins, *Current Anthropology,* **31**: 233-261.

Livingstone, Alasdair, 1986: *Mystical and Mythological Explanatory Works of Assyrian and Babylonian Scholars.* – Oxford, UK: Oxford University Press.

Lloyd, Seton, 1984: *The Archaeology of Mesopotamia: From the Old Stone Age to the Persian Conquest* (revised). – London: Thames & Hudson.

Lockyer, Sir Joseph Norman, 1894: *The Dawn of Astronomy.* - London: Cassell. – Reprint: Cambridge, MA: MIT Press, 1965.

Lum, Peter, 1948: *The Stars in our Heaven: Myths and fables.* – New York: Pantheon Books.

MacDonald, John, 1998: *The Arctic Sky: Inuit Astronomy, Star Lore, and Legend.* – Toronto: Royal Ontario Museum.

Macey, Samuel L. (Ed.), 1994: *Encyclopedia of Time*. - New York & London: Garland.

Mackay, Damien F., 1995: The Sothic star theory of the Egyptian calendar (A Critical Evaluation), *MA Thesis* (University of Sydney).

Macrobius [c. 410 CE], 1990: *Commentary on the Dream of Scipio* (Records of Western Civilization). - New York: Columbia University Press.

Málek, Jaromír, 1999: *Egyptian art*. - London: Phaidon.

Malinowsky, Bronislaw, 1944: *A Scientific Theory of Culture and other essays*. - Chapel Hill: University of North Carolina Press.

Malinowsky, Bronislaw, 1948: *Magic, Science and Religion and other essays*. – Boston: Beacon.

Mallory, James P., 1989: *In Search of the Indo-Europeans: Language, Archaeology and Myth*. - London: Thames and Hudson.

Malloroy, James P. and D.Q. Adams, 1997: *Encyclopedia of Indo-European Culture*. - London and Chicago: Fitzroy Dearborn.

Malville, J. McKim, Fred Wendorf, Ali A.Mazar, and Romuald Schild, 1998: Megaliths and Neolithic astronomy in southern Egypt, *Nature*, 392: 488-491.

Manetho [3rd century BCE], 1940: *History of Egypt and Other Works* (Loeb Classical Library). - Cambridge, MA: Harvard University Press.

Manetho, *see* Verbrugghe, Wickersham, 1996.

Manilius, Marcus [1st century CE], 1977: *Astronomica* (Loeb Classical Library). - Cambridge, MA and London: Harvard University Press and William Heinemann.

Markey, Thomas L. and John A.C. Greppin (Eds.), 1990: *When Worlds Collide: Indo-Europeans and non-Indo-Europeans. The Bellagio Papers*. - Ann Arbor, MI: Karoma.

Marshack, Alexander, 1964: Lunar Notation on Upper Paleolithic Remains, *Science*, **146**, 3645: 743-745.

Marshack, Alexander, 1972: *The Roots of Civilization*. - New York: McGraw-Hill. 2nd ed. - *The Roots of Civilizations: the cognitive beginnings of man's first art, symbol and notation*. - Mount Kisco, NY: Moyer Bell, 1991.

Martin, Geoffrey Thorndike, 1990: *A Bibliography of the Amarna Period and Its Aftermath*. - London & New York: Kegan Paul.

Martin, Thomas R., 1996: *Ancient Greece: From Prehistoric to Hellenistic Times*. - New Haven, CT & London: Yale University Press.

Maunder, Edward Walter, 1908: *The Astronomy of Bible. An elementary commentary on the astronomical references of Holy Scripture*. - London: T.S.Clark.

Maunder, Edward Walter,1913:The Origin of Constellations, *Observatory*, 36.

McCluskey, Stephen C., 1997: *Astronomies and Cultures in Early Medieval Europe*. - Cambridge: Cambridge University Press.

McDonald, Daniel McLean, 1992: *The Origins of Metrology*. - Cambridge, UK: McDonald Institute for Archaeological Research.

McDonald, Marianne, 2000: *Mythology of the Zodiac: Tales of the Constellations*. - New York: MetroBooks.

Megarry, Tim, 1996: *Society in Prehistory: The Origins of Human Culture*. – New York: New York University Press.

Meletinsky, E.M. (Ed.), 1991: *Mythological Dictionary*. - Moscow: Soviet Encyclopedia (In Russian).

Mellaart, James, 1965: *Earliest civilizations of the Near East*. - London: Thames and Hudson.

Mellaart, James, 1979: Egyptian and Near Eastern chronology: a dilemma? *Antiquity*, 53: 6-19.

Mellars, Paul A. (Ed.), 1990: *The Emergence of Modern Humans: An Archaeological Perspective*. - Ithica, NY: Cornell University Press.

Mellars, Paul A., 1996: *The Neanderthal Legacy: An Archaeological Perspective from Western Europe*. - Princeton, NJ: Princeton University Press (For another volume see Trinkaus).

Mellars, Paul A. & Chris Stringer (Eds.), 1989: *The Human Revolution: Behavioural and Biological Perspectives on the Origins of Modern Humans*. – Princeton, NJ: Princeton University Press.

Mendelssohn, Kurt, 1974: *The Riddles of the Pyramids*. - New York: Praeger.

Meyer, Eduard, 1904: *Aegyptische Chronologie*. - Berlin: Verlag der Königl. Akad. der Wissenschaften (In German).

Meyer, Eduard, 1908: *Nachtraege zur Aegyptischen Chronologie*. – Berlin (In German).

Meyer, Eduard, 1931: *Die ältere chronologie Babyloniens, Assyriens und Ägyptens*; nachtrag zum ersten bande der Geschichte des alterums. - Stuttgart und Berlin: J.G.Gotta'sche buchhandlung nachfolger.

Militarev, Alexander V., 1995: Some thoughts in respect to the Gurshtein's hypothesis, *Herald of Ancient History*, 1(212): 170-172 (In Russian).

Mithen, Steven J., 1990: *Thoughtful foragers: a study of prehistoric decision making*. - Cambridge, New York: Harvard University Press.

Mithen, Steven J., 1996: *The Prehistory of the Mind: The cognitive origins of art, religion and science*. - London: Thames & Hudson.

Mithen, Steven J. (Ed.), 1998: *Creativity in Human Evolution and Prehistory*. - London, New York: Routledge.

Mithen, Steven J., 2004: *After the Ice: A Global Human History 20,000-5000 BC*. - Boston, MA: Harvard University Press.

Mohen, Jean-Pierre and Christiane Eluère, 2000: *The Bronze Age in Europe* (Discoveries). - New York: Harry N. Abrams.

Morozov, Nicolai Alexandrovich, 1928: *Christ*, Book I, *Celestial Marks of the Earthly History of Mankind*. – Moscow, Leningrad (In Russian).

Mowinckel, Sigmund, 1928: Die Sternnamen im alten Testament, *Offprint from Norsk Teologisk Tidsskrift 29*. - Oslo, Norway (In German).

Needham, J., W. Ling, et al., 1954-94: *Science and Civilization in China*. 6 vols. - Cambridge, MA: Cambridge University Press.

Nelson, Kit and Associates, 2002, see *Holocene Settlement of the Egyptian Sahara*.

Ness, Lester J., 1999: *Written in the stars: ancient zodiac mosaics*. - Warren Center, PA: Shangri-La Publications.

Neugebauer, Otto, 1942: The Origin of the Egyptian Calendar, *Journal of Near Eastern Studies* **1**: 396-403.

Neugebauer, Otto, 1951: *The Exact Sciences in Antiquity*. - Copenhagen. – 2nd edition, 1957: Providence, RI: Brown University Press.

Neugebauer, Otto, 1955: *Astronomical Cuneiform Texts*, 3 vols. - London: Lund Humphries (Institute for Advanced Study, Princeton, NJ)

Neugebauer, Otto, 1975: *A History of Ancient Mathematical Astronomy*, 3 vols. - Berlin, Heidelberg and New York: Springer.

Neugebauer, Otto, 1983: *Astronomy and History: Selected Essays.* - New York: Springer.

Neugebauer, Otto and Richard A.Parker, 1960-1969: *Egyptian Astronomical Texts,* 4 vols. - Providence, RI: Brown University Press; London: Lund Humphries.

Neugebauer, Paul Victor, 1929: *Astronomische Chronologie,* 2 Vols. - Berlin: W. de Gruyter.

Nilsson, Martin Persson, 1920: *Primitive Time-reckoning: A Study in the Origins and First Development of the Art of Counting Time among the Primitive and Early Culture Peoples.* - Lund, Sweeden: C.W.K.Gleerup.

Noegel, Scott B., 1996: Moses and Magic: Notes on the Book of Exodus, *Journal of the Ancient Near Eastern Society* 24: 45-59.

North, John D., 1989: *Stars, Mind and Fate.* – London: Hambledon Continuum.

O'Connor, David and Eric H. Cline (Eds.), 1998: *Amenhotep III: Perspectives on his Reign.* – Ann Arbor: University of Michigan Press.

Olcott, William Tyler, 1911: *Star lore of all ages: a collection of myths, legends, and facts concerning the constellations of the Northern Hemisphere.* - New York, London: G.P.Putnam's sons.

O'Neil, William Matthew, 1971: *Time and the Calendars.* - Sydney: Sydney University Press.

O'Neil, William Matthew, 1986: *Early Astronomy from Babylonia to Copernicus.* - Sidney: Sidney University Press.

Ong, Walter J., 1988: *Orality and Literacy: The Technologizing of the Word.* - New York: Methuen.

Oppenheim, A. Leo, 1977: *Ancient Mesopotamia: Portrait of a Dead Civilization.* - Chicago: University of Chicago Press.

Orekhov, Roman Alexandrovich, 2014: *The world of pyramid builders. The epoch of the Old Kingdom.* – St.-Petersburg: Contrast.

Ovenden, Michael W., 1960-61: The Origin of the Constellations, *Journal of the British Astronomical Association,* 71: 91-95.

Ovenden, Michael W., 1966: The Origin of the Constellations, *The Philosophical Journal,* **3**, 1: 1-18.

Pande, G.C. (Ed.), 1998: *Science and Civilization in India,* vol. 1, *The Dawn of Indian civilization.* - Oxford: Oxford University Press.

Pannekoek, Anton, 1961: *A History of Astronomy*. - New York: Interscience.

Papke W., 1978: Die Keilschriftseria MUL.APIN. *Dissertation*. - Tübingen.

Parker, Richard A., 1950: *The Calendars of Ancient Egypt* (Studies in Ancient Oriental Civilization, 26). - Chicago: University of Chicago Press.

Parker, Richard A., 1974: Ancient Egyptian Astronomy, *Philosophical Transactions of the Royal Society of London* A.276: 51-64.

Parker, Richard A., 1978: Egyptian Astronomy, Astrology and Calendrical Reckoning. In: C.C.Gillispie (Ed.), *Dictionary of Scientific Biographies*, **15**, 1978: 706-727.

Parker, Richard A. and Waldo H. Dubberstein, 1956: *Babylonian Chronology*. 2nd edition (Brown University Studies, 19). - Providence, RI: Brown University Press.

Partridge, Archibald E., 1936: *The story of the Heavens. How the 48 ancient constellations got their names 5000 years ago*. - Seattle, WA: The Simplex Publishing Company.

Peters, C.H.F. & Knobel, E.B., 1915: *Ptolemy's catalogue of stars*. - Washington, DC: Carnegie Institute of Washington (Publication 86).

Piazzi Smyth, Charles, 1867: *Life and Work at the Great Pyramid*. - Edinburgh.

Pingree, David, 1963: Astronomy and Astrology in India and Iran, *Isis*, 54: 229-246.

Pingree, David and Hermann Hunger, 1999: *Astral sciences in Mesopotamia*. - Leiden, Boston: Brill.

Pluche, Noël Antoine, 1740: *The history of heavens considered according to the notions of the poets and philosophers, compared with the doctrines of Moses*, 2 vols. - London: J.Osborn.

Plunket, Emmeline Mary, 1903: *Calendars and Constellations*. - London: John Murray.

Poincaré, Henri, 1982: *The foundations of science. Science and Hypothesis. The Value of Science. Science and Method*. - Washington, D.C.: University Press of America.

Popper, Karl, 1949: *The Open Society and its Enemies*. - London: Routledge & Kegan Paul.

Porada E., 1987: On the Origin of Aquarius. In: Rochberg-Halton, Francesca (Ed.) *Language, Literature and History: Philological and Historical Studies Presented to Erica Reiner.* - New York: Eisenbrauns.

Powell, Robert A., 2007: *History of the Zodiac.* – San Rafael, CA: Sophia.

Propp, William H., 1988: Did Moses Have Horns? *Bible Review*, **IV**, 1: 30-37.

Prosecký, Jiří (Ed.), 1998: *Intellectual Life of the Ancient Near East.* Papers Presented at the 43rd Recontre assyriologique internationale. - Prague: Academy of Sciences of the Czech Republic.

Ptolemaeus, Claudius [2nd century CE], 1940: *Tetrabiblos* (The Loeb Classical Library, 435). - Cambridge, MA: Harvard University Press & London: William Heinemann Ltd.

Quirke, Stephen, 2001: *The Cult of Ra: Sun-Worship in Ancient Egypt.* - New York: Thames and Hudson.

Quirke, Stephen & Spencer, Jeffrey (Eds.), 1992: *The British Museum Book of Ancient Egypt.* - London and New York: Thames and Hudson.

Rabinovich, E.G., 1978: The Type of a Calendar and the Typology of a Culture. In: *Studies in History of Astronomy*, **XIV**: 141-154. - Moscow: Nauka (In Russian).

Raevsky, Dmitry Sergeevich, 1995: History of Zodiac: Facts, Hypotheses, Reconstructions, *Vestnik Drevnei Istorii (The Herald of Ancient History)*, 1 (212): 193-199 (In Russian).

Rappenglück, Michael A., 1999: *Eine Himmelskarte aus der Eiszeit? Ein Beitrag zur Urgeschichte der Himmelskunde und zur paläoastronomischen Methodik.* - Frankfurt am Main: Peter Lang.

Rawlinson, George, 1910: *History of Herodotus* (Everyman's Library). – London: Dent.

Redford, Donald B., 1967: *History and Chronology of the Eighteenth Dynasty of Egypt; Seven Studies.* - Toronto: University of Toronto Press.

Redford, Donald B., 1984: *Akhenaten, the heretic king.* - Princeton, NJ: Princeton University Press.

Redford, Donald B., 1992: *Egypt, Canaan, and Israel in Ancient Times.* – Princeton, NJ: Princeton University Press.

Redford, Donald B., 1999: The Beginning of the Heresy. In: *Pharaohs of the Sun*, edited by Freed, Markowitz and D'Auria: 50-59.

Redford, Donald B. (Ed.), 2001: *The Oxford encyclopedia of ancient Egypt*, 3 vols. - New York: Oxford University Press.

Reeves, Carl Nicholas, 1990: *The Complete Tutankhamun: The King, The Tomb, The Royal Treasure.* - London and New York: Thames & Hudson.

Reeves, Carl Nicholas, 2000: *Ancient Egypt: The Great Discoveries. A year-by-Year Chronicle.* - London: Thames & Hudson.

Reeves, Carl Nicholas, 2001: *Akhenaten the false prophet.* - New York: Thames & Hudson.

Reeves, Carl Nicholas & Richard Wilkinson, 1996: *The Complete Valley of the Kings: Tombs and Treasures of Egypt's Great Pharaohs.* - London: Thames & Hudson.

Reiner, Erica, 1975: *Babylonian planetary omens.* - Malibu, CA: Undena.

Reiner, Erica, 1995: *Astral Magic in Babylonia.* – Philadelphia: American Philosophical Society.

Renan, Ernest, 1991: *The life of Jesus* (Great minds series). - Buffalo, NY: Prometheus Books.

Renfrew, Colin, 1988: *Archaeology and Language: The Puzzle of Indo-European Origins.* - Cambridge: Cambridge University Press.

Renfrew, Colin & Chris Scarre (Eds.), 1998: *Cognition and Material Culture: the Archaeology of Symbolic Storage* (McDonald Institute Monographs). - Cambridge, UK: McDonald Institute.

Rice, Michael, 1990: *Egypt's Making: The Origins of Ancient Egypt, 5,000-2,000 B.C.* - London and New York: Routledge.

Rice, Michael, 1998: *The Power of the Bull.* - London and New York: Routledge.

Ridpath, Ian, 1988: *Star Tales.* - Cambridge, MA: Lutterworth.

Roaf, Michael, 1990: *Cultural Atlas of Mesopotamia and the Ancient Near East.* – New York: Facts on File.

Roberts, J.M., 2004: *Ancient History: From the First Civilizations to the Renaissance.* The 1st edition: London: Duncan Baird.

Rochberg, F., 1995: Astronomy and Calendars in Ancient Mesopotamia. In: *Civilizations of the Ancient Near East,* **3** (Ed. J.M.Sasson). - New York: Charles Scribner's Sons.

Rochberg, Francesca, 2004: *The Heavenly Writing: Divination, Horoscopy, and Astronomy in Mesopotamian Culture.-* Cambridge: Cambridge University Press.

Rogers, John H., 1998: Origins of the ancient constellations: I.The Mesopotamian traditions; II.The Mediterranean traditions, *Journal of the British Astronomical Association* **108**, 1: 9–28; 2: 79-89.

Rohl, David M., 1995: *Pharaohs and Kings: A Biblical Quest.* – New York: Crown.

Rolleston, Frances, 1862-1865: *Mazzaroth; or, the Constellations, 4 pts.* - London: Rivingtons, Waterloo Place.

Room, Adrian, 1988: *Dictionary of Astronomical Names.* - London and New York: Routledge.

Roy, Archie E., 1984: The Origin of Constellations, *Vistas in Astronomy,* **27**: 171-197.

Ruggles, C.L.N., 1984: *Megalithic Astronomy : A New Archaeological and Statistical Study of 300 Western Scottish Sites* (BAR Series, 123). – Oxford, UK: British Archaeological Reports.

Ruggles, C.L.N. and Saunders, N.J. (Eds.), 1993: *Astronomies and Cultures.* - Niwot, CO: University Press of Colorado.

Ruggles, C.L.N., 1999: *Astronomy in Prehistoric Britain and Ireland.* - New Haven and London: Yale University Press.

Ruggles, Clive, Frank Prendergast, and Tom Ray, (eds.), 2001: *Astronomy, Cosmology and Landscape.* - Bognor Regis, UK: Ocarina Books.

Ruggles, C.L.N., 2005: *Ancient Astronomy: An Encyclopedia of Cosmologies and Myth.* - Santa Barbara, CA: ABC-CLIO.

Ruggles Clive, Gary Urton, Anthony F. Aveni, 2007: *Skywatching in the Ancient World: New Perspectives in Cultural Astronomy.* - Norman, OK: University of Oklahoma Press.

Ruggles, C.L.N. (ed.), 2014: *Handbook of Archaeoastronomy and Ethnoastronomy.-* New York, NY: Springer Science+Business Media.

Ryan, William B.R. and Walter C.Pitman III, 1998: *Noah's Flood: The New Scientific Discoveries About the Event That Changed History.* - New York: Simon & Schuster.

Sachs, A.J. and Hunger, H., 1988-96: *Astronomical Diaries and Related Text from Babylonia*, 3 vols. - Vienna: Osterreichische Academie der Wissenschaften.

Sallmann, N, 1983: *Censorini de die natali liber ad Q.Caerellium.* - Leipzig: Teubner.

Santillana, Giorgio de & Dechend, Hertha von, 1969: *Hamlet's Mill: An Essay on Myth and the Frame of Time.* - Ipswich: Gambit.

Schaefer, Bradley E., 2000a: The heliacal rise of Sirius and ancient Egyptian chronology, *Journal for the History of Astronomy,* **31**, 2: 149-155.

Schaefer, Bradley E., 2000b: Date and place of origin of the Asian Lunar lodge systems. – In: César Esteban & Juan Antonio Belmonte (Eds.), *Oxford VI and SEAC 99: Astronomy and cultural diversity.* - La Laguna: 283-287.

Schaefer, Bradley E., 2004: The Epoch of the Constellations on the Farnese Atlas and their Origin in Hipparchus' Lost Catalog, *Journal for the History of Astronomy* **36**, 167.

Schafer, Edward H., 1977: An Ancient Chinese Star Map, *JBAA*, 87: 162.

Schlögl, Hermann Alexander, 1993: *Echnaton - Tutankhamun: Daten, Fakten, Literatur*, 4th ed. – Wiesbaden: Harrassowitz (In German).

Schmandt-Besserat, Denise, 1992: *Before Writing.* Vol. 1, *From Counting to Cuneiform.* - Austin: University of Texas Press.

Schmandt-Besserat, Denise, 1996: *How Writing Came About.* - Austin: University of Texas Press.

Schmidt, Klaus, 2010: Göbekli Tepe – the Stone Age Sanctuaries: New Results of Ongoing Excavations with a Special Focus on Sculptures and High Reliefs, *Documenta Praehistorica*, 37: 239-256.

Schoch, Robert M., with Robert Aquinas McNally, 1999: *Voices of the rocks: a scientist looks at catastrophes and ancient civilizations.* - New York: Harmony Books.

Scholem, G.G., 1965: *On the Kabbalah and its Symbolism.* - New York: Schocken.

Schoelm, G.G., 1974: *Major Trends in Jewish Mysticism.* - New York: Schocken.

Sedgwick, Charlalee B., 1976: *Discussions of the Meaning of the Zodiac in ancient Palestinian synagogues.* A Thesis Submitted to the Graduate Faculty of the University of Georgia. - Athens, GA.

Selin, Helaine (Ed.) and Xiaochun Sun (Advisory Ed.), 2000: *Astronomy Across Cultures: The History of Non-Western Astronomy* (Science Across Cultures, Vol.1). - Dordrecht/Boston/London: Kluwer.

Senard, M., 1948: *Le Zodiaque.* – Paris, La Colonne Vendome (In French).

Sesti, Giuseppe Maria, 1991: *The Glorious Constellations: History and Mythology.* - New York: Harry N. Abrams.

Shaw, Ian (Ed.), 2000: *The Oxford History of Ancient Egypt.* - Oxford, UK: Oxford University Press.

Sheler, Jeffery L., 1999: *Is the Bible True?* - San Francisco, CA: HarperSanFrancisco.

Sheler, Jeffery L., 2001: The Fight for History, *U.S.News & World Report*, **131**, 26 (December 24): 38-46.

Shukla, Kripa Shankar, 1987: Main Characteristics and Achievements of Ancient Indian Astronomy in Historical Perspective. In: *History of Oriental Astronomy*, ed. by G.Swarup, A.K.Bag, and K.S.Shukla: 9-22. - Cambridge, UK: Cambridge University Press.

Silberman, Neil Asher, 1998: *Heavenly Powers: Unraveling the Secret History of the Kabbalah.* - Grosset & Dunlap.

Silverman, David P. (Ed.), 1997: *Ancient Egypt.* - London and New York: Duncan Baird.

Sivin, N., 1976: Giorgio Diaz de Santillana (1902-1974), *Isis*, **67**: 439-443.

Sklenář, Karel, 1984: *Za jeskynním člověkem: neformální encyklopedie.* - Praha: Československý spisovatel.

Skomal, Susan Naccv and Edgar C. Polome (Eds.), 1987: *Proto-Indo-European: The Archaeology of a Linguistic Problem.* Studies in Honor of Marija Gimbutas. - Washington, DC: The Institute for the Study of Man.

Snodgrass, Mary Ellen, 1997: *Signs of the Zodiac: A Reference Guide to Historical, Mythological, and Cultural Associations.* – Greenwood.

Solis, Ruth Shady, Jonothan Haas, Winifred Creamer, 2001: Dating Caral, a Preceramic Site in the Supe Valley on the Central Coast of Peru, *Science,* **292**, 5517: 723-726.

Spalinger, Anthony J. (Ed.), 1994: *Revolutions in Time: Studies in Ancient Egyptian Calendrics* (Varia Aegyptiaca Supplement 6). - San Antonio, TX: Van Siclen Books.

Speake, Graham (Ed.), 1994: *Dictionary of Ancient History.* – Cambridge: Blackwell.

Spencer, Jeffrey, 1993: *Early Egypt: The Rise of Civilization in the Nile Valley.* - London.

Stearns, Peter N. (Ed.), 2001: *The Encyclopedia of World History: Ancient, Medieval, and Modern Chronologically Arranged.* 6th ed., revised and updated. - Boston, New York: Houghton Mifflin.

Stepugina T.V. and E.N.Kaurov, 1995: Ancient Chinese Myth and Mythological Grounds of Zodiacal Constellations. In: Zodiac History in the History of Culture (collection of papers on Gurshtein's concept), *Journal of Ancient History (Vestnik Drevnei Istorii),* 1 (212): 172-175 (In Russian).

Stolyar, Abram Davidovich, 1985: *The Genesis of Visual Arts.* - Moscow: Iskusstvo (In Russian).

Tacitus, P.Cornelius [1 century CE], 1952: *The Annals and The Histories.* - Chicago: Encyclopedia Britannica (Great Books of the Western World, 15).

Takho-Godi, Aza Alibekovna, 1989: *Greek Mythology.* - Moscow: Iskusstvo (In Russian).

Tattersall, Ian, 1993: *The Human Odyssey: Four Million Years of Human Evolution.* - New York: Prentice Hall.

Tattersall, Ian, 1998: *Becoming Human: Evolution and Human Uniqueness.* - Harcourt Brace.

Tattersall, I., E.Delson, and J. Van Couvering (Eds.), 1988: *Encyclopedia of Human Evolution and Prehistory.* - New York: Garland.

Teilhard de Chardin, Pierre, 1959: *Phenomenon of Man.* - New York: Harper.

Tester, S. Jim, 1987: *A History of Western Astrology.* - New York: Ballantine.

Thompson, Thomas L., 1999: *The Mythic Past. Biblical Archaeology and the Myth of Israel*. - New York: Basic (Perseus).

Tomasello, Michael, 1999: *The Cultural Origins of Human Cognition*. - Cambridge: Harvard University Press.

Toomer, G.J., 1984: *Ptolemy's Almagest*. - London: Duckworth.

Toomer, G.J., 1988: Hipparchus and Babylonian astronomy. A Scientific Humanist. In: *Studies in Memory of Abracham Sachs* (eds. E. Leichty et al): 353-62. – Philadelphia: Publications of the Kramer Fund, 9.

Toporov, Vladimir Nikolaevich, 1982: Premordial concepts of the world (general view). In: *Essays on history of knowledge of Nature in Antiquity* (The Library of World History of Natural Sciences). - Moscow: Nauka: 8-40 (In Russian).

Trinkaus, Erik (Ed.), 1989: *The Emergence of Modern Humans: Biocultural Adaptations in the Later Pleistocene* (School of American Research Advanced Seminar Series). - Cambridge; New York: Cambridge University Press. For another volume see Mellars.

Tyldesley, Joyce, 1999: *Nefertiti: Egypt's Sun Queen*. - New York: Viking.

Tylor, Edward Burnet, 1865: *Researches into the Early History of Mankind and the Development of Civilization*. - London: J. Murray.

Tylor, Edward Burnet, 1871: *Primitive Culture: Researches into the Development of Mythology, Philosophy, Religion, Language, Art, and Custom*. - London: J. Murray. The 4th edition, revised - London, 1903, in 2 vols.

Ulansey, David, 1989: *The Origins of the Mitraic Mysteries: Cosmology and Salvation in the Ancient World*. - New York: Oxford University.

Ulansey, David, 1994: Solving the Mithraic Mysteries, *Biblical Archeology Review*, **20**, 5 (September-October): 41-53.

Van Riper, A. Bowdoin, 1993: *Men among the Mammoths (Victorian Science and the Discovery of Human Prehistory)*. - Chicago & London: The University of Chicago Press.

Van Seters, John, 1994: *The life of Moses: the Yahwist as historian in Exodus - Numbers*. - Louisville, KY: Westminster / John Knox Press.

Verbrugghe, Gerald P., John M. Wickersham, 1996: *Berossos and Manetho, Introduced and Translated. Native Traditions in*

Ancient Mesopotamia and Egypt. - Ann Arbor, MI: University of Michigan.

Vercoutter, Jean, 1992: *The search for ancient Egypt.* - New York: Harry N. Abrams, and London: Thames & Hudson.

Vermaseren, Maarten J., 1956: *Corpus Inscriptionum et Monumentorum Religionis Mithriacae.* - The Hague: Martinus Nijhoff.

Vermaseren, Maarten J., 1963: *Mithras, The Secret God.* - London: Chatto & Windus.

Wade, Nicholas, 2006: *Before the Dawn.* – New York: Penguin Press.

Waerden, Bertil L. van der, 1953: History of the Zodiac, *Archiv fur Orientforschung,* **16**: 216-230.

Waerden, Bertil L. van der, 1966: *Die Anfange der Astronomie: Envachende Wissenschaft II.* - Groningen. Translation *Science Awakening 2. The Birth of Astronomy,* 1974. - Leiden & New York: Noordhoff and Oxford University Press.

Waerden, Bertil L. van der, 1978: Mathematics and Astronomy in Mesopotamia. In: *Dictionary of Scientific Biography* (ed. C.C.Gillespie), **15**, Supplement I, Topical Essays: 667-680. - New York: Charles Scribner's Sons.

Waerden, Bertil L. van der, 1984: Greek astronomical calendars, 1; *Archive for history of exact science,* 2.

Walker, Christopher (Ed.), 1996: *Astronomy before the Telescope.* - London: British Museum.

Walker, C.B.F, Hunger, H., 1977: Zwoelfmaldrei, *Mitteilungen der Deutsches Orientalisches Gesellschaft,* **109:** 27-34 (In German).

Ward, Donald, 1968: *The Divine Twins. An Indo-European Myth in Germanic Tradition* (Folklore studies, 19). - Berkeley and Los Angeles: University of California.

Ward, F.A.B., 1970: *Time Measurement: Historical Review* (3rd impression with amendments). - London: Science Museum.

Warner, Deborah J., 1979: *The Sky Explored. Celestial Cartography 1500-1800.* – New York: Alan R. Liss & Amsterdam: Theatrum Orbis Terrarium.

Watterson, Barbara, 1999: *Amarna. Ancient Egypt's Age of Revolution.* - Stroud, UK: Tempus.

Weinberg, I.P., 1986: *Man in the Culture of the Ancient Near East.* - Moscow: Nauka (In Russian).

Wells, R.A., 1985: Sothis and the Satet Temple on Elephantine: a direct connection, *Studien zur Altagyptischen Kultur*, 12: 255-302.

Wells, R.A., 1990: The 5th Dynasty Sun Temples at Abu Ghurab as Old Kingdom star clocks: examples of applied Ancient Egyptian astronomy, *Beiheft zu Studien zur Altagyptischen Kultur, Akten des Vierten Internationalen Agyptologen Kongresses Munchen 1985*, 4: 95-104.

Wells, R.A., 1990: Sothis and the Satet Temple on Elephantine: An Egyptian Stonehenge? *Beiheft zu Studien zur Altagyptischen Kultur, Akten des Vierten Internationalen Agyptologen Kongresses Munchen 1985*, 4: 107-15.

Wells, R.A., 1992: The mythology of Nut and the birth of Ra, *Studien zur Altagyptischen Kultur*, 19: 305-21.

Wells, R.A., 1993: Origin of the Hour and the Gates of the Duat, *Studien zur Altagyptischen Kultur*, 20: 305-26.

Wente, Edward F. and Charles C.Van Siclen III, 1976: A chronology of the New Kingdom. In: *Studies in Honor of George R.Hughes* (*Studies in Ancient Oriental Civilization*, 39. – Chicago: The Oriental Institute.

Werner, Helmut, 1967: Problems and Results of Comparative Studies of the Celestial Constellations, *Vistas in Astronomy*, **9**: 135-143.

Wesley, Walter G., 1978: The Accuracy of Tycho Brahe's Instruments, *Journal for the History of Astronomy*, **9**: 42-53.

Whitefield, Peter, 1995: *The Mapping of the Heavens*. - London: The British Library.

Whitfield, Peter, 2001: *Astrology: A History*. - London: The British Library.

Whyte, Charles, 1928: *The Constellations and Their History*. - London: Charles Griffin.

Wilkinson, Toby, 2003: *Genesis of the Pharaohs: Dramatic new discoveries that rewrite the origins of ancient Egypt*. - London: Thames & Hudson.

Wilson, Edith R., 1913: The Story of the Zodiac, *Popular Astronomy*, **21**: 151-158; 216-225.

Wolbarsht, M.L. and Lichtenberg, J.D., 1961: Freud and the Moses of Michelangelo, *American Imago*, 18: 263-268.

Wu, K.C., 1982: *The Chinese Heritage*. - New York: Crown.

Xiaochun, Sun & Jacob Kistemaker, 1997: *The Chinese sky during the Han: constellating stars and society* (Sinica Leidensia, 38). - Leiden: Brill.

Zeuner, Frederick E., 1963: *A History of Domesticated Animals*. - New York and Evanston: Harper & Row.

Zerubavel, Eviater, 1989: *The Seven Day Circle: The History and Meaning of the Week*. - Chicago: Chicago University Press.

Zivie-Coche, Christiane, 2002: *Sphinx: History of a Monument*. - Ithaca & London: Cornell University Press.

Zodiac History in the History of Culture (Collection of 10 papers in form of a discussion on Gurshtein's concept), 1995. - *Herald of Ancient History [Vestnik Drevnei Istorii]*, 1 (212): 153-200 (In Russian).

Zolotarev, Alexander Michailovich, 1964: *The Tribal System and the Primitive Mythology*. - Moscow: Nauka (In Russian).

Zvelebil, Marek (Ed.), 1986: *Hunters in transition*. - Cambridge: Cambridge University Press.

Zvelebil, Marek, 1996: Ideology, Society and Economy of the Mesolithic Communities in Temperate and Northern Europe, *Origini: Preistoria e Protostoria delle civilta antiche*, **20:** 39-70.

Zvelebil, Marek, 1997: Hunter-gatherer ritual landscapes: spatial organization, social structure, *etc, Analecta Praehistorica Leidensia*, **29:** 33-50.

CHRONOLOGICAL SUMMARY OF ASTRONOMICAL MILESTONES IN PRE-WRITTEN AND ANCIENT HISTORY ON THE BACKGROUND OF THE GENERAL HISTORY OF MANKIND

The purpose of this appendix is to single out the basic mindsteps of mankind in forming archaic and ancient astronomy. To make the story more explicable, it is exposed on the background of the general history of human culture up to modernity. Some debatable concepts and dating in pre-written history of astronomy are given in accordance with results derived in previous publications of this author (*see* Selected Bibliography).

About **200,000-150,000** BCE. Out of Africa. The early humans started to leave their ancestral African homeland. The DNA of present-day Africans is more diverse than that of people on other continents, indicating that humans have lived in Africa the longest. The limited extent of modern human genetic diversity implies that all living humans share a common ancestor (Wade, 2006).

About **70,000-50,000** BCE. Humans journeyed from Africa into the Middle East. In multiple migrations, they spread east into Asia and northwest into Europe. Pierre Teilhard de Chardin (1881-1955) in *The Phenomenon of Man* put emphasis on what he considered to be Early Man's most amazing feature – his restless mobility. Archaic people were in need of advanced navigation, which could be based on astronomical practice only. THIS WAS THE INITIATION OF PRIMITIVE ASTRONOMY.

After **60,000** BCE. The end of the Lower Paleolithic and the heyday of the Mousterian Culture (70,000-40,000 BCE) associated with Neanderthal Man. In climate, the last glacial (Wurm) period started 70,000 years ago and lasted up to 10,000 BCE. Artifacts tell about regulated burial habits (Robbins in Selin, 2000). This reflects some kind of common outlook among hunting tribes. There are traces of a three-fold model for the world with a division among the lower, middle, and upper worlds. Astronomically, the FOUR CARDINAL POINTS OF THE HORIZON were determined by the rising and setting of luminaries. In art (Stolyar, 1985), man went a long way from a 'natural creative issue' (ritual exhibition of animal bodies or their parts: a head, extremities, a fell) to a 'natural mock-up' (a natural or rough artificial frame covered with a head, a fell, extremities). The roots of the cave's bear cult are known from many of the European *bears' caves*. The name 'bear' is taboo in many languages. The domination of a male by a female, and, as a result, the domination of the She-bear (Sklenář, 1984).

60,000-40,000 BCE. Middle Paleolithic. Dawn of an anthropological type of human being who is learning to think and to speak (according to the skull's structure). The emergence and spread of fully modern humans. The skill of moving upon water. Human beings are ready to conquer fire. In art, there are full-scale sculptures with a transition to profile bas-reliefs.

Some attributes of fully modern human behavior detectable in the archaeological record beginning 50,000-40,000 years ago (Klein, 1999, p.589):
- substantial growth in the diversity and standardization of artifact types;
- earliest appearance of incontrovertible art;
- oldest undeniable evidence for spatial organization of camp floors;

- oldest evidence for the transport of large quantities of highly desirable stone raw material over scores or even hundreds of kilometers;
- earliest secure evidence for ceremony or ritual;
- first evidence for human ability to live in the coldest, most continental parts of Eurasia;
- first evidence for human population densities approaching those of historic hunter-gatherers in similar environments;
- first evidence for fishing and for other significant advances in human ability to acquire energy.

After **40,000** BCE. The Aurignacian Culture of Cro-Magnon inhabitants starts in Eastern Europe: the first phase of the Upper Paleolithic in Europe (after Mousterian flake-based stoneworking industry associated in Europe with the Neanderthals).

Features (Tattersall, 1993): Elaborate burial of the dead; bodily ornamentation; the use of bone, antler, ivory, shell and other materials for tools; subtle toolmaking methods; the extensive use of nonlocal, exotic raw materials from distant sources; complex hunting methods including fishing; complex use of fire; decoration of objects (the appearance of art in the form of naturalistic paintings, fanciful sculptures, and engraved bone and antler); musical instruments; notation (symbolism).

30,000-26,000 BCE. The Aurignacian of Western Europe. An engraved plaque with complex markings has come from the Abri Blanchard Cave that Alexander Marshack (1964; 1991) has interpreted as *a lunar calendar*. The same is confirmed by rock paintings.

Astronomical accomplishments. UTILIZATION OF LUNAR PHASES: A LUNATION AS A UNIT OF TIME (lunar month). THE FIGURE SEVEN (etimologically it probably means *the most honorable*) BECAME A FAVORITE CELESTIAL SACRED NUMBER (Gurshtein, 1997). NOT LATER THAN THIS TIME, THE SKY WAS PATTERNED WITH STABLE GROUPS OF

SEVEN ATTRIBUTIVE STARS (some proto-constellations; the name of one of them derived from a totem of a great she-bear).

26,000-20,000 BCE. The Gravettian period. The Gravettians produce the first portable art. The first people are arriving in North America by way of Siberia and the Bering Strait land bridge.

20,000-16,000 BCE. The Solutrean period in France appears when the art of flint-working is brought to its highest level of excellence. The production of female figurines implies a fertility cult (some of them came even from the Gravettian period: for example, 11-cm- high 'Venus of Willendorf', Austria, or 44-cm-high 'Venus of Laussel' - a sculpture of a woman holding a bison horn with 'calendrial' markings, Dordogne, France). The celestial Virgo could originate from the same time.

16,000 BCE. Last glacial maximum. Some linguists date *Proto-Nostratic* as a speculative distinct pre-language ('mother tongue') for all other language families to spread after this time.

Astronomical accomplishments (Gurshtein, 1995): CONSTELLATIONS ARE ARRANGED INTO THREE SYMBOLIC STRATA OF THE SKY: THE LOWER, MIDDLE, & UPPER WORLDS (with water, land & air symbolism, respectively).

16,000-8,000 BCE. The Magdalenian, the final phase of the European Upper Paleolithic.

Ca. **13,500** BCE. A sea level rise of about 40 meters floods large areas of lowland – the result of the melting of the overall world ice shields. Soon afterward the Bering Strait opens and hunter migration via Siberia to North America is stopped.

Ca. **10,500** BCE. People settle in southern South America.

After **10,000** BCE. The end of the Ice Age in Europe; a warming trend begins to usher in the replacement of European steppe/ grasslands by forests. Goats are domesticated in Mesopotamia by the hunter-gatherer community that earlier domesticated the dog from the Asian wolf. (The so-called Younger Dryas climate episode, which followed the last glaciations, is now dated from 10,900 to 9,600 BCE).

A key Mesolithic culture (the Natufian) emerges in the Near East (southwest Asia). The Natufian communities abandon seasonally nomadic hunting and gathering activities and replace these with plant cultivation and animal husbandry (Kottak, 2005). They bury their dead ceremoniously with ornaments, beads and headdresses. The consequences of this agricultural revolution include increases in population growth, full-time craft specialization, and class formation, each the result of the ability to generate and deploy agricultural surpluses.

Between **10,000** and **8,000** BCE. The primitive temple Göbekli Tepe in the northern Fertile Crescent (southeastern Turkey) is evidence that elements of religious rituals existed among hunter-gatherers before village life started (Schmidt, 2010).

9-7 millennia BCE. Origination of the world's seat for agriculture and cattle-rearing in South-Eastern Asia (proto-Chinese civilization).

Ca. **8,000** BCE. The end of the Mesolithic and spread of the Neolithic (or Food-Producing) revolution. In the Near East, permanent settlement in mudbrick villages becomes regular. Jericho (about 15 miles to the east of Jerusalem), perhaps the first attempt in human history at a walled town, is built. Emmer wheat is domesticated in the Fertile Crescent.

Between **6,500** and **3,500** BCE. Neolithic art flourishes in various areas of 'Old Europe' that extends from the Aegean and Adriatic, including the islands, as far north as Czechia and Slovakia, southern Poland and western Ukraine (Anthony, 2010). The dominant subject of this influential art is the female figurine ('Venus'), which is considered to be a creative principle: the Great Mother-Goddess, or Goddess of Life, Death and Regeneration (Gimbutas, 1982). The divine pantheon of the time mirrors a society dominated by the mother. This feminine world was superimposed upon with a masculine world born outside Old Europe by Indo-European newcomers.

Ca. **6,500** BCE. The last time that the land bridge joining Britain to Europe is flooded: Britain becomes an island (though only in about 4,000 BCE did the seas reach their present level).

The *astronomical Age of Gemini* starts. The extraordinary symbols of the ongoing time would be Twins, the Goddess of Fertility (the Great Goddess), the Hunter, and Fishes (Gurshtein, 2005).

Ca. **6,400** BCE. The wheel is invented by Sumerians in the Tigris-Euphrates basin.

About **6,000-5,000** BCE. In accordance with DNA findings, at the beginning of the Neolithic period in Europe closely related groups of newcomers - early farmers - appeared in Germany, Hungary, and Spain, different from indigenous hunter-gatherers (Haak, Lazaridis, Patterson, et al., 2015).

Ca. **5,600** BCE. The hypothetical *Noah's Flood* (Ryan and Pitman, 1999). According to this approach, rising global sea levels following the last ice age caused the Mediterranean to overflow through what is now the Bosporus Straight in a flood that created much of the modern Black Sea, previously a lake. This catastrophic event, the authors contend, played a pivotal role in the spread of early farming into Europe and much of Asia. Memory of it, they say, was handed down in stories that reached historical times as the legend of Noah's flood.

Fertile Crescent and Old Europe: with the inception of regular agriculture, the cultivator of plants starts to observe annual events more attentively than the previous hunter-gatherer had done. The *solar calendar* becomes of great significance for his agronomic purposes. For this, he has to pay close attention to the stars along the annual path of the Sun.

Astronomical accomplishments (Gurshtein, 2005): AMONG OTHER CONSTELLATIONS, FOUR STARRY GROUPS ON THE ECLIPTIC TO MARK THE SUN'S TRACK (THE FIRST GENERATION OF THE PROTO-ZODIAC). THESE FOUR CONSTELLATIONS CONTINUE TO REFLECT THREE STRATA OF THE SKY EARLIER INSTITUTED, SO THREE OF THEM ARE EARTH SYMBOLS (HUMANS: GEMINI, VIRGO, AND SAGITTARIUS) WHILE ONE IS OF AN AQUATIC NATURE (PISCES). THE MOST PROBABLE LOCATION OF THIS ACCOMPLISHMENT IS OLD EUROPE.

5,508 BCE. The Year of Creation as adopted by the Third Ecumenical Council of Constantinople (the 7th century CE) and now in use by the Eastern Orthodox Church.

5,300 BCE. A small archaeological site from this time was discovered in southern Egypt in the early 1990s by the American archaeologist Fred Wendorf and interpreted by the astronomer McKim Malville, of Colorado (Malville et al., 1998). It seems to have astronomical alignments marking cardinal directions and the summer-solstice sunrise by widely separated slabs. Radiocarbon dating suggests it was used over a 1,700-year-long period. Its origin predates the earliest astronomical sites of Europe by one thousand years. THE FIRST DIRECT EVIDENCE OF ASTRONOMY ALONG THE HORIZON.

Approximately after the same time (ca. 5,000 BCE) agriculture starts in Egypt.

After **5th millennium** BCE. The so-called *Age of Metals* gradually starts to replace the New Stone (Neolithic) Age in the Near East.

Men first begin to use *copper* (well-known in 4,000 BCE). Then they use *bronze*, an alloy of copper and tin (3,500-3,000 BCE). Then follows the use of *iron*, beginning probably in Asia Minor (1,500 BCE).

Approximately at the same time the dominant social role of females begins to yield its significance to males. As a result, pagan religious mentality in various cultures starts to move from supremacy of the Great Mother-Goddess (the Goddess of Fertility) to potency of a male god. This process will be later reflected in symbolism of the second ecliptic quartet for the *Age of Taurus* (Gurshtein, 1993).

4,500-2,000 BCE. Supposed entrance of Indo-European people into Old Europe. This movement could have, too, contributed to the superimposition of the masculine mythic world upon the feminine world.

4,400 BCE. The *astronomical Age of Gemini* ends, the *Age of Taurus* starts (the extraordinary symbols of a new era will be basically animalistic emblems of power: a Bull, a Lion, a Scorpion, a Manly Water-bearer. A little bit later the Scorpion is substituted with the Eagle in some places).

4,250-3,250 BCE. The period of passage grave construction in Brittany.

4,000-3,000 BCE. Copper metallurgy under way in the Balkan region.

4,000-1,500 BCE. In Europe, megalithic monuments partially with an astronomical meaning (Great Britain, Brittany, Iberian peninsula) are erected. The most ancient of them are probably on Malta (for example, the megalithic temple of Hagar Qim, 3,500-3,000 BCE).

Ca. **4,000** BCE. The Al Ubaid period of Mesopotamia, which is characterized by a simple agricultural economy and the use of painted pottery with geometric designs. The Uruk period, which followed, saw the first development of monumental architecture and pictographic writing.

4th millennium BCE. The astronomical lore in Vedic literature suggests that the Rg-Veda was completed in this millennium, that the core text of the Mahabharata was composed at the end of this millennium, and that Brahmanas and Sutras are products of the high Harappan period towards the end of the 3rd millennium BCE (Elst, 1999).

Ca. **3,500** BCE. A *potter's wheel* in Mesopotamia.

Ca. **3,500-3,300** BCE. Gradual evolution of graphic markings for communication into early writing systems, although a genuine cradle and date still remain uncertain (the dominance of Mesopotamia is now in question). Various scholars give the edge to one of three possibilities: artisans of Abydos (Egypt), priests of Uruk (Mesopotamia), or the unknown makers of Indus script (Harappan civilization). It appears that writing has a much deeper pedigree than was previously thought (Lawler, 2001).

Ca. **3,200-3,100** BCE. The unification of Upper and Lower Egypt under a single crown (Bunson, 1999). Egypt emerges as an agricultural superpower (the date is different in various chronological scales).

Ca. **3,100-2,900** BCE. Construction of Newgrange (Ireland) – the Megalithic Passage Tomb that is known for the illumination of its passage and chamber by the winter solstice Sun (Hoskin, 1997). (One of the World Heritage Sites).

Ca. **3,000** BCE. Reconstructed date of the origin of *Gilgamesh*, which is the first known written legend with astral allusions.

Construction of Stonehenge 1 – the prominent British monument with astronomical alignments.

3,000-1,750 BCE. (The start of the period is very uncertain). An early urban civilization in the Indus Valley (Harappa, Mohenjo Daro, and other sites) produces polished stone, metals, incised seals, and pictographs. From this epoch, there are artifacts with astral meanings (Pande, 1998).

Definite roots of Indo-European languages traced by linguists.

Ca. **2,900** BCE. The Sahara Desert begins as over-grazing and over-cultivation lead to soil exhaustion.

Between **2,900** and **2,650** BCE. In Egypt, the time of the Pharaoh Djoser (Zoser) and his vizier Imhotep. The Step Pyramid at Saqqara, built for Djoser by Imhotep, is the world's largest stone structure (in time it is later than the temples on Malta).

After **2,850** BCE. The First Dynasty of Ur in Mesopotamia.

Around **2,800** BCE. The yin and yang philosophy of nature is supposedly originated in China by the legendary Emperor Fu Hsi; health and peace require equilibrium among the 5 elements: wood, fire, earth, metal, water. Fu Hsi is credited as the inventor of writing, hunting, trapping, and fishing. A while later, another cultural hero, Shen Nung, is credited as the inventor of agriculture and mercantilism.

2,776 BCE. In Egypt, the first solar (so called *civil*) calendar in history with 12 equal months is introduced. Its neighbors continue to use lunar and luni-solar calendars.

Astronomical accomplishments (Gurshtein, 1998): TO IMPROVE SOLAR YEAR RECKONING, THE SECOND QUARTET OF LABELS ON THE ECLIPTIC WITH THE EGYPTIAN SYMBOLISM IS INTRODUCED TO MARK FOUR SEASONAL POINTS ON THE SUN'S YEARLY TRACK. THESE CONSTELLATIONS ARE THE CIRCLE OF BEASTS (TAURUS, LEO, SCORPIO, AND AQUARIUS), CONTRARY TO

THE PREVIOUS CIRCLE OF HUMANS WITH A MOTHER-GODDESS ATOP. NEW SYMBOLS HELP TO MAINTAIN THE FIRST IN THE WORLD PURELY SOLAR CALENDAR.

THE FIGURE OF EIGHT BECOMES A VERY PECULIAR SACRED NUMBER IN EGYPT.

THE BIRTH OF ASTROLOGY either in Egypt or in Mesopotamia.

Around **2,700** BCE. In China, the Yellow Emperor (Xuanyuan Gonsun), the third legendary cultural hero, is credited with inventing (through his teacher and advisor Danao) the *ganzhi* system, which is often called the calendar *system of cyclic characters*. The latter contains 10 *tiangan* (celestial trunk, or stem) and 12 *dizhi* (terrestrial branch). The rationale behind the invention of these symbols was to name the years, the months, and the days alike. Such a system demanded at least 60 elements: 12 animals of the so-called Chinese zodiac and 5 (duplicated) primal elements (wood, fire, earth, metal, water). While Western historians dismiss the historicity of the Yellow Emperor as legend, he is regarded as a historical persona for most of Chinese history. Soon after his time, 12 animals of the Chinese zodiac surface in real historic documents (Wu, 1982). It is customary to number the 60-year cycles from 2637 BCE, when the Chinese calendar was supposedly invented. There is an alternative starting date of 2697 BCE, which is one cycle earlier than 2637 BCE. Of course, both dates are very questionable.

Ca. **2,600** BCE. Caral, a site in the Supe Valley, about 200 km north of Lima, Peru (23 km inland from the Pacific coast). It is the first urban center in the Americas with monumental architecture covering over 65 ha (about 160 acres). Caral, discovered in 1948, is the largest recorded site in the Andean region with dates older than 2000 BCE and appears to be the model for the urban design adopted by Andean civilizations that rose and fell over the span of four millennia. It is one of 18 large preceramic sites in the Supe Valley indicating a start of monumental corporate architecture, urban settlements, and irrigating agriculture (Solis *et al.*, 2001).

Ca. **2,600 - 2,500** BCE. Three Great Pyramids and the Sphinx are erected as sacred monuments in honor of the Sun's track as decoded by the Egyptians.

Ca. **2,500** BCE. The Sumerians develop a cuneiform script alphabet of some 600 simplified signs.

Ca. **2,350** BCE. The Akkadian Empire is founded by Sargon I of Sumer. Sumer's city-state civilization reaches its peak.

About **2,200** BCE. Earliest Cretan palaces of the Minoan civilization.

About **2,100** BCE. The Carnac alignments (France).

Sarsen Circle and Trilithons of Stonehenge (UK).

Temple of Enlil and ziggurat at Nippur (Iraq).

West Kennet post circles, near Avebury (UK).

THE FLOURISH OF THE OBSERVATIONAL PRACTICE CALLED ASTRONOMY ALONG THE HORIZON.

About **2,000** BCE. The beginning of Hebrew history when Habiru nomadic tribes enter the land between the Tigris and Euphrates rivers.

Decimal notation appears in Babylonia (which has replaced Sumer).

Start of a great Maya civilization in Central America.

Ca. **1,950** BCE. Hammurabi, the King of Babylon, who ruled 42 years, conquers the whole of Mesopotamia and imposes a code of laws, the first one in the world's history, with some astronomical features.

THE DEFINITIVE RULE FOR INTERCALATIONS TO COORDINATE LUNAR AND SOLAR CALENDARS.

Between **1,900** and **1,800** BCE. The alphabet in Egypt. Two short limestone inscriptions about a dozen characters each are found at Wadi el-Hol. Until this discovery, the earliest alphabet had been traced to Semites in Sinai, who left writing sometime between 1,700 and 1,500 BCE. The new inscriptions demonstrate how letters were derived from hieroglyphics (*Science*, 1999, **286**, 5445: 1675).

Ca. **1,800** BCE. The *astronomical Age of Taurus* ends, the *Age of Aries* starts (the previous seasonal symbols would be gradually replaced with Bible-type allegories: a Ram, a Crab, a Balance, and a Fish-goat. They are instituted centuries later, when the transition to the new age has become obvious).

About **1,700** BCE. Legendary Abraham, who moved from Ur to Canaan, is said to found Judaism. It is the first monotheistic religion. Abraham replaces human sacrifice with a ram sacrifice.

ROOTSTOCKS OF THE HEBREWS' ASTRONOMICAL KNOWLEDGE DURING THE PATRIARCH AGE.

Ca. **1,650** BCE (or one-two centuries later). A catastrophic eruption of the Santorini Volcano on the island of Thera, close to the island of Crete. It is accompanied with tsunamis nearly 100 m high. The event is usually associated with the decline of the Minoan culture on Crete, although the latter is estimated to have taken place about two centuries later (Friedrich, 2000). Speculative authors like to attach the Santorini eruption to the submersion of Atlantis.

Ca. **1,600** BCE. Nebra Sky Disc found in Germany - the best artifact we have so far to attest to astronomical knowledge in Europe.

Crete's celebrated Phaistos Disk, which is Europe's oldest documented literary read.

About **1,500** BCE (with an uncertainty of some hundreds of years). Nomads of central Asia, Aryans of uncertain antecedents, push into the Indian subcontinent, bringing flocks of sheep and herds of cattle.

Ca. **1,410** BCE. The Egyptian pharaoh, Tuthmosis IV, grandfather of the forthcoming Akhenaten, cleans the Sphinx of sand and restores it. The present author believes this was a provision for the future great Feast of Eternity.

Ca. **1,380** BCE. The Egyptian pharaoh Amenhotep III, father of the forthcoming Akhenaten, institutes some innovations, which are actually returns to the religious ideas of the Great Pyramid Age.

1,368 BCE. For the first time in Egypt, the civil calendar's New Year Day returns to its initial position.

In Egypt, the Pharaoh Amenhotep IV (Akhenaten) has started his reign on the eve of the first Great Calendar Cycle of Egypt ending. The present author (1998) believes Akhenaten's solar overturn was motivated by the celebration of this tremendous event.

Astronomical accomplishments (Gurshtein, 1998): AN IDEA FOR THE THIRD ECLIPTIC QUARTET EMERGES; THE TOTAL NUMBER OF LABELS TO MARK THE ANNUAL SOLAR TRACK THROUGHOUT THE SKY BECOMES TWELVE.

Ca. **1,300** BCE. Alphabetical writing is originated in Syria as a simplification of Mesopotamian cuneiform writing from 2,500

BCE. It appears on the crossroads of cultural influences from Egypt, Mesopotamia and Asia Minor. The earliest samples of the Phoenician alphabet with 22 letters (without vowels) are dated from the 12th century BCE. In the 9th century BCE the Greeks become acquainted with the Phoenician alphabet.

Between **1,300** and **1,200** BCE. Moses and the Exodus of the Hebrews out of Egyptian bondage. Moses steps down from Mount Sinai with ram's horns and prohibits his people to call upon the Golden Calf. This could be a signal of the transition from the *Age of Taurus* to the *Age of Aries*.

THE SPREAD OF THE IDEA FOR THE NEW ECLIPTICAL QUARTET OUT OF EGYPT.

THE FIGURE OF TWELVE BECOMES SACRED AFTER THE NUMBER OF THE ZODIACAL CONSTELLATIONS (BUT THE CORRECT ORDER OF THE ZODIACAL CONSTELLATIONS IS NOT OFTEN WELL REMEMBERED YET).

Ca. **1,200** BCE. Priam's city of Troy falls to Greek armies after a 10-year siege (the Trojan War of Homer).

Wuxian, a legendary Chinese astronomer, is claimed to be the author of 44 new asterisms out of ancient traditions, but in reality all of them are probably of a later origin.

Ca. **1,100** BCE. THE FIRST REGULAR ASTRONOMICAL OBSERVATORY IN CHINA.

Estimated date for origination of *mul*APIN, THE MOST PROMINENT CUNEIFORM SUMERIAN TEXT ON ASTRONOMY.

The Tower of Babylon, used partially for ASTRONOMICAL OBSERVATIONS.

Ca. **1,000** BCE. Destruction of Mycenaean palace culture is complete.

During the first millennium BCE. THE FINAL FORMING OF THE 12-STRONG WESTERN ZODIAC.

8ᵗʰ century BCE. The life of the legendary epic poet Homer who mentions only a few constellations. Homeric poetry recorded later on in writing using a Phoenician alphabet modified with vowels.

Ca. **700** BCE. The Greek poet Hesiod is supposed to have lived a little later than Homer. His *Theogony* is an account of the origin of the world and of the gods. The Greek mythology echoes more ancient celestial mythologies, and relationships between Greek gods reflect certain celestial events.

Ca. **625-546** BCE. Thales of Miletus in Asia Minor, who is said to have predicted an eclipse of the Sun in 585 BCE and introduced the constellation of Ursa Minor in Greece, which was primarily of Phoenician origin.

Ca. **409-356** BCE. Eudoxus of Cnidos, according to the common story, brings the constellations from Egypt and is the first to publish them in the original prose *Phainomena;* three centuries later Cicero calls him the greatest astronomer that ever lived. The constellations "unquestionably are in many cases variations of long antecedent, perhaps prehistoric, legends and observations from the Euphrates, Ganges, and Nile; indeed the Greek astronomers always acknowledged their indebtedness to Chaldaea and Egypt, but gave most of the credit to the latter" (Allen, 1963).

387 BCE. Inauguration of Plato's Academy in Athens.

Ca. **370-340** BCE. Shi Shen, a Chinese astronomer, is said to be the creator of the oldest known catalogue of star positions. A set of

92 new asterisms is claimed to be his invention, but in reality it seems to be of a later origin.

331 BCE. Alexander the Great conquers Egypt and founds Egyptian Alexandria.

305-282 BCE. The rule of Ptolemy I Soter of Egypt, the son of Lagus - Alexander the Great's boyhood friend at Pella, the capital of Macedonia, who later becomes one of his trusted generals. During his reign, the Museum and the Library of Alexandria become the greatest centers of Hellenistic learning.

Ca. **290** BCE. Under Ptolemy I Soter of Egypt, Aristyllos and Timocharis begin the Alexandrian astronomical school. They manage the observations of star positions that are generally supposed to have led Hipparchus to the discovery of precession (Evans, 1998).

Aristarchus of Samos (ca. 310-264 BCE), a Greek astronomer of the Alexandrian school, forerunner to Copernicus, is the first to argue that the Earth moves around the Sun. His views fail because society is too immature to absorb such an advanced idea.

Ca. **275** BCE. Aratus of Soli becomes the first Greek poetical writer on astronomy whose works are still extant. Following the order of Antigonus Gonatas, the king of Macedonia and his patron, Aratus, who knows nothing of astronomy, describes the ancient patterns of the starry sky in a poem in accordance with Eudoxus' description. Meanwhile, the Aratus account seems to be very inexact and leads to well-founded criticism starting with Hipparchus. According to modern analysis, Aratus' description fits the heavens of about 2,000 to 2,200 BCE.

Ca. **276-194** BCE. Eratosthenes, who was the keeper of the Alexandrian Library. He calculates the Earth's circumference. His map of the world is the first to contain lines of latitude and longitude.

He seems to be the inventor of the armillary sphere, a device for celestial position measurements.

After **200** BCE. The reshuffling of the Chinese Sky into the form a celestial 'megalopolis.' Instead of the earlier episodic ancient constellations, Chinese court astrologers of the Han Dynasty pepper the sky with a pattern of 283 petty asterisms, often comprised of only one or two hard-to-distinguish stars. The network of these asterisms is molded into the likeness of the Chinese imperial court: the Emperor, Celestial Officials, the Emperor's Facilities, etc. The previous genuine star repertoire is abandoned for good. This is the unique case of such a revolution in the history of world astronomy.

Ca. **190-120** BCE. Hipparchus is the acknowledged pioneer of many avenues of modern science. He invents trigonometry, calculates the duration of the solar year and the lunar month, probably discovers precession, makes a catalogue of 1080 'fixed' stars in 49 constellations, and advances Eratosthenes' method of determining places on the Earth's surface by latitude and longitude. In Alexandria, he is followed by Conon and Sosigenes (1st century BCE), the latter to be a consultant to Julius Caesar for a calendar reform.

Ca. **145-87** BCE. Sima Qian, a Chinese historian and astronomer. He compiles the earliest manuscript with uniformly described stars in the whole sky, *Tianguan shu (A Monograph on Celestial Officials)*. A court astrologer, he leads appreciable astronomical activities preparing for the calendar reform during the reign of Emperor Wu (140-87 BCE).

1st century BCE. Mithraism, an enigmatic oriental religion and the most influential foe to Christendom. It originated centuries earlier, probably in Persia. The ancient images of the Western Zodiac come out mostly of Mithraic shrines. D.Ulancey (1989) claimed Mithraists' cryptic doctrines were a *celestial code*, and the cult began as a religious response to a startling astronomical discovery: the end of the *astronomical Age of Taurus*. An open address to celestial links by Mithraism forces the competitor, early Christianity, to conceal and, later, practically to erase its astronomical connotations.

60 BCE. The *Age of Aries* ends, the *astronomical Age of Pisces* begins (fishes are among meaningful symbols again).

45 BCE. In Rome, Julius Caesar administers the calendar reform for millennia to come modeled after Egypt. Caesar's heir, the Emperor Octavianus Augustus, finalizes the reform a few decades later.

Ca. **12** BCE – **33** CE. The presumable lifetime of Jesus of Nazareth, the Christ. Among his important emblems are a ram and fishes; both are substantial astral embodiments of the transient period from the *Age of Aries* to the *Age of Pisces*.

Ca. **15** CE. Important astrological compendium, *Astronomica*, by Marcus Manilius (Rome).

Ca. **100-170** CE. Claudius Ptolemy ends a sequence of prominent Alexandrian astronomers and completes the development of Hellenistic astronomy by creating his outstanding geocentric system of the world in the manuscript called *The Great Mathematical Syntaxis (Almagest)*. He is the author of the famous astrological tractate *Tetrabiblos* as well. Ptolemy has remained as the superlative authority in astronomy (and astrology) up to Copernicus.

Ca. **220-300** CE. Chen Zhuo, a Chinese astronomer, completes the composition of the Chinese starry map with 283 asterisms comprised of 1464 individual stars. From then on the original Chinese celestial map is without changes.

1307-1321 In his invaluable epitome of medieval civilization, the *Divina Commedia*, the greatest poet in the world, the Italian

Dante Alighiere (1265-1321), reproduces the tripartite vertical structure of the archaic Cosmos: Paradise, Purgatory, and Inferno. Dante's worldview is the last grandiose artisan reflection of a millennia-long tradition.

1543 The catholic monk and the greatest scientific visionary, Nicolaus Copernicus (1473-1543) of Poland, "stopped the Sun and moved the Earth" *(De Revolutionibus orbium coelestium. Libri VI)*. He disintegrates the Earth-centered Cosmos and, as a result, discredits the medieval tripartite world of Dante, which starts gradually to deteriorate.

1609 With a telescope in his hands, acclaimed Italian experimentalist, Galileo Galilei (1564-1642), validates the heliocentric vision of the Cosmos by Copernicus *(Sidereus nuncius magna…)*. In his honor, the UN declared 2009 to be the International Year of Astronomy.

1687 Briton Isaac Newton (1642-1727), the genius of physics, finds the prime mover of the Universe's motions – the force of gravity – and describes its performance in mathematical terms *(Philosophiae naturalis principia mathematica)*. After him, for educated people there is no more way to restore the archaic worldview.

Modernity. Shamans of indigenous tribes in various parts of the Earth continue to represent the world with four corners and in the form of a tripartite vertical structure.

Despite their complete scientific failure and sharp religious criticism, astrological writings continue to flourish among the common public.

The twelve-strong Western Zodiac is often utilized as an ornamentation to represent a material apotheosis to the spiritual achievements of ancients. The same is true of the Chinese Zodiac.

The *Age of Pisces* being close to the end, the astronomical *Age of Aquarius* is coming soon!

ABOUT THE AUTHOR

Alexander A. GURSHTEIN was born in Moscow, Russia and graduated from the Moscow University for Geodesy and Cartography with a major in astrometry and theoretical geodesy. His career dawned as an observer in the Sternberg State Astronomical Institute (Moscow University), where he got the degree of Candidate of Science (Physics & Mathematics). For years he worked for the space industry: Korolev's Design Bureau, hailed for the creation of Sputnik and manned spaceships, and the Institute for Space Research (Academy of Sciences).

His extended book *Eternal Enigmas of the Heaven* appeared in 1973; two editions followed with a circulation of about half a million and a translation into Spanish. He has authored books, hundreds of research papers, reviews and 5 certificates of inventions. He got a Ph.D. (Doctor of Science in Physics & Mathematics) from the Main Astronomical Observatory of the Academy of Sciences in St. Petersburg (Pulkovo) and moved to the Vavilov Institute for History of Science & Technology (Moscow). His contributions on history of astronomy and the Zodiac have appeared in Russian, English, Chinese, German, Italian, and Polish.

A scientific activist, he served as the Editor-in-Chief for the annual on History of Astronomy and Space, Deputy Editor-in-Chief for the Russian Academy's *Nature,* the Head of the Board for Astronomical Education (Ministry of Education), and as the Vice Director for the Institute for History of Science & Technology (Academy of Sciences). In 1995, he departed for the US to teach in Colorado. A member of several scientific unions, he was honoured as the President for the Commission on History of Astronomy (International Astronomical Union). In this capacity, he proposed to declare 2009 as the International Year of Astronomy, the initiative being promoted by the IAU, UNESCO, and the UN.

Printed in the United States
By Bookmasters